How Good Policies and Business Ethics Enhance Good Quality of Life

Alex C. Michalos

How Good Policies and Business Ethics Enhance Good Quality of Life

The Selected Works of Alex C. Michalos

Springer

Alex C. Michalos
University of Northern British Columbia
Prince George, BC
Canada

ISBN 978-3-319-50723-1 ISBN 978-3-319-50724-8 (eBook)
DOI 10.1007/978-3-319-50724-8

Library of Congress Control Number: 2017934320

Printed on acid-free paper

This Springer imprint is published by Springer Nature
The registered company is Springer International Publishing AG
The registered company address is: Gewerbestrasse 11, 6330 Cham, Switzerland

Other Books by Alex C. Michalos

North American Social Report, 5 volumes
Global Report on Student Well-Being, 4 volumes
Essays on the Quality of Life
Ancient Views on the Quality of Life
Militarism and the Quality of Life
Foundations of Decision Making
Trade Barriers to the Public Good
Good Taxes
A Pragmatic Approach to Business Ethics
Principles of Logic
Improving Your Reasoning
The Popper-Carnap Controversy

For Deborah, with love

Acknowledgements

Most of the previously published papers in this set of four volumes (and most of my books) appeared in a publication of Springer, Kluwer, Reidel, or Nijhoff, a chain of publishers that I have had the opportunity to work with since the 1960s. Since the original source of each paper in the collection is given on its first page in this collection, there is no need to repeat all these sources and express my thanks for permission to reprint them in each occurrence. I am happy to express here my gratitude for the lot and for the many years of our pleasant and productive work together.

In each of the volumes in this set, I will acknowledge permission to reprint each of the previously published papers appearing in scholarly journals, books, or newspapers apart from the chain of publishers listed above. In this second volume, I would like to thank John Wiley and Sons Ltd. for Chap. 1. Michalos, A.C. (1997). Social sciences and business ethics. In P.H. Werhane & R.E. Freeman (Eds.). *Encyclopedic Dictionary of Business Ethics*, (pp. 595–597). Oxford: Blackwell; Elsevier Pub. for Chap. 2. Michalos, A.C. (2012). Business ethics and the quality of life. In R. Chadwick (Ed.). *Encyclopedia of Applied Ethics*, (pp. 361–364). Amsterdam: Elsevier; Pearson Canada for Chap. 6. Michalos, A.C. (2005). The loyal agent's argument. In D.C. Poff (Ed.). *Business Ethics in Canada*, 4th ed. (pp. 200–206). Toronto: Pearson Canada; Pearson Canada for Chap. 7. Michalos, A.C. (2005). Moral responsibility in business. In D.C. Poff (Ed.). *Business Ethics in Canada*, 4th ed. (pp. 30–46). Toronto: Pearson Canada; University of Illinois Press for Chap. 8. Michalos, A.C. (1988). A case for a progressive annual net wealth tax. *Public Affairs Quarterly*, 2: 105–140; New York Academy of Sciences for Chap. 9. Michalos, A.C. (1989). Militarism and the quality of life. *Annals of the New York Academy of Sciences*, 577: 216–230; newspapers *Globe and Mail, Prince George Citizen*, and *Guelph Mercury* for several letters in Chap. 22. Michalos, A.C.

In the Appendix of each volume, I included some photographs and pictures to provide a somewhat different kind of historical context to my narrative. What I have been able to contribute over the past 50 years or so has been influenced by many more people than I have been able to picture here, but when I reflect on what I have done, most of the people pictured here are very much a part of the story. Most of the photographs and pictures are from my family albums, but some have come from friends and a couple newspapers. I would like to express my thanks to the following for allowing me to reprint their items: Wolfgang Glatzer for photographs in How Good Policies and Business Ethics Enhance Good Quality of Life, numbered v2.1 (short for photo #1, volume 2), in Development of the Quality of Life Theory and its Instruments (v3.3, v3.5, and v3.6), and in Connecting the Quality of Life Theory to Health, Well-Being and Education (v4.1); to Ferran Casas for photographs v2.6, v3.1, v3.2 and v3.4; to Filomena Maggino for v4.4, v4.5 and v4.6; to Anna L.D. Lau and Robert A. Cummins for v4.3, v4.8 and v4.9, to Valerie Moller for v3.7 and v3.8; to Joanna Kit-Chun Lam for v3.11; to Daniel T.L. Shek for v4.2; to the *Cleveland Plain Dealer* for Philosophical Foundations of Quality of Life (v1.4), and to the *Detroit Free Press* for v1.7.

Contents

Overview of the "The Selected Works of Alex C. Michalos"

Philosophical Foundations of Quality of Life

Development of Quality of Life Theory and Its Instruments

Connecting the Quality of Life Theory to Health, Well-Being and Education

Introduction to "Selected Works of Alex C. Michalos"

Biographical Notes

The central aim of this set of volumes is to describe and explain the context and connections among a subset of papers and books produced over the past 50 years. Rather than a mere reproduction of work already published, this will be an attempt to disclose the productive processes in their various historic contexts that led to the various research projects and publications. In Michalos (2003), I published a collection called *Essays on the Quality of Life* containing 20 articles focused on the quality of life, 3 of which appear in other volumes of this set because they seemed to be so central to the array of issues in the 70 articles in these volumes. For completeness, I mention articles from the earlier collection and books that are directly relevant to the themes in these volumes.

Some years ago (these days, it seems that most things begin with "some years ago," unfortunately), in a debate about the existence of God, a member of the audience put the question to us "Why would God want to watch re-runs?". The question made sense from the point of view of one of the debaters, since God was supposed to know everything that is going to happen before it happens. As the atheist in the debate, I could only say that I have no idea why, although a lot of people seem to enjoy them.

While I also enjoy some reruns, I would not find much joy in rebinding some old papers for a new audience. I do, however, find the idea of describing the historical context in which similar research questions more or less simultaneously appeared to people in diverse parts of the globe and were addressed first individually and then collectively. Here, the historical context includes some of my own biographical material. This is offered as a kind of second-best effort substituting for an autobiography that I have never had the courage to write, notwithstanding having thought about it many times.

My father ended his formal education in the sixth grade, and my mother ended hers in the eighth grade. As far as I have been able to discern, in 1917, when he was about 17, my father, Charles K. Michalos, emigrated from the island of Chios,

Greece, to work in the steel mills of Gary, Indiana. He arrived with a pocket-sized Greek–English dictionary, learned to speak English with a heavy Greek accent, moved from the mills to driving a Nabisco bread and pastry truck for another 17 years, bought a small hamburger joint, then a somewhat bigger one and finally something more like a diner on Euclid Avenue in Cleveland, Ohio. Its claim to fame was the fact that many of the Cleveland Browns ate there, which was quite a big deal in 1947 when the Browns were the All American Football Conference champions and I was one of their biggest junior high school fans. My father died in January 1951, at about 51. We were never sure, because he was never sure, how old he was. I was daddy's boy, and his loss was a great loss to me.

My mother, Josephine Pucci, was born in Akron, Ohio, one of eight children of immigrants from Palermo, Sicily. She worked at the May Company Department store, sang in the chorus of the Cleveland Opera Company, married my father in 1931, produced my brother in 1932 and me in 1935, and provided the mom part of our mom and pop diner. Unlike my dad, she was not a particularly happy person, but she lived to be 93 years of age, dying in June 1998. Like my dad, and the rest of us I guess, she did the best she could with what she had.

I was generally an above average but not outstanding primary and secondary school student. In secondary school and the first half of university, I was more interested in sports and girls than scholarship, though I enjoyed mathematics and history. I went to what was then Western Reserve University (now Case-Western Reserve University) in 1953, majoring in history with minors in philosophy and religion. When I read Plato's *Republic*, I felt as if he was talking directly to me. It had never occurred to me to ask what a good life might be, but the more I thought about it, the more I *had* to think about it.

I grew up in a very mixed religious family. The story my mother told was that her family were Catholics until the local priest did something that led my grandfather to tell him to go to hell and he took the whole gene pool into a more friendly Baptist church. My father seemed to practice the religion of washing his car on Sundays, but he thought his sons had to be baptized Greek Orthodox in order to preserve something or other that was important to him. So, we were. However, because our house was one block away from a small Quaker church, my brother, Chuck Michalos, and I were sent off together as soon as we were old enough to find our way there and back. I have a gold medal showing that I accumulated three years of Sundays without missing Quaker Sunday school.

Given this background, when I began to think seriously about a good life, I thought I should make my peace with God if there were one. So, besides studying philosophy, I studied the history of religions. Then, I went to graduate school at the University of Chicago. Because I was what one would have called a doubter, I wanted to study religion in a school of believers, assuming that if anyone could convince me that I was wrong, they could. At least they would be inclined to try. So, in 1957, I enrolled in the Divinity School, which seemed to have the most diverse faculty, including visiting experts in Buddhism, which especially interested me.

I also married in the summer of 1957, a marriage that lasted about 23 years and produced Cyndi (1960), Ted (1961), and Stephanie (1963). In 1985, I married the love of my life, Deborah Poff, a lucky break for both of us at the time and ever since.

While studying the history of religions, I took courses in philosophy and it seemed to me that philosophers had more precise and decisive methods of pursuing the truth than theologians. The University of Chicago had a wonderfully flexible approach to higher education, allowing students to pursue more than one degree at a time. To get a bachelor of divinity degree, a student was required to pass 7 comprehensive examinations and have a year internship in some relevant field of practice. I took some courses designed to prepare one to take the examinations and some courses in philosophy that I found interesting. At the 1961 convocation, I received a B.D. and an M.A. in philosophy and then proceeded to pursue a Ph.D. in philosophy of science. I completed the latter in 1965 with a dissertation on a dispute between Rudolf Carnap and Karl Popper on the nature and use of probability theory in the assessment of scientific theories (Michalos 1971).

Many of the most salient and important features of the following 50 years of research and other activities may be regarded as relatively natural developments of these earlier initiatives. In a memorable essay on the best teacher he ever had, Keyfitz (2003) said that scholars should replace the metaphor of providing building blocks for a relatively durable corporate body of knowledge with that of providing biodegradable nutrition out of which new knowledge would grow. In a sense, today's nutrient is tomorrow's fertilizer. What I did until 1965 provided the ingredients for what followed, just as the latter will feed what comes afterward. Most importantly, I think my general approach has been informed by a pragmatic and philosophic interest in a holistic, comprehensive understanding of any particular object of investigation. I will try to explain this approach in the next few paragraphs.

Broadly speaking, there are two ways to define "*philosophy*." From a *functional* point of view, philosophy may be identified as critical thinking about anything at all, from asphalt to zebras. From a *content* point of view, philosophy may be identified as a body of knowledge answering three questions: What is it? What good is it? and How do you know?

Answering the question 'What is it?' gives one a discussion of the nature or being of something. In short, it gives one an *ontology*, a word derived from the Greek "on," meaning nature or being, and logos, meaning discourse (among other things). Descriptions of the nature of things, ontologies, have at least two aspects. Everything has, after all, a form, structure, morphology, or anatomy on the one hand and a function, activity, or physiology on the other. A duck, smile, or football game, for example, can be described at a minimum by describing their structural parts and how the parts function. What Isaac Newton might have referred to as natural philosophy and we now would call natural science is close to what philosophers would call ontology.

Answering the question 'What good is it?' gives one a discussion of the value, worth, or goodness in some sense of something. In short, it gives one an *axiology*, a word derived from the Greek "axios" meaning worthy or valuable, and logos. Of the variety of kinds of value that may be described, it is most useful to distinguish intrinsic from instrumental value. *Intrinsic value* refers to the worth or goodness of a thing in itself, its value as an end in itself rather than as a means to something else. *Instrumental value* refers to the worth or goodness of a thing as a means to something else, not as a thing in itself. Standard examples include things like eating an apple or throwing a ball at a target having instrumental value insofar as the former produces nutrition and the latter scores points, which in this context have intrinsic value.

Since practically anything might be a useful means to something else for someone in some circumstances for some purposes, practically anything can have instrumental value. However, some people believe that all alleged sorts of intrinsic value may be reduced to a single one. For example, they would argue that the nutrition obtained from eating an apple is really only instrumentally valuable as a means to good health, which is itself instrumentally valuable for a life of pleasure, happiness, or satisfaction. Those who believe that there is finally only one intrinsically valuable thing such as pleasure, happiness, or satisfaction may be called monists with respect to the ultimate nature (ontological status) of value, while those who believe that there are many intrinsically valuable things may be called *pluralists*.

For a monist, then, it may be said that ontologically distinct things such as music, cheese, and justice have different degrees of some sort of values such as pleasure, happiness, or satisfaction, while for a pluralist, such ontologically distinct things have ontologically distinct values (music value, cheese value, and justice value) regardless of how much pleasure, happiness, or satisfaction these things produce. From an ontological point of view, then, a monist would have a numerically smaller number of ontologically distinct things in his or her world (e.g., music, cheese, justice, and some degree of pleasure, happiness, or satisfaction generated by the other three), while a pluralist's world would have music, cheese, and justice plus music value, cheese value, and justice value.

For a monist, the task of measuring the total value of something, a person, event, object, attitude, belief, proposition, action, or life itself, is in principle straightforward. One simply needs to measure the degree of intrinsic value generated by that thing in terms of or operationalized as pleasure, happiness, or satisfaction. For pluralists, the task of measuring the total value of something is not at all straightforward because there may be no way to compare ontologically distinct values such as the value of music versus the value of cheese or justice. There does not appear to be any common measure, scale, or instrument available to answer questions such as "How much is music worth compared to the value of justice or cheese?" or "What is the value of this piece of music in terms of the value of justice or cheese?"

Given the severe comparability problems faced by all value pluralists, it is not surprising that the most frequently studied theories of economists and decision theorists, namely preference theory, choice theory, utility theory, and game theory, and one of the most popular ethical theories studied by philosophers, utilitarianism, assume value monism of some sort. As we will see in many of the papers in this collection and many more cited in those papers, scholars have invented a great variety of methods for living in and managing a world apparently containing a plurality of values. In particular, I will describe my own efforts over about 50 years, which have been interesting but largely unsuccessful.

Answering the question 'How do you know?' gives a discussion of one's knowledge of something. In short, it gives one an *epistemology*, a word derived from the Greek "episteme" meaning knowledge and logos, hence a theory of knowledge. Strictly speaking, one ought, prudentially and morally, to have a fairly clear answer to the epistemological question before one attempts to answer the ontological and axiological questions. Since a philosopher aims to obtain a body of knowledge about the nature and value of things to be used in the practice of living a good life, a patently necessary condition of achieving that aim is clarity with respect to knowledge itself and its production. That is why the earliest essays in these 4 volumes concern epistemological issues.

Comments on the Articles

All of the papers in this set of volumes are arranged partly in chronological order and partly by their logical connections. Each volume has its own major themes, and within those themes, articles have been selected and arranged to provide some idea of the time at which they appeared and its relation to my own and others' research agendas around that time.

Following this introduction, the first two articles in this volume provide bridges from the social sciences to business ethics and from the latter to the quality of life. Among several ways of revealing the impact of social sciences on business ethics, in Chap. 1, it is reported that the 1992 *Journal Citation Reports* of the *Social Sciences Citation Index* shows that "only one (8%) of the 12 journals that are listed as citing *JOBE* [the *Journal of Business Ethics*] in 1992, 1991, and 1990 was not a social science journal…[and] every one of the 48 journals cited by authors in *JOBE* was a social science journal."

About a third of the 151 articles published in JOBE in 1994 used some sort of consequentialist moral theory. Generally speaking, advocates of such theories typically hold that one ought to try to act so that one's actions tend to impartially improve the happiness, well-being, utility, welfare, or quality of life of those affected by the actions. As explained in Michalos (2015), ideas about the nature of well-being, happiness, and so on have been contested since roughly the eighth century BCE. What creates a set of critical issues that must be resolved by any consequentialist measuring the quality of life is the fact that they begin with the qualification, *all things considered,* but there is no generally agreed upon criteria for determining exactly which things, in what period, in what way, by whom, and many other things. Chapter 2 lists many of the critical issues, effectively showing why many business ethicists and quality-of-life researchers face similar problems and should draw on each other's resources. A more robust account and illustration of the role played by different explications of the critical issues may be found in Michalos (2008).

In Chap. 3, I describe "the rudiments of a system of cost accounting to be used in the evaluation of the costs" of decision making. Aspects of this system are incorporated into the comprehensive set of explications in Michalos (1978). Most importantly, a thorough accounting for all potential costs and benefits of a decision or decision procedure reveals the essential contribution of moral considerations to any plausible measure of efficiency. This, in Chap. 4, provides the inescapable conceptual link between rationality as a kind of efficiency and morality, a link that the well-known praxiologists Tadeusz Kotarbinski and Henryk Skolimowski denied or rejected.

Having disclosed the logically necessary connection between rationality as a kind of efficiency and morality, there was a need to show that Herbert Simon's notion of satisficing rationality was as deficient as the more frequently employed notion of maximizing rationality. In Chap. 5 and more fully in Michalos (1978), I show that the satisficers ask too little and the maximizers ask too much for a workable concept of rationality, and I sketch a notion of consensual rationality that is a reasonable blend of morality and efficiency. I still think I made a compelling case for a somewhat novel foundation for economics and other decision sciences, although I am not aware of anyone else who felt compelled by it.

When we founded the *Journal of Business Ethics* in 1982, the field hardly existed. People often quipped "Isn't that an oxymoron, a contradiction in terms?" They still do, though not quite as often, but probably with as much justification. The Volkswagen scandal is only months away now. Michalos and Poff (2012) reviewed the first 30 years of publishing JOBE, reprinted 33 of its most frequently cited articles, and provided short assessments of the impact of the journal by over 100 scholars in the field. Chapters 7 and 8 are relatively early attempts to dispose of frequently used unsound arguments against business ethics, against the field and even more disturbing, and against the very idea of introducing ethical considerations into the assessment of business practice. In Chap. 6, I analyze what I call "the Loyal Agent's Argument," which is based on the assumption that it is morally acceptable to perform immoral and even illegal acts designed in the interest of or to prove one's loyalty to someone else, a person, company, or country, for example. This is one of 14 arguments considered briefly in Chap. 7. Others erroneously purport to show, for example, that introducing ethical considerations into business practices would undermine Adam Smith's invisible hand, violate certain rights, be beyond one's competence, decrease efficiency, increase government control, and undermine moral pluralism.

Chapter 8 contains an analysis of the case for "the introduction of a progressive annual net wealth tax in Canada." I present 19 arguments in favor of such a tax and try to show that 31 arguments against such a tax are unsound. As this paragraph is being written (December 2015), no political party in Canada is advocating such a tax, although in the 1970s I helped get the policy adopted by the New Democratic

Party of Canada. However, political environments change and what seemed possible at one time and impossible at another seems possible again. Only a few months ago, Atkinson (2015) recommended reconsideration of an annual net wealth tax for the UK, and the year before, Piketty (2014) recommended the same for the European Community. As the world becomes increasingly alarmed by the enormous concentration of wealth and its implications for democracy, the prospects of such taxation become much brighter than they were nearly 30 years ago when my paper came out.

In Chap. 9, I present 15 arguments for resisting further Canadian commercialization (i.e., production and export) of military arms broadly construed. While there is certainly money to be made in this industry, as some of its greatest producers continue to demonstrate, there are serious costs that tend to be neglected by its proponents. The analyses presented in this chapter are roughly half of the case made in my Science for Peace monograph, *Militarism and the Quality of Life* (1989). Unfortunately, Canada's largest sale of military equipment ever ($15 billion) was made this year to Saudi Arabia under less than properly scrutinized circumstances.

Chapter 10 brings together "three lines of research that I have been engaged in for some years in relative isolation, namely, research on social indicators and quality of life measurement, research on peace and security, and business ethics." Among other things, I tried to show that the disciplines of psychology and sociology had important contributions to make to peace and security research, contributions that scientists and policy makers working in different silos seemed to neglect. Generally speaking, I concluded that human beings (strangers at least) probably merited greater trust than most people seemed willing or able to grant and that the world would be a better place if more of us could risk granting greater trust. In fact, following up a line of argument suggested by William James and analyzed in the first volume of this set, because trusting people is a necessary condition of living in a world characterized as trustworthy, one ought morally and prudentially to give people the benefit of doubt and risk granting them trust before they have had an opportunity to show that they merit it.

In all democratically developed countries, commercial polling has become a standard practice for exploring voters' views about issues that are up for or some people think should be up for public debate. According to Lepore (2015), in the USA, "From the late nineteen-nineties to 2012, twelve hundred polling organizations conducted nearly thirty-seven thousand polls by making more than three billion phone calls." In Canada, there has been serious discussion about the possibility and wisdom of banning such polling during elections. In Chap. 11, I present and try to demolish 16 arguments in favor of such bans and then give 16 arguments against such bans. In the final section of the article, I offer a "model set of disclosure standards for the publication of poll results during election campaigns." While the model has not been formally adopted or legislated here, routine reading of our national media suggests that some modest progress has been made in the direction of meeting the requirements of the model. I remain hopeful for greater progress.

I was a candidate in the federal parliamentary elections of November 1988, October 1993, and June 1997, running with the New Democratic Party in the riding of Guelph-Wellington in the first two elections and in Prince George Peace River in the third. I lost in all three elections, winning 20% of the vote in 1988, 5% in 1993, and 9% in 1997. In the 1988 election, the main issue was the Canada–US Free Trade Agreement (FTA), and in the 1993 election, it was the North American Free Trade Agreement (NAFTA), involving Canada, the USA, and Mexico. New Democrats opposed the FTA and NAFTA, but a Conservative majority government passed the FTA in 1988 and a Liberal majority passed the NAFTA in 1994. I presented briefs to the Sub-Committee on International Trade of the Standing Committee on External Affairs and International Trade in the House of Commons in December 1992 and to the Ontario Cabinet Committee on North American Free Trade in April 1993. Chapter 12 is a copy of my Ontario Brief, in which I tried to explain why I and my party opposed many of the salient controversial provisions of the NAFTA. According to its proponents, the jewel of the agreement was supposed to be the Dispute Settlement Provisions that were intended to make some sort of level-playing field for the three countries. I addressed these provisions in my brief and later in my book *Trade Barriers to the Public Good: Free Trade and Environmental Protection* (2008).

Specifically, in Michalos (2008, p. 346), I concluded,

> I began with the question: In the NAFTA dispute settlement involving [the fuel additive] MMT, were the broader community interests of most people in Canada served better or worse than the relatively narrower commercial trade interests of investors? My attempt to answer that question was complicated by the initiation of the AIT [Agreement on Internal Trade] dispute settlement. However, the answer to the basic question is that broader community interests, as assessed and defended by the Government of Canada, were crushed in favor of the narrower trade interests of the Ethyl Corporation and the petroleum industry, defended in one arena by the Ethyl Corporation and in the other by the Government of Alberta with the support of Saskatchewan and Québec.

Regarding these so-called free trade deals, it should always be remembered that these deals are designed with a bias in favor of commercial interests over all others. So once a dispute is moved to adjudication by a trade panel, any case for other interests such as environmental protection, human, or community rights will be significantly handicapped and probably fail.

In Chap. 13, written in the second half of the 1990s, I looked into the future and recommended some issues that seemed to me to warrant more attention from business ethicists and practitioners. These included the role and impact of labor unions on the ethical culture of business, social dumping (companies dumping their products on foreign markets at prices in those markets lower than the costs of production in order to drive out competitors), international finance and Third-World debt, tobacco promotion, arms trade, wealth concentration and its taxation, pollution and resource depletion, international trading blocks, and quasi-cabals of CEOs of transnational corporations. Reflecting on this list 20 years later, it looks as if I mainly projected my own primary interests on the field, hoping if not assuming, that others would take up explorations that I had begun. It is fair to say that most of these issues are being actively investigated, whether or not anyone noticed my initiatives.

Chapters 14 and 15 were the products of two conferences in which social indicators used as performance or outcome measures were examined in relation to public policy making and management. Chapter 14 was written for a 1997 conference in Naples, Italy, on the introduction of performance-based management in public administration. I argued that it was a welcome innovation that would likely have significant benefits within and beyond regions where it was implemented, although I doubted that it required a "whole new and different type of manageriality in public administration." More critically, I expressed doubt that "a purely or even a primarily market-oriented theory would be progressive enough to be sustainable or worth sustaining in the long run." Chapter 15 was written for a 1998 conference in Kingston, Ontario, on the likely usefulness of six different outcome measures "for improving the coherence and integration of public policy-making." The measures involved the use of Pacific herring stocks for building a sustainable fishery on Canada's west coast, alternative measures of poverty, comparative energy efficiency of four modes of passenger transportation (automobile, bus, train, and plane), federal government debt, provincial government deficits, and the efficient market hypothesis.

Chapter 16 is a paper presented at a Conference on New Rules for the New Millennium sponsored by Mani Tese in Florence, Italy, in March 2000. It is based on my monograph *Good Taxes: The Case for Taxing Foreign Currency Exchange and Other Financial Transactions* (1997). The 1981 Nobel Laureate James Tobin suggested such taxes in 1978, following up on a recommendation by John Maynard Keynes in 1936 (Desir and Ford 2000). In 1998, a group called ATTAC (Association pour une Taxation des Transactions financieres pour l'Aide aux Citoyens) was founded, and before the end of 1999, it had grown to over 100 chapters in France with a total membership of over 10,000 people. In March 1999, the Canadian House of Commons endorsed a New Democrat's Private Member's Motion by a vote of 164 to 83 which said: "that, in the opinion of the House, the government should enact a tax on financial transactions in concert with the international community." Over 100 participants from members of the European Union and other countries met in June 2000 to endorse such taxes in the First Interparliamentary Meeting on the Tobin Tax in Brussels. In my concluding Speaker's comments to the Brussels meeting, I said that "Tobin Taxes represent a concrete vehicle by which civil society can re-assert its right to control its financial and therefore its political future." Twelve years later, in May 2012, the European Parliament voted 487 to 152 for a financial transactions tax, and in May 2014, 11 European Union countries committed to initiating "a financial transactions tax by the beginning of 2016 at the latest," only two weeks away from what I am writing now (http://www.english.rfi.fr/economy/20140506-11-eu-states-implement-tobin-tax-january-2016). In 2000, I predicted that some members of the European Union would be the first to introduce a sustainable Tobin-type tax (there are many variations), would make a lot of money (currently modest annual estimates of 30 to 50 billion euros), and continue to attract more proponents and participants. I am pleased to say my crystal ball has proven to be fairly accurate so far. I am also pleased to report that the former head of Britain's Financial Services Authority recently claimed that the great global financial crisis of 2008 was driven in part by economists' commitment to the "efficient market hypothesis" (Turner 2016), a hypothesis I roundly criticized in Chap. 16 and Michalos (1997).

The article reprinted as Chap. 17 expresses some worries I had and still have that "there is such a diversity of opinion about so many fundamental issues that most ethical appraisals, especially in committees, are probably very shallow and barely warranted." Like most academics, I spent a lot of time working in committees and I think this paper was probably a result of an overload of unpleasant experiences. I tried to bring some order to the pluralistic axiological world that most of us are working in. In its intent, the effort was a bit like the more formal Science Court procedures that I wrote about twenty years earlier in 1980 (see Philosophical Foundations of Quality of Life.) and Diener's (2005) effort to bring some conceptual order to the field of well-being and ill-being studies. While the views expressed in this chapter are uncharacteristically pessimistic for me, they do reveal some genuine concerns that are still relevant.

Chapter 18 is based on a 2004 submission to the B.C. Citizen's Assembly that was formed to hold consultations with British Columbians leading to a referendum in May 2005 on a new electoral system. The proposed single transferable vote (STV) system required at least 60% support of voters for passage and it received 58%. I added my voice to the opposition of STV. In the federal election of October 2015, the winning Liberal Party promised to introduce a new electoral system in time for the next federal election. Since some sort of STV system is already being talked about as a live option, it seems worthwhile to include my observations here.

A version of Chap. 19 was presented at the World Business Ethics Forum held at Hong Kong Baptist University in November 2006. I reviewed several examples of ancient writers who addressed issues of business ethics over two thousand years ago. The most interesting problems were discussed by the great lawyer and statesman, and sometimes friend of Julius Caesar, Marcus Tulius Cicero (106-43 BCE). Most importantly, Cicero was the first writer in antiquity to present and demolish the business case for business ethics. He "clearly saw that if morally right actions are finally only warranted by their financial profitability then they could be undermined and over-ridden by immoral actions whenever the latter promised greater profitability." I have much more to say about the business case in Chap. 21.

In 2007, Robert Reich, the former US Secretary of Labor in the Clinton Administration, published a book called *Supercapitalism: The Transformation of Business, Democracy and Everyday Life* in which, among other things, he tried to show that and why business ethicists are largely engaged in relatively unproductive exercises. In his view, the interests of such people would be better served "if they undertook the hard work of engagement in democratic political processes leading to legislation that would force corporations to pursue the public interest as well as their own." In Chap. 20, I describe what I call Reich's Monster of Supercapitalism, analyze his arguments for believing that the Monster is inherently stronger than democracy and democratic practices, and finally demonstrate that his "understanding of democracy and democratic process are flawed" as well as "his understanding of CSR [corporate social responsibility] and its relation to the law."

Chapter 21 was provoked by some featured articles in *Maclean's Magazine*, one in particular called "Corporate Social Responsibility Report 2010: Good for Business," celebrating the award winners of Jantzi-Sustainalytic analysts' competition. I explained my lack of success in trying to find out exactly what measures were used in what ways in the adjudication process, why any alleged measure of sustainability could not satisfy the demands of its name without good measures of what is to be sustained, with what resources, given what rates of change for each, and that given our inability to sort out and measure people's motives and the payoffs for all actions, exercises like the Jantzi-Sustainalytic competition are misleading at best and probably dangerously so. In Development of the Quality of Life Theory and its Instruments, I will have more to say about the world's problems identifying and measuring sustainable development.

Earlier in this chapter, I mentioned that I ran for office in Canada's House of Commons. When I was 9 years of age, I joined a local youth group of the YMCA (Young Man's Christian Association), not because I was a Christian but because the group included my brother and a lot of my friends, played basketball and baseball, and ran summer camps. To practically everyone's surprise, I was elected president shortly after joining the group, mainly I think because I came in with many other 9-year-old friends who voted as a block for one of their own. I was much impressed by this success, as was my father, who had one eye on Alexander the Great when he and my mother picked my name. From that time on, I had the idea that I should one day be elected to public office. I never thought I would be the president of the USA or prime minister of Canada. I just thought I had a future in public, political service. So, I often joined interest groups, professional associations, and a political party, ran for and served as an officer, and finally ran for and lost parliamentary elections. I also wrote a lot of letters to the editors of many newspapers and a few magazines, expressing my views on events and other people's views. In the interests of rounding out the biographical aspects of this particular volume of this set, I have included 24 published letters in Chap. 22. They are only a few of many and many more unpublished letters. Together they cover the years from 1989 to 2001, and they provide a rich context for my academic work and show how the latter influenced and was influenced by my political work. Here, a brief overview of their topics is sufficient to suggest my politics.

I wrote letters urging cessation of cruise missile test flights over Canada, supporting a march against poverty, resisting purchase of new submarines, undertaking much more conservation before building more nuclear reactors, understanding women's right to therapeutic abortion, settling native land claims prior to resource extraction, cessation of low-level bomber test flights over Labrador, suggesting a more recession-resistant federal budget, resisting the Gulf War and increased sale of arms made in Canada, supporting pay equity, opposing NAFTA with formal presentations to elected officials and leading a huge public protest march in Ottawa, documenting the growth of business ethics, replacing ad hoc philanthropy with fair taxation, addressing the problem of wealth inequality with annual net wealth taxes and financial transaction taxes, showing the pernicious bias in "Tax freedom day," supporting the Seattle protests against the World Trade Organization, meeting the successor to South Africa's Bishop Tutu, and organizing a conference in Pentagon City on the quality of life of US military personnel and their families. The latter conference was held the month before the planes flew into the Pentagon and the World Trade Center.

References

Atkinson, A. B. (2015). *Inequality: What can be done?* Cambridge, MA: Harvard University Press.

Desir, H. & Ford, G. (2000). Introduction. In H. Desir & G. Ford (Eds.), *Time for Tobin: Proceedings of the Conference of the First Interparliamentary Meeting on the Tobin Tax, 28 June 2000* (pp. 5–13). Brussels: European Parliament Intergroup on Capital Tax, Fiscal Systems and Globalization.

Diener, E. (2005). Guidelines for national indicators of subjective well-being and ill-being. *Journal of Happiness Studies, 7*, 397–404.

Keyfitz, N. (2003). Nathan Keyfitz on Mr. Somerville and others. In A. C. Michalos (Ed.), *The best teacher I ever had: Personal reports from highly productive scholars* (pp. 126–131). London, ON: Althouse Press.

Lepore, J. (2015). Politics and the new machine. *The New Yorker*, XCI:36-44. Advance Magazine Publishers: New York.

Michalos, A. C. (1971). *The Popper-Carnap controversy*. Hague: Martinus Nijhoff.

Michalos, A. C. (1978). *Foundations of decision making*. Ottawa: Canadian Library of Philosophy.

Michalos, A. C. (1989). *Militarism and the quality of life*. Toronto: Science for Peace and Samuel Stevens.

Michalos, A. C. (1997). *Good taxes: The case for taxing foreign currency exchange and other financial transactions*. Toronto: Science for Peace and Dundern Press.

Michalos, A. C. (2003). *Essays on the quality of life*. Dordrecht: Kluwer Academic Publishers.

Michalos, A. C. (2008). *Trade barriers to the public good*. Montreal: McGill-Queen's University Press.

Michalos, A. C. & Poff, D. C. (Eds.). (2012). *Citation classics from the Journal of Business Ethics: Celebrating the first thirty years of publication*. Dordrecht: Springer.

Piketty, T. (2014). *Capital in the twenty-first century*. Cambridge, MA: Harvard University Press.

Reich, R. B. (2007). *Supercapitalism: The transformation of business, democracy, and everyday life*. New York: Alfred A. Knopf.

Turner, A. (2016). *Between debt and the devil*. Princeton: Princeton University Press.

Chapter 1
Social Sciences and Business Ethics

Alex C. Michalos

It is convenient to think of the social sciences as the organized pursuit of law-like regularities and theories regarding human action, and to think of BUSINESS ETHICS as the theory and practice of human action aimed at securing a good life in a market, a mixed market, or an exchange economy. Perhaps the most important word in the preceding brief definition of our headword is "convenient," because it emphasizes the fact that what is being offered is merely a stipulative definition or conventional understanding about the key words designating this subject-matter.

Although there is no general agreement about the proper way to define the social sciences and its diverse disciplines, there are different identifiable, self-defined, specialized research communities (i.e., professional or learned societies), academic departments, and scholarly journals. So, one way to proceed to an exhaustive analysis of our subject would be to list the appropriate social-science societies, types of academic departments, and journals, and then examine their particular relations to business ethics. One would still have borderline cases, one of the oldest being history and one of the newest being evaluation science (Michalos 1992). Among the social sciences, one would include family studies, geography (especially economic and social geography), political science, policy science, planning (urban, rural, and regional), sociology (especially criminology, quality of work life, sociology of work or labor studies, industrial relations and social indicators), psychology, economics, organizational behavior and anthropology.

Unfortunately, the suggested strategy of approaching our subject is oversimplified because it assumes that we are confronted with a many-one relation, many

---

Michalos, A.C.: 1997. Social sciences and business ethics. In P.H. Werhane & R.E. Freeman (Eds.) Encyclopedic Dictionary of Business Ethics (pp. 595–597). © Wiley-Blackwell 1999.

A.C. Michalos (✉)
University of Northern British Columbia, Prince George, BC, Canada
e-mail: michalos@brandonu.ca

A.C. Michalos, *How Good Policies and Business Ethics Enhance Good Quality of Life*, DOI 10.1007/978-3-319-50724-8_1

disciplines to one business ethics, when in fact we are faced with a many-to-many relationship, because different people construe ETHICS and business ethics in different ways. One theoretical approach in the study of ethics is CONSEQUENTIALISM (including UTILITARIANISM as a particular species). However, it too comes in many forms, which increases the variety of subheadings on the business ethics side of the relationship to be correlated with the social-sciences side. A few examples will suffice to illustrate the great importance of social-scientific research to con-sequentialism. Ruut Veenhoven published three fine collections of research studies on HAPPINESS, any one of which shows a world of difference between the primitive musings of JEREMY BENTHAM, with his felicific calculus and contemporary research. The first, Veenhoven (1993a), is a bibliography of 2,472 studies on the "subjective appreciation of life," and the second, Veenhoven (1993b) is a review of national surveys on the same topic for 56 countries in the 1946–1992 period. These were an extension of work begun earlier. Michalos (1991a, b, 1993a, b) reviews the research literature for the past twenty years on happiness and satisfaction with life as a whole and on satisfaction in a dozen domains of life (e.g., satisfaction with one's job, housing, family relations, etc.), and reports the results of testing his explanatory Multiple Discrepancies Theory (MDT) on over 18,000 undergraduates in 39 countries. MDT was designed to provide a new empirical foundation for consequentialist ethics, choice and DECISION THEORY, and microeconomics.

In Michalos (1991a) it was reported that biennial computer searches of the research literature carried out over the past dozen years on the key words "happiness" and "satisfaction" had revealed an average annual publication rate of over 1,100 titles for nearly 20 years. In February 1994 a search was made through Social SciSearch for the single year of 1990 using the original two key words plus "social indicators," "well-being" and "quality of life." To the researcher's astonishment, 11,256 titles were discovered. Electronic databases often have duplicates and other kinds of "noise" in them, but most of the titles would have some relevance to one or another of the key words which, depending on one's particular project, may or may not be useful.

Although few philosophers have ventured into this empirical work in the consequentialist moral tradition, social scientists have been very active and social scientists working on business ethics are increasingly drawing on this tradition. For example, inspecting the most recent past 12 months of publications in the *Journal of Business Ethics* (*JOBE*, July 1993–June 1994), one finds that 34 (23%) of the total 151 articles appearing employed some sort of consequentialist analysis.

Another way to assess the impact of social science on business ethics was suggested by Robertson (1993). She reviewed the articles in *JOBE* in the years from 1982 to 1990, and found that 2.9% of them were empirical in the former year compared to 32.6% in the latter year. In the three years for which she presented detailed classifications of topics considered, 1988, 1989, and 1990, the most frequently mentioned was "theory." At the end of her review, she offered eight recommendations, including giving more care to connecting empirical research to normative assumptions, emphasizing behavior instead of mere attitudes as a dependent variable, testing theoretical models of ethical decision-making, building more and better theories, developing longer-term research programs, using more diverse experimental designs, and building "links to managerial and public policy applications".

A third way to measure the impact of social science on business ethics is by means of the most recent issue of the *Journal Citation Reports* of the *Social Sciences Citation Index*. Examining the "Cited Journal Listing" for 1992 (Grid: M5), one finds that only one (8%) of the 12 journals that are listed as citing *JOBE* in 1992, 1991, and 1990 was not a social science journal. Going in the other direction, one finds that every one of the 48 journals cited by authors in *JOBE* was a social-science journal (Grid: H9, 19).

A fourth way to assess the impact of social science on business ethics is to examine the empirical studies attempting to measure the influence of personal and situational factors on people's ethical decision-making in business contexts. Besides providing information that is interesting in itself, such information has significant instrumental value in helping people understand and train ethical decision-makers. Ford and Richardson (1994) published a splendid analysis of precisely this issue based on a review of 62 articles drawn from a wide variety of journals. Among other things, they found that one study showed that "strength of religious belief was significantly and positively related to strength of ethical standards," 7 studies found that "females are more likely to act more ethically than males," and 7 others found sex had no significant influence on ethical beliefs, a couple of studies found "managers were more ethical than students," 3 studies found Machiavellian managers "perceive ethical problems as less serious than others," 11 studies reported that "respondents saw themselves as more ethical than their peers, supervisors, or other people they knew," 5 studies found that people believed the "behavior of superiors" most influenced their own ethical behavior, 4 studies found a positive "relationship between rewards and the ethical behavior of the individual decision maker," and 2 studies found ethical decision-making inversely related to organization size and 3 others to a person's occupational level. As one would expect, there were often conflicting findings, but the preceding list of findings tended to be most representative of the total set.

Finally, then, it is worthwhile to mention that although the focus of the present essay was on different ways of measuring the impact of social science on business ethics, the causal arrows of influence obviously run in both directions. Business ethics has had and will likely continue to have a profound impact on social science. Indeed, it does not seem to be an exaggeration to say that we have not witnessed such a morally provocative influence on the social sciences since the turn of the century when virtually all of these sciences were driven by reform-minded researchers committed to improving the human condition with the help of their new tools of social analysis.

References

Ford, R. C., & Richardson, W. D. (1994). Ethical decision making: A review of the empirical literature. *Journal of Business Ethics, 13*, 205–221.

Michalos, A. C. (1980). Philosophy of science: Historical, social and value aspects. In P. T. Durbin (Ed.), *A Guide to the culture of science, technology and medicine* (pp. 197–281). New York: The Free Press.

Michalos, A. C. (1991a). *Global report on student well-being, vol. I: Life satisfaction and happiness*. New York: Springer.

Michalos, A. C. (1991b). *Global report on student well-being, vol. II: Family, friends, living partner and self-esteem*. New York: Springer.

Michalos, A. C. (1992). Ethical considerations in evaluation. *The Canadian Journal of Program Evaluation, 7*, 61–75.

Michalos, A. C. (1993a). *Global report on student well-being, vol. Ill: Employment, finances, housing and transportation*. New York: Springer.

Michalos, A. C. (1993b). *Global report on student well-being, vol. IV: Religion, education, recreation and health*. New York: Springer.

Robertson, D. C. (1993). Empiricism in business ethics: Suggested research directions. *Journal of Business Ethics, 8*, 585–600.

Veenhoven, R. (1993a). *Bibliography of happiness: 2472 contemporary studies on subjective appreciation of life*. Rotterdam: Erasmus University, Department of Social Sciences, Center for Socio-Cultural Transformation.

Veenhoven, R. (1993b). *Happiness in nations: Subjective appreciation of life in 56 nations 1946–1992*. Rotterdam: Erasmus University, Department of Social Sciences, Center for Socio-Cultural Transformation.

Chapter 2
Business Ethics and the Quality of Life

Alex C. Michalos

Ethical Foundations

For a moral consequentialist, the connection between business ethics and quality of life is very close and direct. In general, moral philosophers may be divided into two very broad groups: deontologists and consequentialists. Deontologists hold that some human actions are inherently morally good or evil—for example, murder is inherently bad, whereas telling the truth is inherently good. Consequentialists hold that no human actions are inherently morally good or evil, but all human actions are subject to evaluation from a moral point of view. The moral point of view may be based on one of the following principles:

1. Principle of beneficence: One ought to try to act so that one's actions tend to impartially improve the quality of life of those affected by the actions.
2. No harm principle: One ought to try to act so that one's actions tend not to harm anyone affected by the actions.

Depending on how one regards one's basic moral principles, there may not be much difference between a deontologist and a consequentialist. If, for example, a consequentialist believes that either the principle of beneficence or the no harm principle specifies a kind of action that is inherently moral, then at that level the consequentialist is also a deontologist. If, on the other hand, a consequentialist believes that the institution of morality is constructed by human beings, for

---

Michalos, A.C.: 2012. Business ethics and the quality of life. In R. Chadwick (Ed.) Encyclopedia of Applied Ethics (pp. 361–364). Amsterdam: Elsevier.

A.C. Michalos (✉)
University of Northern British Columbia, Prince George, BC, Canada
e-mail: michalos@brandonu.ca

A.C. Michalos, *How Good Policies and Business Ethics Enhance Good Quality of Life*, DOI 10.1007/978-3-319-50724-8_2

whatever reason, then that sort of consequentialist is not a deontologist. This article is written from the perspective of the latter sort of consequentialism.

Assuming that one is going to try to act in accordance with the principle of beneficence, again broadly speaking, there are two ways to go:

1. One can try to improve relatively objective circumstances that are measured by things such as ensuring that people have access to freshwater and clean air, full employment with fair wages, cleaner and safer workplaces, and longer lives free of disability and disease, as well as elimination of poverty and homelessness and the reduction of crime.
2. One can try to improve relatively subjective circumstances that are measured by people's reported peace of mind, contentment, happiness, and satisfaction.

Clearly, if one's relatively objective and subjective circumstances are improved, then the quality of one's life is improved. Since the fifth century before Christ, people have haggled about what is objective, what is subjective, and which is more important. However, it is evidently trivially true that if one's total circumstances are improved, one is better off and the quality of one's life has improved. Thus, in general, one's moral obligation is to try to act so that the quality of people's lives is improved objectively and subjectively.

Because actions performed by businesspeople are a species of human actions, morally speaking, one ought to conduct one's business activities in accordance with the principle of beneficence. Bertrand Russell once complained about John Dewey's consequentialist moral point of view on the grounds that the latter left no moral holidays. Insofar as any human activity can be examined and appraised from a moral point of view, Russell accurately saw how intrusive Dewey's and anyone else's consequentialism can be. Unlike Russell, however, most consequentialists probably believe it is a good thing, pragmatically speaking, to have a robust and demanding moral point of view, for businesspeople no less than for everyone else. If one believes that a world populated by people who actively try to improve each others' well-being is preferable to any other, and that the more people actively try to reach that goal, the more likely it is that the goal will be reached, then the absence of relief from the pursuit of this goal seems to be a very good thing indeed—morally, prudentially, and pragmatically.

The Quality of Life

When people use the phrase 'quality of life,' they sometimes intend to contrast it with quantities or numbers of something. There are, then, two quite different sorts of things that one might want to refer to when using the phrase 'quality of life.' First, one might want to refer to sorts, types, or kinds of things rather than to mere numbers of things. For example, one might want to know nor merely how many people were admitted to a hospital last year and for how long but also what sorts of people they were, male or female, young or old, rich or poor, and so on. When the term 'quality' in the phrase 'quality of life' is used in this sense, one may say that it and the phrase in which it occurs are intended to be primarily descriptive. Second, one might want to refer to the value or worth of things by using the term 'quality' in the phrase 'quality of life.' For example, one frequently hears of people making a trade-off between, for example, a high salary and better working or living conditions. Presumably, the exchange here involves monetary and some other value. That is, one exchanges the value of a certain amount of money for the value of a certain set of working or living conditions. When the term 'quality' in the phrase 'quality of life' is used in this sense, one may say that it and the phrase in which it occurs are intended to be primarily evaluative.

Both senses of the phrase 'quality of life' are important. It is important to be able to describe human existence in a fairly reliable and valid manner, and it is important to be able to evaluate human existence in the same way. The philosopher Plato is still celebrated for raising the evaluative question at least 2300 years ago when he asked, "What is a good life for an individual person and what is a good society?" However, it is often forgotten that he also raised the descriptive question, "What is the nature of an individual's or a society's life?".

The term 'social indicator' denotes a statistic that is supposed to have some significance for measuring the quality of life. The term 'social report' designates an organized collection of social indicators, and 'social accounts' designates some sort of balance sheet in which costs and benefits are assigned to the indicators in a social report. Briefly, the main difference between social reports and accounts is that the former answers the question, "How are we doing?" and the latter answers the question, "At what price?" where price might be measured in dollars, energy, personal satisfaction or dissatisfaction, or some other generally applicable medium. Social indicators that refer to personal feelings, attitudes, preferences, opinions, judgments, or beliefs of some sort are called subjective indicators—for example, satisfaction with one's health, attitudes toward exercise, and beliefs about the benefits of some therapy. Social indicators that refer to things that are relatively easily observable and measurable are called objective indicators—for example, the height and weight of people, number of people admitted to the hospital, and number of people dying per year.

From Pleasure and Pain to the Quality of Life

There is a long historical tradition of moral consequentialists that may be traced back fairly directly to Jeremy Bentham's ideas about a 'felicific calculus' that would allow decision makers to calculate the net pleasure or pain connected to every action for everyone affected by that action, with public policy choices made to get the greatest net pleasure or least net pain for the greatest number of people. Because pleasure and pain are relatively transient experiences, something more durable would better suit Bentham's purpose. If happiness is regarded as a relatively long-lasting positive experience and/or attitude, then that would distinguish it from transient pleasurable mood states and would justify moving from Bentham's greatest pleasure principle to Mill's greatest happiness for the greatest number. For economists, utility theory is the apparent heir of Bentham and Mill. Utility theory is formally elegant and has been an enormously fruitful source of research programs in individual and group decision making related to commercial markets, social and political relations, bargaining, conflict resolution, gaming, and scarce resource allocation in practically all areas. It is the heart of microeconomics. Unfortunately, utility theory (as is the case for many other theories) is much better on paper and in classroom exercises than it is in practice, especially in public policy making. Worse, utility theory begins with revealed preferences that are the mere tips of socially, psychologically, and pragmatically constructed icebergs of more or less coherent systems of knowledge, opinions, attitudes, desires, and needs. However, for present purposes, the defects of utility theory as a psychosocial theory of perceived well-being are not its major problem. Its major problem is that it merely provides information about the subjective states of people, although we know that people's objectively measurable circumstances are also important features of the quality of their lives. Because, morally speaking, our commitment ought to be not merely to improving people's (subjective) feelings and attitudes about their lives but also to improving the very (objective) conditions in which they live their lives, defining our basic principle of beneficence in terms of the quality of life seems to be most appropriate.

Critical Issues for Consequentialist Quality of Life Assessment

The main disadvantage of accepting the principle of beneficence as one's fundamental moral principle is that it is far from clear how one ought to measure the quality of life for an individual or group. In fact, because the vast majority of—if not all—human actions affect other people as well as the individual actors, it is primarily the quality of life of groups that actors have to try to assess. At least since Simon's pioneering work leading to his notion of 'satisficing behavior,' we have known that all attempts at thoroughly synoptic, comprehensive assessments of any human action are impossible. We are bound to stop measuring whenever we think we have measured enough for the particular problem before us. Although Simon and others seemed to think that meant that the ideal of comprehensive assessment ought to be abandoned, Michalos argued that the ideal is still a good guide to principled and deliberate human action. One just has to grant that despite one's best efforts, one will most likely fall short of the ideal.

An ideal consequentialist assessment of the quality of life of an individual or group would have to satisfactorily address the following critical issues:

1. Affected population: Who will be affected by the action, from the actor alone to everyone else? Can one know all the people more or less affected?
2. Spatial coordinates: Across what amount of space should one look, from one's own home to the whole world?
3. Temporal coordinates: Across what length of time should one look, how far into the future?
4. Population composition: How should the affected individuals be characterized, if at all, in terms of sex, age, education, ethnic background, income, etc.?
5. Domains of life composition: What domains of life should be examined—for example, health, job, family life, and housing?
6. Objective versus subjective indicators: Supposing one grants that both kinds of indicators are important, how should one decide exactly which kind to use for which domains?
7. Input versus output indicators: Should one measure only what one invests, what comes of the investment, or both?
8. Benefits and costs: What particular benefits and costs should be counted, for which individuals and groups?
9. Discount rates: How much should one discount costs and benefits delivered some time in the future compared to those delivered today?
10. Measurement scales: There are usually different ways to measure the same and different things. How should one choose the best sort of scale or measuring device?
11. Distributions: How should central tendencies and variation be measured in diverse fields?
12. Interaction effects: How should one measure causal interactions in any particular array of phenomena?
13. Confidence levels: Because one often lacks complete certainty regarding the truth of claims, what level of confidence should one require to accept any particular claim?
14. Research procedures: Because one's data are as good as one's search and research procedures, what adequacy criteria should be used to assess procedures?
15. Research personnel: The procedures one uses are likely to be as reliable as the people doing the research. How should one choose one's experts, if indeed experts are to be chosen at all?
16. Aggregation function: How should all the diverse elements of the assessment be aggregated?
17. Assessment assessor: Who should decide (audit) if the assessment is adequate or appropriate?
18. Assessment criteria: What criteria should be used to assess (audit) the adequacy of the assessment?

Some Problems

In the presence of so many questions to be answered, it is not surprising that even people who share the same general approach to moral appraisal might reach different conclusions about the same cases. In such cases, those who answer different questions in different ways will have to negotiate a common approach, which of course may or may not work, depending on the cases and the appraisers.

Although the fundamental moral principle of beneficence articulated previously prescribes a kind of act consequentialism, most consequentialists probably operate as rule consequentialists most of the time and only attempt comprehensive moral assessment when conventional rules conflict or appear too blunt or unsophisticated for especially complicated cases.

Apart from the difficulties in applying or operationalizing the principle of beneficence, some people might object that the principle is irrelevant to business ethics because businesspeople have their own ethical principles. This problem was addressed by Michalos (1987). Briefly, the argument he presented was that the idea that there are different moral principles for different fields of endeavor (e.g., business, baseball, and chess) is logically incoherent. Because one of the conditions for an acceptable moral theory is that it should be able to resolve conflicts of interest (without resorting to civil or criminal laws), there must be a single, supreme moral principle. Without such a principle to adjudicate between conflicting interests or lower level maxims, moral appeals are useless. When conflicts arise involving businesspeople and environmentalists, for example, people in each group can retreat to their own special code, making it impossible to use either code to resolve the conflict. Thus, at that point, one must either reject the idea that moral theories must be able to resolve conflicts of interest or reject the idea that both of the two codes in conflict are moral codes. Because rejection of the former alternative would allow us to have useless moral theories, the latter alternative should be rejected. Thus, although there may be no objection to anyone saying that they will live by this or that code of conduct, it is nonsensical (literally logically absurd) to suppose that any old code of conduct qualifies as a moral code.

Conclusion

The aim of this article was to show how business ethics is connected to the quality of people's lives. For a consequentialist moral theory based on the principle of beneficence, the connection is close and direct. Although such a theory certainly has its disadvantages, they are not more troublesome than the disadvantages of other theories.

See also: Consequentialism and Deontology.

Further Reading

Michalos, A. C. (1978). *Foundations of decision-making*. Ottawa, ON: Canadian Library of Philosophy.
Michalos, A. C. (1980a). *North American social report, Vol. 1: Foundations, population and health*. Dordrecht: Reidel.
Michalos, A. C. (1980b). *North American social report, Vol. 2: Crime, justice and politics*. Dordrecht: Reidel.
Michalos, A. C. (1981a). *North American social report, Vol. 3: Science, education and recreation*. Dordrecht: Reidel.
Michalos, A. C. (1981b). *North American social report, Vol. 4: Environment, transportation and housing*. Dordrecht: Reidel.
Michalos, A. C. (1982). *North American social report, Vol. 5: Economics, religion and morality*. Dordrecht: Reidel.
Michalos, A. C. (1985). Multiple discrepancies theory (MDT). *Social Indicators Research, 16*, 347–413.
Michalos, A. C. (1987). Moral responsibility in business. In D. C. Poff & W. Waluchow (Eds.), *Business ethics in Canada* (pp. 12–25). Scarborough, ON: Prentice-Hall Canada.
Michalos, A. C. (1991a). *Global report on student well-being, Vol. 1: Life satisfaction and happiness*. New York: Springer.
Michalos, A. C. (1991b). *Global report on student well-being, Vol. 2: Family, friends, living partner and self-esteem*. New York: Springer.
Michalos, A. C. (1993a). *Global report on student well-being, Vol. 3: Employment, finances, housing and transportation*. New York: Springer.
Michalos, A. C. (1993b). *Global report on student well-being, Vol. 4: Religion, education, recreation and health*. New York: Springer.
Michalos, A. C. (1995). *A pragmatic approach to business ethics*. Thousand Oaks, CA: Sage.
Michalos, A. C. (2003). *Essays on the quality of life*. Dordrecht, The Netherlands: Kiuwer.
Michalos, A. C. (Ed.). (2005). *Citation classics from social indicators research*. Dordrecht: Springer.

Relevant Website

http://www.isqols.org—International Society for Quality-of-Life Srudies.

Chapter 3
The Costs of Decision-Making

Alex C. Michalos

In this paper an attempt is made to construct the rudiments of a system of cost accounting to be used in the evaluation of the costs of employing decision makers and decision procedures. By "decision makers" I mean any individual, group, or mechanical device from whom or which decisions may be obtained, e.g., ordinary people, public officials, managers, committees, the United States Senate, a computer program, etc. By "decision procedures" I mean any techniques that may be used to obtain a decision, i.e., majority rule by a show of hands, scanning an encyclopedia, flipping a coin, asking an expert, natural deduction, etc. By "a system of cost accounting" I mean a classification scheme whose divisions and subdivisions could be useful in the systematic search for and organization of all those costs that may arise as a result of employing certain decision makers and/or procedures.

In section "Production, Implementation and Failure", production, implementation and failure costs are distinguished. Sections "Production Costs", "Implementation Costs", and "Failure Costs" are devoted to a more thorough analysis of each of these three types of costs. Section "Overview" contains a brief overview of the preceding sections. This is followed by an examination and modification of certain results of other theorists regarding the relations between bargaining and protection (section "Bargaining and Protection"). Finally, we investigate the costs of over-and underplanning from the point of view of inventory problems (section "Planning Costs").

Michalos, A.C.: 1970. The costs of decision making. Public Choice, 9, pp. 39–51.

A.C. Michalos (✉)
University of Northern British Columbia, Prince George, BC, Canada
e-mail: michalos@brandonu.ca

A.C. Michalos, *How Good Policies and Business Ethics Enhance Good Quality of Life*, DOI 10.1007/978-3-319-50724-8_3

Production, Implementation and Failure

When one sets out to determine the cost of employing a decision-maker or procedure to make a particular decision, one is immediately confronted with a threefold ambiguity. First, one is tempted to focus on the costs of reaching a decision in a certain way, say, with the help of a certain decision-maker or procedure. So one considers such things as research techniques, equipment, organization, personnel, time, labor, insurance, etc. Such costs will be called *production costs* because they are, after all, nothing more than the costs of producing a particular decision. Alternatively one is tempted to focus on the costs of action based on the decisions produced. Interestingly enough these admit of broad classifications virtually identical to production costs, i.e., time, labor, equipment, etc. We call all those costs involved in acting on a particular decision *implementation costs.*

The third sort of costs that one is tempted to focus on are those that result from the failure of one's efforts of production or implementation or both. We call these *failure costs.* Failure costs become isolated because relative to a given set of resources, production and/or implementation costs tend to be fixed while failure costs tend to be extremely variable. For example, the production and/or implementation costs of a football team selecting and carrying out a particular play would generally be very much the same in practice and in a game. Indeed, one of the primary goals of practice sessions is to reduce the differences between such sessions and ordinary game conditions with respect to such costs in order to increase predictability. Moreover, even though a coach will try to simulate game conditions by instructing, scolding, screaming, etc. to impress players with the costs of their failing to perform in a certain way, everyone knows that it is usually much less costly to fail in practice than in a game. Similarly the reason management trainees are drilled in business games, cadets play war games, medical students carve cadavers, etc. is that the costs of errors (failure) in such situations is considerably less than in "real life."

Let us consider each of these three kinds of costs more carefully.

Production Costs

This class of costs may be divided into four subclasses: methods, materials, personnel and overhead costs. We will consider each in turn.

By *methods costs* we mean all those costs which are incurred as a result of a particular method being used by a decision maker and/or with the application of a decision procedure in order to produce some decision. Clearly the costs of employing a certain person to produce a particular decision will vary with the methods he uses and the way he uses them. A careless and the unsystematic decision maker will produce fewer acceptable decisions per unit of cost than a careful and systematic one. Similar remarks are applicable to the employment of procedures. A simple group decision procedure like majority rule by a show of hands can become extremely costly if the method of applying it is perverse. For example, if pertinent information is withheld from some members of the group, time for preparation or research is shortened, discussions limited or individuals coerced, the procedure loses some of its strength and the per unit cost of acceptable decisions increases. Hence, whether we are considering the production costs of employing people or a procedure, we must investigate the methods costs involved.

Materials costs cover all those incurred for raw material and necessary equipment. These include everything from pencils and paper to highspeed computers. Materials costs for decision-makers working on sociological problems might involve the purchase of standardized questionnaires, recording and transcribing hardware, and some means of transportation. Similarly, different procedures have different materials costs. The procedure of testing syllogisms for validity by syllogistic rules does not require any material. The use of Venn diagrams for the same purpose creates a small paper and pencil costs. Thus, whether we are considering the production costs of employing people or procedures, we must investigate the materials costs involved.

By *personnel costs* we mean all those that are more or less directly attached to individuals employed to produce a decision or to produce a decision using a particular procedure. Alternatively we might use the term human costs since what is involved are costs which have specific reference to such distinctively human characteristics as intelligence; the ability to communicate, persuade and bargain; sensitivity to moral, esthetic and religious values, etc.

The most obvious sort of personnel costs that may be incurred pertain to formal education and informal experience. The former might be quite general such as the cost of a college education, or it might be more specific such as the cost of a six-week course in computer programming for certain employees. Because this sort of training is fairly standardized, the task of appraising its cost is comparatively straightforward, i.e., straightforward in comparison to the determination of informal experience costs. The latter can be extremely difficult. The authors of the Constitution of the United States required Senators to have reached an age of thirty years and Presidents thirty-five. Presumably they believed that a certain amount of experience is an important asset for public officials and that a necessary condition for obtaining such experience is a certain amount of time. Whatever the merits of this view, what must be granted is that experience has its own costs and someone has to be stuck with the bill.

The next sort of personnel costs to be noticed has received a considerable amount of attention by Buchanan and Tullock (1962). They are bargaining or persuasion costs. These authors examined the relations between such costs and group decision procedures requiring various proportions of group agreement in order to produce a decision that would be binding on the whole group. They concluded correctly, if all other things are equal, that as the necessary proportion increases, bargaining or persuasion costs increase. It costs less to persuade a simple majority than an absolute one, less an absolute one than 2/3, less 2/3 than 3/4 and less 3/4 than the whole group (unanimous decision). What must be emphasized here is that many other things are frequently not equal. Indeed, bargaining or persuasion costs seem to vary more with the peculiar qualities of group members than with their quantity. As every school teacher knows, the cost of "selling" a particular idea to three different classes of roughly the same size can vary considerably. What is vitally important to these costs is the past experience, training, industry, interest, ability, temperament, manners, etc. of both students and teacher. Similarly, the crucial variables involved in the bargaining and persuasion costs required for a particular group to employ a particular procedure are those that reflect these qualities. Buchanan and Tullock insist that one cannot answer the question "What proportion of a group must agree in order to bind the whole group to their decision?" until one knows what issue is before them. I would insist that the question cannot be answered until one *also* knows what personal qualities (education, temperament, experience, etc.) are required and possessed by the group members.

A third important sort of personnel costs are those resulting from the violation of an individual's or group's moral principles, rules or norms. If, for example, a South Vietnamese voter is opposed to allowing communists (criminals for him) to vote or to hold a seat in the legislature, then the employment of election procedures permitting universal adult suffrage or of communists in the law-making assembly must have additional costs for that voter. While he might recognize the enormous costs of instability and war that arise in preventing "the other side" from having a voice in governmental decision-making, such costs may not seem as high to him as those incurred by the abandonment of his moral principles. He might prefer to be dead rather than red.

Finally, we should mention labor costs as a fourth important species of personnel cost. In the simplest cases, these would be measured by the time required by a particular decision maker to make certain kinds of decisions or by the average time required by people employing a particular procedure. Alternatively we might measure the amount of human activity required in order to employ some decision maker or procedure.

All businessmen are familiar with *overhead costs*. These are more or less unavoidable costs that are not readily attached to the production of any specific item. For example, whether we manufacture balloons, baskets or baseball bats we would have to pay for our factories, land, power, heat, water, taxes, insurance, labor, etc. whether business was booming or not. These expenses are incurred just for being in business, even though business might be bad. Moreover, it seems to be the case that an analogous set of costs arises for the production of decisions by a particular decision-maker or procedure. A decision-maker will have to be somewhere for some time. So someone will have to pay for his upkeep which may be high, low or medium depending on his tastes, the company budget and their mutual bargaining strengths. Similarly a procedure can only be applied somewhere for some time, and someone will have to pay for the time and the place, e.g., a town meeting type of government must tie up people's spare time and may even require the construction of a Town Hall.

The problem of protecting oneself from the "external effects" of other people's decisions has been given considerable attention by political scientists and philosophers. The costs incurred for such protection may be regarded as a fundamental species of overhead cost. It might involve expenses resulting from prevention policies or programs, insurance or retention. These are merely three ways of protecting oneself against losses due to unexpected occurrences. (See: Denenberg 1964.) Clearly "unexpected occurrences" include many phenomena that are not the result of anyone's decisions, design or activity. If we employ Smith as our decision-maker for a certain set of problems, no one can be blamed if he develops a brain tumor that destroys his ability to make decisions or if he suddenly drops dead. Nevertheless, if the decisions Smith is supposed to make are important, then in one way or another we must protect ourselves against these eventualities. Let us briefly examine the three means of protection suggested above; namely, retention, insurance and prevention.

When one protects himself against losses incurred through the employment of some decision-maker or procedure by maintaining enough assets to be able to sustain any loss arising from the employment, he is protecting himself by *retention* of the risk. That is, rather than transferring the risk of loss to someone else (taking out insurance), he is retaining it himself. When one protects himself against losses resulting from the employment of some decision-maker or procedure by transferring the risk of such losses to someone else, he is protecting himself by *insurance.* The advantage of insurance over retention is primarily the reduction of assets that one must maintain more or less secure and, therefore, more or less idle and unproductive. With insurance one obtains the protection he needs for a relatively small price, which allows him to use the remainder of his assets for other things. The most thorough way to protect oneself against losses resulting from the employment of a particular decision-maker or procedure is through prevention, i.e., the elimination of the sources of risk. For example, one way to protect oneself against losses resulting from urban renewal programs is to slow down urban deterioration by strengthening building and maintenance codes and their enforcement. Concomitantly one could initiate clean-up programs with teach-ins, contests, prizes and other sorts of propaganda and incentives in order to secure the support of the citizenry.

These then, are the three basic means of protecting oneself against losses arising from the employment of a particular person or procedure to produce a decision. In appraising the overhead costs of employing a person or procedure, one must select the most efficient means available (the one which yields the greatest amount of protection for the smallest price) and add its cost to the other production costs.

Implementation Costs

Even when implementation costs are clearly distinguishable from production costs, the former may be subdivided exactly like the latter. That is to say, the former will have methods, material, personnel, and overhead costs. We need not spend much time analyzing these subdivisions, because at the level at which we are working our remarks would be quite similar to those made with respect to production costs.

In order to illustrate my claim that the subdivisions of these two sorts of costs are basically the same, we shall consider Lyndon Johnson's decision to increase the number of United States servicemen in Vietnam to over 500 thousand. Having employed certain methods to reach this difficult decision (which methods no doubt included an appraisal of the implementation and possible failure costs of various alternatives), it is apparent that some other methods are necessarily involved in its implementation. For example, the latter include costs incurred as a result of using particular logistical formulae and techniques of transporting troops and supplies. While the material costs of production and implementation probably both include expenses for computers, only the latter involve tanks, fighter planes, cannons, rifles, etc. Similarly, personnel costs of production and implementation include secretarial fees, but the latter also includes special fees for fighter pilots, spies, tactical engineers, propagandists, etc. And finally, the overhead costs (food, clothing, ordinary medical care, etc.) of just maintaining an army of 500 thousand men on the other side of the world obviously dwarf the overhead costs of reaching the decision to do it. Hence, although the subdivisions of the implementation costs of Johnson's decision are like those of its production costs, the specific cost-incurring items appearing in the subdivisions are not the same. Furthermore, this discrepancy is quite typical. Indeed, it is the existence of this discrepancy in specific items that drives one to the more general division between production and implementation costs in the first place.

Failure Costs

Having paid the price of employing a particular decision-maker or procedure to reach and implement a certain decision, the final costs that one is liable to incur willy-nilly are those resulting from a failure to produce a "correct" decision or to implement it properly or both. It has already been noted that failure costs may be distinguished from production and implementation costs because the former tend to be variable while the latter tend to be fixed. We could also draw a distinction between these costs on the grounds that the latter must be paid whether or not failure occurs. Failure costs may be usefully subdivided into classes of direct losses, indirect losses and the estimated-value-of-success losses. We will consider each of these in turn.

By *direct losses* we mean those that are incurred more or less overtly and immediately by reaching an "incorrect" decision and/or failing to implement it appropriately. For example, a man who is fired after informing his employer that he had decided to form a shop union might say that the decision cost him his job. Alternatively he might simply have begun to organize the work force without informing his employer, and still have lost his job. In this case he might say that it was his implementing activity that cost him his job rather than the mere decision to form the union. Perhaps, he might reason, he could have been spared that cost if he had ventured to tell his boss of his decision before attempting to implement it.

Indirect losses are those that are incurred more or less covertly and precariously as a result of reaching and/or implementing an "incorrect" decision. Of course there is quite a vague area between such losses and direct ones, but it seems worthwhile to draw the distinction for the sake of the fairly clear-cut extremes. For example, if after losing his job for supporting union organizers, a man slowly withdrew his support from social organizations or tended to mistrust people or to doubt his own principles or to question his manliness, etc. we might regard any of these effects as indirect losses resulting from his earlier decision. They are probably due to a combination of things, but the fact that they seem to have been initiated by that decision makes them candidates for inclusion in its class of indirect losses. By calling them "indirect losses" we suggest that their full value might be appropriately weighted (and, therefore, discounted) by a personal probability value indicating the degree of uncertainty regarding their connection to that decision.

By the *estimated-value-of-success losses* we mean an individual or group's best estimate of the total value of reaching a "correct" decision, or of implementing it successfully, or both. This requires some explanation. We assume that every "correct" decision and/or successful implementation of it may be assigned some more or less plausible value, sometimes in quantitative terms and sometimes not. To take a trivial example, we might say that a person who wins a thousand dollars on a quiz program for making the "right" decision has produced a decision worth about a thousand dollars. If his partner wins another thousand for appropriately implementing the announced decision, we might say that the value of the implementation is also about a thousand dollars. These are nice neat quantifiable cases (provided that we do not push the analysis more deeply to "real income," etc.). The following is considerably less tidy. Suppose a general makes a decision regarding a strategic maneuver which subsequently leads to the complete rout of the enemy. There might be some question as to whether it was "really" his decision or those of his subordinates or their implementing activities or some combination of these things or something else that deserves credit for the victory. But, more importantly for our purposes, the evaluation of an event like the rout of an enemy would be extremely complicated. Although one can put a fairly reliable price (in dollars and cents) on weapons, clothing, food, communication and transportation equipment, an appraisal of the value of the lives lost and of the effects on morale and determination (of winners and losers) is more difficult. Nevertheless, we are assuming that some sort of an evaluation of all these aspects may be made. Moreover, we are assuming that in the absence of success, people are able to and frequently do estimate the value that success would have been to them. In the midst of failure, people form an image of what might have been and, depending on their attitudes toward "spilt milk" or "birds in the bush" of various sorts (i.e., toward the present value of lost benefits or benefits weighted by a personal probability indicating their presumed proximity to possession), they ascribe value to it. Then their assessment of the failure costs of employing this or that decision-maker or procedure to reach and/or implement the faulty decision is formed by adding their estimated-value-of-success loss to their direct and indirect losses.

Overview

What we have now is a classification of decision making costs that contains eleven main subdivisions. Production and implementation costs are subdivided into methods, materials, personnel (or human) and overhead costs, while failure costs are subdivided into direct, indirect and estimated-value-of-success losses. From a practical point of view, the classificatory scheme may be regarded as exhaustive, i.e., all costs may be located in one of the subdivisions. Moreover, practically speaking there would seem to be no problem in regarding the classes as exclusive, i.e., an item taken account of in one class could unambiguously be omitted from all others. From a logical point of view, I would doubt both the exhaustiveness of the analysis and the exclusiveness of the subdivisions, i.e., there seems to be nothing self-contradictory about the idea that one could construct a scheme that captured more items more precisely. Since my primary aim is to open, broaden or increase the scope of investigations of decision making costs, the former (practical) point of view is of fundamental importance. Hence, the logical incompleteness of my scheme (if indeed it *is* logically incomplete) is tolerable. In the next section. I will consider an immediate benefit of my analysis.

Bargaining and Protection

We have already made reference to bargaining and protection costs in section "Implementation Costs". In *The Calculus of Consent,* Buchanan and Tullock show that bargaining costs and the special costs that an individual must bear to protect himself against the activity of others in a group tend to be inversely related to the proportion (majority, two-thirds, etc.) whose consent is required to bind the whole group. Bargaining costs increase with the size of this proportion, while protection costs decrease.

Although it must be granted that the cost of protecting oneself against *some* of the activities of others decreases as the decisive proportion increases, the cost of protecting oneself against some of these activities must increase. Moreover, the latter increase cannot be regarded as a product of bargaining or persuasion. For example, consider the training costs for members of some decision-making group. Generally, the larger the group, the higher the training costs. If we assume that these costs are born by someone outside the group, then we have no problem. But suppose the group must pay its own way. Then in one way or another (by insurance, prevention or retention) each member must obtain protection against losses resulting from the activities of group members in their training programs. Training costs usually include some raw materials,—textbooks, reference libraries, teachers, administrators, rooms, furniture, etc.—and the quantity and total cost of these resources must increase with the number of trained people required. Therefore, the amount of protection costs one must incur in order to be covered against losses arising from the use of these resources must also increase with the required number of trained people. (Within limits, of course, we may reduce some of the costs per individual by training more people at the same time, but this does not alter our claim with respect to total costs). Similarly, as more resources of *any* sort are required, more protection is required, and more resources are usually required whenever the size of the decisive proportion increases. Hence, contrary to the view suggested by Buchanan and Tullock, some protection costs vary in the *same* direction as bargaining costs with respect to the decisive proportion.

The conclusion we have just reached constitutes an important modification of Buchanan and Tullock's perceptive analysis of the relations between bargaining and protection costs and decisive proportions. It is apparent now that one cannot hope to merely balance protection and bargaining costs in order to select the optimal decisive proportion. One must determine exactly which protection costs should be balanced against bargaining costs and add the remaining protection costs to the result of the balancing.

Planning Costs

It may be assumed that any or all of the species of costs considered so far may be incurred while employing a decision-maker or procedure to reach and/or implement decisions with respect to problems or issues immediately present. We call these *immediate use* costs, e.g., the costs of studying a menu to determine what one should order for dinner (what would give one the most satisfaction), of a group of people trying to reach some agreement on the particular stock their club should purchase this month, or a doctor weighing the arguments for and against using a new drug on a patient, etc.

Immediate use costs may be contrasted with those which arise as a result of reaching and/or implementing decisions regarding problems or issues that are not immediate. We call the latter *planning costs,* e.g., the cost incurred by a man outlining his vacation itinerary; by a firm selecting and purchasing locations for branch offices in case of expansion; by a mayor organizing anti-riot strategies including the construction of temporary blockades and fences, increasing his staff of policemen, private detectives, special assistants, etc. All of these decision-makers are faced with the task of preparing for events whose occurrences are more or less probable. Whether or not they are under any particular stress now, they almost certainly will be later if they do not invest some resources in planning for the future.

Planning costs may be analyzed along the lines of ordinary inventory problems, e.g., problems of stocking retail goods in a supermarket, raw materials and tools in the production division of a factory, available servicemen to look after the various types of machines in a large office building, etc. The essential characteristic of such problems is that they involve a balancing of two types of costs, namely, carrying costs and out-of-stock costs. *Carrying costs* are those that arise from keeping a supply of items on hand for future contingencies. *Out-of-stock costs* are those that arise from not keeping a sufficient supply of items on hand. Since these terms seem a bit foreign to our discussion, we will use the more descriptive analogues "overplanning" and "underplanning" costs.

The primary sources of *overplanning costs* are those arising from obsolescence and from unnecessary "handling and storage." When a procedure or person is employed to reach and/or implement decisions that will be effective or not in the future depending on how events transpire, there is some danger that much of the product of the invested resources will be obsolete, out-dated or just inappropriate for the time of need. For example, a married couple might spend a lot of their spare time planning for the college education of their three-year-old child, only to have their decisions for his welfare overruled by his own decisions. Similarly, precautions taken by a mayor and his staff today may be completely inadequate to meet the sort of tactics employed by demonstrators tomorrow. Procedures used today by college administrators to reach decisions for incoming students five years from today may be largely unacceptable to those students primarily because of the very nature of those procedures.

Unnecessary "handling and storage" costs include all those that arise from keeping more decisions (or sets of them in the form of multiphased strategies) or products of these of one sort or another on hand than one can use. They involve extra costs of organizing or systematically classifying this data, designing special searching and sorting devices to make appropriate selections for various purposes, periodic reviewing and renewing systems, etc.

The primary sources of *underplanning costs* may be regarded as those resulting from lost opportunities and goodwill, from production and/or implementation disruption and from special expedition. To take a trivial example of the first of these sources of loss, we frequently think of the "perfect" response to someone's remarks when the conversation is over. (What is worse, thereafter we find ourselves paying exorbitant overplanning costs for that response in order to be prepared for the next time which may never come.) When other people are relying on a decision-maker or procedure for a certain amount of preparation, failure to display such preparation may result in a serious loss of goodwill. The candidate without an answer to some questions loses votes as well as "face."

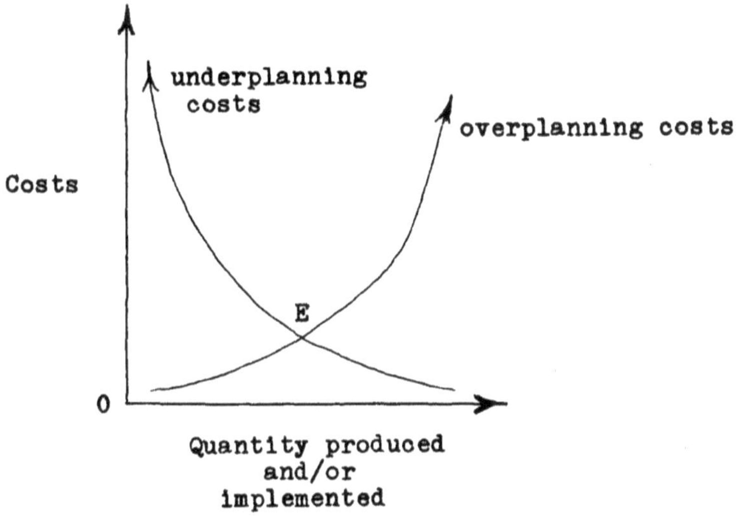

Fig. 3.1 Planning Costs

If certain decisions cannot be made and/or implemented until certain others have been, then the production and/or implementation of the former will be disrupted unless the latter are delivered on schedule. If production and/or implementation of the latter falls behind, then special expediting costs will be incurred. Such costs would include increased risks of and even commissions of errors resulting from pressures to think fast with insufficient data and the limited use of usual quality control techniques.

The main advantage of thinking about the problems of over- and underplanning from the point of view of inventory problems is that an enormous amount of operations research theory becomes *prima facie* applicable to problems of individual and group decision making. (A good idea of the amount of potentially useful theory that is available may be found in Wagner 1969.) For example, consider the general question: What is the optimal amount of planning to undertake in order to be adequately prepared for certain contingencies? One way to tackle this problem is to employ a fundamental theorem of inventory accumulation. We know that overplanning and underplanning costs tend to be inversely related to the quantity of decisions produced and/or implemented for future contingencies. That is, as the quantity of decisions produced and/or implemented for future contingencies is increased, the overplanning costs increase while the underplanning costs decrease. As that quantity is decreased, the overplanning costs decrease while the underplanning costs increase. These relations are illustrated in Fig. 3.1.

The optimal quantity to produce and/or implement for a certain period of time is evidently represented by the intersection of the underplanning and overplanning cost curves at E. This quantity may be shown to be

$$E = \sqrt{\frac{2Q\bar{c}}{\bar{r}}} \tag{3.1}$$

where $\bar{r}$ represents the average cost of carrying (in one's mind, on paper, in a library or a machine, etc.) a decision for a given period of time, $\bar{c}$ the average cost of producing and/or implementing such a decision and Q the quantity of such decisions to be used in that period (Horngren and Accounting 1967). It may be noted that E increases as Q or $\bar{c}$ increases, and as $\bar{r}$ decreases. E decreases as $\bar{r}$ increases, and as Q or $\bar{c}$ decreases.

Using $\bar{r}$ as in the last paragraph and $\bar{r}_u$ as the average underplanning cost, we may represent the *allowable rate of unpreparedness* or the relative frequency with which one may be allowed to be caught with insufficient planning by another inventory theorem:

$$A = \frac{\bar{r}}{\bar{r} + \bar{r}_u} \tag{3.2}$$

As the cost of poor preparation increases, our tolerance of such preparation decreases. Hence, for example, a mayor who envisaged extremely high costs resulting from the lack of preparation for certain kinds of demonstrations, would have a very low A-value; and we would expect to see his precautionary efforts vary inversely with the size of that value. As A increases, he should reduce his efforts. As it decreases, his efforts should increase.

Concluding Remarks

In this paper an attempt has been made to construct the rudiments of a system of cost accounting to be used in the evaluation of the costs of employing decision-makers and decision procedures. Distinctions were drawn among production, implementation and failure costs, and these three types of costs were then examined thoroughly. A brief comparison of our results with others regarding the relations between bargaining and protection costs was considered, and over- and underplanning costs were examined from the point of view of inventory problems. The comparison suggested an important modification of Buchanan and Tullock's analysis of bargaining and protection costs, while certain analogies with inventory problems suggested that research in planning theory could be aided by models from inventory theory.

References

Buchanan, J. M., & Tullock, G. (1962). *The calculus of consent*. Ann Arbor, MI: University of Michigan Press.

Denenberg, H. S. et al. (1964). *Risk and insurance*. Englewood Cliffs, New Jersey: Prentice-Hall, Inc.

Horngren, C. T. (1967). *Cost accounting*. Englewood Cliffs, NJ: Prentice-Hall, Inc.

Wagner, H. M. (1969). *Principles of operations research*. Englewood Cliffs, NJ: Prentice-Hall Inc.

Chapter 4
Efficiency and Morality

Alex C. Michalos

Praxiology is the (still very primitive) science of efficient human action. Its most prolific proponents have been the contemporary Polish philosopher Tadeusz Kotarbinski[1] and more recently Henryk Skolimowski.[2] According to both of these philosophers, praxiologists are and should be *as* praxiologists concerned with practical values but not moral values. Skolimowski tells us that:

> Praxiology does use a system of *values* to assess various deeds, but practical values are different from ethical as well as from aesthetic values. The deed, excellently performed from a praxiological point of view, can be aesthetically neutral and at the same time morally repulsive.[3]

And Kotarbinski claims that

> … what may be good from the praxiological point of view may be justly condemned on ethical grounds.[4]

Because I share the enthusiasm of these philosophers for this infant. science, I would like to persuade them and other students that the elimination of moral values

Michalos, A.C.: 1972. Efficiency and morality. Journal of Value Inquiry, 6, pp. 137–143.

[1]Tadeusz Kotarbinski, *Praxiology: An Introduction to the Sciences of Efficient Action*. Oxford: Pergamon Press, 1965.
[2]Henryk Skolimowski, "Praxiology—the science of accomplished acting," *The Personalist,* Vol. 46, No. 3, 1965. "The structure of thinking in technology," *Technology and Culture,* Vol. 7, No. 3, 1966.
[3]"Praxiology—the science of accomplished acting," p. 355.
[4]*Op. cit.*, p. 159.

A.C. Michalos (✉)
University of Northern British Columbia, Prince George, BC, Canada
e-mail: michalos@brandonu.ca

A.C. Michalos, *How Good Policies and Business Ethics Enhance Good Quality of Life*, DOI 10.1007/978-3-319-50724-8_4

from the essential concerns of a praxiologist is a demonstrably serious mistake.[5] Or, to put my thesis positively and provisionally, whenever a human action has any moral value, that value must be included in or taken account of in the appraisal of its practical value. Human beings certainly *can* perform actions that have little or nothing to do with moral values, e.g, they can scratch their heads, put on their socks, blow their noses, etc. But when moral value *is* present in an action, it is not irrelevant to but essentially partially constitutive of practical value.

Lest any reader be kept in suspense unnecessarily, the argument for my thesis may be roughly summarized as follows. In order to determine the practical value of an action, we must assess it from the point of view of efficiency. Its efficiency is some function of the benefits and costs attached to it. It *may* involve typically moral benefits and costs such as the strengthening or weakening of one's integrity, honesty, fairness, kindness, thoughtfulness, courage, benevolence, etc. But the only way to know whether or to what extent such values are involved in any action is to include an inquiry into their presence in our system of cost-benefit accounting. Hence, in order to determine the practical value of a human action, we must include an inquiry into its moral value, i.e. its moral benefits and costs. In the remaining paragraphs of this paper I will develop this argument more carefully.

By the *practical value* of a human action I mean its effectiveness and efficiency as a means of achieving some end. For example, the practical value of swatting flies is nothing more than the effectiveness and efficiency with which swatting eliminates flies; the practical value of spraying flies with some insecticide is the effectiveness and efficiency with which spraying eliminates flies; etc.

I say "effectiveness *and* efficiency" because, although some philosophers seem to use the two terms interchangeably,[6] they certainly designate two different but essentially related ideas. An action which is intended to accomplish a certain task for some agent is *effective* for that task exactly insofar as the latter is actually accomplished by the former. Fly swatting is an effective action insofar as a given swatter's swat (a direct hit) obliterates the swattee, i.e, the fly. Spraying insecticide is an effective action insofar as it kills or prevents the growth of insects.

The *efficiency* of an action is defined and measured by the ratio of its benefits (including effectiveness) to its performance costs, i.e, by the ratio of what we get (benefits) to what we pay for (costs).[7] My son and I find that the action of pounding a nail with a hammer is an effective means of driving a nail into a board, but it is a more efficient procedure for me than for him. He swings more and hits less, not

---

[5]Unfortunately, it is a mistake which I have also made in "Decision-making in committees," *American Philosophical Quarterly* Vol. 7, No. 2, 1970.

[6]For examples, see Skolimowski, "The structure of thinking in technology," p. 376; Mario Bunge, "Towards a philosophy of technology," *Technology and Culture,* Vol. 7, No. 3, 1966, third section: John C. Harsanyi, "Individualistic and functionalistic explanations in the light of game theory: the example of social status," *Problems in the Philosophy of Science,* ed. I. Lakatos and A. Musgrave, Amsterdam: North-Holland Publishing Co., 1968. pp. 306–307.

[7]Alternatively, one could use a more subtle marginal definition involving the ratio of the rate of increase of benefits per unit increase of cost.

counting fingers. If he could get his father to pound nails for him as often as he likes (which is virtually impossible) his most efficient means of driving nails would be to simply ask his father to drive them. Unfortunately, he knows that procedure is practically worthless because it is almost always completely ineffective. My wife, on the other hand, is a much more efficient nail driver than my son, provided that we do not count pain costs incurred (directly by her and indirectly by the rest of us, especially me) when she smashes her fingers. Her ratio of direct (nail) hits to misses is nearly the same as mine, but she puts a very high price on smashed fingers and that drives her efficiency ratio down. Since, unlike my son's requests, hers do produce the desired results (often enough), the practical value of her asking me to pound some nails here or there is substantial. Her requests are practically speaking more valuable than her own nail-driving activity. The former are finally as effective as the latter, and considerably more efficient.

I gather that by now the important difference between effectiveness and efficiency is clear. Effectiveness is a property which an action may have or not have, perhaps to a certain degree. Efficiency is a relation (more precisely a ratio) between benefits (including effectiveness) and costs.

I have already suggested that and illustrated how the efficiency ratio, and hence, practical value of an action is determined by what we count as and how we count benefits and costs. I shall now give an outline of a system of cost accounting which will provide a framework for appraising the costs of human action.[8] Parts of the system would be applicable to an analysis of benefits, but I have not examined its utility from this point of view and will not pursue the matter now. Hereafter our discussion will be focused on costs rather than benefits and costs.

The costs of an action may be divided first into the three broad categories of production, implementation and failure costs. *Production costs* are those that are incurred in order to reach a decision to act. In terms of one of the homely examples we have been using, production costs might involve examining various types of insecticides and fly swatters, estimating the scope of the problem (perhaps there are already too many flies in the house to attempt a massive swatting campaign), reviewing past experience, etc. *Implementation costs* are those that are incurred through acting on a particular decision. They might, for example, include the dollars and cents cost of purchasing an insecticide, a sprayer or a fly swatter, the time required to swat or spray all the flies in the house, the labour involved in spraying or swatting, etc. *Failure costs* are those that result from the failure of one's efforts of production or implementation or both. Failure costs must be distinguished because relative to a given set of resources, production and implementation costs tend to be *fixed* while failure costs tend to be extremely variable. If my wife drives her thumb into the wall instead of the nail when she is all alone, her failure cost consists mainly of physical pain. If she drives her thumb into the wall while I am

[8] A more thorough discussion may be found in my "An analysis of decision making costs," *Methodology and Science* (Forthcoming) and "A theory of decision making evaluation" which is at present unpublished.

watching, her costs zoom upward as embarrassment (not to say insult) is added to injury. The football player who drops a pass in practice loses the confidence of his quarterback, but in a game he might lose six points as well.

Production and implementation costs may be subdivided into four identically labeled classes; namely, methods, materials, human and overhead costs. While the four general rubrics are the same, the particular kinds of items that are included in, say, production methods costs as opposed to implementation methods costs are typically different. Each of these subclasses shall be briefly examined.

Methods costs are those that are incurred as a result of the particular methods of production and implementation used by a given agent. Given a house full of flies, one person might try to decide what to do by consulting his neighbor, another by consulting a book on insecticides, another by reviewing his past experience, another by combining some of these procedures. Having reached the decision to, say, attack the problem with an insecticide, one person might spray lightly while another would spray heavily, one might concentrate on likely breeding areas while another would concentrate on areas most used by the family, one might proceed systematically while another proceeded randomly, etc. Clearly different methods of deciding and doing this or that frequently involve different costs.

Materials costs are those incurred as a result of using some sort of equipment and/or raw materials to produce and act upon a decision. The cost of deciding how to attack the fly problem might include a slight automobile expense incurred while driving to and from a hardware store, a handbook on insecticides, a dictionary to help translate the handbook, or perhaps a ten cent telephone call to a knowledgeable friend. The implementation materials might include a fly swatter, can of insecticide, sprayer, flypaper, etc.

Human costs are those which arise in exchange for typically human abilities and characteristics that are involved in the production and implementation of decisions. Broadly speaking they include the costs of education; communication; moral and religious principles; social and political views; psychological idiosyncracies (personal images, systematic behavior, drive, etc.) esthetic sensitivities and economic propensities (risk taking, entrepreneurship, etc.). Even such banal activities as pounding a nail into a wall may become fraught with human costs, costs which logically could not arise for, say, an ordinary nail-pounding machine. The machine cannot be embarrassed or frustrated by missing a nail. It cannot be insulted, morally troubled or disturbed by being put to work at a certain time, e.g. Sunday morning. It has nothing else to do, no interesting opportunities to forgo. It cannot feel unjustly overworked or underpaid, etc. Win or lose John Henry must pay a higher price for his performance than a spike-driving machine, just as Charley Gordon paid more dearly than Algernon the mouse every time they matched wits in the maze. Machines and mice do not care if they are somehow superior or inferior to human beings—which causes some of the latter to believe that the former "really" are superior and others to believe that they "really" are inferior. For our purposes it is enough to notice that if all other things are ever equal (which is hardly ever), it is trivially true that machines and mice will perform certain tasks more efficiently than humans because the latter will while the former will not have human costs on top of all the others. The efficiency ratio of the action of humans will be smaller than that for the machines and mice because of the greater costs (denominator) incurred by the humans.

Incidentally, it is perhaps worthwhile to point out that Kant's maxim that we ought to "use humanity… always at the same time as an end, never simply as a means"[9] is roughly supported by the fact which I have just cited, i.e, that when all other things are equal, men are less efficient and therefore, practically speaking, less valuable "instruments" or "means" than machines and dumb animals. Whatever one thinks about the moral justification of Kant's dictum, it makes perfectly good sense from a practical point of view.

Overhead costs are more or less unavoidable expenses that are not readily attributable to any specific decision or action. The term is borrowed, of course, from the businessman's vocabulary. Whether one's business happens to be manufacturing balloons, biscuits, baskets or birthday cards, one must pay for the factory, land, power, heat, light, water, taxes, insurance, etc. whether business is booming or not. These costs are incurred merely for being in business, even though business might be bad. Similarly, a human being must live somewhere, sleep on something, eat and drink something, breathe fresh air, exercise, enjoy some leisure and security, etc. no matter what specific actions we imagine him performing. Whether or not you drive nails or kill flies, you must incur certain general expenses to stay alive and healthy, and it is just these expenses that we regard as the overhead costs of human action.

Production and implementation costs must be borne even if a decision reached is a poor one or if an action performed is unsuccessful, or both. These costs are incurred given any outcome, favorable or not. This is only another way of reaffirming my view that such costs tend to be fixed, and that in this respect they differ from failure costs which tend to be highly variable. Failure costs may be subdivided into the three classes of direct losses, indirect losses and estimated-value-of-success losses.

Direct losses are those that arise more or less overtly and immediately as a result of reaching an "incorrect" decision and/or failing to implement it appropriately. For example, a man who is fired after informing his employer that he has decided to form a shop union might say that that decision cost him his job. Alternatively he might simply have begun to organize the work force without informing his employer, and still have lost his job. In this case he might say that it was his implementing activity that cost him his job rather than the mere decision to form the union. Perhaps, he might reason, he could have been spared that cost if he had ventured to tell his boss of his decision before attempting to implement it.

Indirect losses are those that are incurred more or less covertly and precariously as a result of reaching and/or implementing an "incorrect" decision. Of course there is quite a vague area between such losses and direct ones, but it seems worthwhile

[9]Quoted from H. J. Paton, *The Categorical Imperative: A Study in Kant's Moral Philosophy*, London: Hutchinson, 1958, p. 165.

to draw the distinction for the sake of the fairly clear-cut extremes. For example, if after losing his job for supporting union organizers, a man slowly withdrew his support from social organizations or tended to mistrust people or to doubt his own principles or to question his manliness, etc. we might regard any of these effects as indirect losses resulting from his earlier decision. They are probably due to a combination of things, but the fact that they seem to have been initiated by that decision makes them candidates for inclusion in its class of indirect losses. By calling them "indirect losses" we suggest that their full value might be appropriately weighted (and, therefore, discounted) by a personal probability value indicating the degree of uncertainty regarding their connection to that decision.

Estimated-value-of-success losses are an individual's (or group's) best estimate of the total value of reaching a "correct" decision and/or of implementing it successfully. This is not a loss that one finds discussed by cost accountants or economists, but it seems quite essential for a complete picture of the costs of human action. People become attached to their dreams, and place some value on them prior to their realization. When the hour is passed and their dreams are crushed by failure, they are left with their image of what might have been, for whatever that is worth. For some people such images are worth very little. They place very little value on "birds in the bush" and have no inclination to "cry over spilt milk." That is, their discount rates for time preferences are such that the present value of benefits for them in virtually any future period is negligible and, consequently, they have almost nothing to regret when their plans do not materialize. For other people such images may be worth even more than their successful realization. They obtain more satisfaction from and place a greater value on their dreams than the "real world." So they pay dearly for shattered dreams, and it is this expense that we wish to include under the rubric of "estimated—value-of-success losses."

This completes my outline of a general system of cost accounting for human action. While I would not want to claim that it provides an exhaustive classification of mutually exclusive *kinds* of costs that arise in relation to such action, I believe it does provide a framework which is broad enough and precise enough to capture as much data as most people would ever require. I have not examined any of the difficult operational problems involved in establishing meaningful rank orderings (much less metrics) among the multitude of perhaps occasionally incomparable values introduced here, and I would be the first to admit that the problems are formidable to say the least. This is not to say, of course, that I regard the problems as insurmountable, uninteresting or unworthy of serious consideration. They are technological problems which current research suggests do admit of more or less plausible and corrigible solutions.[10] But for the purposes of this paper, it would not be useful to tackle the issues now. Instead I shall proceed immediately to tie up the threads of my argument.

---

[10]Two excellent surveys of this research are: A.R. Prest and R. Turvey, "Cost—benefit analysis: a survey," *The Economic Journal,* Vol. 75, No. 300, 1965; and G.M. Becker and C.G. McClintock, "Value: behavioral decision theory," *Annual Review of Psychology,* vol. 18, 1967.

It is trivially true that human action involves human costs as these have been analyzed above. This is a result of the logic of my analysis, not of any empirical observation. Moral costs are a particular species of human costs which may or may not be attached to this or that action. In order to determine whether or not a given action creates moral costs for a certain agent in a certain circumstance, we must examine the action, agent and situation from the moral point of view. When there are moral costs, they must be added to the total cost appraisal for that action if a complete assessment is to be obtained. In order to obtain an unbiased estimate or measure of the efficiency of an action, its total costs must be included in our calculations. Then, since the practical value of an action will be determined by its efficiency and effectiveness, this value will always be partially determined by moral values in the form of benefits and costs whenever such benefits and costs arise. Hence, *if a human action has any moral value at all, then that value will constitute an essential aspect of its practical value.* In short, contrary to the views of those who would want to *contrast* moral and practical values or the requirements of efficiency and morality, this investigation leads us to the conclusion that moral values partially *constitute* practical values for all those actions that possess both kinds.

Chapter 5
Rationality Between the Maximizers and the Satisficers

Alex C. Michalos

Introduction

Rational action generally and rational decision-making in particular have been identified with two distinct kinds of policies, namely, that of maximizing and that of satisficing. In this paper it is argued that both views are inadequate, and a third alternative is outlined. Sections Two and Three consist of four arguments against the identification of rationality with the maximization of anything. In Section Four satisficer's objections to the maximizer's position are reviewed and the former's views are sketched. The fifth section is devoted to a decisive objection to the satisficer's proposal. Finally, the last section contains a brief statement of my alternative proposal. A more complete statement of this view may be found in my *Foundations of Decision-Making* (American Elsevier, in press).

The Regress of Maximization

Any proposed explication of rationality that requires the maximization of something must be unsatisfactory because the prescription to maximize this or that cannot (in fact) be satisfactorily specified. For example, consider the identification of rational action with maximally efficient action, i.e., an action is supposed to be rational if and only if (very roughly speaking) it seems and/or is likely to produce a ratio of

---

Michalos, A.C.: 1973. Rationality between the maximizers and the satisficers. Policy Sciences, 4, pp. 229–244.

A.C. Michalos (✉)
University of Northern British Columbia, Prince George, BC, Canada
e-mail: michalos@brandonu.ca

A.C. Michalos, *How Good Policies and Business Ethics Enhance Good Quality of Life*, DOI 10.1007/978-3-319-50724-8_5

benefits to costs that is at least as great as any available alternative. According to this rough definition then, what one is supposed to do to act rationally is to choose those courses of action that are or, at least, seem to be maximally efficient for one's ends. (This view is supported by the overwhelming majority of writers; e.g., Savage 1954; Miller and Starr 1960; Churchman 1961; Good 1962 and Wagner 1969). Ignoring the problem of choosing ends and the fact that lots of actions ordinarily regarded as rational do not seem to involve any choice or decision, the question is: From what set of alternative courses of action *should* a maximally efficient one be chosen? The answer offered by classical economics, statistical decision theory and most management science textbooks is *the given set.* (See, for example, Luce and Raiffa 1957 and Wagner 1969). But whether this set is supposed to be socially (MacRae 1968), organizationally or environmentally 'given' (March and Simon 1958), such a response to the *normative* question raised is practically worthless. The question is a request for a *rational policy* with respect to the selection of a set of alternatives from which a rational course of action can be selected. Looked at in another way, it is a request for a general normative criterion of relevance for the selection of sets of alternatives which would be *analogous to* a general normative criterion of rational action given an appropriate set of alternatives. It cannot, therefore, be answered by a mere report or description of the way such sets are usually determined. (No one has done a better descriptive job than March and Simon 1958). Nor can it be answered by strategies that are question-begging in the sense that they assume one can always or often enough find 'experts' or 'rational managers' who, by suitably exposing their ideas to each other, will finally make appropriate selections (Helmer 1966; Mason 1969). Unfortunately, the more seriously one takes the normative aspect of the question, the more dubious one becomes about the possibility of providing an answer that is satisfactory from the point of view of a policy of maximization.

Suppose, for example, that one is reflecting upon the enormous mortgage payments that he is saddled with every month and wondering whether or not it is rational for him to continue paying them or to sell out and buy a new house. How should he specify his alternatives? For the sake of completeness, one might suggest that he should consider all *logically* possible alternatives. This would certainly be a fatuous piece of advice to give anyone, because there are an infinite number of such alternatives and no one could examine all of them. Moreover, a similar condemnation is applicable to the suggestion that all *factually* possible alternatives should be examined. To see that this is so, consider his options with respect to consulting a single realtor. He might call the realtor at any time, on any day, from any place and standing or sitting in any position, so long as no contradiction is involved in the description of the time, day, place and position. If the set of alternatives that is factually possible to construct on the basis of this handful of variables is not infinite, it is still ridiculously too large to be recommended as a *desideratum.* (See also Diesing 1955; Duncan-Jones 1957 and Kuhn 1963, on 'the complexity of a simple decision').

At this point one is tempted to say that in any real decision situation a multitude of restrictions come into play to eliminate *prima facie* factually possible alternatives (Dror 1968). Thus, what one *ought* to do is let such restrictions generate a preferred set of alternatives. But this will not do. Even if, for example, it is assumed that realtors work a 5 day and 40 h week, and that our prospective buyer is not going to leave town to make a phone call, we are still left with thousands of factual possibilities. There are, for example, 144,000 mutually exclusive seconds in the given work-week, any one of which might be chosen as the time to place the call. Clearly then, the appeal to de facto restrictions to solve our problem is hopeless.

What one hankers to say now is that only *relevant* alternatives should be considered. But this too is abortive. When one is thinking about buying a new house, one of the most relevant questions that can be raised concerns the price one can afford to pay for it. Normally one thinks of very round figures and intervals, e.g., anything in the $27,000–$30,000 range would be possible. Hence, it is usually the case that as a matter of fact many more relevant alternative possible prices could be afforded than are ever examined individually. The $3000 range mentioned in the previous sentence, for instance, implies 300,000 live options, namely, $27,000.01, $27,000.02, etc.

One might insist now that because it is highly unlikely that anyone is going to ask or offer a sum like $27,000.02 for a house, such sums are not 'really' relevant. 'Really' relevant sums, it might be claimed, are those that have a *fairly high probability* of being asked or offered, e.g., $27,000, $27,500, etc. This strips our alleged 300,000 live options down to about 7.

The suggestion that 'really' relevant alternatives are those with fairly high probabilities of being adopted seems to be rather promising and reminiscent of Schelling's (1963) analysis of tacit bargaining and Braybrooke and Lindblom's (1963) analysis of disjointed incrementalism. As a rule, however, it is seriously deficient. In the first place, normally one must already have a set of alternatives (a reference class or universe of discourse) before any probability values can be determined. Needless to say then, the selection of the latter set raises precisely the kind of problem the present recommendation was supposed to solve. Second, when unique events are involved, there may be no probability values worth measuring, e.g., one may feel that one's psychological or logical probability assessments of what price he might offer or be asked to pay are not useful pieces of information to have. Third, insofar as these interpretations of 'probability' are applied, the more candidates for relevant alternatives one discloses, the less likely it becomes that any of them will have fairly high initial probability values. Thus, in order to obtain alternatives with high psychological or logical probabilities, one ought to generate as few as possible. Hence, an unattractive corollary of the present recommendation would be: The fewer alternatives one uncovers, the better! Finally, insofar as the proposal might be construed as identifying the relative frequency of occurrence of something with its relevance, it would seem to be a recipe for stagnation and misjudgment. It would be a recipe for stagnation because it brands all highly novel alternatives as irrelevant, and it would be a recipe for misjudgment because frequently the very uniqueness or scarcity of many events (e.g., one's own death) makes them extremely important rather than simply irrelevant (see also Bauer 1966).

In response to the barrage of objections presented in the preceding paragraph, it might be insisted that the criterion of relevance employed there is perverse. One *should*, it might be claimed, attempt to consider only those alternatives that are 'really' relevant, but nobody in his right mind would use the criterion of relevance that I have just used. Instead of appealing to the probability (in some sense) of an item's being selected, one ought to appeal to its *value* (in some sense) or, perhaps, to its probabilistically-weighted value. One might say then, that 'really' relevant alternatives are those that have a certain kind of value or expected value. (See, for example, Lyons 1965; Dror 1968 and Sobel 1970). The so-called 'cost of search' approach to alternative-set selection is a sophisticated species of this strategy (Raiffa 1968).

This idea sounds promising, but it is useless for an efficiency maximizer. For the latter it must lead directly to the prescription to search through all logically or factually possible alternatives to discover those with the appropriate sort of value. To demand less than this is to admit that any selected set of 'really' relevant alternatives might fail to include plenty of other 'really' relevant alternatives, some of which could well be much more valuable than any of those in the finally selected set. In other words, to demand less than this is, as Simon (1945, 1957) has insisted, to abandon the *policy* of maximization in favor of a weaker policy. Hence, a maximizer cannot escape from his herculean prescriptions. For reasons which have already been cited, however, he cannot hope to fulfill such prescriptions either.

Having gone up all these hopeless garden paths, one begins to realize that what a maximizer is seeking is a set of alternatives that is itself maximally efficient in the sense that it contains the maximally efficient alternative from the set of all logically possible alternatives and as little extra as possible. That is to say then, that according to the maximizers what one is supposed to do to act rationally is (roughly speaking still) to choose maximally efficient courses of action from sets of alternatives which are themselves maximally efficient. But this is the beginning of an infinite regress. Once again one cannot examine an infinite number of logically possible or an unmanageably large finite number of factually possible sets of alternatives to find the maximally efficient set. So one must find some smaller, more manageable set of sets of alternatives. But which set of sets in particular should one choose? Again it is the set that contains the maximally efficient set of alternatives and as few others as possible, i.e., again one finds oneself chasing an ever-elusive maximally efficient set of alternatives. Thus, since there can be no end to the search for a maximally efficient set of alternatives, there can be no choice of a maximally efficient course of action from such a set of alternatives. Hence, there can be no rational action according to the maximizer's proposal. But this, I should think, is patently absurd and certainly not intended by most defenders of the proposal. The typical maximizer's textbook generally contains plenty of illustrations of allegedly rational actions and I have yet to see anyone attempt to defend the view that any satisfactory explication of rationality must be such that rational actions are as a matter of fact or logic impossible to perform.

This rather long regress argument against maximization with respect to sets of alternative courses of action is applicable (making suitable trivial changes) to any sets of alternatives that one might be required to have, e.g., sets of alternative decision processes, allocations of resources, possible states of the world and goals. Insofar as one must be in possession of a maximally efficient set of alternatives in order to act rationally, one cannot act rationally because one cannot possess such a set.

Recently Bales (1971) has attacked shorter but roughly similar regress arguments on the ground that they fail to distinguish criteria of application from meaning. Addressing his remarks to the problem of what makes an act morally right, he claims correctly that "...a proposed ethical theory... *could* provide a correct account of right-making characteristics *without* spelling out a procedure which, if followed, would crank out in practice a correct and immediately helpful answer to questions like, 'Ought I in this case to use enough gas and electricity to keep my home warm?" (Bales 1971, pp. 261–262). Therefore, he believes, it would be a mistake to reject an account of 'right-making characteristics' if, as a matter of fact, it failed to provide a satisfactory decision procedure as well.

I imagine that some people have probably committed the *non sequitur* to which Bales has called our attention. But the argument I have just advanced is certainly free of that error. My argument rests on the assumption that it would be a mistake to accept an account of the meaning of any term if, as a matter of fact, no satisfactory criterion of application could be specified for it. I am not claiming that an account of the meaning of a term should *provide* a criterion of application as well. What I am claiming is that an account of the meaning of a term should *permit* a criterion of application. In other words, I am claiming that it is self-defeating to propose explications of concepts which by their very nature preclude their application. To take a well-worked example, it would be a mistake to explicate 'complete verification' such that a priori one knows that no proposition could ever be completely verified (Malcolm 1950). Similarly, it would be self-defeating to explicate the concepts of a morally right act or a rational act such that a priori one knows that no acts could ever be morally right or rational.

Blunt-Rationality, Self-sufficiency and Excessive Costs

Supposing that the regress argument against maximization could be demolished, there are still three serious problems to be faced. In the first place, rationality is ordinarily thought to admit of gradations, i.e., there are supposed to be 'degrees of rationality' (Diesing 1950; Friedrich 1964). One's actions can be more or less, very, hardly, somewhat, slightly or highly rational or irrational. In this respect rationality is analogous to preference. However, when rationality is defined in terms of maximal efficiency, the result is a concept with a logical structure that is, for want of a better word, 'blunter' than the ordinary concept. More precisely, if 'x' and 'y' are placeholders for the names or descriptions of any actions, then

x is more rational than y

can only by analyzed as

x is rational and y is irrational,

never as

x is rational and y is rational and x is more rational than y.

For example, if all other things are equal and one is confronted by a set of four alternative courses of action with efficiency ratios of 1, 2, 3 and 4, then according to the maximizer's proposal, one is acting rationally if and only if one chooses that course of action with the ratio of 4. Any other choice in the given circumstances would be irrational. One who chose the action with a ratio of 4 would be more rational than one who chose the action with a ratio of 3 only in the sense that the former was rational and the latter was *not*. Moreover, one who chose the action with a ratio of 4 could only be described as choosing *the most rational action* in the set in the sense that he chose the one and only rational action in the set. Furthermore, it could not be said that one who chose the action with a ratio of 3 was more rational than one who chose the action with 2, because anyone choosing either action would be irrational. Of course, it could be said that one who chose the action with 3 was less irrational than one who chose the action with 2, but this does not eliminate the peculiarity that I am citing. Ordinarily *both* rationality and irrationality admit of gradations, but on the maximizer's proposal there are no gradations of rationality. In this respect then, the maximizer's explication of rationality does not capture an important nuance of the ordinary concept. Instead, it merely provides us with a concept that is somewhere between what we might call 'blunt rationality' and ordinary rationality.

Another problem raised by the maximizer's proposal is that if all other things are equal, the choice of self-sustaining over self-developing actions is always irrational. Roughly speaking, an action is self-sustaining if its B/C ratio is one and self-developing if its B/C ratio is greater than one. I have used the term 'self-developing' rather than 'self-aggrandizing' because the latter has a slightly pejorative connotation that the former lacks and I do not want to suggest that growth itself is necessarily undesirable (Grauhan and Strubelt 1971, use 'self-enhancement'). The point that must be insisted upon is that contrary to the maximizer's proposal, it does not seem to be a logical truism that if all other things are equal, it is irrational to choose to maintain the status quo rather than to develop it. Just as one might want to say that something is *good enough* in some sense although something else would be better, one might want to say that some action is *rational enough* although some other action would be more rational. On the present proposal however, in the presence of an alternative with a higher efficiency ratio than that of the action chosen, the latter cannot (logically) be rational enough. Indeed, it cannot be rational at all!

It might be objected, following Diesing (1962, p. 44), that "it is reasonable to achieve the larger end as far as possible... because that is what it means to have an end." If this were true then it would be self-contradictory to assert that one has an end or goal which is not as large as it could (logically and factually) be but is large enough. The very idea of ends or goals that are just large enough would be logically incoherent. However, for reasons already cited, it seems to me that this idea not only makes perfectly good sense but it is absolutely essential for an adequate explication of the concept of rationality.

Finally, it is an unacceptable consequence of explications of rationality in terms of the maximization of something that, if all other things are equal, then no matter what the cost of an action, it is rational so long as it is not more costly than its 'available' alternatives. For example, confronted by the alternatives of waging a war leading to 40 million casualties or one leading to 30 million casualties, a maximizer can act rationally by waging the latter rather than the former. Although I would agree that it is peculiarly less evil to destroy 30 million rather than 40 million people, the destruction of 30 million people still strikes me as the kind of action that ought (rationally in some sense) to be regarded as irrational if not downright insane. The reason I think it should be regarded this way is that I have grave doubts that the benefits of such a war could (as matter of fact) outweigh the enormous costs of 30 million lives. Again, consider the plight of Creon in Sophocles' *Antigone.* Creon must either uphold his own edict and destroy his daughter or else spare his daughter and undermine the law. What makes his situation tragic is the fact that the costs of any action he can perform are almost certainly going to outweigh the benefits. And this is typical of many tragedies. Man, the rational animal, finds himself in situations such that whatever he does is, as it were, contrary to his own nature. Whatever he does is 'less' than it ought to be. In short then, I am suggesting that explications of rationality ought to require more than making the best of any situation. In this world, it seems that the 'best' actions in some situations can be so horrible that they cannot be described as rational without making a travesty of the concept. (See also Schwartz 1970; Wolff 1970 and Watkins 1970).

Satisficing Rationality

While the arguments presented in the last two sections against explications of rationality in terms of the maximization of something may be new, their conclusions are not. Maximization models of rationality have been under attack for some time, most notably by Simon (1945, 1957) and March and Simon (1958). According to Simon (1957, p. 202), "the approach taken in the theory of games and in statistical decision theory to the problem of rational choice is fundamentally wrongheaded. … It is wrong… in seeking to erect a theory of human choice on the unrealistic assumptions of virtual omniscience and unlimited computational power." Furthermore, he claims that "the key to the simplification of the choice process in both cases is the replacement of the goal of *maximizing* with the goal of *satisficing*, of finding a course of action that is 'good enough'" (Simon 1957, pp. 204–205). It will be instructive then, to provide at least a rough outline of the alternative these writers are suggesting in order to be able to evaluate and compare it with the proposal to be elucidated in the final section.

To begin with, it should be noted that although March and Simon claim to be primarily concerned with the 'adequate' description of rational decision-making rather than with prescriptions about how people ought rationally to make decisions, it is doubtful that they or anyone else can keep these two tasks separate. The fact is that 'rationality' is an evaluatively loaded word in the English language. Whatever they mean by the words, people like to think of themselves as and believe that they *ought* to be rational. While few of us would go so far as to assert that rationality in a human being is everything, it is almost certainly a necessary condition of many of the attributes that we regard as important and distinctively human (e.g., moral virtue), and practically everyone regards it is a very good thing—whatever it is. Thus, for example, to say that a man is rational or irrational is not at all like saying that he is hairy or bald. Take away a man's hair and you have a bald man, but take away his rationality and you are on the verge of taking away his humanity. Again, to say that someone is acting irrationally is to say that he is not acting as he *should* act, that his action departs from some *norm.* Moreover, since the farther and longer he departs from that norm the more he tends to become less human, it must not be imagined that in specifying the norm or classifying his behaviour in one way or another with respect to it, one is merely engaged in description. To say that a man has the wits of a mule, or conversely, that a mule has the wits of a man, is to make an *unfavorable appraisal* of the man and a *favorable appraisal* of the mule. In short, with respect to the properties of rationality and irrationality, there is no such thing as a non-evaluative description.

The main difficulties with the so-called classical model of rational man, according to March and Simon (1958, pp. 138–139), are as follows. (1) The model postulates as *given* a set of 'all' available alternative courses of action, a set of 'all' possible consequences attached to each alternative and a utility function completely ranking each consequence according to its value to the actor. But in fact these features are typically not given or even obtainable. (2) It grants that one may have certain, risky or uncertain information concerning possible consequences, but does not recognize that one's information concerning available alternatives and the value of consequences may be similarly complicated. (3) By admitting that one's information concerning a situation may be less than perfect, the model implies a distinction between subjective and objective rationality. But so-called subjective rationality then seems to be a poor substitute for 'real' rationality and hardly worthy of the name 'rationality' at all. (4) The model fails to agree with 'common-sense notions of rationality'.

In the light of these objections to the classical model of rationality, March and Simon propose an alternative with the following simplifying features.

(1) Optimizing is replaced by satisficing—the requirement that satisfactory levels of the criterion variables be attained.
(2) Alternatives of action and consequences of action are discovered sequentially through search processes.
(3) Repertories of action programs are developed by organizations and individuals, and these serve as alternatives of choice in recurrent situations.
(4) Each specific action program deals with a restricted range of situations and a restricted range of consequences.
(5) Each action program is capable of being executed in semiindependence of the others—they are only loosely coupled together (March and Simon 1958, p. 169).

Again, the 'key' to the model of rationality proposed by March and Simon is satisficing instead of maximizing. Moreover, as this idea is unpacked by these writers and Simon independently, the "criteria of satisfaction is closely related to the psychological notion of 'aspiration levels'" (March and Simon 1958, p. 182). Hence, the decisive factors in the determination of satisfactory solutions to problems or satisfactory levels of performance or achievement tend to be somewhat vague and, for want of a better word, subjective. What one regards as good enough depends upon what one is typically able to obtain. There is, in Simon's (1957, p. 260) words, a "rational adjustment that humans find 'good enough'," and there is apparently no means of deciding in an intersub-jectively confirmable fashion just what sort of an adjustment this or that human *ought* to find rational or 'good enough'.

The Inadequacy of Satisficing Rationality

It seems to me that although March and Simon's proposal represents a distinct improvement over the classical model of rationality, it is still not an adequate view. I shall explain its inadequacy in this section and then outline what I take to be a more plausible alternative in the next.

The trouble with the satisficing proposal is that according to it virtually *any* kind of action or behaviour is rational provided that the actor thinks it is good enough. This is a direct consequence of their explication of rationality in terms of individual satisfaction or aspiration levels, and it logically cannot be avoided unless some additional criterion of preferable levels is introduced, a criterion by means of which one can decide (probably roughly and precariously) that a certain individually selected level is too high or too low. Clearly, 'too high or too low' is merely an abbreviation for something like 'higher or lower than it rationally or reasonably ought to be'. In that case then, rather than having rationality defined purely in terms of satisfaction or aspiration levels, it would be defined *circularly* in terms of rational or reasonable satisfaction or aspiration levels. But anyone in doubt about the meaning of 'rational action' would not be enlightened by an account which requires an understanding of 'rational satisfaction or aspiration levels'. Hence, no appeal to an additional criterion of preferable levels can be introduced and, therefore, any old satisfaction or aspiration level must be regarded as acceptable. Thus, for example, if Charles Lamb's fool burns down his house to roast pork, then we should regard his action as perfectly rational provided that he is satisfied with the exchange. Similarly, if he makes love to his pig and keeps his wife in a pen, then that behaviour too must be sanctioned as long as he regards it as good enough. In sum, no matter what action science or common sense tells us is strange, stupid or horrendous, we shall be obliged to regard it as rational provided that the actor regards it as satisfactory or satisfactorily suited to his levels of aspiration. If this fact is not sufficient to demolish the March and Simon proposal, I do not know what is (See also Dror 1968 and Grauhan and Strubelt 1971).

It might be thought that the way to dispose of the preceding objection is to distinguish subjective from objective rationality. That is, one might say, for example, that while Lamb's fool is not objectively rational (because almost everyone believes that the price he pays to roast pork is outrageously high), he is still subjectively rational (because as far as he is concerned the price is fair). Although I quite agree that such a division can be usefully made, it is a mistake to think that it eliminates the force of my objection. My objection is, briefly, that to identify rational action with satisficing action is to allow every individual to be the final judge of his own rationality. Even if it is granted that every individual is the final judge of his subjective rationality, it cannot be granted that every person is the final judge of his objective rationality. The question is then: Which kind of rationality is it that people like to think they have and believe that they ought to have? The answer to this question is undoubtedly *both kinds.* Since everyone knows that damn fools and psychopaths are capable of subjectively rational action, to be rational in that sense is hardly enough. One ought and would like to be objectively rational, i.e., not merely sensible in one's own eyes but in the eyes of the rest of the human race as well. Nevertheless, if one's objectively rational behaviour were never subjectively rational, never satisficing or suited to one's aspirational levels, then one would probably have a serious psychological problem. Such a person would be at best a very disturbed martinet, always doing what ought rationally to be done but never finding it personally satisfying or rational in his own eyes. Clearly then, granted that it is useful to distinguish subjective from objective rationality in some sense, no one should be inclined to abandon one in favor of the other. Hence, no one should be inclined to believe that anyone can be the final judge of his own rationality in every significant sense of the term. Having cut the pie of rationality for analytic purposes, one must still have both pieces in order to remain a 'normal' member of the human race.

A Third View of Rationality

Supposing now, that satisficing action cannot be identified with rational action (in the full sense of 'rational') and that, for reasons presented earlier, maximizing action also cannot be identified with rational action, what is left? Briefly and roughly, what is left is action such that its benefits balance or outweigh its costs. This is the halfway house between the maximizer's and the satisficer's proposals. More precisely, if 'A' is a placeholder for the names or descriptions of any actions, then

(1) A is rational $=_{df}$ the *accurately and consistently estimated resulting benefits* of A *reveal a tendency* (directly or indirectly with precedence given to the former in case of conflicts) to *balance* or *outweigh* the *accurately and consistently*

estimated resulting costs for *every individual affected* by A in a *situation-determined region of analysis.*

(2) A is irrational $=_{df}$ the accurately and consistently estimated resulting costs of A reveal a tendency (directly or indirectly with precedence given to the former in case of conflicts) to outweigh the accurately and consistently estimated resulting benefits for every individual affected by A in a situation-determined region of analysis.

and

(3) A is more rational than A′ $=_{df}$ A and A′ are rational and the accurately and consistently estimated resulting B/C ratio of A reveals a tendency (directly or indirectly with precedence given to the former in case of conflicts) to be greater than that of A′ for every individual affected by A and A′ in a situation-determined region of analysis, *or else* A is rational and A′ is irrational.

Each of the italicized terms in (1) requires some explanation. First, I speak of *estimated* benefits and costs in A because one seldom has the resources to do anything but estimate benefits and costs, and it would be self-defeating to offer an explication which made the actual determination of the rationality of an action virtually impossible. Moreover, since estimates may be careful, careless, skillful, amateurish, wise or foolish, it is necessary to specify that the estimates required by A must be obtained by methods that tend to be *accurate and consistent.* That is, the estimating techniques employed by a rational actor must be such that they tend to obtain estimates that accurately represent the states of affairs that they are supposed to represent and these estimates must be consistently obtainable from the same kind of data. So far as I can tell, my views about the nature and role of estimates in determining rational action is basically similar to March and Simon's, and any maximizer's that I have encountered.

Second, the phrase '*reveal* a *tendency*' is supposed to indicate two requirements, one pertaining to evidence and the other to what is to be evidenced. More precisely, it is intended to indicate the need for at least an introspectable disclosure of a propensity or disposition to generate a certain pattern of benefits and costs. Fairly hard evidence rather than, say, hunch or hearsay is demanded in the interests of intersubjective testability and confirmability, while the identification of tendencies as well as mere occurrences is demanded as a means of taking *some* account of the benefits and costs of dependencies *beyond* given regions of analysis. Dror's (1968, p. 60) claim that "a change between past and present net output is insignificant and misleading unless it indicates a trend that can be extrapolated into the future" is probably too strong (since information about a present state of affairs may be accurate and significant for certain purposes), but it is in the spirit of the proposal being made here. From a logical point of view there is no reason why a maximizer or satisficer could not share my interest in tendencies, dispositions or propensities. But as a matter of fact, since most maximizers and certainly March and Simon tend to be behavioristically oriented, they would probably tend to avoid the sort of deeper analysis of benefits and costs that I am suggesting.

Third, the senses in which benefits may be said to *balance* or *outweigh* costs are primarily the ones designated when people talk about various kinds of considerations balancing or outweighing others. For example, we talk of considerations of needs, morality and self-satisfaction balancing or outweighing preferences, monetary gain and public acclaim, respectively.

It should be noticed that the requirement that estimated resulting benefits should *balance* or *outweigh* resulting costs represents a genuine alternative to the maximizer's and satisficer's proposals. (1) does not *require* anyone to seek out the single 'best' course of action from any set of alternatives and it does not *allow* one merely to satisfy oneself that the value of an action is 'good enough'. In other words, (1) provides an objective 'standard of quality' (Dror 1968) that is not impossible to realize.

In effect this requirement is close to the 'survival quality' standard discussed at length by Dror (1968) and strongly recommended by Grauhan and Strubelt (1971). According to the latter,

> The fact that an individual can deliberately commit suicide shows that the more conscious he is about his own choices, the more clearly he has to choose existence first in order to choose any other goal. It is not by chance that even the proponents of a procedural concept of rationality give as the only material standard of appraisal, the survival quality.... The pathological choice par excellence would be, in the last resort, the choice of self-destruction. In this conception the elements of rational and pathological choice are mutually exclusive (Grauhan and Strubelt 1971, p. 254).

Dror (1968) criticizes the survival quality standard on the grounds that mere psycho-physical survival does not entail worthwhile existence. What is required, according to Dror, is not merely the preservation of people, but also the preservation of their ideals or values. For example, most of us would want to have 'survival plus freedom' instead of just survival. It seems to me that a distinction between existence *simpliciter* and worthwhile existence is of fundamental importance. Therefore, I have tried to accommodate this view in my analysis of costs and benefits.

Another writer who has come very close to articulating the requirement proposed here is Ladd (1964). "I think," he tells us, "that when we call an action 'irrational', we usually mean that, although it is an effective means to the end sought (and thus rational in the broad sense), the outrageous price that has to be paid for using that particular means is completely ignored by the agent, that is, the means are unsuitable" (Ladd 1964, p. 141. See also Stein and Denison 1960 and Taylor 1970.)

The requirement that estimated resulting benefits should *balance* or *outweigh* resulting costs may be regarded as opposed to maximization policies in another way. According to utility maximizers like Davidson et al. (1957) and Luce and Raiffa (1957), following von Neumann and Morgenstern (1944), rational choice is logically impossible in the presence of cyclical preferences, because there is no alternative to which no other is preferred, i.e., there is no 'best' or maximally efficient alternative. On the contrary, the question of cyclical or non-cyclical preferences is here logically irrelevant to the rationality of actions or choices, because the rationality of any alternative is not viewed as a function of its status in comparison with others but as a function of its own net output.

Fourth, the qualifying term *resulting* which appears before *benefits* and *costs* marks a distinction between, as it were, the *direction* and the *net outcome* of the B/C ratio change. Suppose, for example, that an alteration in a particular sort of action lowers its typical B/C ratio from 4 to 3. In that case it is still a rational action according to (1), but it is less rational than it was, according to (3). In other words, the net outcome of the B/C ratio change is such that the modified action is still rational, but the direction of the change is unfavorable or destructive. Generally speaking then, according to (l)–(3) the B/C ratios of prime importance for the determination of rationality are resulting or net outcomes rather than transitional ratios.

Fourth, the parenthetical remark 'directly or indirectly with precedence given to the former in case of conflicts' is included in order to indicate my position on an issue that has received a considerable amount of attention by philosophers for the past 30 years. The problem arises as follows. On the one hand, a tendency may be revealed by a *direct* assessment of the benefits and costs arising from A itself, and on the other, such a tendency may be revealed *indirectly* by classifying A as a *kind* of action that usually yields a certain distribution of benefits and costs. For example, suppose A is interpreted as keeping a promise in a particular situation. Then one could appraise A directly by examining the benefits and costs it yields this time, or one could appraise A indirectly by regarding it as one of many instances of keeping a promise and noting the benefits and costs usually emerging from acts like A. As long as the direct and indirect assessments of A agree, there is no need to consider the question whether one type of assessment is in some sense superior to the other. However, the assessments do not always agree. It might be the case, for example, that although promise-keeping usually yields estimated benefits outweighing costs, a particular act of promise-keeping may not and one may be practically certain that it does not. Confronted by cases like this then, the question of the possible superiority of direct or indirect assessment becomes acute. So what should our judgment be?

The basic considerations seem to be as follows. One who uses only indirect appraisals must be prepared to admit that an eccentric particular action may be correctly regarded as rational although one knows that it in no way contributes to the production of estimated benefits balancing or outweighing costs. That is, one knows that although actions which are like it in significant respects usually have desirable results, such results are not even partially dependent upon it. The *relative frequency* of such results is partially dependent upon it, but the *desirability* of the results themselves are independent of it. Alternatively, one who uses direct appraisals only must be prepared to admit that an eccentric particular action may be correctly regarded as rational although one knows that actions which are like it in significant respects usually produce estimated costs outweighing benefits. That is, one knows that although actions which are like it in significant respects usually have undesirable results (and there might be plenty like it yet to come), such results are not even partially dependent upon it. And lastly, one who insists upon agreement between direct and indirect assessments must be prepared to admit that in his view rational action is impossible (logically) in the presence of the kind of conflicts in question.

In the light of these considerations then, it seems to me that an explication of rationality as applied to actions should require *either* direct *or* indirect appraisals and in case of conflict, give precedence to the former over the latter. Obviously this view is not logically entailed by the considerations reviewed in the preceding paragraph, but it seems to be warranted by those considerations plus the following. The main risks involved with direct appraisal seem to be that it departs from and may undermine the rules, policies or lawlike (statistical or non-statistical) generalizations that one's own and others' past experiences have already vindicated. However, in order to avoid intellectual and moral stagnation or dogmatism, these risks must be taken. To refuse a priori to take them is to commit oneself to the view that rules, policies or generalizations should be used but never *posited*, as if long run data relevant to particular kinds could be accumulated without anyone ever specifying the kinds.

Fifth, the terms *benefits* and *costs* have been used in (1) and throughout this paper primarily in order to avoid the highly ambiguous term 'utility'. Since 'utility' has been used by other writers to designate pleasure, happiness, satisfaction, anything enhancing personal and social welfare, anything good or valuable, anything believed to be good or valuable (whether or not it is), anything useful, anything preferred to something else, anything preferable (i.e., that ought to be preferred to something else) and anything chosen, there is not much point in denying that what I have been calling 'costs' and 'benefits' have been called 'utilities' by *someone.* (Historical reviews of these alternatives may be found in Kauder 1965; Narveson 1967 and Werkmeister 1970). But there is not much point in asserting it either, because without considerable qualifications it is hardly an informative assertion. It will be worthwhile, however, to give you some idea of the 'breadth' of the concepts of benefits and costs as I understand them, especially since my views on this subject seem to diverge from those of most other writers.

I begin with the heuristically useful and ontologically innocuous concept of a *point of view*, perspective or way of looking at the world. In March and Simon's terminology, I begin with a concept of a 'frame of reference'. There are several ways to characterize points of view. For example, they may be regarded as *sources of reasons* for believing or knowing things about the world. They might also be thought of as 'conceptual nets' thrown over amorphous futures or, to use a different metaphor, as 'intellectual handles' by means of which one attempts to take hold of or grasp the world. Again, they provide systems of rules, policies, procedures and roles of behavior for individuals and groups in various situations. Finally, employing Pfiffner and Sherwood's (1960) suggestive metaphor, one might think of points of view as 'transparent overlays' through which the world is observed in an actor's mind.

While March and Simon refer specifically to three broad points of view, namely, that of the individual, his social environment and the organization of which he is a member, I make use of eleven. There are logical, physical (including biological and chemical), technological, economic, legal, moral, political, social, psychological, esthetic and religious points of view. In order to exhaustively determine the benefits and costs involved in any action then, what one would do is examine it in the light of these eleven points of view. Typically, of course, only a few of the points of view yield significant data, and one learns with experience which points of view may be safely neglected in which situations. The key word in the last sentence, however, is *experience.* One literally learns from experience where and when to look at a situation from a certain point of view in order to uncover important benefits and costs.

Evidently this plethora of alternative points of view creates king-sized measurement and amalgamation problems. Somehow people must be able to apprehend enormously complicated and disparate bits of information with some precision and 'process' them with the aim of deciding whether or not the benefits of an action balance or outweigh the costs. As Arrow (1951) and others have shown us, there is at least a serious question as to the logical possibility of constructing a neat mechanical procedure for aggregating such information. But the psychological possibilities remain largely obscure. It may well be the case, as I suspect it is, that human intuition far outstrips any of the formalized instruments available for measuring, weighing and balancing complex considerations that are pertinent to many kinds of problems. At any rate, it is not my intention to try to solve these problems here or even to try to persuade you that they are not serious problems. I merely want to make it clear that they exist and that I am aware of them.

Sixth, supposing that one is committed to an examination of the benefits and costs of an action as these arise from eleven generic points of view, one must still select a certain region of analysis within which one's investigation will be conducted. A *region of analysis* may be thought of as a spatio-temporal cut of the world with which one is prepared to reflect upon. That is, since one cannot count benefits and costs forever, one must select some particular region within which all benefits and costs will be counted. The *size* and *composition* of these regions depends heavily upon the kinds of actions contemplated and upon the kinds of *situations* in which they will occur. For example, if most of the costs of becoming a physician are borne during medical school and internship while most of the benefits are received in the years following these periods, then a region of analysis used in the evaluation of the extended activity of becoming a physician ought to be large enough to include both the costly and the beneficial years. Obviously, by carefully selecting the size and composition of one's region of analysis one can simply rule out certain kinds of data from one's concern, which is precisely what individuals, organizations and governments do.

Finally, closely related to the selection of regions of analysis, there is the problem of selecting an appropriate *recipient population.* Since nothing can be beneficial or costly *simpliciter*, but only beneficial or costly *for someone*, a decision must be made regarding those who ought to bear the costs or enjoy the benefits of any action. Generally, if there are N individuals (in the broad sense including 'corporate persons') in a certain region of analysis, then there are $2^N - 1$ mutually exclusive possible recipient populations. For example, if you and I are the only individuals in some region under consideration, then the three possible recipient populations are

you *and* I
you *and* not I
not you *and* I.

The overwhelming majority of people who talk about rational action seem to assume that rationality only demands that one looks after one's own interests. The interests of others, it seems to be assumed, should only be considered insofar as they affect one's own. I call this view *egoistic rationality*, and so far as I can tell it is the view of March and Simon. In contrast to this view, I hold that every individual affected by an action in a situation-determined region of analysis ought to be considered as a member of the recipient population for that action. This position I call *consensual rationality.*

My basic objection to egoistic rationality is that it is essentially immoral, because selfishness is immoral. Contrary to the impression that one might receive by reading contemporary literature on rational decision making, egoistically rational action is not neutral or logically independent of non-egoistic morality. Those who hold that in conflict situations one ought (rationally) to look after one's own interests are committed to the view that in such situations one ought to act immorally, i.e., selfishly. In such situations there is simply no difference between self-interested and selfish action. Where there is a difference, there is no real conflict. Thus, primarily because I would like to have a concept of rational action that is not inherently immoral, I reject egoistic rationality in favor of consensual rationality. The latter has its own problems, but immorality is not one of them.

Acknowledgements I would like to thank Myles Brand, Hugh Lehman, Michael Martin, Ian Mitroff, Michael Ruse and Gordon Welty for their thoughtful comments and encouragement.

References

Arrow, K. J. (1951). *Social choice and individual values*. New York: Wiley.
Bales, R. E. (1971). Act-utilitarianism: Account of right-making characteristics or decision-making procedure? *American Philosophical Quarterly, 8,* 257–265.
Bauer, R. A. (1966). Detection and anticipation of impact: The nature of the task. In R. A. Bauer (Ed.), *Social indicators* (pp. 1–67). Cambridge: MIT Press.
Braybrooke, D., & Lindblom, C. E. (1963). *A strategy of decision*. New York: Macmillan Co.
Churchman, C. W. (1961). *Prediction and optimal decision*. Englewood Cliffs: Prentice-Hall Inc.
Davidson, D., Suppes, P., & Siegel, S. (1957). *Decision-making: An experimental approach*. Stanford: Stanford University Press.
Diesing, P. (1950). The nature and limitations of economic rationality. *Ethics, 61,* 12–26.
Diesing, P. (1955). Non-economic decision-making. *Ethics, 66,* 18–35.
Diesing, P. (1962). *Reason in society*. Urbana: University of Illinois Press.
Dror, Y. (1968). *Public policymaking reexamined*. San Francisco: Chandler Publ. Co.

Duncan-Jones, A. (1957). Utilitarianism and rules. *The Philosophical Quarterly, 8,* 364–367.
Friedrich, C. J., (1964). On rereading machiavelli and althusius: Reason, rationality, and religion. In C. J. Friedrich (Ed.), *Rational Decision* pp. 1977–196. New York: Atherton Press.
Good, I. J. (1962). How rational should a manager be? *Management Science, 8,* 383–393.
Grauhan, R. R., & Strubelt, W. (1971). Political rationality, reconsidered: notes on an integrated evaluative scheme for policy choices. *Policy Sciences, 2,* 249–270.
Helmer, O. (1966). *Social technology*. New York: Basic Books Inc.
Kauder, E. (1965). *A history of marginal utility theory*. Princeton: Princeton University Press.
Knight, F. H. (1921). *Risk, uncertainty and profit*. New York: Houghton Mifflin Co.
Kuhn, A. (1963). *The study of society*. Irwin Inc, Homewood: R. D.
Ladd, J. (1964). The place of practical reason in judicial decision. In C. J. Friedrich (Ed.), *Rational decision* (pp. 126–144).New York: Atherton Press.
Luce, R. D., & Raiffa, H. (1957). *Games and Decisions*. New York: Wiley.
Lyons, D. (1965). *Forms and limits of utilitarianism*. Oxford: Clarendon Press.
MacRae, D. (1968). Utilitarian ethics and social change. *Ethics, 78,* 188–198.
Malcolm, N. (1950). The verification argument. In M. Black (Ed.), *Philosophical analysis* (pp. 244–298). Englewood Cliffs: Prentice-Hall, Inc.
March, J. G., & Simon, H. A. (1958). *Organizations*. New York: Wiley.
Mason, R. O. (1969). A dialectical approach to strategic planning. *Management Science, 15*(1), B403–B414.
Miller, D. W., & Starr, M. K. (1960). *Executive Decisions and Operations Research*. Englewood Cliffs: Prentice-Hall Inc.
Narveson, J. (1967). *Morality and utility*. Baltimore: The Johns Hopkins Press.
von Neumann, J., & Morgenstern, O. (1944). *Theory of games and economic behavior*. Princeton: Princeton University Press.
Pfiffner, J. M., & Sherwood, F. P. (1960). *Administrative organization*. Englewood Cliffs: Prentice-Hall Inc.
Raiffa, H. (1968). *Decision analysis*. Reading, MA: Addison-Wesley Publ. Co.
Savage, L. J. (1954). *The foundations of statistics*. New York: Wiley.
Schelling, T. C. (1963). *The strategy of conflict*. New York: Oxford University Press.
Schwartz, T. (1970). On the possibility of rational policy evaluation. *Theory and Decision, 1,* 89–106.
Simon, H. A. (1945). *Administrative behavior*. New York: Macmillan Co.
Simon, H. A. (1957). *Models of man*. New York: Wiley.
Sobel, J. H. (1970). Utilitarianisms: simple and general. *Inquiry, 13,* 394–449.
Stein, H. (Ed.) (1952) *Public administration and policy development*. New York: Harcourt, Brace and Co.
Taylor, V. (1970). How much is good health worth? *Policy Sciences, 1,* 49–72.
Wagner, H. M. (1969). *Principles of operations research*. Englewood Cliffs: Prentice-Hall Inc.
Watkins, J. (1970). Imperfect rationality. In R. Borger & F. Cioffi (Eds.), *Explanation in the behavioral sciences*. Cambridge: Cambridge University Press.
Werkmeister, W. H. (1970). *Historical spectrum of value theories*. Lincoln: Johnson Pub. Co.
Wolff, R. P. (1970). Maximization of expected utility as a criterion of rationality in military strategy and foreign policy. *Social Theory and Practice, 1,* 99–111.

Chapter 6
The Loyal Agent's Argument

Alex C. Michalos

Introduction

According to the Report of the Special Review Committee of the Board of Directors of Gulf Oil Corporation:

> It is not too much to say that the activity of those Gulf officials involved in making domestic political contributions with corporate funds during the period of approximately fourteen years under review [1960–1974] was shot through with illegality. The activity was generally clandestine and in disregard of federal, as well as a number of state, statutes.[1]

Nevertheless, and more importantly for our purposes, the Committee apparently endorsed the following judgment, which was submitted by their lawyers to the U.S. Securities and Exchange Commission.

> No evidence has been uncovered or disclosed which establishes that any officer, director or employee of Gulf personally profited or benefited by or through any use of corporate funds for contributions, gifts, entertainment or other expenses related to political activity. Further, Gulf has no reason to believe or suspect that *the motive of the employee or officer* involved in such use of corporate funds was anything other than a *desire to act solely in what he considered to be the best interests of Gulf and its shareholders.*[2] [Emphasis added.]

Michalos, A.C.: 2005. The loyal agent's argument. In D.C. Poff (Ed.) Business Ethics in Canada, 4th ed. (pp. 200–206). Toronto: Pearson Canada.

[1] J.J. McCloy, N.W. Pearson, and B. Matthews, *The Great Oil Spill* (New York: Chelsea House, 1976), p. 31.
[2] Ibid., p. 13.

A.C. Michalos (✉)
University of Northern British Columbia, Ottawa, ON, Canada
e-mail: michalos@brandonu.ca

A.C. Michalos, *How Good Policies and Business Ethics Enhance Good Quality of Life*, DOI 10.1007/978-3-319-50724-8_6

If we accept the views of the Committee and their lawyers, then we have before us an interesting case of individuals performing illegal actions with altruistic motives. What they did was admittedly illegal, but they meant well. They had good intentions, namely, to further "the best interests of Gulf and its shareholders." Furthermore, there is no suggestion in these passages or in the rest of the report that the officials were ordered to commit such acts. They were not ordered. On the contrary, the acts seem to have emerged as practically natural by-products of some employees' zeal in looking after their employer's interests. They are, we might say, the result of overzealous attempts of agents to fulfill their fiducial obligations.

In the following paragraphs I am going to pursue this apparently plausible account of overzealous behavior to its bitter end. That is, I'm going to assume for the sake of argument that there really are reasonable people who would and do perform immoral and illegal actions with altruistic motives, i.e., there are people who would and do perform such actions with reasons that they regard as good in some fairly general sense. It's not to be assumed that they are shrewd enough to see that their own interests lie in the advancement of their employer's or client's interests. They are not, I'm assuming, cleverly egoistic. If anything, they are stupidly altruistic by hypothesis. But that's beside the point now. What I want to do is construct a generalized form of an argument that I imagine would be attractive to such agents, whether or not any of them has or will ever formulate it exactly so. Then I want to try to demolish it once and for all.

The Argument

What I will call the Loyal Agent's Argument (LAA) runs as follows:

1. As a loyal agent of some principal, I ought to serve his interests as he would serve them himself if he had my expertise.
2. He would serve his own interests in a thoroughly egoistic way.
3. Therefore, as a loyal agent of this principal, I ought to operate in a thoroughly egoistic way in his behalf.

Some clarification is in order. First, in order to make full use of the fairly substantial body of legal literature related to the *law of agency*, I have adopted some of the standard legal jargon. In particular, following Powell, I'm assuming that *"an agent is a person who is authorised to act for a principal and has agreed so to act, and who has power to affect the legal relations of his principal with a third party."*[3] The standard model is an insurance agent who acts in behalf of an insurance company, his principal, to negotiate insurance contracts with third parties. More

[3]R. Powell, *The Law of Agency* (London: Sir Isaac Pitman and Sons, Ltd., 1965), p. 7.

generally, lawyers, real estate agents, engineers, doctors, dentists, stockbrokers, and the Gulf Oil zealots may all be regarded as agents of some principal. Although for some purposes one might want to distinguish agents from employees, such a distinction will not be necessary here. The definition given above is broad enough to allow us to think of coal miners, Avon Ladies, zoo attendants, and Ministers of Parliament as agents.

Second, as our definition suggests, there are typically three important relationships involved in agency transactions, namely, those between agent and principal, agent and third party, and principal and third party. The law of agency has plenty to say about each of these relationships, while LAA is primarily concerned with only the first, the fiducial relation between agent and principal. It would be a mistake to regard this as mere oversight. Few of us are immune to the buck-passing syndrome. Most of us are inclined to try to narrow the range of activities for which we are prepared to accept responsibility and, at the same time, widen the range of activities over which we are prepared to exercise authority. Notwithstanding the psychological theory of cognitive dissonance, most human beings seem to have sufficient mental magnanimity to accommodate this particular pair of incompatible inclinations. Like the insects, we are very adaptable creatures.

Third, I imagine that someone using an argument like LAA would, in the first place, be interested in trying to establish the fact that agents have a moral obligation to operate in a thoroughly egoistic way in their principals' behalf. If most LAA users in fact are primarily concerned with establishing their legal obligations, then perhaps what I have to say will be less interesting than I imagine to most people. Nevertheless, I'm assuming that the force of "ought" in the first premise and conclusion is moral rather than legal. For our purposes it doesn't matter what sort of an ontological analysis one gives to such obligations or what sort of a moral theory one might want to use to justify one's moral principles. It only has to be appreciated that LAA is designed to provide a moral justification for the behavior prescribed in its conclusion.

Fourth, an agent may be regarded as operating in a thoroughly egoistic way if all his actions are designed to optimize his own interests and he has no inclination at all to identify the interests of anyone else with his own. (Throughout the essay I usually let the masculine "he" abbreviate "he or she.") He may very well be a self-confident, self-starting, self-sustaining, and self-controlled individual. These are all commendable personal characteristics. But he must be selfish, self-centered, and/or self-serving. In conflict situations when there are not enough benefits to satisfy everyone, he will try to see that his own needs are satisfied, whatever happens to the needs of others. He is more interested in being first than in being nice, and he assumes that everyone else is too. He may harbor the suspicion that if everyone behaved as he does, the world's resources would be used in a maximally efficient way and everyone would be materially better off. But these are secondary considerations at best. His first consideration, which he regards as only prudent or smart, is to look out for *Numero Uno*, himself.

Fifth, to say that an agent is supposed to operate in a thoroughly egoistic way in behalf of his principal is just to say that the agent is supposed to act as he believes his principal would act if his principal were an egoist. The agent is supposed to conduct the affairs of his principal with the single-minded purpose of optimizing the latter's interests and not yielding them to anyone else's interests.

The Second Premise

Now we should be talking the same language. The question is: Is the Loyal Agent's Argument sound? Can its conclusion be established or even well-supported by its premises? I think there are good reasons for giving a negative answer to these questions. Moreover, since the argument has been deliberately formulated in a logically valid form, we may proceed immediately to a closer investigation of the content of its premises.

Let's consider the second premise first. This premise can only be regarded as true of people a priori if one of the assumptions we have made for the sake of argument about human motivation is false. Following the quotations from the Special Review Committee, it was pointed out that the case involved agents who apparently performed illegal actions with altruistic motives. What they did wrong, they did in behalf of Gulf Oil Corporation. Fair enough. However, if it's possible to perform illegal but altruistically motivated acts, it must be possible to perform legal but altruistically motivated acts as well. The very assumption required to give the argument initial plausibility also ensures that its second premise cannot be assumed to be generally true a priori. Since some people can perform nonegoistically motivated actions, the second premise of LAA requires some defense. Moreover, broadly speaking there are two directions such a defense might take, and I will consider each in turn.

Granted that users of LAA cannot consistently regard every individual as a thoroughly egoistic operator and hence guarantee the truth of the second premise a priori, it is still possible to try to defend this premise as a well-confirmed empirical hypothesis. That is, admitting that there are exceptions, one might still claim that if one acted as if the second premise were true, much more often than not one would be right. This is the sort of line economists have traditionally taken toward their idealized rational economic man. They realize that people are capable of altruistic action, but they figure that the capability is seldom exercised and they design their hypotheses, laws, and theories accordingly.

So far as business is concerned, the egoistic line seems to be translated into profit maximization. According to Goodman, for example:

> The Wall Street rule for persons legally charged with the management of other people's money runs as follows: Invest funds in a company with the aim of gaining the best financial return with the least financial risk for the trust beneficiaries. If you later come to disagree with the company's management, sell the stock.[4]

Similarly, in a cautious version of LAA, Friedman has claimed that:

> In a free-enterprise, private-property system, a corporate executive is an employee of the owners of the business. He has a direct responsibility to his employers. That responsibility is to conduct the business in accordance with their desires, which generally will be to make as much money as possible while conforming to the basic rules of the society, both those embodied in law and those embodied in ethical customs.[5]

Instead of challenging the accuracy of these assessments of the motives of people generally or of businessmen in the marketplace in particular now, I want to grant it straightaway for the sake of the argument. The question is: How does that affect LAA?

As you may have guessed, users of LAA are not much better off than they were. If it's a good bet that the second premise is true, then it's an equally good bet that anyone inclined to defend his actions with LAA is not an altruistic operator. No one can have it both ways. Evidence for the empirical hypothesis that people generally act as egoists is evidence for the truth of the second premise and the falsehood of the alleged altruistic motives of anyone using LAA. In short, the premise is still self-defeating.

Corporate Principals

Instead of regarding the second premise as an empirical claim about real people and attempting to support it inductively, one might treat it as a logical claim justifiable by an appeal to the definitions of some of its key terms. This looks like a very promising strategy when one considers the fact that many contemporary principals, like Gulf Oil Corporation, for example, are abstract entities. Corporate persons are, after all, nothing but fictional persons invented by people with fairly specific aims. In particular, corporations have been invented to assist in the accumulation of material assets. While they typically accomplish many different tasks, the accumulation of assets is generally regarded as their basic aim. Thus, if one's principal happens to be a corporation, one might reasonably argue that it is by definition thoroughly egoistic. The business of such entities is certainly business, because that is their very reason for being, the very point of inventing them in the first place. So, the second premise of LAA could be substantiated by definitional fiat....

---

[4]W. Goodman, "Stocks Without Sin," Minneapolis Star and Tribune Co., Inc. Reprinted in R. Baum (ed.), *Ethical Arguments for Analysis* (New York: Holt, Rinehart and Winston, 1975), p. 206.

[5]M. Friedman, "The Social Responsibility of Business Is to Increase Its Profits," see p. 18ff. of this book.

Apparently, then, morally conscientious corporate agents may find themselves facing lawsuits if they assume their principals are not self-serving profit maximizers and act accordingly. Legal niceties aside, there is a thought-provoking moral argument in favor of agents acting as if their principals were just as the designers of corporate law imagine them. That is, if any particular stockholder wants to give his money away or to pursue any aims other than profit maximization, he is free to do so. Investors should be and almost certainly are aware that corporations are designed to make money. If they have other aims, they shouldn't be investing in corporations. If they don't have other aims and they go into corporations with their eyes wide open, then they should appreciate and respect the interests of others who have gone in with them.

In principle, the defense of the second premise of LAA on the grounds of the defining characteristic of corporations may be challenged as before. Insofar as corporations are defined as egoistic corporate persons (a rough abbreviated definition, to be sure), a serious question arises concerning the morality of becoming an agent for them—not to mention inventing them in the first place. The evils of unbridled egoism are well known and they aren't mitigated by the fact that the egoist in question is a corporate person. If anything, they are magnified because of the difficulties involved in assigning responsibility and holding corporations liable to their activities. It is demonstrably certain that if everyone only attends to what he perceives as his own interests, a socially self-destructive result may occur. That is the clear message of prisoner's dilemma studies. It's also the message of two kids in a playpen who finally tear the toys apart rather than share them.

`As before, it will not help to argue that in developed countries most people work for corporations or they don't work at all. Again, self-preservation is not altruism. To serve an evil master in the interests of survival is not to serve in the interests of altruism, and users of LAA are supposed to be motivated by altruism. On the other hand, insofar as corporations are not defined as egoistic corporate persons and are granted more or less benevolent if not downright altruistic aims, the truth of the second premise of LAA is again open to question. In either case, then, an agent trying to salvage LAA with this sort of definitional defense is bound to find the task self-defeating.

The First Premise

Let's turn now to the first premise of LAA. In a way it's as innocuous as motherhood and apple pie. Every discussion I've read of the duties of agents according to agency law in North America and the United Kingdom has included some form of this premise. For example, Powell says, "An agent has a general duty to act solely for the benefit of his principal in all matters connected with the execution of his authority."[6] The *American Restatement of the Law of Agency* says that "an agent is subject to a duty to his principal to act solely for the benefit of the principal in all

[6]Powell, *The Law of Agency*, p. 312.

matters connected with his agency."[7] According to a standard Canadian textbook on business law, "Good faith requires that the agent place the interest of his principal above all else except the law."[8]

The only trouble with the premise is that its limitations are not clearly built into it. In this respect it is like most moral principles and rules of law. Short of turning every principle and rule into a self-contained treatise, it's impossible to indicate every possible exception.... However, the *American Restatement of the Law of Agency* makes it quite clear that "In no event would it be implied that an agent has a duty to perform acts which...are illegal or unethical."[9] Moreover, "In determining whether or not the orders of the principal to the agent are reasonable...business or professional ethics...are considered."[10] Powell also remarks that agents have no duty "to carry out an illegal act."[11]...Thus, there is no doubt at all that the first premise of LAA cannot be regarded as a licence to break the law. No respectable court would permit it. In fact, although the courts have no special jurisdiction over moral law, they have shown no reluctance to condemn immoral acts allegedly performed in the interests of fulfilling fiduciary obligations.

Illegality and immorality aside, the first premise still gives up much more than any sane person should be willing to give up. It virtually gives a principal licence to use an agent in any way the principal pleases, so long as the agent's activity serves the principal's interest. For example, suppose a life insurance agent agrees to sell State Farm Insurance on commission. It would be ludicrous to assume that the agent has also committed himself to painting houses, washing dogs, or doing anything else that happened to give his principal pleasure. It would also be misleading to describe such an open-ended commitment as an agreement to sell insurance. It would more accurately be described as selling oneself into bondage. Clearly, then, one must assume that the first premise of LAA presupposes some important restrictions that may have nothing to do with any sort of law.

Since they are apparently drawn from and applicable to ordinary affairs and usage, perhaps it would be instructive to mention some of the principles developed in the law of agency to address this problem. You may recall that the definition of an agent that we borrowed from Powell explicitly referred to a person being "authorised to act for a principal." An agent's duties are typically limited to a set of activities over which he is granted authority by his principal.... [This]... would be sufficient to prevent the exploitation of the hypothetical insurance agent in the preceding paragraph.

---

[7]Section 387 as quoted in P.I. Blumberg. "Corporate Responsibility and the Employee's Duty of Loyalty and Obedience: A Preliminary Inquiry," *The Corporate Dilemma,* D. Votaw and S. P. Sethi (eds.) (Englewood Cliffs, NJ: Prentice-Hall, Inc., 1973), p. 87.

[8]J.E. Smyth and D.A. Soberman, *The Law and Business Administration in Canada* (Toronto: Prentice-Hall of Canada, Ltd., 1968), p. 360.

[9]Section 385 as quoted in Blumberg, "Corporate Responsibility," p. 86.

[10]Ibid.

[11]Powell, *The Law of Agency,* p. 302.

Besides a carefully developed set of principles related to the granting of authority, the law of agency recognizes some other general duties of agents like the previously considered duty of good faith. For example, an agent is expected to "exercise due care and skill in executing his authority."[12] This obviously serves the interests of all concerned, and there are plenty of principles and precedents available to explain "due care and skill."...He is expected to "keep proper accounts," i.e., accounts that clearly distinguish his principal's assets from his own....[13]

Keeping the preceding guidelines in mind, perhaps some form of LAA can be salvaged by tightening up the first premise. Let's suppose I'm in the advertising business and I want to use LAA by suitably restricting the scope of the first premise thus:

> 1a. *As a loyal advertising agent of some company, I ought to advertise its products as they would advertise them if they had my expertise.*

That would require a consistent modification of the second premise and conclusion, but we need not worry about that. The question is: Does this reformulated premise la escape the kinds of criticism leveled against premise 1?

Certainly not. If the company happens to be run by a bunch of thoroughly unscrupulous thugs, it could be immoral and illegal to advertise their products as they would if they had the agent's expertise. Even if the company is run by fools who really don't know what they make, it could be immoral and illegal to advertise their products as they would if they had the agent's expertise. For example, if the company's directors are smart enough to know that they can make more money selling drugs than they can make selling candy, but dumb enough to think that the candy they make is an effective drug, an agent could hardly be under any obligation to advertise their product as a marvelous new drug, i.e., assuming that the agent was smart enough to know that his employers were only capable of producing candy.

If you think the agent could have such an obligation, what would be its source?

Clearly it is not enough to say that the agent is employed by the company. That would be tantamount to appealing to LAA in order to establish a version of its own first premise, i.e., it would be a circular salvaging effort. Something else is required to support premise la...

Conclusion

The announced aim of this essay was to destroy LAA once and for all. I think that has been done. It is perhaps worthwhile to emphasize that if people use LAA when, as we saw earlier, the real reason for their actions is fear (or job preservation) then

[12]Ibid., p. 303.

[13]Ibid., p. 321.

they will be circulating a distorted view of the world and decreasing the chances of reform. Thus, in the interests of a clear perception and resolution of social problems related to responsible human agency, LAA deserves the sort of treatment it has received here.

Chapter 7
Moral Responsibility in Business, or Fourteen Unsuccessful Ways to Pass the Buck

Alex C. Michalos

Introduction

In the Middle Ages, philosophic essays had a standard form. An author would begin by stating a thesis to be proved. Then arguments opposed to that thesis would be presented and systematically demolished. Following the demolition, the author would present arguments in favour of the thesis. If all went according to plan, nothing further could be done. There would be no good reasons left supporting the other side, and only good reasons left supporting the author's thesis. It's a tedious process to be sure, but effective. By the time one reaches the end, one is pretty sure of one's conclusion.

This is not the Middle Ages, so I am not going to provide that sort of analysis. Instead, I am going to undertake the first half only. My thesis is that businesspeople should be morally responsible agents *as* businesspeople. In other words, my thesis is that businesspeople ought to be morally responsible agents not merely in their role as citizens of a moral community, but in their role as people engaged in competitive enterprise. My strategy of defence will be to present apparently plausible arguments opposed to my thesis, and to show that these arguments are defective. If I am successful, you will be persuaded that, so far as we know, there

---

Michalos, A.C.: 2005. Moral responsibility in business. In D.C. Poff (Ed.) Business Ethics in Canada, 4th ed. (pp. 30–46). Toronto: Pearson Canada.

This essay first appeared in the first edition of this text; an earlier version was presented at the 17th World Congress of Philosophy In Montreal, Quebec, August 1983. Most of the 14 arguments presented here were suggested in T. Beauchamp and N. Bowie's *Ethical Theory and Business* (Prentice-Hall, 1983). The author of this essay would like to express his thanks to the editors and authors of that volume.

A.C. Michalos (✉)
University of Northern British Columbia, Prince George, BC, Canada
e-mail: michalos@brandonu.ca

A.C. Michalos, *How Good Policies and Business Ethics Enhance Good Quality of Life*, DOI 10.1007/978-3-319-50724-8_7

are no good reasons to deny or reject my thesis. I leave it to another occasion to persuade you that there are, in addition, good reasons to accept it.

Before I get to those defective arguments, however, let me clarify some terminology.

Complementary versus Contrary Terms

The words 'moral' and 'ethical' in English are ambiguous insofar as they may be used merely to designate classifications or to designate evaluations. So it will be useful to eliminate this ambiguity. First, it is necessary to distinguish complementary from contrary terms. *Complementary terms* are used to divide the world, the whole world, into two mutually exclusive and exhaustive classes. For example, everything in the world is a competitor or a non-competitor, a horse or a non-horse, a banana or a non-banana. Quite generally, take any word at all and then put a 'non' in front of it, and you have a pair of complementary terms. Thus, whatever 'moral' and 'ethical' mean, one may divide the whole world into things that are moral and non-moral, or ethical and non-ethical. To say that actions are moral or non-moral, when these words are used as complementary terms, is not necessarily to make a moral appraisal of those actions; it is, or may be, merely to classify the actions prior to a moral evaluation. To perform the latter task, one would make use of contrary terms.

Contrary terms are used to divide only a part of the world into mutually exclusive and exhaustive classes. For example, within the subset of the world known as competitors, there are winners and losers. All competitors are winners or losers. Similarly, within the subset of actions appraised from a moral point of view, there are morally good and morally bad (evil) actions. Unfortunately, in English one may use the words 'moral' and 'ethical' alone as abbreviations of 'morally good' and 'ethically good', respectively. In such cases, the words are used as contrary terms and their opposites are 'morally bad' and 'ethically bad'. Thus, in the next section when social are distinguished from moral responsibilities, it is the complementary or classificatory sense of the word 'moral' that is intended. The distinction is not between morally good and bad responsibilities, but between moral responsibilities and non-moral responsibilities.

Social versus Moral Responsibilities

In most of the literature on business ethics, people refer to social responsibilities and contrast them with other kinds of responsibilities. In virtually all cases, the phrase 'social responsibilities' is used to designate what are really moral responsibilities, roughly as these will be defined shortly. The issues typically discussed under the rubric 'social responsibilities' are usually not merely matters of good manners or etiquette, but of something much more serious. So, it will be useful to clarify this distinction.

Roughly speaking, one may say that human action is socially responsible insofar as it does not violate any rules of etiquette, good manners, good taste or generally accepted social practice. Examples of socially responsible behaviour include such things as thanking people for gifts received, arriving at and leaving parties at suitable times, answering letters or other messages requesting acknowledgment, and so on. Socially responsible action is necessary for human community, and in one way or another appropriate criteria of evaluation and sanctions for irresponsible action are routinely developed in all societies.

There are at least two ways to identify morally responsible action, a narrow way and a broad way. Narrowly speaking, one may say that human action is morally responsible, or simply moral, insofar as it does not violate any generally accepted moral maxims. Examples of moral maxims include such things as "One should not steal," "One should always tell the truth" and "One should avoid harming innocent people." Broadly speaking, one may say that human action is morally responsible or moral insofar as it is reasonably intended to impartially maximize human wellbeing. Since the actual consequences of action often involve unexpected, unintended and uncontrollable elements, one cannot require the actual maximization of well-being with every action of every agent every moment of every day. Instead, one requires a reasonable amount of attention to the likely consequences of one's action, a reasonable amount of care with one's performance and a relatively clear intention to act so as to produce a fairly specific sort of result. In particular, one should intend and try to act so that everyone affected by one's actions is affected in an even-handed, unbiased, impartial or a similar way unless there are good reasons for affecting some people in different ways.

Perhaps the easiest and most morally neutral way to understand the terms "impartial," "even-handed" and "unbiased" in the preceding sentence is probabilistically. That is, these terms should be understood as indicating that one is intending and trying to act such that every person affected by one's action has the same probability or chance of being affected in roughly the same way. More precisely, one is trying to give every affected person both an equal probability and as high a probability as possible (consistent with the former) to maximize their well-being. Since there is a generally accepted formal principle of justice that demands that similar people and similar actions should be treated in similar ways unless there are good reasons for treating them in different ways, the broad criterion of morally responsible action includes a condition of justice. Thus, on this broad account of moral action, one who acts morally must also act justly to some extent. It is not clear (to me at least) that morality and justice are entirely coextensive domains, but there is some overlap.

Clearly, what I have called the narrow and broad ways to identify morally responsible action might not define exactly the same set of actions. What's more, this might not be merely the result of a semantic disagreement or the fact that people have just never gotten around to articulating all the moral maxims they implicitly accept. On the contrary, the narrow and broad ways to identify morally responsible action might be based on significantly different views of what is required for such action. In particular, some people might believe that no one is ever morally required to try to maximize anyone's well-being. They might say that morality is essentially concerned with trying to prevent certain kinds of harm from certain kinds of people, and that while universal beneficence is praiseworthy, it cannot be morally required. In short, they might say such beneficence is appropriate for saints or those who aspire to sainthood, but it has no essential role to play in the morality of ordinary people.

There is no rule book to consult now in order to decide whether a reasonable and morally good person should adopt the narrow or broad way to identify morally responsible action. In fact, I prefer the broad way because I think a world populated by people holding such a view would be a better place to live in than a world populated by people holding the other view, all things considered. In other words, I think a world populated by people motivated by universal beneficence would be better than one motivated merely by a desire to prevent certain harms. Moreover; since morality is to some extent always a matter of aspiration rather than achievement and the latter may easily be constrained by limitations in the former, I think wisdom is on the side of taking a broad view of morally responsible action.

Moral Maxims Versus Moral Theories

It will be worthwhile to draw one other fundamental distinction before proceeding to the main part of my story. I have already referred to moral maxims such as "One should tell the truth," "One should not steal," and so on. In all countries around the world maxims of this kind are recommended. Students are sometimes shocked by this assertion, for they often have the mistaken belief that in some far-off places radically different maxims are accepted. Of course there are *some* contradictory moral maxims recommended in different countries, e.g., that women should or should not have to cover their faces, or that men should or should not be allowed to have more than one wife. However, that is entirely consistent with my claim that there are some universally accepted maxims. To take the simplest example just to prove my point: around the world it is universally accepted that it is morally wrong to kill innocent babies for pleasure. Such actions, including the particular motive mentioned, are always condemned. Furthermore, there are no societies in which a contradictory maxim would be recommended. That is, there are no societies (and I would be willing to bet there never have been any) in which the following maxim is part of their moral codes: "It is morally right to kill innocent babies for pleasure" or, briefly, "One ought to kill innocent babies for pleasure."

Although there is universal agreement about some moral maxims, there is no such agreement about the justification, reason or warrant for accepting these maxims. Much of moral philosophy is concerned with questions of justification. We want to explain why it is reasonable to accept some maxims and not others. As rational beings, we want to have good reasons, warrants, or justifications for accepting some maxims and rejecting others. In other words, we want our moral judgements to be well-grounded or well-supported rather than capricious, unprincipled or ad hoc. In short, we want to have our moral maxims derivable from moral theories. Just as any scientist wants to have generally acceptable theories to account for observable facts and law-like regularities, moral philosophers want to have generally acceptable moral theories to account for moral claims and maxims.

Moreover, just as all scientific theories are fallible and limited, so are all moral theories. In truth, there are few, if any, scientific theories that can claim the longevity of some moral theories, which also surprises some people. In particular, for better or worse, no scientific theory has lasted as long as the theory that moral maxims ought to be accepted because they are legislated by God. But longevity is beside the point here. The main point is that while there is some universal agreement about some moral maxims, there is no universal agreement about moral theories. Thus, it is obvious that whenever one is engaged in any moral controversy, it is a wise strategy to try to resolve issues at the level of moral maxims. If that is impossible and one must resort to higher-level moral theories, one is bound to encounter more problems. Again, as rational beings, we must have theories, and occasionally theoretical agreement is precisely what is required to solve some lower-level problems. But, to paraphrase a remark made by Martin Luther King Jr. concerning violence, when you resort to theories, the main issues tend to be theoretical, and practical questions of right and wrong may be swept aside.

Let's now examine in detail the 14 arguments already alluded to.

Arguments and Replies

1. Adam Smith's Argument

Whether or not the 18th century economist endorsed exactly the following argument, it is often attributed to him and is generally consistent with his views. Simply stated, the argument is that if each person would pursue his or her own interests in a fairly enlightened way, then in the long run social well-being or welfare would be maximized. Moreover, people do seem to be naturally inclined to pursue their own interests rather than anyone else's. Therefore, it is pointless for businesspeople or anyone else to concern themselves with morally responsible action. In short, if people would do what comes naturally instead of trying to perform the relatively unnatural actions recommended by moralists, the very results that the latter desire would be achieved. Clearly then, the recommendations of the moralists are at best redundant.

Reply The trouble with this argument is that its premises are empirically incorrect. If it is true that people are naturally inclined to pursue their own interests and it is also true that such activity will naturally maximize social well-being, then why has the latter not occurred? Presumably, a world that has recessions and depressions, unemployment, poverty and inefficiencies resulting from near-monopolies is not a world in which social well-being is being maximized. Moreover, it cannot plausibly be argued that we have not waited long enough to obtain the benefits of unbridled, universal, self-interested action, because virtually all of the restraints and remedial activities introduced into allegedly free markets have only been introduced when the destructiveness of unbridled self-interested action was obvious to everyone. For example, since self-interested monopolists would try to exploit everyone else (as long as that was perceived to be in their own interests), practically everyone has been willing to introduce anti-monopoly laws a priori into allegedly free-enterprise systems. What's more, empirical research has repeatedly shown that the closer one comes to monopolistic domination of a market (in food, cars, fuel, etc.), the more consumers are robbed through gross inefficiencies in production and inflated prices. Again, unemployment insurance was introduced only after it became clear that the unbridled avarice of some people would keep many other people without any adequate means of support. Similarly, social insurance systems were initiated only after it became clear that many old people, single-parent mothers and children would live and die in poverty unless the state intervened for them.

Instead of arguing that we have not waited long enough to obtain the benefits of unbridled self-interested action, one might argue, following Plato nearly four hundred years before Christ, that people don't always know what is really in their own interests. Whatever their natural inclinations might be, people tend to misperceive, misrepresent and generally make mistakes when they try to look out for themselves. In fact, one might add a heavy dose of stupidity to human avarice to account for the fact that things haven't turned out as Smith predicted. That, I suppose, is a bit extravagant. It's bad enough to have a theory that leads to false predictions. To suggest that one's theory leads to false predictions because most people are too stupid to make the most of their avarice really adds insult to injury. It would be simpler and wiser to just abandon the theory altogether.

2. Agnosticism Regarding Ends

A second argument that might be used to argue that businesspeople should not be concerned with morally responsible action involves agnosticism regarding the appropriate ends of such action. According to this view, no one knows exactly what goals, objectives, aims or ideal ends are really desirable for all the people in any society. Therefore, it is pointless at best and possibly dangerous, at worst, to try to get businesspeople (or anyone else, for that matter) to pursue such allegedly desirable ends.

Reply Given the great variety of human interests, abilities and resources, as well as what the economist Frank Knight called the "perversity of folks," it is indeed unlikely that there are many ideal ends that are desirable for every person in every society. Fortunately, however, it is also irrelevant. Just as it would be silly to abandon rules of the road because some people can't tell their right hand from their left, it would be silly to abandon the pursuit of all ideals because some people can't benefit from their pursuit or realization. There are plenty of identifiable goals whose realization *would* be desirable for the vast majority of people in any society, i.e., there are plenty of socially and morally desirable goals. For example, most people would benefit from full employment, an equitable distribution of wealth and incomes, safety from environmental pollutants, the elimination of dangerous food additives and unsafe consumer durables (cars, toys, household appliances, etc.), universal and adequate health care and education, good housing and transportation, and equitable access to political power.

3. Agnosticism Regarding Means

Supposing it is granted that there are clearly identifiable socially and morally desirable ends to pursue, it might be argued that it is pointless and perhaps even dangerous to urge businesspeople to pursue them because no one knows exactly what any particular person, in particular circumstances, must do to achieve such ends. The road to hell is certainly paved with good intentions. Among those who believe that full employment is a desirable goal, for example, some seem to think the most efficient means of achieving this would involve government regulation only to prevent monopolies or obviously harmful activities; others think some government planning can be useful in the allocation of private resources and public resources; and some think total government control of all means of production is the best strategy. Again, according to some people, children are most likely to get an adequate education if schools are controlled by local communities, while others believe that because of the great disparities in local community resources, the best strategy involves some national intervention and contribution. Thus, in view of such controversies over the appropriate means to obtain recognized desirable ends, agnosticism is justifiable, for businesspeople as well as everyone else.

Reply This argument proceeds from relatively reasonable premises to an unreasonable conclusion. From the facts of controversies and difficulties regarding the identification of optimal strategies to be used to pursue shared ends, it is concluded that total agnosticism is warranted. But if such agnosticism means the denial of any knowledge regarding appropriate means to obtain shared desirable ends, then the argument involves a *non sequitur*. It is plainly false that we know of no appropriate strategies to follow to try to realize our goals. In the case of the pursuit of full employment, for example, we know that it is useful in the first place for governments to obtain reliable and valid labour force statistics, including numbers of available workers by geographic region, age, sex, education, skill training and employment status. It is useful to have a thorough understanding of a nation's resource production and consumption, past, present and estimated future supplies and demands. In the third place it is useful to set relatively realistic employment targets and finally to experiment with a variety of tactics for hitting those targets. Of course, there will be controversies and difficulties in the pursuit of shared goals since all knowledge is fallible, all activities have some unintended consequences and very often the intended consequences of social engineering will not equally satisfy every affected person. Still, to grant all this is to grant nothing sufficient to warrant total agnosticism and abandonment of attempts to find optimally desirable means to obtain similar ends.

4. Absence of Right

Roughly speaking, we may say that one has a right to something insofar as one has a special entitlement or claim to it which everyone else has a duty or obligation to recognize. Rights may be described as positive or negative, depending on whether people have a duty to provide things in someone else's interests, or merely to avoid doing some things or to prevent some things that would harm someone else from being done. For example, in Canada, children are supposed to have a positive right to at least a primary school education, which means that adults have an obligation to provide it. All people are supposed to have a negative right to life, which means, at a minimum, that all of us have a duty to avoid wantonly destroying other people's lives, or at a maximum, that all of us have a duty to prevent the wanton destruction of people's lives. Hence, in the interests of insuring that Canadians have these rights protected, we are taxed to pay for the operation of educational institutions, our systems of criminal justice punish people legally for intentionally taking people's lives, and in some instances we morally condemn people for failing to prevent such destruction.

A fourth argument leading to the conclusion that businesspeople should not be concerned with morally responsible action *as* businesspeople is based on the simple premise that businesspeople do not have a right to engage in such action. According to this view, there is nothing in the special role, expertise or character of such people that would give them such a right, and in any case few people outside the class would recognize any obligation to provide or prevent anything in the interest of protecting the alleged right.

The idea behind this argument is that businesspeople have certain roles to play and a certain kind of expertise which are relatively limited. To suppose or demand that an obligation to perform morally responsible action can or should be included in the definition of those roles, or in every sort of expertise is a mistake. Thus, for example, the business of selling shoes, insurance or cars can and should be defined without any appeal to moral responsibilities, and one may be a good shoe salesperson, insurance agent or car dealer without having anything to do with such responsibilities. On the contrary, one's responsibilities would include, say, knowledge of the different qualities of shoes, the requirements of different people for different shoe styles, the appropriate prices to pay to suppliers and to charge to consumers, and so on. These sorts of things, it would be said, cannot reasonably be expected to create rights to making moral decisions.

Reply In response to this argument, it may be insisted that businesspeople *as* businesspeople certainly have a right to act rationally. This may be regarded as a positive right insofar as some education, training and socialization is a necessary condition of rational action, and initially someone (without specifying the particular agent) has to provide it. Indeed, it may be said that education, training and socialization must be provided precisely in the interest of protecting people's right to act rationally. Without some of the former, most human babies would not even survive to adulthood, since rational action is typically necessary for survival.

If it is granted that businesspeople have a right to act rationally, then it must be granted that they have a right to estimate all the consequences of their actions, as far as that is possible in different circumstances. Without such estimates, people could not assess the ratio of benefits achieved to costs expended. In other words, without such estimates, people couldn't determine if their actions were self-constructive or self-destructive, i.e., they couldn't assess the survival value of their actions. That ignorance, of course, should be resisted. Thus, it must be insisted that people have a right to estimate all the consequences of their actions, and that must include all the moral and immoral consequences of their actions too. Insofar as businesspeople are interested in performing rational actions, they must also have a right to perform them. Moreover, this implies a right to consider and perform morally responsible actions, since these also produce benefits and costs.

5. Level of Competence

Supposing it is granted that businesspeople have a right to perform morally responsible actions *as* businesspeople, it might still be argued that since they will have such low levels of competence regarding moral actions, they should not be encouraged to perform them. Given a society in which most people are relatively free to choose their occupations, it is likely that people who choose the world of business or competitive enterprise probably are more interested in engaging in the activities characteristic of this world than in those of its alternatives. Similarly, those who choose careers in government service, social work or, broadly speaking, in any of the "helping professions" (such as the ministry or priesthood, teaching, lawyers working in legal aid and public health personnel) probably are more interested in engaging in the activities characteristic of these occupations than in those of business. Clearly, the career interests of those in the helping professions are more compatible with those of moralists than the career interests of businesspeople. Moreover, it is likely that interest is usually a necessary condition of competence, since people are not likely to be or become good at doing things that they are not interested in doing. Thus, in fact the most competent people regarding morally responsible actions will probably be outside the world of business and, therefore, these are the people who should be urged to perform such actions rather than businesspeople. The latter will almost certainly botch the job.

Reply Those who use the preceding argument incorrectly assume that competence in performing morally responsible actions is an exclusive trait which people develop at the expense of other traits. On this view, becoming a morally responsible person is analogous to developing a special skill or becoming a specialist in a particular area of knowledge. Becoming a morally responsible person, on this view, is like becoming a good dentist or historian. It is simply another kind of specialization. On this view, if, for example, *Maclean's* or *Time* wanted to include reports of morally responsible actions, they would merely add another section. Besides their traditional sections on business, sports, books, international affairs, and so on, there would be a section on morality. Presumably, it would be a section reporting on who did what morally good or bad thing to whom, for what and with what interesting consequences.

If one adopts what I earlier called the narrow way to identify morally responsible actions, there is a strong tendency to think of morality in precisely this way, that is, as a specialized field with special interests, principles and practitioners. Then one is hard-pressed to find good reasons for most people, who typically would not think of themselves as specialists in moral matters, to be interested in such matters. Short of striving to become some sort of new renaissance person or the local champion at *Trivial Pursuits* [sic] there would appear to be little motivation for most people to try to keep up with the news in yet another area of specialization. Might as well leave it to those who go in for that sort of thing.

As you might have expected, the unhappy scenario just described provided one of the motivating factors for my adoption of what I called the broad way of identifying morally responsible actions. With this view of such actions, there would be no special section of *Maclean's* devoted to morality because there is no such specialization. On this view, *any* action has moral significance insofar as it is appraised from a moral point of view. In other words, *any* action has moral significance insofar as it is assessed from the point of view of its being reasonably intended to impartially maximize human well-being. Thus, if, to continue my illustration, the editors of *Maclean's* wanted to include reports of morally responsible actions, they would not add any new reports or any new sections. Instead, they would merely appraise the actions routinely reported in their specialized sections from a moral point of view. Competence in making such appraisals is not, therefore, an exclusive trait of moral specialists. On the contrary, since such appraisals involve the most comprehensive review of any and every human action, urging people to adopt a moral point of view is tantamount to urging them to develop a uniquely inclusive trait. It is a habit of mind, a mental set or disposition to think of all actions from the point of view of their moral impact, which is thoroughly inclusive rather than exclusive.

6. Reduced Economic Efficiency

In the interest of trying to impartially maximize human well-being, one might fail to maximize profits. In that case, one would also fail to be economically maximally efficient. Insofar as one fails to be economically maximally efficient, one is being wasteful, since inefficiency simply means there is less output per unit of input than there could be. Thus, since wastefulness is inexcusable, it should not be allowed to occur for the sake of achieving other goals.

Reply This objection represents the tip of an iceberg involving a variety of more or less controversial arguments concerning an alleged trade-off between the aims of economic efficiency and morality. In the fifth volume of my *North American Social Report* (D. Reidel 1982), I presented nearly two dozen arguments that have been used by proponents of one side or the other. For present purposes, it is enough to report two main conclusions of that analysis. First, it is of course possible to imagine situations arising in which one would be faced with a choice between economic efficiency and morality. Second, given the distribution of wealth and income in Canada (and even more in the United States), it is highly probable that such choices do not arise. Since the richest 20% of Canadians own around 70% of the wealth, the other 80% of the population has to get along on the remaining 30%. Under these circumstances, it is virtually impossible for the wealthy fifth to actually use much of their wealth. In the simplest terms, one can only consume so much lobster and champagne, take so many trips, wear so many suits and dresses, live in so many houses, and even enjoy the natural beauty of one's own land, to a certain point of saturation.

Moreover, except for the very needy, few people make the maximum use of things they own. So one would expect that those who can accumulate goods at the relatively lowest personal cost would also be the most wasteful. They would have more things lying around idle and they would be least concerned with apparent waste. In short, given the current distribution of wealth and the likely uses to which that wealth can be and is put, it is highly probable that *any* activity that would tend to redistribute wealth in the direction of greater equality (in the interest of morality) would reduce waste and would, therefore, be economically efficient. Put more bluntly, I think that the current distribution of wealth in Canada creates such gross economic inefficiency that it is practically impossible to make adjustments toward greater equality in the interest of morality that would not create greater economic efficiency.

7. Increased Government Control

Ignoring my first reply to the argument concerning reduced economic efficiency, further developments in that scenario may be elucidated. In particular, the "non-moralists" may argue that the immediate result of excessive wastefulness will be shortages, and that excessive shortages will lead directly to increased demands for government intervention. When the government finally intervenes. if will probably be in the form of regulating production and prices, and rationing consumption. The latter combination of activities, then will probably lead directly to so-called black markets, that is, to illegal transactions in which the unscrupulous few rip off those who may or may not be able to afford to be ripped off. Increased illegal activities, of course, tend to generate increased demands for greater law enforcement, meaning additional government bureaucracy to manage additional taxation, to pay for more salaries of more law enforcement personnel (police officers, clerks, court officials, correctional officers and institutions), and to pay for more buildings and the sophisticated technological hardware characteristic of our modern enforcement agencies. Thus, since no one in his or her right mind wants to live through this scenario, everyone should be reluctant to suffer economic inefficiency even if it requires ignoring alleged moral responsibilities. Indeed, faced with the spectre of such an outrageous scenario, many people would be inclined to describe their perceived obligations in fairly moralistic terms. That is, they would be inclined to insist that in the interests of humanity, civilization or a free society such a scenario should be resisted.

Reply Naturally, I would welcome the move from the talk about economic efficiency to talk about humanity or, more particularly, morality. It is always helpful to have agreement about relatively ultimate aims, or about that for the sake of which relatively immediate actions are being performed or recommended. However, for present purposes, it will be wise to concentrate on those who might not.

Since, for the sake of argument (i.e., Argument #6), I have allowed the other side to assume that actions performed in the interest of morality would lead to reduced economic efficiency, it is worthwhile to remember that standard practices allegedly leading to increased efficiency are notoriously inefficient. In order to avoid any misunderstanding or confusion about apparent paradoxes, one must never forget that all measures of efficiency are ratios of benefits to costs, and that there is no standard rule book to tell people exactly *how* to measure *which* benefits and costs to *whom* in *what* time period. Thus, it is easy for an employer to replace relatively expensive human labour (people, that is) with relatively cheap machines, and to increase efficiency defined as a greater benefit to cost ratio *for the employer.* On the other hand, since the very same replacement (by hypothesis) puts some people out of work, it is easy for these employees to show a decrease in efficiency defined as a smaller benefit to cost ratio *for the employee.* Hence, the fact that efficiency measures are essentially ratios with controversial numerators and denominators largely explains the apparent paradoxes involved when certain actions are claimed to be both efficient and inefficient. Without first getting some agreement about how to measure which benefits, etc., it is logically impossible to obtain generally recognized definitive answers.

In the absence of the required agreement about how to measure whose benefits, I would merely remind those who use this seventh argument that widespread poverty and unemployment are two extremely wasteful by-products of the sort of economic efficiency they are recommending. As the economists of the "small is beautiful" or "appropriate technology" view have argued, it cannot be rational to try to continually replace labour with capital when there is relatively plenty of the former and little of the latter. In more human terms, it cannot be reasonable to insist on capital accumulation for a few in the interest of a kind of "efficiency" that makes relative paupers of many others.

Consideration of waste aside, the main reply I would offer to the argument before us is that the alleged choice between a free society and a society highly controlled by government is a false dichotomy. All highly industrialized societies are characterized by high levels of functional interdependence. In such societies almost everyone is more or less dependent on many other people to maintain his or her lifestyle. Although it is possible for people to raise their own sheep, spin the wool, weave cloth, manufacture needles, design clothes, carve buttons, make clothes, etc., few people have the inclination to engage in such activities. The vast majority of people prefer a style that makes them more dependent on the productive activities of others. In highly industrialized societies, this preference has the unfortunate by-product that most people are probably even more dependent on others than they would like to be or should be for their own best interests. Indeed, the whole field of business ethics is largely a response to the realization that a system of production, distribution and consumption of goods and services is almost synonymous with a way of life.

Such a system necessarily socializes, conditions and, finally, even controls people in fundamental ways. Thus, if one were going to insist on any dichotomy, I would suggest at the risk of oversimplification, that between control by elected officials in the public interest, and control by private industrial officials in their own interests. Given the fact that people will certainly become socialized with certain kinds of expectations, aspirations and ideas about a good life, the real issue is how such a life should be defined and what strategies should be used to achieve it. It is a raw red herring to suggest that it is possible to just let everyone do whatever turns them on. That never happens. Moreover, as argued earlier, it is highly unlikely that the result of such unconditioned activity would benefit most people. Finally, granted that in fact elected officials do not always act in the interests of society as a whole and that private industrial officials do not always act in their own interests narrowly defined, this sort of dichotomized thinking is probably not particularly helpful in the long run.

8. Loyal Agent's Argument

Elsewhere I have examined this argument in considerable detail. I will summarize that discussion here. [See this text, p. 200 ff.] The argument runs as follows. (1) As a loyal agent of some principal (i.e., employer), I ought to serve his or her interest as he or she would serve them if the latter had my expertise. (2) Such a principal would serve his or her own interests in a thoroughly egoistic way. Therefore, (3) as a loyal agent of such a principal, I ought to operate in a thoroughly egoistic way in the interests of that principal. In other words, loyal agency seems not only to permit but to require that people should be selfish in the interests of their employers.

Reply One may be regarded as operating in a thoroughly egoistic way if all one's actions are designed to optimize one's own interests and one has no inclination at all to identify the interests of anyone else with one's own. One may very well be a self-confident, self-starting, self-sustaining and self-controlled individual. These are all commendable personal characteristics. But one must be selfish, self-centred and/or self-serving. In conflict situations when there are not enough benefits to satisfy everyone, an egoist will try to see that his or her own needs are satisfied whatever happens to the needs of others. One is more interested in being first than in being nice, and one assumes that everyone else is too. One may even believe that if everyone behaved this way, the world's resources would be used in a maximally efficient way and everyone would be materially better off. But that is a secondary consideration. One's first consideration—the only prudent one—is to look out for Numero Uno, oneself.

The trouble with the loyal agent's argument is that both premises are problematic. The second premise assumes that all people are egoists; but people who try to defend their actions are *not* egoistic. Their basic assumption is that they are loyal agents motivated by a desire to serve the best interests of their employers. However, if it is possible for them to have such nonegoistic motives, then it must be possible for other people to have such motives too. Hence, the very assumption required to make the argument look plausible in the first place makes the second premise look implausible. So the argument is self-defeating.

The first premise—that an employee's responsibility is to the employer alone—looks as innocuous as motherhood and apple pie, and in a way it is. Its only weakness is that its limitations are not built into it. In this respect it is like most moral principles and rules of law. Short of turning every principle and rule into a self-contained treatise, it is impossible to indicate every possible exception. For example, no one should kill anyone, except *maybe* in self-defence, war, capital punishment, euthanasia or suicide. Similarly, a loyal agent ought to pursue the interests of his or her employer except…. In the famous Nuremburg trials, the Charter of the International Military Tribunal recognized, for instance,

> …that one who has committed criminal acts may not take refuge in superior orders nor in the doctrine that his crimes were acts of states. These twin principles working together have heretofore resulted in immunity for practically everyone concerned in the really great crimes against peace and mankind. Those in lower ranks are protected against liability by the orders of their superiors. The superiors were protected because their orders were called acts of the state. Under the Charter, no defence based on either of these doctrines can be entertained.

Canadian and American laws relating to loyal agency do not sanction any illegal or unethical actions. Thus, there is no doubt at all that the first premise of the loyal agent's argument cannot be regarded as a licence to break laws. No respectable court would permit it. In fact, although the courts have no special jurisdiction over moral law, they have shown no reluctance to condemn immoral acts allegedly performed in the interests of fulfilling fiduciary obligations.

9. Materialist Orientation

In the fifth argument above it was indicated that people whose primary interests are in business would probably have low levels of competence in performing morally responsible actions. I replied that the flaw in this argument was the assumption that competence in performing morally responsible actions was an exclusive trait or skill, and that the broad way of understanding morality which I have adopted is more inclusive than exclusive. One might still argue that, given the materialistic orientation of businesspeople, when they try to make a broad benefit-cost analysis in the interest of morality, they are bound to spoil it. As Aristotle said a long time ago, as a person's character is, so is the world seen. People who spend most of their time evaluating things from a materialistic point of view will tend to make moral evaluations from the same point of view. So, when they try to do things in the interests of everyone impartially, they will probably not be doing the sorts of things moralists would like them to be doing. For example, from the point of view of Canadian businesspeople, the support of economic research designed to show that Adam Smith's argument (Argument #1) was basically sound might be regarded as impartially benefiting everyone. Quite generally, then, such people might regard anything that reinforces their view of the world as impartially benefiting everyone.

Thus, urging these people to be universally beneficent might lead to universal materialism, which most moralists would find unacceptable.

Reply As suggested earlier, it is almost certainly an oversimplification to say that businesspeople usually have a materialistic orientation. Given the variety of businesses that people can enter, the variety and ambiguity of human motivations, and the variety of personal philosophies of life and lifestyles, it is unlikely that people in business, broadly construed, are uniformly materialistic. If there is any reliable and valid research indicating such bias, I haven't seen it. Secondly, it (would be a mistake to think that all materialism is dangerous and objectionable. Some material goods do make positive contributions to the quality of life, e.g., reliable consumer durables such as cars, household appliances, dwelling units and communications hardware (telephones, radio, television). Finally, Aristotle's remark is obviously not the whole truth. As much as people's interests influence what they perceive and believe, what they perceive and believe also influences their interests. Indeed, my reading of the evidence accumulated so far indicates that perception and belief contribute more to interest than the reverse. But the literature on this subject is diverse, complicated and controversial.

10. Need for Pluralism

In a pluralistic society like Canada, there are many perspectives from which controversial issues may be viewed. There are many important issues about which various people have unsettled opinions, and there are others about which there are solid and contradictory opinions. To expect business people to have uniform and settled opinions, and to urge them to see that these are predominant is unwarranted and unwise. It is unwarranted because there is no good reason to expect businesspeople as such to be intellectually more tidy or clearheaded than the rest of the population and, therefore, it is unwise to urge these people to strive to make their views predominant over all others. Given the enormous overt and covert power of businesspeople, they might go even farther than they already have to create a onedimensional society. The only reasonable course to follow is a pluralistic one.

Reply This argument, too, is a red herring. To urge businesspeople to engage in morally responsible action is to urge *only* businesspeople to engage in such action. Of course pluralism will and ought to continue, if that means that there should be a variety of perspectives from which important issues may be viewed. No one in his or her right mind would insist on silencing all voices but one, or on excluding all points of view but one. It would be as bad to have only businesspeople steering the ship of state as it would be to have only philosophers, moralists or gymnasts doing so.

The other problem with this argument is that it is self-defeating. If it is true that businesspeople are so powerful that they represent a threat to the rest of society, then morally irresponsible businesspeople would represent an even greater threat. Hence, if this argument has any value at all, it is only to reinforce the view that urges businesspeople to be morally responsible.

11. Overload

The world of competitive enterprise is notoriously complicated already. Compared to those in other occupations, business executives have a relatively high incidence of heart attacks and strokes. To insist that such overloaded people should take on yet another responsibility and, indeed, such a controversial and inherently complex one as moral decision-making, is to risk complete systemic failure. Quite apart from the arguable facts that the engagement of businesspeople as such in morally responsible action would be redundant and incompetent, there is no good reason to risk destroying currently reasonable business practices by overloading decision-makers.

Reply If this argument proves anything, it proves too much. Life, after all, is complicated. So, if complexity were sufficient to eliminate the burden of attending to moral responsibilities, then all of us could take a permanent moral holiday. Clearly, however, a society in which no one attended to any moral responsibilities would have virtually nothing to recommend it as a human and humane community. In such a society, if it could ever be called that, life would be "nasty, brutish and short," as the 17th century British philosopher Thomas Hobbes said. Secondly, the argument still seems to presuppose that morality is some kind of specialization which people can get into or not, as they choose. As I have indicated above, this is a mistake. The moral point of view is not another specialized perspective, but is inherent in all major decisions.

12. Inconsistency

Perhaps one of the most frequently heard arguments against businesspeople engaging in morally responsible action is that such action is logically inconsistent with competitive enterprise. To engage in competition in an open market is essentially to try to do better than others. The rough rule is to buy cheap and sell dear. To engage in morally responsible action is essentially to try *not* to have some come out better than others. The rule then is to buy and sell at no monetary gain. Thus, those who recommend that businesspeople as such should be morally responsible are talking literal nonsense and recommending that businesspeople should perform actions that are aimed both to make someone and no one come out better, which is absurd.

Reply I believe the unsoundness of this argument may be demonstrated by consideration of competitive games of fair play. For example, there is apparently nothing immoral about such competitive games as chess, tennis, golf and track-and-field events, to name only a few. Rules are designed to insure that, in principle, all competitors have an equal probability of winning. Each chess player gets the same number of pieces, uses the same board, has the same time constraints and so on. Moreover, each player is free to play, or not, depending on the relative benefits and costs of playing. Hence, since chess games are thoroughly competitive and morally unobjectionable, it is logically possible for something to be so. Thus, those who think there is some logical absurdity involved in recommending that businesspeople should be moral and competitive are plainly wrong. If there is any inconsistency involved, it is certainly not a matter of logic or conceptualization.

13. The Godfather's Argument

The Godfather's argument in that excellent book and series of movies was simply that as long as a business provides goods and services demanded by some consumers and a substantial family income for producers, few people should ask anything more of it. After all, business is business, and businesspeople are not saints any more than the rest of us. Life, as the great British-American philosopher Alfred North Whitehead said, is robbery. All living things draw their sustenance from other living things. So, a Godfather-type disciple might have concluded, we are doomed to be predators. The most we can hope for is to make a reasonable living for ourselves and our families, granting always that there is an unattractive aspect to our business activities.

Reply Dazzling—and pragmatic—as the rhetoric may sound, it's still nonsense. Granting that all living things live by consuming the corpses of other living things, it does not follow that we are all robbers, thieves or murderers. Poetic licence is not a licence to commit logical fallacies. There are important differences between, for example, chopping up vegetables for a Caesar salad and chopping up Caesar. The facts that some people may be willing to pay to have someone murdered and that some other people are willing to perform the murder are not sufficient to justify the transaction. The person whose life is being negotiated also has an interest that ought to be protected, as do the rest of us whose lives would be at risk if such business transactions were legal.

14. Particular Morality

Finally, one might argue that the basic presupposition of this essay is a red herring, because few if any businesspeople have to be persuaded to be morally responsible. How many people in business have you ever heard saying that they should be morally irresponsible, immoral, morally bad or evil? Not many, probably. No one is born a businessperson. Most people in business were taught roughly the same moral maxims at home and in school, and most of these maxims had roughly the same origins in the Judeo-Christian religions. So most people have been socialized to be morally responsible. Businesspeople generally intend to act and are expected to act the same as everyone else. Thus, to assume that businesspeople are in need of special remedial training, encouragement or admonitions to be nice is simply to make a false assumption.

On the other hand, it is true that the moral maxims to which virtually everyone is exposed are not necessarily predominant in the world of competitive enterprise. Just as chess players and golfers agree to accept particular rules of behaviour for the sake of their games, businesspeople also adopt special rules for the sake of their work. Like chess players, then, businesspeople may be said to have particular codes of ethics in addition to and occasionally in opposition to ordinary or universal ethics. Many actions that would appear to have questionable moral status, judged by the maxims of universal morality, may be morally good judged by the maxims of the particular morality of the world of business. Therefore, instead of condemning businesspeople for acting immorally, one ought at least to appreciate their particular ethical positions and perhaps praise them for steadfastly adhering to the rules of their own game.

Reply This apparently tolerant approach to the identification and appraisal of morally responsible action is yet another self-defeating argument. Insofar as the argument has any strength at all, it tends to undermine *all* morality. One of the basic aims and functions of morality or codes of ethics is the resolution of disputes involving conflicting interests. Moral maxims and, more importantly, the ideal of universal beneficence are designed to provide rules for settling disputes without resorting to legislated civil or criminal laws. The recognition of a supreme moral principle of action, namely, the intention to impartially maximize human well-being, is a necessary condition of morality achieving its basic aims. Without such a tie-breaking principle, a principle to adjudicate between conflicting interests or lower level maxims, appeals to morality are useless.

Thus, the concept of particular moralities is logically incoherent, for it entails maxims of action which both include and exclude a supreme principle. In other words, it posits a set of maxims which are relatively equal in status but also not relatively equal to one supreme principle. Unless the maxims of any so-called particular morality are roughly equal to those of other particular moralities, one cannot use them to claim special privileges for one's behaviour. However, granting them such equal status implies eliminating the possibility of appealing to them to resolve conflicts. If, for example, businesspeople, bandits and baseball players all have equally important ethical codes to live by, then, when there are conflicts between people in different groups, each can retreat to his or her own special code, with the result that no resolution of the conflict is possible. If one would take the additional step that some people seem to recommend, namely, that everyone should have his or her own moral code, then morality would be radically relativized and absolutely useless. Clearly, the way out of this logical and moral morass is simply to abandon the idea of particular morality. There can be only one kind of morality, and it is universal. Businesspeople, like everyone else, must be judged morally responsible or irresponsible in terms of this morality. There is no third option.

Chapter 8
A Case for a Progressive Annual Net Wealth Tax

Alex C. Michalos

Introduction

The basic aim of this paper is to make a case for the introduction of a progressive annual net wealth tax in Canada. I begin with a review of some national public opinion polls indicating the attitudes of Canadians toward taxation and government spending (section "Taxation"). Section "Distributions of Wealth and Income" provides an overview of the distributions of wealth and income and emphasizes the significantly greater inequalities in the former compared to the latter. A progressive annual net wealth tax is briefly described and then proposed as a means to reducing wealth disparities (section "Outline of the Proposed Tax"). In the next section "Arguments for a Net Wealth Tax", I present 19 arguments in favor of such a tax. Following that, I present 31 arguments opposed to a net wealth tax, and I try to show that none of these arguments can be sustained (section "Replies to Arguments Against a Net Wealth Tax"). For reasons explained in some detail in the body of the paper, the redistribution of wealth should be regarded as a fundamental feature of any national socio-economic development plan.

Michalos, A.C.: 1988. A case for a progressive annual net wealth tax. Public Affairs Quarterly, 2, pp. 105–140.

A.C. Michalos (✉)
University of Northern British Columbia, Prince George, BC, Canada
e-mail: michalos@brandonu.ca

A.C. Michalos, *How Good Policies and Business Ethics Enhance Good Quality of Life*, DOI 10.1007/978-3-319-50724-8_8

Taxation

Galbraith (1975, p. 57) wrote "Where taxes were concerned, the (American) colonists were exceptionally obdurate; they were opposed to taxation without representation, as greatly remarked, and they were also, a less celebrated quality, opposed to taxation with representation." There is some evidence that Canadians are also not particularly enthusiastic about taxation. Since 1962, on five occasions, the Canadian Institute for Public Opinion (Gallup Polls) has put the following question to national samples of Canadians, "Do you think taxes are too high or about right?" On every occasion more people answered "Too high" than "About right." (See Table 8.1.) (Gallup Polls are typically designed so that reported percentages should be within 4% points of the true percentages 95% of the time. Thus a very conservative interpretation of reported percentages would require differences of about 8% points between two figures in order to judge that the differences indicate more than mere measurement error. Hence, for example, although in 1962 47% of respondents answered 'Too high" and 43% answered "About right," a conservative interpretation would allow that the 4% point difference between these figures might be merely the result of measurement error or, briefly, that the difference was not statistically significant. I generally favour a conservative interpretation of poll results.)

In 1980, 71% of a national sample of Canadians thought that "if the average Canadian felt he or she could get away with it he or she would be likely to attempt [tax] evasion." (Reported in *Canadian Taxation*, Spring 1980, p. 38) On May 12, 1983, the CIPO released results of asking the following question, "As you may know, the current Federal deficit is approaching 30 billion dollars. Where do you think the government should look for additional funds—Do you think the Federal government should raise taxes, should introduce economy measures or should borrow more money abroad? What should be done first? And in second place?" In first place, 85% of a national sample, said, "Introduce economy measures." and in first or second place 92% said, "Introduce economy measures." Three percent favored raising taxes as their first or second choice.

Lest one is inclined to jump to the conclusion that the basis for Canadians' attitudes toward taxation is merely some sort of an innate reluctance to part with their cash, it is worthwhile to notice the results of some other relevant national

Table 8.1 Do you think taxes are too high or about right?

Year	Percent answering		
	Too high	About right	Can't say
1962	47	43	10
1965	49	39	12
1970	75	21	4
1975	66	27	7
1985	69	24	7

Source The Gallup Report, May 6, 1985

Table 8.2 Do you think the Federal government's polices for tackling the country's economic situation gives you a feeling that they are or are not handling the situation properly?

Year	Percent answering		
	Yes, handling properly	Not handling properly	Don't know
1977	28	54	18
1978	27	59	14
1979	27	62	11
1981, January	25	61	14
1981, June	18	67	15
1981, November	20	69	11
1982, June	14	76	9
1983, June	27	61	12
1984, May	23	62	15

Source The Gallup Report, July 19, 1984

opinion polls. The CIPO had nine polls including the question, "Do you think the Federal government's policies for tackling the country's economic situation gives you a feeling that they are or are not handling the situation properly?" In every case, from 1977 to May 1984, most people said they had the feeling that the government was not handling the economic situation properly. (See Table 8.2.) In 1968, the Federal Task Force on Government Information found that 45% of a national sample of Canadians had "low" or "fairly low" levels of faith in the Federal government, and 45% thought it was "inefficient" or "somewhat inefficient" (Michalos 1980, p. 163). The CIPO reported that 70% of Canadians believed that "People are asked to make great sacrifices, but government officials themselves live in luxury" (January 2, 1984). Granted that there may be some inclination to hold on to their cash, there is also some suspicion that the Federal government (of Liberals or Progressive Conservatives) is not completely in control of its fiscal house.

Taxes are the means of effecting compulsory transfers of assets from the private to the public sector. While most taxes are called just that (for example, income taxes and sales taxes), some go by other names, for example, premiums for unemployment insurance and social security. Two main principles govern the levying of taxes, namely, that levies should be made according to (a) benefits received or (b) ability to pay. Since many of the benefits received from paying taxes are public goods (for example, national defense), it is difficult to operate exclusively on this principle. Still, unemployment insurance premiums, for example, are warranted by it. In order to apply the second principle, some measure of ability to pay must be selected. "Ideally, this measure would reflect the entire welfare which a person can derive from all the options available to him or her, including consumption (present and future), holding of wealth, and the enjoyment of leisure. Unfortunately, such a comprehensive measure is not practicable" (Musgrave and Musgrave 1984, p. 233). Generally speaking, the measures used are based on income, expenditures or wealth. Thus, there are income taxes (using income as the measure of the ability to pay), sales taxes (using expenditures) and property taxes (using some wealth as the measure). A tax on incomes is said to be "progressive" if the ratio of the tax to any particular income rises as incomes rise. It is "proportional" if the ratio remains constant for any income changes, and it is "regressive" if the ratio falls as incomes rise. If all other things are equal and a scheme of income taxation is progressive, then the distribution of after-tax incomes will be more equal than the distribution of before-tax incomes. Similarly, a scheme of net wealth taxation that is progressive would leave the distribution of after-tax net wealth more equal than the distribution of before-tax wealth. That is precisely the sort of net wealth tax that is being recommended here.

Distributions of Wealth and Income

Since 1952, Statistics Canada has collected data on the net wealth of Canadians in its Surveys of Consumer Finances. However, as a result of changes in basic definitions and other technicalities, only the survey data from 1970, 1977 and 1984 are reasonably comparable (Statistics Canada 1986, pp. 7–9). The 1970 and 1977 data-sets have been more thoroughly analyzed than the 1984 dataset, but because the figures regarding net wealth are so stable, much of what was found in the earlier surveys is very similar to what has been and probably will be found in the later survey.

The key definitions in these surveys are as follows:

> The concept of the wealth of families… is rather narrowly defined as the value of total selected assets *less* total debt…. Total asset holdings which comprise wealth … consist of deposits and savings certificates in chartered banks, trust companies and other institutions, cash on hand, Canada Savings Bonds, other Government of Canada bonds, all other bonds, publicly traded stocks and shares, mortgages, loans to other persons and businesses, amounts (including accrued interest) held in RRSP's (Registered Retirement Savings Plans) and RHOSP's (Registered Home Ownership Savings Plans), other financial assets such as trust funds, cars, market value of owner-occupied homes, equity in vacation homes, other real estate and business/farm/professional interests… the value of only one consumer durable good, i.e., cars, has been included in total asset holdings whereas the value of all other consumer durables such as coloured televisions, yachts, sail boats, skidoos and other household furnishings and equipment has been excluded. Also excluded is the value of jewelry, art, stamps, coins, etc.
>
> Total debt, which is subtracted from total asset holdings in order to define the wealth of a family unit, consists of money owed on credit cards, charge accounts and instalment debts, bank loans secured by stocks and bonds and household goods, student loans, all other bank loans, loans from sales finance and consumer loan companies, credit unions and caisses populaires, other institutions such as savings banks, life insurance companies, other miscellaneous debts and mortgage debt on the owner-occupied homes. (Statistics Canada 1979a, pp. 8–9.)

The 1977 sample covered about 17,000 households, with some over-sampling of high-income households because "survey data on incomes or other financial items seriously underestimate income or other items at the upper end of the distribution because small samples do not adequately measure the high incomes and because refusal rates may be higher among high income groups or high asset holders" (Statistics Canada 1979a, p. 11). The overall response rate was 80% and the response rate for the high-income sample was about 45% (Oja 1983, p. 170). Details regarding sampling frames, response rates, accuracy of estimates, random and systematic errors, sizes of standard errors, and so on, are given in Statistics Canada (1979a, b, 1980, 1986).

Basic results of the 1970, 1977 and 1984 surveys are given in Fig. 8.1. This Figure includes detailed breakdowns for individuals living alone (unattached individuals), families of two or more members, and aggregates of families and unattached individuals. In 1984 if all Canadians (unattached individuals and families) were lined up from the very poorest to the very richest and divided into five groups containing 20% (a quintile) of the population in each group, and if the total net wealth of all the units was determined and its distribution among the five groups was calculated, then the result would be as indicated in Fig. 8.1. The poorest 20% of Canadians (i.e., the lowest quintile) had less than nothing; they were in debt, which is indicated in the Figure as—0.3% of the net wealth of all units. The next poorest 20% had only 2.4% of the whole pie, and so on. The wealthiest quintile had about 69%, and the wealthiest 10% (decile) had just over half (51%) of the wealth of all Canadians.

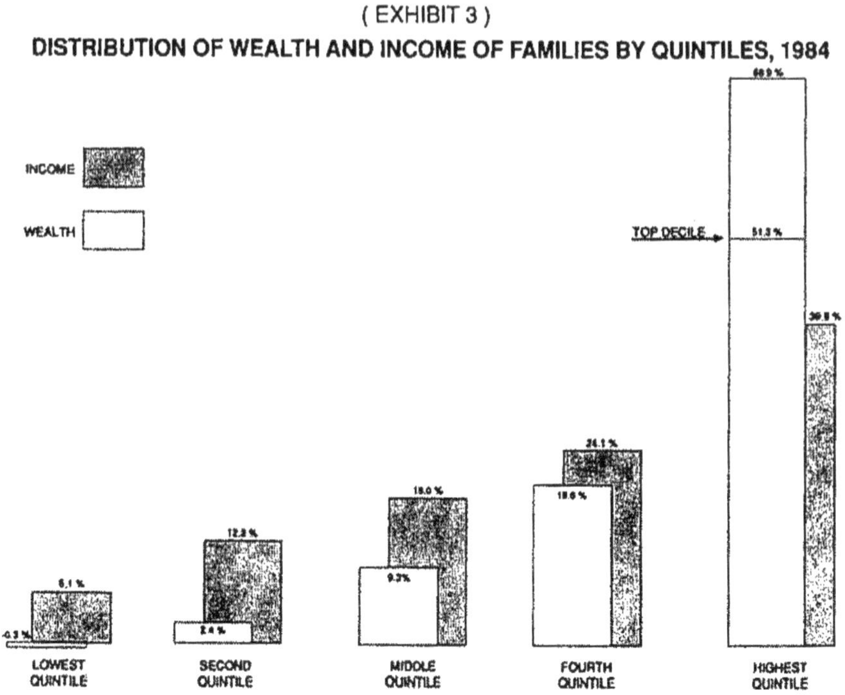

Fig. 8.1 Distribution of wealth and income of families by quintiles, 1984

For purposes of comparison, Fig. 8.1 also includes figures regarding the distribution of incomes. The figure clearly shows that the 1984 distributions of incomes for all units, families or unattached individuals were not as unequal or skewed as the distributions of net wealth. For example, considering all units, the poorest quintile had 4.5% and the richest quintile had 43% of the total income of all Canadians.

For a variety of reasons regarding the sample response rates, missing values, imputed values, extreme skewness of the net wealth distribution, and so on, it is difficult to estimate the accuracy of the figures on the basis of which the percentages in Fig. 8.1 were determined. According to Oja (1983, p. 172) the 1977 "survey estimates of financial assets and debts may come to 60–70% of the true balances of the household sector." Given the likelihood of such substantial under-estimations, any differences of 1 or 2% points in our figures should be regarded with caution. Thus, it is best to think of the net wealth distributions from 1970 to 1984 as essentially unchanged. Insofar as one is prepared to take the figures at face value, the indicated change of about 2% points in 14 years implies that, if the future were fairly similar to the past, it would take about 70 years to reduce the top decile's wealth 10% points.

Concerning the distributions of income, much more can be said. According to Gillespie (1980a, b, pp. 27, 31), "the distribution of income in Canada became considerably less unequal between 1930 and 1951… and remained virtually unchanged between 1951 and 1977…. The empirical evidence for the 1970–77 period demonstrates that federal budgets have not substantially altered the economic position of lowest-income families relative to highest—income families … Rather, it seems that federal budgets have provided larger benefits for the latter compared with the former—although both have gained—financed primarily by lower-middle- and upper-middle-income families" (See also Michalos 1982, pp. 38–41).

The first time I saw figures concerning the distribution of wealth and income in Canada, I was shocked. like most other Canadians, I knew that there were people in this country with much less and much more money than I had, and I knew that some of the former were very poor while some of the latter were very rich. I naturally wondered how my country compared to similar other countries, for example, the USA and the UK. Good comparisons were and are very difficult to find. Harrison (1980) presented evidence indicating that the UK's wealth distribution was skewed much more than that of Canada and the USA, partly as a result of the persistence of large fortunes through inheritance. Although I addressed some of the problems related to poverty and wealth in Canada and the USA in Michalos (1982), I was not able to try to make the case for a net wealth tax which would effectively reduce the great and continuing disparities of wealth and, among other things, provide the revenue to eliminate poverty. It is now time to make that case.

Outline of the Proposed Tax

More details of the proposal are given below in the course of considering arguments for and against it. However, a brief overview will be useful now. What is being proposed is a progressive annual tax on net wealth which, to some extent, would both supplement and supplant current income, consumption and wealth taxes. The net wealth tax would be part of a comprehensive tax scheme that would be more efficient to administer and would obtain more revenue more equitably than the current system. The administration of the tax would be combined with the current income tax, and the two kinds of taxes would be calculated together. Thus, the Federal government would be primarily responsible for gathering the tax with the cooperation of Provincial governments. The revenues obtained would be shared somehow, as current income tax revenues are shared.

Net wealth would be comprehensively defined as what is left over when total debts are subtracted from total assets. The unit of taxation would be individuals or families. Consistent with current income taxes, there would be deductions for dependents and the aged, and exemptions for some housing, household and personal effects, pension rights, insurance policies, patents and copyrights. There would be starting and ending points (floors and ceilings) for tax liabilities based on the national distribution of average net wealth holdings and these points would be periodically adjusted. For example, consider the 1984 distribution of wealth illustrated in Fig. 8.1. Since the lowest three quintiles' share of the nation's total wealth is far below, the fourth quintile's share is about even with and the highest quintile's share is far above what it would be in an egalitarian society, a reasonably progressive net wealth tax would have starting points or floors for tax liability set so that no tax would be paid by families in the lowest four quintiles. The 2% or 3% tax levied on families in the highest quintile would be divided so that the wealthiest decile paid more than the second wealthiest decile, and the total revenue would be distributed so that families in the lowest quintile received more than those in the second quintile, and so on. It is likely that the tax would never exceed 5% of any individual's or family's net wealth, and it would most likely be under 3%.

According to a report of the Organization for Economic Cooperation and Development (OECD 1979), in 1976 there were 11 member countries with a net wealth tax, namely, Austria, Denmark, Finland, Federal Republic of Germany, Iceland, Ireland, Luxembourg, Netherlands, Norway, Sweden and Switzerland. Musgrave and Musgrave (1984, p. 476) claimed that there were 17 countries with such a tax, including the OECD countries, India and some Latin American countries. The OECD report mentioned above was based on a survey of all member countries regarding the costs and benefits of net wealth taxes with a wide variety of provisions. Several related studies have been carried out by the OECD and should be carefully reviewed by anyone interested in following up my proposal. References may be found in OECD (1979).

Arguments for a Net Wealth Tax

The following arguments may be offered in support of the establishment of an annual progressive net wealth tax applicable to all Canadians.

1. Net wealth is the best measure of an individual's ability to pay taxes (Sazama 1980, p. 20; Bird 1980, pp. 35–36; Bale 1980, p. 39).
2. Net wealth is much more unequally distributed than income, so a nation that is nominally committed to egalitarianism should be more concerned with the distribution of wealth than of income. In the words of the Ontario Committee on Taxation in 1967, "A democratic society such as ours, espousing political equality for all its citizens, cannot permit undue concentration of wealth in the hands of a few" (Quoted from Bale 1980, p. 48).
3. It is practically impossible for Canadians to focus attention on the existence of the enormous wealth of this country, of the great disparities in the distribution of that wealth and of the consequences of such disparities without the official, routine and public accounting required through an annual tax on net wealth. As indicated above, we have had three roughly comparable surveys examining net wealth and their results certainly under-estimate the real net wealth in this country. Since the Survey of Consumer Finances estimates depend "not only on the willingness of respondents to provide financial data but also on their ability to recall amounts accurately, voluntary cooperation to consult their records, clear understanding of the questions asked and their rapport with the interviewers, etc.," the estimates **obtained** from such surveys cannot be regarded as adequate for the development of public policy (Statistics Canada 1979b, p. 50). Furthermore, public policy on such a sensitive matter as the distribution of wealth cannot be allowed to be periodically manipulated by half-baked Royal Commissions like the 1978 Royal Commission on Corporate Concentration. (A rapid review of the *Report* of this Commission may be found in Michalos 1982, pp. 30–34.)
4. It is practically impossible to mobilize interest and support for the initiation of remedial measures to eliminate harmful consequences of significantly unequal distributions of wealth unless there has been relatively continuous monitoring and public discussion. As Sazama (Panel 1980, p. 54) remarked, "By talking about net wealth taxation we are raising fundamental issues about how the economic system is organized. To have full popular control of economic power it will be necessary (but not sufficient) to transform private wealth to social wealth. The process of working for a net wealth tax will make those conclusions obvious to more people."
5. The current unequal distribution of net wealth contributes to the unequal distribution in incomes (Ward 1980, p. 32; Michalos 1982, pp. 26–30).
6. The unequal distribution of net wealth prevents the equalization of opportunities for employment and other necessities of a good life (Bird 1980, pp. 35–36; Bale 1980, p. 40).

7. The unequal distribution of net wealth creates unequal access to political power. This undermines democracy (Sazama 1980, p. 20; Ward 1980, p. 32; Bird 1980, p. 36; Bale 1980, p. 40).
8. The unequal distribution of wealth and incomes must distort markets and economic development in the interests of monopolies and oligopolies, which tend to be characterized by relatively inefficient production and overpricing (Michalos 1981b, pp. 17–21; 1982, pp. 19, 30–34).
9. The current emphasis on income taxes as a source of government revenue places a greater burden on labor than on capital, which therefore requires a net wealth tax to correct the inequity (Bird 1980, p. 35; Ward 1980, p. 33; Musgrave and Musgrave 1984, pp. 238, 245).
10. Unlike significantly progressive income taxes which perpetuate current concentrations of wealth by preventing new accumulations, a progressive net wealth tax would reduce the size of and even eliminate some current concentrations (Bird 1980, p. 36; Bale 1980, p. 40).
11. An appropriately designed net wealth tax would allow the government to reduce income taxes without loss of revenue, and that would allow relatively poorer Canadians to accumulate some wealth and reduce the current wealth disparities.
12. The sum total of net wealth is so much larger than the sum total of annual incomes that the former provides a much larger tax base and a much better source of national revenue. The total estimated net wealth of Canadians in 1977 was about $400 billion, compared to the estimated Gross National Product of about $200 billion (*National Income and Expenditure Accounts 1970–1984*, p. 2, Table 1; Statistics Canada 1979b, pp. 41, 44). Net wealth in the USA in 1980 was about three times the GNP (Musgrave and Musgrave 1984, p. 463).
13. A progressive net wealth tax would have the effect of redistributing the wealth of Canada to the whole community, where it can be more effectively used in the interests of that community. In other words, it would "encourage decision making which is responsible to the community as a whole" rather than that which emphasizes "profits and corporate power" (Canadian Mental Health Association 1985, p. 82).
14. Current taxes that touch net wealth are notoriously regressive. "For example, the municipal real property tax, in effect a gross wealth tax confined to one kind of asset, is regressive over all income levels. The same is generally true of the provincial retail sales taxes, the federal sales tax and the selective excise taxes" (Bale 1980, p. 39). To say that these taxes are regressive is to say that they violate the principle of taxation according to ability to pay and that they tend to increase rather than decrease wealth disparities. As a source of revenue, their sustaining virtue is convenience.
15. The making of large fortunes is largely the result of good luck for winners and bad luck for losers, but the making of civilized communities requires reasonable and compassionate alterations in the circumstances resulting from mere luck, which alterations could be initiated by a net wealth tax (Bird 1980, p. 36; Bale 1980, p. 40; Michalos 1982, p. 29). It is perhaps worthwhile to mention

here that even if large fortunes were the result of great skill, hard work or special virtues of some sort, it would not follow that such fortunes should be preserved. After all, the virtues that allow one to accumulate wealth may be entirely irrelevant to or even incompatible with its wise and compassionate use. Presumably the preservation of civilized communities should take precedence over the preservation of large fortunes no matter how virtuously the latter were made.

16. Optimistically, perhaps, one might expect that the reduction of great disparities in the distribution of net wealth might help reduce envy, greed, selfishness and competitiveness on the one hand, and encourage sympathy, empathy, compassion and cooperation on the other hand, as human characteristics and motives of social behavior. Of course, those who are severely taxed might become more envious, greedy and so on, but since they are fewer in number than the others, there should be a net gain.
17. For political, economic and moral reasons, it is reasonable to expect Canadians to set their own house in order as part of a global effort to improve the total human condition. Given the relatively greater influence Canadian voters have on their own elected representatives and the relatively greater concern they have for less fortunate fellow citizens, if significant changes cannot be made at home, it is highly unlikely that significant changes can he made in the distribution of wealth from developed to developing or Third World countries.
18. Great disparities in the distribution of net wealth are inefficient and wasteful insofar as they contribute to unemployment and create incentives for people to drop out of a patently unfair race for an acceptable share of the good things in life, which shrinks the size of one important factor of production (that is, labor) and any output that might have come from it. It was estimated that the "unutilized component of the available labor supply" in Canada in 1982 was about 12% of GNP or $39 billions (Manitoba Political Economy Group 1985, pp. 36, 41; Michalos 1982, p. 19). Obviously, unemployment also tends to increase wealth disparities.
19. People without hope of having socially acceptable means of obtaining a reasonable share of a community's wealth may resort to socially unacceptable means (for example property crime); to self- destruction with drugs, alcohol and more violent forms of selfabuse; or to violent crimes against other members of their families and community (Michalos 1980, Chap. 4; Canadian Mental Health Association 1985, p. 81).

Replies to Arguments Against a Net Wealth Tax

A number of arguments may be and have been raised against the establishment of a tax on net wealth. These will now be presented along with replies that seem sufficient to either destroy or at least seriously undermine them.

1. The sum total of the net wealth of the wealthiest quintile of Canadians is so small that even if it were heavily taxed the revenue would not be sufficient to solve any important problems (Walker 1980, p. 15).
   Reply (1) On the contrary, some rough calculations indicate that if only 2% of the net wealth of the wealthiest quintile was taxed, there would be enough revenue to lift all low income families in Canada out of poverty. Indeed, if the previously mentioned substantial under-estimations of net wealth are anywhere near accurate, it would be possible to lift the total low income population out of poverty without altering the *reported* net wealth of the wealthiest quintile at all! (2) We have already seen that the purposes of a net wealth tax go far beyond the collection of revenue to the prevention of harms such as undermining political democracy, protecting illegitimate special privilege, distorting markets and social and economic development.

2. The sum total of the net wealth of the wealthiest quintile of Canadians is so big that a tax large enough to break up such concentrations would never be politically feasible or tolerated in this country (Tinker in Panel 1980, p. 52).
   Reply (1) As indicated in section "Outline of the Proposed Tax" above, no one is recommending a single lump-sum tax on the wealthiest quintile that would rapidly and radically reduce their share of the total wealth in the nation. What is being recommended is an annual progressive tax on net wealth of under 5%. (2) It is also recommended that there should be continuous monitoring of national net wealth by percentiles so that the wealth tax can be levied at a rate sufficiently large to guarantee some annual reduction of the current wealth disparities. As a starting point for discussion, one might think of redistributing net wealth from the wealthiest decile to the poorest two or three quintiles at a rate of one percent a year for ten years, always serving the needs of the poorest quintile first.

3. Insofar as the aim of a net wealth tax is to raise funds in order to pay for programs to help the needy, the aim can be better served by allowing capital to flow to its most efficient users, which will finally result in the most rapid growth in output and a bigger pie for everyone (Walker 1980, p. 15).

   Reply (1) The size of the economic pie has increased, but there are more Canadians living in poverty and unemployed. In 1973 the GNP was about $120 billions, 12% of the population was living in poverty and the unemployment rate was 5.6%. In 1984 the GNP was about $420 billions, 18% of the population was living in poverty and the unemployment rate was 11% (Michalos 1982, pp. 81, 117, 124; National Council of Welfare 1985, p. 7; *Canadian Social Trends*, Autumn 1986, pp. 7, 43). In constant 1971 dollars, the GNP increased 31% from 1973 ($108 billions) to 1984 ($141 billions) (*Canadian Statistical Review*, June 1985, p. 8). At the same time, the poverty rate increased 50% and the unemployment rate increased 96%. Hence, increases in the size of the economic pie are not sufficient for the elimination of poverty or unemployment. (2) As already indicated, poverty can be eliminated by redistributing only a fraction of the total net wealth of the richest quintile of Canadians. Hence, any growth in the size of the economic pie is not even necessary to serve the interests of the needy. (3) I am in favor of the most efficient use of all resources and believe that the current practice of allowing capital to flow to the most powerful private corporate or personal hands is much more wasteful than the proposed redistribution (Manitoba Political Economy Group 1985; Matziorinis 1980). (4) Evidence from several studies of many other countries indicates a positive correlation between productivity and economic growth on the one hand and relatively less skewed distributions of wealth and greater government spending for social programs on the other (Social Planning Council of Metropolitan Toronto 1985, pp. 12–17). For example, Levin (1986, p. 234) wrote that, "Income and wealth are more evenly distributed in Japan than in the United States, and in Japan as well as in those European countries with a better productivity record than the United States government spending on social programs represents a larger share of gross national product than it does here [i.e., in the USA]. That equality is harmful to growth is an article of faith, not a confirmed hypothesis."

4. A net tax on wealth is essentially a way of destroying wealth (Walker 1980, p. 15; Ward 1980, p. 31).

   Reply The mere shifting of wealth from rich people to poor people or to the public purse to be used in the interest of the vast majority of Canadians clearly does not destroy wealth (Bird in Panel 1980, p. 49).

5. Economic growth requires investment, and investors need the security of large supplies of wealth accumulated through saving and the incentive of the possibility of relatively large profits. Hence, a net wealth tax is bound to undermine saving, investment and growth (Walker 1980, p. 15; Wagner 1980, p. 26; Ward 1980, pp. 31, 33).

   Reply (1) It has already been noted above (section "Arguments for a Net Wealth Tax", #15) that great fortunes are not the result of careful saving but of good luck. (2) The wealthiest quintile has enjoyed about 70% of the net wealth in Canada for over 30 years (assumed that distributions of net wealth are at least as stable as distributions of income), while investments have gone up and down. (3) It has been demonstrated that special tax incentives given to businesses in the period from 1972 to 1975 yielded net losses to the public purse of from 50 to 80%. Summarizing the results of a comprehensive survey of the impact of tax incentives, Matziorinis (1980, p. 178) wrote,

   > Business investment experience in Canada does not support the hypothesis that tax incentives have been effective in promoting higher levels of investment... that the additional investment induced by the measures was only a fraction of their cost... [and that] ... tax incentives seem to have served mainly as an instrument for granting tax relief by lowering the effective corporate income tax rate significantly below the statutory rate.

   (4) Similarly, McIntyre (1987, p. 26) claimed,

> In 1981 [the US] Congress enacted tax breaks that essentially exempted from taxation the profits from new capital investments. The new loopholes were supposed to produce an investment boom, by lowering the cost of capital. But, again, it didn't happen. From 1981 to 1985 the kinds of investment in business equipment that were to be made more attractive grew at only a quarter the rate at which they had grown from 1976 to 1980. Companies did save on taxes but then spent the money on everything but new investment, including increases in dividends, higher executive pay, and a record-breaking wave of giant corporate mergers.

(5) Taking a broader view, Levin (1986, p. 491) wrote,

> Of course, economic theory tells us that lowering the price of capital services by means of lowering interest rates or taxes will lead to more capital formation. But it remains one of the great puzzles of economic science that, after more than 20 years of careful econometric research, the data simply do not provide strong confirmation for this proposition. And the more complex linkage between capital taxation and productivity growth is even more difficult to confirm empirically.

(6) It is an incredible oversimplification to suggest that investment decisions are made primarily on the basis of the size of a potential investor's net wealth or of taxes on that wealth. Matziorinis (1980, pp. 178–179) wrote,

> To attribute a firm's investment decision to tax factors alone is to ignore the relatively greater importance of such factors as the demand for the firm's product in relation to its capacity, the cost and availability of credit to finance the firm's investment, market share and market strategy considerations, capacity constraints, the state of business confidence or a firm's predisposition to invest in light of current and expected business conditions, structural considerations such as the degree of foreign ownership, and the effect of government policies such as the anit-inflation program, among others.

(7) It is a mistake to suppose that only private persons or corporations can accumulate capital and make investments, especially in a country like Canada which has so many successful Crown Corporations. Hence, it is question-begging in favor of private capital to assert that if private investment were to be reduced then all investment would be reduced (Canadian Union of Public Employees 1985).

6. Property taxes already tax wealth (Ward 1980, p. 33).
   Reply As already indicated above (section "Arguments for a Net Wealth Tax", #14), property taxes reach only one segment of wealth and are highly regressive. The proposed progressive net wealth tax should replace such regressive taxes to some extent.

7. The great disparities in net wealth are finally maintained by the legitimized force of the state in a relatively capitalistic country like Canada. Hence, it is a mistake to imagine that some sort of a tax scheme can alter such disparities (Sazama 1980, p. 22).
   Reply If this argument is sound, then potential reformers are wasting their time. Since pessimism only leads to despair and inaction, wisdom is on the side of optimism and action.

8. Given the current connections between economic and political power, any new taxes are likely to be designed to continue to favor the rich over the poor (Sazama in Panel 1980, p. 54).

   Reply As with the previous objection, it is difficult for a potential reformer to give an entirely satisfactory reply to this sort of radical pessimism or cynicism. Again, one can only say that wisdom is on the side of optimism and action in spite of the unfortunate but real possibility indicated by the pessimists and cynics.

9. Since wealth is equivalent to income insofar as the former can be regarded as potentially generating the latter, income taxes are indirect taxes on net wealth (Wagner 1980, p. 24; Fiekowsky in Panel 1980, p. 54).

   Reply There is a theoretical equivalence between income and wealth which can be wisely or unwisely applied to the real world. Musgrave and Musgrave (1984, p. 470) explain the relationship as follows.

   > Given *perfect capital markets and assessment procedures*, a 5 percent tax imposed on the value of an asset may readily be translated into an income tax on the income derived from the asset. Suppose that an asset worth $1,000 yields an annual income of $100, in line with a 10 percent market rate of interest. The liability under a 5 percent tax on the asset value is $50. Expressed as a percentage of the asset's income, it equals 50 percent. The 5 percent tax on the asset value (or property tax) is thus equivalent to a 50 percent tax on the property income (or income tax). Putting it more generally, the value of an asset *in a perfect capital market* is given by $Y = iV$, so that $V = Y/i$ where V is its value, Y is its annual income, and i is the market rate of interest obtainable on other investments. If the same yield is to be obtained from a property tax at rate tp and a tax on income therefrom at rate ty, we must have $tpY/i = ty$ or $tp = ity$. (Emphasis added.)

   The theoretical relationships are instructive. One might prefer a 5% net wealth tax to a 50% income tax generating the same amount of revenue. In fact, in 1966 the Canadian Royal Commission on Taxation was apparently so inclined (OECD 1979, p. 27). Nevertheless, it must be remembered that in the real world there are no "perfect capital markets and assessment procedures." In this world wealth is not equivalent to income because

   > Capital confers an income independent of the health of the owner and attainable without any current sacrifice of leisure; and, over and above any income derived from it, it gives its possessor independence, security, and the opportunity for advantageous purchase or for a spending spree. These advantages confer additional taxable capacity on the owner of capital. To some extent this additional taxable capacity can be recognised by taxing income from wealth more heavily than income from work; but this method is imperfect, for it takes no account of the advantages which wealth confers even if it yields no money income and it takes insufficient account of such advantages where the money income yield is low (OECD 1979, p. 13).

10. Since physical capital is already taxed twice (that is, once when it is obtained in the form of earned income and a second time when either the interest it earns as saving is taxed or the profits it earns from investment are taxed) but income is

taxed only once, a tax on net wealth would unfairly triple the tax bias against saving, capital formation and investment (Wagner 1980, pp. 24–25).
Reply The number of times something is taxed is clearly relatively unimportant compared to the amount of the taxes levied. Granting that physical capital is taxed twice, the fact that the distributions of income and wealth have been practically unchanged for 30 years demonstrates the irrelevance of the number of times such capital is taxed.

11. The unequal genetic inheritance of people is partly responsible for the current disparities in wealth, and no fair tax will ever be able to eliminate the existence and unequal consequences of such inheritance (Wagner 1980, p. 27; Ward 1980, p. 32).
Reply (l) No one is claiming that all of the consequences of unequal genetic inheritance, whatever they are, should be compensated for by a tax on net wealth. (2) As indicated above (#15), there is evidence that large fortunes owe much more to chance than to skill or anything else. (3) It is a mistake to think of the social practice of people leaving wealth to blood relatives as some kind of a biological or, more specifically, genetic phenomenon. (4) Even if biology had some systematic influence on the creation of great wealth, Bale (1980, p. 43) correctly remarked that "… although we can do little about the unequal genetic endowment flowing from the lottery of birth, we can do something about unequal wealth inheritance because such inheritance is entirely a socially created institution."

12. There is no way to measure the degree to which skews in the distribution of wealth are generally harmful because (a) there are too many variables involved to determine causal relations, (b) there are too many value judgments involved and (c) there is no way to assess and compare how people feel about the alleged impact of wealth disparities. Hence, arguments for a net wealth tax on the grounds of the actual or potential harmfulness of wealth disparities must be based on mere ideology or faith, or both (Wagner 1980, p. 29; Ward 1980, pp. 31–32).
Reply (1) If the argument had merit, it would undermine virtually all economic planning, private and public, since all such planning is based on the assumption that many causal relations can be determined with enough certainty to make them worthwhile. (2) No one knows how many value judgements are involved in the arguments for or against the harmfulness of wealth disparities, the number of judgments is relatively unimportant compared to the kinds, and the variety of kinds is also unknown. (3) For over a decade psychologists and sociologists have annually published over 1100 research studies involving the assessment and comparison of perceived net satisfaction and happiness regarding a wide variety of things (Michalos 1986). Hence, arguments for a net wealth tax on the grounds of harmfulness may be based on as much evidence, objectivity, science and reasonable argumentation as arguments against such a tax on such grounds.

13. Economists refer to the question of who pays how much of what tax as the problem of tax incidence. Although there are some settled opinions concerning many issues related to this problem, "controversy and uncertainty still swirl" about the incidence of "sales taxes, corporate profits taxes and … property taxes" (Gillespie 1980a, b, p. 4). For example, "standard incidence assumptions" allow that half of corporate profits (income) taxes are passed on to consumers (Gillespie 1980a, b, p. 6; Sazama 1980, p. 20). However, considering the size and diversity of goods and services produced by multinational firms and conglomerates, the multiplicity of relations among subsidiaries and parents, and the vast opportunities for special pricing and creative accounting, nobody knows how much of the taxes on corporate profits are passed on to consumers. The accepted figure of 50% reflects economists' uncertainty, probably mixed with some optimism regarding the fairness of the system. Since the introduction of a net wealth tax would require the resolution of such very controversial tax incidence issues, it would be wise to avoid introducing such a tax.

    Reply (1) If this argument had any merit, it would undermine virtually all taxation, since one can always find reasons for asserting that there are certain hidden benefits or costs of any tax which significantly alter the apparent incidence. (2) If serious consideration were given to the possibility of introducing a net wealth tax, then there would be improvements in data collection, research and analysis of all options. So, it is likely that reasonable agreements could be reached concerning outstanding issues of tax incidence.

14. Instead of undertaking the difficult task of introducing a whole new tax, it would be better to continue with the present system and introduce laws that would prevent the possible abuses of great wealth disparities (Wagner 1980, p. 30; Piper in Panel 1980, p. 51).
    Reply (1) What is being proposed in this objection is precisely what has been tried for years and found inadequate, namely, allowing great disparities and preventing abuses. (2) It is impossible to have great wealth disparities and prevent abuses because there are limits to the world's resources, goods and services, and typically great accumulations of wealth in one place are possible only by making great withdrawals and leaving poverty in another place (Harrison 1981, pp. 23–41; Michalos 1981b, pp. 6–11, 75–76; United Church of Canada 1985, pp. 178–183; Canadian Conference of Catholic Bishops 1985, pp. 212–213).

15. Those who call for a net wealth tax are motivated by envy which should not be encouraged or rewarded with success.

    Reply (1) There is no evidence that the motives of those who call for a wealth tax are more or less envious than the motives of anyone else. (2) The arguments presented in favor of such a tax appeal to considerations of justice, morality and economic efficiency, and these arguments must be regarded as evidence of the motives of the tax proposers. (3) Even if all of those who called for a net wealth tax were motivated by envy (which is highly unlikely), the costs of failing to introduce such a tax and the benefits of introducing it are far more important than any character flaws in the proposers. (4) Anyone who would characterize poor people lacking the necessities of life as merely envious of rich people enjoying luxuries would exhibit callousness, insensitivity and the lack of fundamental human compassion, which are more serious character flaws that should be condemned.

16. Although there may be great disparities of inherited wealth in some countries, that is not the case in Canada. So, there is no problem here that requires a net wealth tax as a solution (Ward 1980, p. 32).

    Reply (1) According to the OECD (1979, p. 14), "in most countries inheritance is a major source of inequality in the distribution of wealth." (2) The evidence of the studies by Porter (1965), Clement (1975, 1977) and Newman (1975) indicate that there are great disparities of inherited wealth in Canada. (3) Although the origins of great disparities of wealth are important for reasons already indicated, the consequences of such disparities are even more important. Thus, it would be a mistake to ignore the latter as if only the former warranted consideration.

17. Inheritance or so-called death taxes are a kind of net wealth tax, and they have been virtually abandoned in Canada. Their abandonment should be regarded as evidence that they were relatively worthless.

    Reply (1) Canada is almost the only developed country that has abandoned such taxes (Bale 1980, p. 48). (2) Although they typically have been designed here so that people with a moderate degree of foresight and some appreciation of estate planning can easily avoid paying such taxes (Ward 1980, p. 34), inheritance taxes might be designed to successfully redistribute wealth. (3) There is some evidence that the Federal government abandoned such taxes without giving them serious consideration (Bale 1980, p. 48). (A more cynical view would be that they were intentionally designed to be ineffective and then abandoned because they were just that.) (4) The specific kind of a tax on net wealth being argued for here is not a single inheritance or death tax but an annual tax requiring annual accounting similar to that involved in income taxes. Again, a single tax package might be designed that efficiently assessed wealth and income.

18. People who argue for a tax on net wealth would not want such a tax applied to themselves (Ward 1980, p. 32).

    Reply (1) There is no evidence that the proposers of a net wealth tax would want themselves excluded from paying such a tax. (2) Since it would be patently unfair, immoral, self-defeating, inconsistent and apparently irrational to recommend the tax and self-exemption, it is highly unlikely that anyone arguing for the tax would also argue for self-exemption. (3) It is highly likely that anyone who wanted to be exempted from paying such a tax would either never argue for it or argue against it.

19. A significantly progressive tax on net wealth would discriminate against the very wealthy, and such discrimination would be unjust (Ward 1980, p. 32).
Reply At a minimum, justice requires that people should be taxed in accordance with their ability to pay, which is precisely what is being proposed here. The greater burden falling to the very wealthy is not the result of discrimination but of their greater ability to pay.

20. Insofar as equality of opportunity is an aim of a net wealth tax, that aim can be better served by improvements in the education system and by the elimination of social discrimination (Ward 1980, p. 32).

    Reply (1) Several studies have shown that disparities in income and wealth cannot be accounted for by disparities in educational achievement. (2) Great disparities in wealth are at least as much and probably more the cause than the effect of social discrimination (Michalos 1981a, pp. 96–98; 1982, pp. 26–30). (3) All three problems of wealth disparities, inadequate education and social discrimination merit attention.

21. A tax on net wealth must be unfair because such wealth includes human capital (for example, native intelligence, personal skills or attractiveness), which cannot be taxed (Ward 1980, p. 32; Royal Commission on Taxation *Report* (1967) according to Bale 1980, p. 41).

    Reply (1) The fact that all wealth cannot be directly taxed is not a good reason for failing to tax any wealth or for failing to tax a broader range of wealth than is currently taxed (Bale 1980, p. 41). (2) The fact that all wealth cannot be taxed makes a net wealth tax similar to practically all other taxes, since it is unlikely that any tax captures everything in fact that it might capture in principle (Bird in Panel 1980, p. 50). (3) Human wealth is taxed when it is transformed into income, and a net wealth tax is supposed to supplement rather than supplant income taxes.

22. Insofar as a net wealth tax must include the taxation of homes and property, which are municipally taxed, a wealth tax would create jurisdictional problems (Ward 1980, p. 33).

    Reply (1) There are many Canadian precedents regarding problems of jurisdiction and many relatively straightforward solutions, for example, Federal and Provincial income taxes are easily administered at the same time. (2) Given the regressive nature of municipal property taxes and the progressive nature of the proposed net wealth tax, it is likely that the inclusion of property taxes in a comprehensive tax package would result in a more equitable as well as a more profitable source of revenue. (3) There might even be some administrative cost saving resulting from the development of a more comprehensive system.

23. Considerable wealth is tied up in things like private homes, automobiles and various consumer durables (for example, appliances, stereo sets, and so on), and such wealth does not represent dangerous economic and political power. Hence a net wealth tax would erroneously identify and tax such power (Sazama in Panel 1980, p. 54).

    Reply (1) As indicated in section "Distributions of Wealth and Income", with the exception of automobiles, consumer durables have been excluded from Statistics Canada's Survey of Consumer Finances; so the measured disparities in wealth have never been based on such things. (2) As indicated earlier in section "Outline of the Proposed Tax" and later in my reply to the objection following this one, the proposed tax would include provisions for standard deductions and exemptions regarding basic necessities. (3) When assessments of the significance of wealth are made from the perspective of the total distribution of wealth from the top decile and quintile of wealth holders to the bottom, it will be easier to determine potential and actual dangers. (4) In the absence of routine accounting procedures established through a wealth tax, it has been, is and will be more difficult to identify any hazards.

24. Net wealth assessment would create too many administrative problems, including those involving the mere discovery of all taxable assets and those involving their evaluation (Bird 1980, p. 38; Bale 1980, p. 42). For example, jewels, stamps and works of art can be kept practically anywhere, and the evaluation of such items can be extremely controversial. While Statistics Canada's Survey of Consumer Finances simply excludes such items, administrators of a tax on net wealth would be obliged to include them. What is worse, it is likely that increases in the administrative problems attached to such a tax would lead directly to increases in government surveillance and litigation. *Reply* (1) Concerning administration, the evidence from the OECD survey is clear and favorable.

> No country with a net wealth tax considered it more difficult to administer than income tax and some specified that it was less so… The view was generally held that the existence of net wealth tax assisted the administration of income tax. The collection of data on wealth enabled investment income to be cross-checked with income-earning assets; the trend in assets-holding might also highlight income discrepancies. (OECD 1979, p. 127.)

    (2) As already suggested, several tactics are used to reduce administrative costs. Besides common returns, standard deductions and exemptions, use is made of evaluations every three or five years instead of every year for certain items, of average values over several years, of insured instead of actually estimated values and of values obtained from taxes on capital gains (OECD 1979, pp. 13, 17, 36–57). (3) Few countries seemed to be willing or able to provide

quantitative estimates of the costs of administration and compliance, but there was no doubt expressed about the benefits of the programs outweighing the costs (OECD 1979, pp. 125–127). (4) There probably would be some increase in surveillance and litigation concerning the wealth of the richest decile or quintile in Canada. (5) However, virtually no public program of taxation is perfect; so the decision to have or not have a tax on net wealth must rest on the particular costs and benefits attached to such a tax. (6) Since the number of families and individuals who might require special surveillance or litigation is relatively small and their potential taxable wealth is relatively great, the benefits of the additional administrative problems would be outweighed by their costs. (7) As already suggested, the introduction of a net wealth tax as part of a comprehensive tax package should decrease the total administrative costs, increase the benefits and make the whole system more efficient than it currently is for most Canadians.

25. Inflation already taxes wealth (Ward 1980, p. 33).
    Reply (1) Since the difference between the amount of wealth possessed by the richest and the poorest quintiles has been steadily increasing for many years, inflation must be operating as yet another regressive tax punishing the poor more than the rich. (2) A suitably designed progressive net wealth tax could reduce the inequitable impact of inflation on people with diverse amounts of wealth.

26. A net wealth tax would tend to undermine family businesses, especially small businesses and farms (Ward 1980, p. 34).

    Reply (1) In all countries with such a tax, special provisions are made for agricultural property (land, livestock, machinery, forestry, woodlands), fishing boats, unincorporated and new businesses (OECD 1979, pp. 49–57). (2) Since the proposed tax is going to be designed to redistribute wealth from the relatively wealthy to the relatively poor, it would not undermine any small businesses or farms. (3) It would undermine large concentrations of wealth controlled by extended family dynasties.

27. An annual tax on net wealth would provoke the flow of capital out and prohibit the flow of capital into Canada, which would shrink the economic pie and the potential for growth, and incidentally leave relatively less wealth to be distributed to anyone. So, even if the resulting distributions of wealth and incomes were more egalitarian, the country would be relatively worse off with the tax than without it.

    Reply (1) There might be some outflow of capital and some arresting of capital inflow following the introduction of a net wealth tax. However, the unattractive scenario hypothesized as a consequence is based on a very oversimplified view of the nature of the wealth that will be taxed, investment in general and capital flows in particular, and national sovereignty. Each issue will be addressed in turn. (2) Over half of the wealth to be taxed is in relatively fixed assets like buildings and land, which is either difficult or impossible to move (Oja 1983, p. 164). (3) There is plenty of theoretical and empirical research on different approaches to the taxation of immovable property. For present purposes, the following remarks are worth quoting from Musgrave and Musgrave (1984, pp. 472–473).

> Just as an increase in property tax rates may reduce property values and induce capital outflows, so may the provision of additional public services raise values and attract capital inflow. Better schools or municipal services may render the town a more attractive place in which to reside or to operate a business. The improvement raises the demand for housing and structures, leading to higher property values, and thus counteracts the effects of increased property tax rates. Thus, expenditure benefits may be capitalized no less than tax burdens, so that the combined tax and expenditure effects may leave housing values reduced, increased, or unaffected, depending on how the revenue is obtained and what it is used for.

(4) In the case of relatively liquid assets (e.g., cash or bonds), it is virtually always possible for one to find some bank or government some place in the world that would give one a higher rate of return for an investment, but people usually do not rush to make such investments. (5) Many countries, including Canada,

> have used temporary bans or limits on certain financial outflows either when the balance of payments was under downward pressure (Canada, the United States) or to prevent the rapid accumulation of liquid, domestic currency assets held by nonresidents, usually when there has been upward pressure on the exchange rate… Japan and the United Kingdom, which even just a few years ago virtually prohibited financial outflows and screened inflows, have now completely liberalised such operations. (OECD 1982, pp. 58–59.)

After a thorough review of capital control practices in OECD countries,

> [t]he main findings … suggest that temporary restrictive controls may at times be an appropriate or inevitable response to cope, in the short run, with difficulties created by large destabilizing capital flows (as far as exchange rate, reserves or monetary objectives are concerned) resulting from divergent economic policies and performances among Member countries or from other non-economic factors. (OECD 1982, p. 60)

(6) Virtually all research and common sense itself indicate that "successful" foreign investors always take more out of a country than they put in. Hence, it is a serious mistake to assume that Canadians would be net losers if new foreign investments are not made here, especially if the investments are made by Americans who have notoriously drained the wealth of this country (Michalos 1982, pp. 58–63). (7) Currency exchange rates can be altered to make capital flows more or less attractive (Bird 1980, p. 37). (8) More importantly, since currency exchange rates are typically much greater than any proposed wealth tax rates are likely to be, the former would have much more influence than a wealth tax on capital flows in and out of the country (Matziorinis 1980, p. 179). For example, the fact that a Canadian dollar loses about 25% of its buying

power by moving to the United States is bound to have much greater influence on its movement than the fact that it is taxed another 2% or 3% in Canada. (9) Economics narrowly and artificially construed aside, serious consideration must be given to the continued erosion of Canada's political sovereignty resulting from efforts "to become more attractive" to very wealthy people whether they are Canadian or not. As short-sighted politicians whittle away at relatively modest health and social security programs, family allowances, unemployment benefits, public housing, educational institutions, research facilities, and so on, the Canadian capacity for autonomous national planning and development is reduced. In the words of the United Auto Workers Brief to the Macdonald Commission (1985, p. 30), "[a]t issue is a meaningful democracy and the collective ability to really—rather than just formally—shape our lives."

28. For over 20 years nation-wide Gallup polls have shown that Canadians regard inflation and unemployment as "the most serious problems facing this country" (Table 8.3), and disparities in wealth are seldom if ever mentioned. Hence, priority should be given to the reduction of inflation and unemployment, rather than to the introduction of a new tax

    Reply (1) The existence of great disparities in wealth has been cited above (section "Arguments for a Net Wealth Tax") as one of the fundamental causes of unemployment and inflation, and the introduction of a net wealth tax is being recommended as a necessary part of a solution to the problem of wealth disparities. (2) The most likely reasons for people not citing wealth disparities as the most serious problem facing this country are because people's judgments about national problems are based on the views presented in the corporate owned and biased popular press and media (Michalos 1981a, pp. 150–156; 1981b, pp. 194–199), on their personal problems and on the perceived problems of their neighbors (Michalos 1986). In all three cases wealth disparities are relatively invisible compared to unemployment and high prices, just as deadly cancerous growths can be relatively invisible compared to the short-term illnesses and accidental injuries of daily life. (3) Although the Gallup Association is not a public interest research group and has never displayed a great interest in questions related to disparities in wealth, it would be misleading to fail to mention the following polls. In response to the question, "In your opinion, do the courts in this country dispense justice impartially or do they favor the rich and influential?", 60% of a national sample of Canadians said they thought the courts favored the rich and influential (*The Gallup Report*, August 12, 1985). Thirteen years earlier, 72% of those who thought that "some of the laws of Canada… favor [a] particular class" mentioned "the upper class, the affluent" as the favored one (February 19, 1972). The same year 54% said they did not think "the big corporations [were] paying their fair share of taxes" (December 2, 1972). (As a matter of fact, the relative shares of personal and corporate income taxes in 1972 were similar to those in 1985 (Table 8.4). Seventy-three

Table 8.3 What do you think is the most important problem facing this country today?

Date	Percent answering	
	Inflation	Unemployment
1963	8	33
1964	3	32
1965	10	14
1966	29	7
1968	38	6
1972	37	34
1973	53	8
1974, April	59	8
1974, October	82	3
1975, July	52	14
1975, November 8	64	8
1976, April	55	12
1976, October 20	50	9
1977, April 13	44	18
1977, July 27	41	28
1978, February 22	38	35
1978, June 17	46	38
1978, October 7	46	30
1979, September 8	50	22
1980, February 6	49	10
1980, August 9	48	16
1981, February 18	55	15
1981, August 22	59	10
1982, January 23	61	12
1982, July 14	54	26
1983, February 7	37	40
1983, July 18	32	47
1983, December 15	33	42
1984, July 9	27	50
1985, January 28	25	56
1985, August 8	21	54
1986, January 13	21	50
1986, July 17	21	44

Sources Norik American Social Report, Vol. 5, pp. 189–198; Gallup Poll Releases for the specific dates cited in the table

percent approved of "equalization payments" giving financial assistance to "have not provinces" (May 13, 1972), a figure that later increased to 84% (September 16, 1981). In 1985, 75% approved of increasing Family Allowances, and 69% approved of increasing Old Age Pensions, provided that they were "paid only to families or people who needed them" (January 21,

Table 8.4 Personal and corporate income taxes, 1962–1985

Year	Personal income taxes	Corporate income taxes	Personal as % of total	Corporate as % of total
	(Current millions)			
1962	2,052	1,302	32.8	20.8
1963	2,018	1,298	31.4	20.2
1964	2,168	1,375	31.6	20.1
1965	2,535	1,669	31.9	21.0
1966	2,638	1,759	30.3	20.2
1967	3,050	1,743	28.8	16.4
1968	3,650	1,821	31.1	15.5
1969	4,334	2,213	32.3	16.8
1970	5,588	2,839	35.3	18.0
1971	6,395	2,427	38.4	14.6
1972	7,227	2,396	38.9	12.9
1973	8,378	2,919	39.1	13.6
1974	9,226	3,710	36.8	14.8
1975	11,710	4,836	36.4	15.0
1976	12,709	5,748	36.6	16.6
1977	14,751	5,377	38.5	14.0
1978	13,562	5,828	34.7	14.9
1979	14,788	5,654	34.7	13.3
1980	17,959	6,951	35.1	14.0
1981	21,296	8,130	36.5	13.9
1982	25,232	8,118	34.5	11.1
1983	27,376	7,139	37.6	9.8
1984	29,290	7,286	38.2	9.5
1985	31,080	9,380	37.1	11.2

Sources (68–211) *Federal Government Finance 1984,* p. 33, T7; *1980,* p. 40, T14; *1977,* p. 38, T14; *1975,* p. 44, T16; *1970,* p. 38, T13; *1965,* pp. 7–8

1985). On the basis of this handful of polls, it is fair to say that Canadians have expressed some concern about some undesirable consequences of wealth disparities, and some willingness to redistribute some wealth from the relatively wealthy to the relatively poor. (4) The best evidence of Canadians' concern with the undesirable consequences of wealth disparities and the need for their reduction may be found in the Briefs presented to the Macdonald Commission which were gathered together in Drache and Cameron's *The Other Macdonald Report* (1985). These Briefs express the views of a wide variety of Canadians, including "churches, trade unions, women's groups, social agencies and organizations representing Native People, farmers and the disadvantaged." Collectively Drache and Cameron (1985, p. ix) refer to this set of people as "the popular sector."

Table 8.5 Inflation and unemployment, 1965–1985

Year	Inflation rate	Unempl. rate	Male Unempl. rate	Female Unempl. rate
1965	2.4	3.9	4.3	2.6
1966	3.7	3.5	3.9	2.6
1967	3.6	4.0	4.5	2.9
1968	4.0	4.8	5.3	3.4
1969	4.6	4.6	5.0	3.6
1970	3.3	5.8	6.4	4.4
1971	2.9	6.3	6.9	5.0
1972	4.8	6.3	6.7	5.3
1973	7.6	5.6	5.7	5.0
1974	10.8	5.4	5.7	4.9
1975	10.8	6.9	6.2	8.1
1976	7.5	7.1	6.3	8.4
1977	8.0	8.1	7.3	9.4
1978	8.9	8.4	7.6	9.6
1979	9.2	7.4	6.6	8.8
1980	10.2	7.5	6.9	8.4
1981	12.5	7.5	7.0	8.3
1982	10.8	11.0	11.1	10.9
1983	5.8	11.9	12.1	11.6
1984	4.4	11.3	11.2	11.4
1985	4.0	10.5	10.3	10.7

Sources North American Social Report, Vol. 5, p. 101, T19, p. 117, t38, p. 118, T39; *Canada Year Book 1980–81,* p. 269, T7.1, T7.2; *1985,* p. 173, T5.6, p. 753, T23.8; *Canadian Social Trends,* Autumn 1986, pp. 7, 43; *Canadian Statistical Review,* May 1986, p. 42, T4

29. Even if a net wealth tax were introduced and additional revenue obtained to create jobs, it is a mistake to think that unemployment can be significantly decreased without concurrent increases in inflation, and the latter hurts everyone.

    Reply (1) As explained in Michalos (1982, pp. 35–38), the alleged inverse relation between unemployment and inflation is one of nine hypotheses frequently invoked to account for inflation. Although it is theoretically plausible, it is certainly empirically false. Inspection of Table 8.5 reveals that in the period from 1965 to 1985 the alleged inverse relation occurred about 60% of the time for males and females taken together, and about 55% of the time for males and females taken separately. Since the figures for unemployment and inflation would have been expected to rise and fall together or inversely about 50% of the time as a result of mere chance, it is clear that the alleged hypothesis is not only plainly false but pretty worthless for the purposes of scientific explanation and prediction. (2) Research from many other countries indicates that it is possible to have relatively full employment and low inflation and that Canada's recent record on this score was not as good as that of many developed countries (Social Planning Council of Metropolitan Toronto 1985, pp. 4–9). (3) There is good evidence indicating that countries with the best performance record regarding full employment and inflation have made the former their top priority. According to Bellemare (1986, pp. 8–10), "... all countries that attain hill employment have made it their primary objective ... [and] ... the pursuit of this objective orients the macro-economic, labor-market and regional development policies."

30. Insofar as one of the main reasons for introducing a net wealth tax is to obtain revenue to transfer to those who are relatively poor and needy, some attention must be given to the possibility that recipients will lose some of their incentive to work for a living. In the now familiar scenario, their withdrawal from the labor force would mean the removal of some productive power and its output, which would in turn yield a smaller total economic pie for everyone. Thus, in order to prevent the initiation of this whole unfortunate scenario, it would be wise to forget about a net wealth tax.

    Reply (1) An adequate response to this objection should begin by drawing a distinction between poor people who are or are not, in principle at least, in the labor force. Clearly, children, the aged and significantly disabled are not under consideration. (2) Concerning the others, although a great deal of research has been devoted toward demonstrating the disincentive effects of relatively moderate programs of social welfare, including unemployment insurance and guaranteed annual incomes, there is still very little evidence of such effects (Michalos 1982, pp. 41–55). (3) According to the National Council of Welfare (1985, p. 40),

> Contrary to what many people believe, most poor families are headed by persons who work or are actively searching for a job. In 1980, 52.4 percent of low-income families were headed by men or women in the labor force, and that percentage increased to 57.8 percent by 1983. In contrast, most poor unattached individuals (64.1 percent in 1983) are not in the labor force.

31. Since corporations have many more assets than families or individuals and the former are already taxed, it is unnecessary to tax the latter and more efficient to simply increase the tax on corporations (Ward in Panel 1980, p. 52).

    Reply (1) As already indicated, there are serious problems concerning the taxation of corporations. The most serious problem is the fact that no one knows how much of corporate income taxes are pased on to consumers. Given the opportunities for passing on such taxes that were mentioned earlier when I discussed the "standard incidence assumptions" (#13), 1 suspect that more than half of these taxes are passed on to consumers. If that suspicion is correct, then increases in corporate income taxes would be counterproductive. Obviously, we desperately need better information about how much of these taxes are

Table 8.6 National product and public debt, 1965–1985

Year	Gross national product	Net public debt	Ratio of NPD to GNP
		(Current millions)	
1965	55,364	15,504	0.28
1970	85,685	16,943	0.20
1971	94,450	17,322	0.18
1972	105,234	17,937	0.17
1973	123,560	17,456	0.14
1974	147,528	18,128	0.12
1975	165,343	19,276	0.12
1976	191,857	23,296	0.12
1977	210,189	29,586	0.14
1978	232,211	39,622	0.17
1979	264,279	55,806	0.21
1980	297,556	68,595	0.23
1981	339,797	84,163	0.25
1982	358,302	98,758	0.28
1983	389,844	122,747	0.32
1984	420,870	154,531	0.37
1985	474,608	191,448	0.40

Sources North American Social Report, Vol. 5, p. 81, Tl; (13–201) *National Income and Expenditure Accounts 1970–1984*, p. 2, Tl; *Canadian Statistical Review*, May 1986; (68–211) *Federal Government Finance 1984*, p. 47, T15

actually passed on to consumers. Granting this, however, in the short run I still think that corporate income should be taxed more heavily than it is, especially compared to the taxation of individuals. (2) Official statistics show that for over 20 years corporate income taxes have been relatively smaller than personal income taxes as a percent of all taxes levied. The figures also show that while the personal income tax share of the total was half again as large as the corporate share in 1962, by 1985 the personal share was over three times the corporate share (Table 8.6). Furthermore, it is worthwhile noticing that while the personal share remained fairly stable from 1975 to 1985, the corporate share steadily decreased and the net public debt significantly increased (Table 8.6). Apparently, then, some of the revenue that governments failed to raise in corporate taxes was raised by borrowing. (Incidentally, the figures in Table 8.6 from 1965 to 1976 show that Keynes was right in claiming that a country can pull itself up by its bootstraps by borrowing and investing in growth. In those years, while the net public debt increased, the GNP increased much faster, with the result that the debt had relatively less significance although it was greater in absolute terms. It is important to keep such things in mind in the presence of people who find the idea of increasing the public debt inherently abhorrent. What is wrong with increasing the public debt is not the extra burden of greater debt but the fact that, as indicated below, to a significant extent the public would be foolishly borrowing from instead of wisely taxing the relatively great wealth-holders.) (3) However, insofar as corporations are the focus of attention, disparities in wealth tend to be depersonalized and the extraordinary power and influence of a relatively few families and individuals tends to be invisible, which invisibility allows them to have even greater influence (Clement 1975, 1977). According to Coyne (1986, p. 15),

> [i]n late 1984,... close to 80 percent of the companies listed in the Toronto Stock Exchange 300 index were controlled by a single family and/or group. And almost 50% of the value of these companies was controlled by only nine families, notably the Thomsons of Hudson's Bay Company and *Globe and Mail* fame, the two branches of the Bronfman family, Paul Desmarais of Power Corporation, the Reichmann brothers, Conrad Black, and George Weston... [s]ome 60 percent of all of our financial assets are held by five financial service conglomerates and the six large banks. More importantly, several of the financial service conglomerates are each owned by one of the major family dynasties.

(4) Depersonalization is also dangerous because it creates and supports the illusion of relatively "natural" and inevitable forces that are responsible for the political economy here and abroad (Poff 1985). (5) This illusion tends to serve the interests of those who want to maintain the status quo, including neo-conservative economists who make their living developing and disseminating the illusion in the form of economic science. (6) What is worse, since nobody in particular is responsible for "natural" and inevitable economic forces, it is pointless to ask who benefits and who loses from the current system, and pointless to ask what we can do, what choices can be made and what actions can be performed to change the status quo in the interests of the vast majority of people. (7) Hence, we are continuously bombarded by a kind of associationist rat-psycholo- gist's rhetoric of the need for "adjustment" and "education for adjustment to a changing world," perhaps the central themes of the Macdonald Commission. It is indeed a pity that long after the battles in the 1940s and 1950s between the associationist and cognitivist psychologists, and the "resounding victory" of the cognitivists (Feather 1982, p. 3), influential people continue to think and talk about human beings as if they were fairly dull organisms capable only of reacting to circumstances that they cannot create or control. (8) In the end, this refusal to see human beings as human agents robs them of their inclination and their capacity to form their own vision of a good life and to actively pursue its realization. In that end, of course, they have lost their humanity and their very lives.

Conclusion

My case for a progressive annual net wealth tax is now complete. It would be redundant and tedious to review the 19 good arguments in favor and the 31 bad arguments opposed to such a tax. It would be remarkable if I managed to address every important consideration and if anyone accepted everything I had to say. That is fair enough. I intended to open discussion, not to close it. According to Thurow

(1971, pp. 122, 134), "[w]ealth taxation is a central component in any ideal system of taxation.... [F]rom both the perspective of potential benefits to be gained and die current costs to be eliminated, wealth taxes merit inclusion in any adequate system of taxes." A net wealth tax should be regarded as only one feature of a national social-economic development plan. Besides recommending a wealth tax to obtain revenue for redistribution, I would favor increased public participation, public planning and public initiatives in the areas of housing, food, clothing, transportation, education, health and social services. The aim and net result of the whole plan should be the maximization of human well-being.

Acknowledgements An earlier version of this paper was presented at the Conference on "Women and Economic Equity: The Canadian Context," at Mount Saint Vincent University, Halifax, Nova Scotia, January 23–25, 1987. Several people have kindly given me helpful suggestions, and I would like to express my thanks to them: G. Bale, F. Cunningham, J. Drewnowski, W.J. Furlong, E.K. Grant, D. Johnston, C.J. Munford, D.C. Poff, M.L. Steele, J. Vanderkamp.

References

Bale, G. (1980). Taxing wealth: Selecting a strategy. *Canadian Taxation, 2,* 39–48.

Bellemare, D. (1986). The birth of a Canadian economy. In *A Paper Presented to Forum 2000: Canada in a Changing World*, November 22, 1986.

Bird, R. M. (1980). Taxing personal wealth. *Canadian Taxation, 2,* 35–38.

Canadian Conference of Catholic Bishops. (1985). Moral vision and political will. In D. Drache & D. Cameron (Eds.), *The other Macdonald report* (pp. 208–213). Toronto: James Lorimer and Co.

Canadian Mental Health Association. (1985). Economic policy and well-being. In D. Drache & D. Cameron (Eds.), *The other Macdonald report* (pp. 80–87). Toronto: James Lorimer and Co.

Canadian Union of Public Employees. (1985). Scapegoating the public sector. In D. Drache & D. Cameron (Eds.), *The other Macdonald report* (pp. 42–48, 196–207). Toronto: James Lorimer and Co.

Clement, W. (1975). *The Canadian corporate elite: An analysis of economic power.* Toronto: McClelland and Stewart Ltd.

Clement, W. (1977). *Continental corporate power: Economic elite linkages between Canada and the United States.* Toronto: McCleland and Stewart Ltd.

Coyne, D. (1986). Corporate over-concentration. *Policy Options Politiques* 14–17.

Drache, D., & Cameron D. (1985). Introduction. In D. Drache & D. Cameron (Eds.), *The other Macdonald report* (pp. ix–xxxix). Toronto: James Lorimer and Co.

Galbraith, J. K. (1975). *Money: Whence it came, where it went.* New York: Bantam Books.

Gillespie, W. I. (1980a). What do we know about tax incidence in Canada? *Canadian Taxation, 2,* 2–7.

Gillespie, W. I. (1980b). Taxes, expenditures and the redistribution of income in Canada, 1951–1977. In Economic Council of Canada (Eds.), *Reflections on Canadian incomes* (pp. 27–41). Ottawa: Minister of Supply and Services Canada.

Harrison, A. (1980). The distribution of personal wealth in Canada, the U.K. and the U.S.A. In Economic Council of Canada (Eds.), *Reflections on Canadian incomes* (pp. 365–380). Ottawa: Minister of Supply and Services Canada.

Harrison, D. (1981). *The limits of liberalism: The making of Canadian sociology.* Montreal: Black Rose Books.

Levin, R. C. (1986). Proposals for economic growth. *Science, 234,* 490–491.

Manitoba Political Economy Group. (1985). The waste economy. In D. Drache & D. Cameron (Eds.), *The other Macdonald report* (pp. 35–41). Toronto: James Lorimer and Co.

Matziorinis, K. N. (1980). The effectiveness of tax-incentives for capital investment. *Canadian Taxation, 2,* 172–179.

McIntyre, R. S. (1987). VAT is a bad idea. *The Atlantic Monthly,* 26–28.

Michalos, A. C. (1980). *North American social report, Vol. 2: Crime, justice and politics.* Dordrecht: D. Reidel Pub. Co.

Michalos, A. C. (1981a). *North American social report, Vol. 3: Science, education and recreation.* Dordrecht: D. Reidel Pub. Co.

Michalos, A. C. (1981b). *North American social report, Vol. 4: Environment, transportation and housing.* Dordrecht: D. Reidel Pub. Co.

Michalos, A. C. (1982). *North American social report, Vol. 5: Economics, religion and morality.* Dordrecht: D. Reidel Pub. Co.

Michalos, A. C. (1986). *Integrated Development Planning Using Socio-Economic and Quality of life Indicators.* Report written for UNESCO, Division of Study and Planning of Development, Bureau of Studies, Action and Coordination for Development; September 1986.

Musgrave, R. A., & Musgrave, P. B. (1984). *Public finance in theory and practice.* New York: McGraw-Hill Book Co.

National Council of Welfare. (1985). *Poverty profile 1985.* Minister of Supply and Services Canada: Ottawa.

Newman, P. C. (1975). *The Canadian establishment: Volume one.* Toronto: McClelland and Stewart Ltd.

OECD. (1979). *The taxation of net wealth, capital transfers and capita/gains of individuals.* Paris: OECD.

OECD. (1982). *Controls on international capital movements.* Paris: OECD.

Oja, G. (1983). The distribution of wealth in Canada. *Review of Income and Wealth, 29*(2), 161–173.

Panel. (1980). Panel discussion: Taxation of personal wealth. *Canadian Taxation, 2,* 49–54. Participants included R. M. Bird, D. A. Ward, G. Bale, M. Wolfson, S. Piper, J. Tinker, P. Setlakwe, S. Fiekowsky & G. W. Sazama.

Poff, D. C. (1985). Feminism flies too. *Resources for Feminist Research, 14,* 6–9.

Porter, J. (1965). *The vertical Mosaic.* Toronto: University of Toronto Press.

Sazama, G. W. (1980). Is the tax system the Robin Hood of our time? *Canadian Taxation, 2,* 16–23.

Social Planning Council of Metropolitan Toronto. (1985). Economic decline in Canada. In D. Drache & D. Cameron (Eds.), *The other Macdonald report* (pp. 3–22, 51–62). Toronto: James Lorimer and Co.

Statistics Canada. (1979a). *The distribution of income and wealth in Canada 1977,* Cat. #13-570. Ottawa: Minister of Supply and Services Canada.

Statistics Canada. (1979b). *Evaluation of data on family assets and debts, 1977.* Ottawa: Minister of Supply and Services Canada.

Statistics Canada. (1980). *Incomes, assets and indebtedness of families in Canada 1977,* Cat. #13-572. Ottawa: Minister of Supply and Services Canada.

Statistics Canada. (1986). *The distribution of wealth in Canada 1984,* Cat. #13-580. Ottawa: Minister of Supply and Services Canada.

Thurow, L. C. (1971). *The impact of taxes on the American economy.* New York: Praeger Pub.

United Auto Workers. (1985). Can Canada compete? In D. Drache & D. Cameron (Eds.), *The other Macdonald report* (pp. 23–34, 151–156). Toronto: James Lorimer and Co.

United Church of Canada. (1985). Economic development and social justice. In D. Drache & D. Cameron (Eds.), *The other Macdonald report* (pp. 169–183). Toronto: James Lorimer and Co.

Wagner, R. E. (1980). Sense versus sensibility in the taxation of personal wealth. *Canadian Taxation, 2,* 23–30.

Walker, M. A. (1980). Measuring and coping with a progressive tax system or Robin Hoodery—A Canadian tradition past its prime. *Canadian Taxation, 2,* 8–15.

Ward, D. A. (1980). The case against capital taxes. *Canadian Taxation, 2,* 31–34.

Chapter 9
Militarism and the Quality of Life

Alex C. Michalos

Introduction

In 1978, the United Nations General Assembly endorsed the Final Document of the First Special Session on Disarmament, which called for the commission of a group of governmental experts to examine the relationships between disarmament and development. Twenty-seven experts were selected from every continent, with Inga Thorsson designated as chairperson. The group's official report was submitted to the Secretary-General of the United Nations in October 1981. The report included nine recommendations, and this essay is a relatively limited attempt to respond to one of them, a quote from which follows below:

> The Group recommends that all governments, but particularly those of the major military powers, should prepare assessments of the nature and magnitude of the short-and long-term economic and social costs attributable to their military preparations, so that the general public can be informed of them (Sanger 1982a).

I will, in the sections that follow, (1) present an overview of some social indicators for Canada and the United States covering the years from about 1963 to 1983; (2) review Canadian federal government expenditures in general for the period from 1974 to 1986; (3) summarize available information on the Canadian

---

This essay is taken from some sections of another essay of the same name that was originally presented at a meeting of the Guelph Chapter of Science for Peace at the University of Guelph, May 24, 1988. The original version was greatly expanded to include responses to 16 arguments opposed to my position, and this expanded version was published in spring 1989 by Science for Peace, University of Toronto.

Michalos, A.C.: 1989. Militarism and the quality of life. Annals of the New York Academy of Sciences, 577, pp. 216–230.

A.C. Michalos (✉)
University of Northern British Columbia, Prince George, BC, Canada
e-mail: michalos@brandonu.ca

A.C. Michalos, *How Good Policies and Business Ethics Enhance Good Quality of Life*, DOI 10.1007/978-3-319-50724-8_9

arms industry, including production and export figures; (4) present 15 arguments against the Canadian production and export of military arms broadly construed; and (5) provide a brief conclusion.

An Overview of Canada and the United States of America

Some of the groundwork for the present investigation was prepared in my *North American Social Report* (Michalos 1980a, b, 1981a, b, 1982a). In this work, I compared the quality of life of Canadians and Americans in the 1964–74 period in the areas of population structure; mortality, morbidity, and health care; criminal justice; politics; science and technology; education; recreation; natural environment and resources; transportation; communication; housing; economics; religion; and morality and social customs. Broadly speaking, three conclusions were reached. First, "on the basis of an examination of over 135 social indicators and over 1659 indicator values, it seems fair to say that the quality of life in the 1964–74 period was comparatively or relatively higher in Canada than in the United States." Second, "if one looks at the first and last recorded stock values for the usable indicators for each country independently of the other country, … [one finds that] both countries improved in more ways than they deteriorated" Third, the responses of national probability samples of Canadians and Americans to over 117 Gallup Poll questions indicate that "the countries were more similar in the 1963–68 period than in the 1969–75 period." In short, "taking the results of my analyses of non-independent paths (social indicator trends) and opinion poll responses together, it seems fair to say that the countries tended to be or become dissimilar in more ways than they tended to be or become similar" (Michalos 1982b).

As for military expenditures, "in the 1965–74 period American military expenditures as a percent of GNP were always two to four times higher than their Canadian counterparts. … In the final year the American figure stood at 6% of the GNP, compared to 2% for Canada" (Michalos 1980c).

Although I planned to update all my figures to 1984 and later, other projects always got in the way. Table 9.1, however, summarizes the results of comparing the rank-order values of Canada and the United States among 142 countries on 13 indicators for 1983 (Sivard 1986a). Canada's rank-orders were preferable to those of the United States on 9 of the 13 indicators. According to Sivard's aggregation procedures, Canada was better off than the United States in "socioeconomic standing" generally and in military expenditures. I suppose these assessments would not have changed much by today. If we may assume that government expenditures for social and economic purposes contribute more to a good quality of life than government expenditures for military purposes, the figures in Table 9.1 suggest that Canadians have been able to make a more favorable trade-off on this score than Americans.

Table 9.1 Ranking of Canada and the United States among 142 countries on military and social indicators, 1983[a]

Indicator[b]	Ranking	
	Canada	United States
Military expenditures		
Per capita (−)	26	7
Per soldier (−)	7	4
Per square km (−)	88	23
Average socioeconomic standing (+)	2	3
Gross national product per capita (+)	10	7
Education		
Public expenditures per capita (+)	4	10
School age population per teacher (−)	13	13
Percentage of school age population in school (+)	3	6
Percentage of women in total university enrollment (+)	11	17
Literacy rate (+)	4	4
Health		
Public expenditures per capita (+)	5	10
Population per physician (−)	26	22
Infant mortality rate (−)	9	17
Life expectancy (+)	7	7
Nutrition		
Calorie supply per capita (+)	20	8
Calories as a percentage of requirements (+)	25	14
Percentage of population with safe water (+)	1	14
Total number of indicators for which each country had a preferable ranking[c]		
Negative	4	1
Positive	5	3
Total	9	4

[a]Data are taken from Sivard (1986a) See Table 9.3 and pp. 36–37 in Sivard for definitions of specific indicators and their sources
[b]Plus signs designate positive indicators, and minus signs designate negative indicators
[c]Excluding the indicator for average socioeconomic standing, and three indicators with tie scores

Canadian Federal Government Expenditures

Table 9.2 lists the Canadian federal government's total and defense expenditures for the 1974–87 period in millions of current Canadian dollars. In the final year, defense expenditures were estimated to be nearly $10 billion or 8.5% of total government expenditures. Although there has been a steady increase in defense expenditures as a percentage of total expenditures since the 1984 election of a Progressive Conservative government, the 1987 figure is still a bit below the 14-year average of 8.6%. However, according to the Tories' white paper on defense

Table 9.2 Federal government and defense expenditures in current millions, 1974–87[a]

Year ended March 31	Total expenditures	Defense expenditures	Percentage of total expenditures on defense
1974	22.839	2232	9.8
1975	29.245	2512	8.6
1976	33.978	2974	8.8
1977	39.011	3371	8.6
1978	42.882	3771	8.8
1979	46.539	4108	8.8
1980	50.416	4391	8.7
1981	58.066	5077	8.7
1982	67.678	6028	8.9
1983	88.521	6938	7.8
1984	96.610	7843	8.1
1985	109.215	8762	8.0
1986	111.227	9094	8.2
1987[b]	116.740	9955	8.5

[a]Data taken from Public Accounts of Canada (1986) and Estimates of the Government of Canada (1986)
[b]Values in this row are estimates

spending, *Challenge and Commitment: A Defence Policy for Canada*, "the Government is committed to a base rate of annual real growth in the defence budget of two per cent per year after inflation, for the (coming 15-year) planning period" (Canada, Department of National Defense 1987). At the same time, "after 1986–87, the budget states that operating costs in all federal departments will not be permitted to rise by more than 2% in nominal terms each year, which, after inflation, is a real cut of 2%" (Prince 1986). If the defense budget does increase at the projected rate, then in 10 years it will be about 10, 5% of total federal government expenditures, which would be roughly its 1972 rate. Putting the 2% real growth rate for defense spending together with the 2% real cut rate for all other federal departments, by 1998 the defense budget would be about 12.5% of the total, or roughly what it was in 1970 (Treddenick 1984).

Table 9.3 puts defense shares of the federal government's total expenditures in the context of the shares of 16 other functional areas and a residual "others". Because *Statistics Canada's accounting procedures* are not exactly the same as those of the federal government, there is roughly a percentage point difference between the figures published by the two agencies. So, on average, for example, the defense share according to Statistics Canada was about 7.6% rather than 8.6%. The Statistics Canada figures are preferable for present purposes because the 16 functional areas are more detailed and easier to identify than their counterparts in successive federal budgets.

Table 9.3 Percentages of total expenditures allocated to different functions, 1974–86[a]

Year ended March 31	Percentage of expenditures																		
	Function[b]																		
	1	2	3	4	5	6	7	8	9	10	11	12	13	14	15	16	17	18	Total
1974	8.8	5.7	7.3	8.0	1.1	12.5	8.9	4.1	3.4	3.8	1.0	0.6	1.8	1.2	7.8	1.5	7.1	15.4	100.0
1975	7.4	5.5	7.1	7.4	1.3	11.1	8.1	5.9	3.1	3.3	0.9	0.7	1.9	1.1	8.7	1.6	7.4	17.5	100.0
1976	7.2	5.1	6.7	7.5	1.6	10.7	9.0	5.3	4.0	3.2	0.8	0.9	2.0	1.4	7.3	1.4	7.7	18.2	100.0
1977	7.8	5.6	6.7	8.0	2.0	10.5	8.9	4.8	4.7	3.3	0.7	1.2	1.9	1.0	8.3	1.4	7.1	16.1	100.0
1978	7.9	5.6	6.4	6.8	2.3	10.6	9.5	4.6	4.0	4.2	0.7	1.1	2.4	1.6	7.6	1.5	7.7	15.5	100.0
1979	8.1	5.5	6.5	7.6	2.6	10.1	9.3	4.1	3.9	4.4	0.8	1.3	1.9	1.4	6.7	1.5	9.3	15.0	100.0
1980	7.7	5.1	5.7	7.3	2.9	11.1	7.2	3.0	3.4	4.2	0.6	1.4	1.8	1.6	7.2	1.7	10.1	18.0	100.0
1981	7.3	5.1	6.3	6.5	3.1	10.9	7.0	2.7	3.3	3.7	0.5	1.5	1.6	1.6	6.5	2.1	10.8	19.5	100.0
1982	7.4	5.1	5.2	6.0	3.2	10.8	7.0	2.6	3.3	3.4	0.4	1.4	1.6	1.4	6.7	1.9	14.2	18.4	100.0
1983	7.2	4.7	3.0	5.0	3.3	10.4	10.8	2.4	3.5	3.1	0.5	1.9	1.7	1.2	6.7	3.1	13.3	18.2	100.0
1984	7.6	4.8	3.1	6.1	3.6	10.2	9.9	2.3	4.1	3.5	0.5	1.6	1.7	1.2	6.4	3.1	12.9	17.4	100.0
1985	7.5	4.7	3.3	6.2	3.8	10.0	9.1	2.1	4.0	3.4	0.4	1.8	1.8	1.0	6.0	2.5	14.7	17.7	100.0
1986	7.4	4.8	3.0	6.1	4.2	10.7	8.9	2.2	3.9	3.4	0.4	1.3	1.8	0.9	5.8	2.8	17.0	15.4	100.0

[a]Data are taken from Statistics Canada (1987)

[b]Column codes: 1: national defense; 2: general government; 3: transportation and communication; 4: health; 5: Canada pension plan; 6: old age security; 7: unemployment insurance; 8: family allowance; 9: assistance to disabled; 10: education; 11: environment; 12: housing; 13: foreign aid and affairs; 14: research establishments; 15: transfer to other levels of government; 16: transfer to own enterprises; 17: debt charges; 18: all other expenditures

Inspection of the figures in Table 9.3 shows that the defense share of the total expenditures is typically greater than 13 of the 16 substantive functional areas. Only old age security payments, unemployment insurance payments, and national debt charges typically take bigger slices of the total pie. While the shares of old age security and unemployment insurance payments typically run from 1 to 3% points above the defense share, the national debt share typically runs about twice as high as that of defense. At a minimum, what these figures suggest is that Canada's defense expenditures constitute a significant share of the federal government's total expenditures and raise provocative questions regarding the actual versus a more desirable distribution. Because most of this paper consists of specific arguments for less spending on the production and export of military arms broadly construed, more will be said about diverse trade-offs as our discussion proceeds.

The Canadian Arms Industry

Because there is no generally accepted definition of "military arms" broadly or narrowly construed, there is bound to be some controversy over any alleged measured level of production or export of such things, The estimates given here am taken mainly from Treddenick (1987a) and Regehr (1987c). According to Treddenick, "the defence industrial base is that part of the nation's economy providing goods and services required to support military activities" (Treddenick 1987b). This definition is very broad, but it becomes more useful when it is operationalized by identifying "the defence industrial base in terms of current demands placed on Canadian industry resulting from expenditures for domestic defence procurement and for exports" (Treddenick 1987b). Refined in this way, the definition suggested by Treddenick comes very close to the one suggested by Regehr: "For purposes of implementing control measures, *the Canadian government should define a military commodity as a commodity purchased by a military force or agency*" (Regehr 1987d). Presumably, both authors would exclude some items like food and housing supplies, and both would include not only weapons but "the support facilities and equipment that make weapons usable" (Regeher 1987b; Treddenick 1987c). Treddenick specifies a "narrow industrial base" within the broader sector, which includes "industries producing specialized military equipment" Operationally, the narrow industrial base includes manufacturers of aircraft, motor vehicles, ships, communications equipment, and some chemicals insofar as the products are sold to military agencies. Applying these rough definitions and some appropriate caveats, he reaches the following conclusions:

> If economic significance means the amount of economic activity generated in the defence industries, then by comparison to total economic activity in Canada, the defence industrial base must be judged to be insignificant. Total defence production accounts for considerably less than one per cent of both gross domestic product and total employment. When the narrow defence industrial base alone is considered, these contributions fall to about one-third of a percentage point in each case. Defence production is also not significant in

> any single provincial economy. Only in Nova Scotia and New Brunswick does employment generated by defence production approximate one per cent of total provincial employment; in most provinces it is considerably less. Defence production must also be considered insignificant in terms of international trade. Defence exports, net of re-exports, currently account for less than one per cent of total merchandise exports while defence imports, including indirect imports, account for just over two per cent of total merchandise imports. Finally, because of its comparatively low level and because it is difficult to make a theoretical case for its transferability to the civilian sector, defence research and development must also be considered insignificant relative to overall economic activity. … The relatively small size of the Canadian defence industrial base makes it extremely difficult to see it as the mainstay of the capitalist system in Canada, in either the Marxian or the Galbraithian sense (Treddenick 1987d).

If Treddenick's estimates are about right, in 1986 about $2.5 billion dollars would have been tied up in arms production. Two and a half billion dollars that year would have matched the federal government's expenditures for family allowances and for research and development in the natural sciences. It would have been 6 times the federal government's expenditure on the environment, 13 times the expenditure on research in the social sciences, and 3 times the expenditure on recreation and leisure. It would have just about matched the country's expenses on community colleges, and it would have added another 22,676 new or renovated housing units to those funded by the federal government in 1986 (Statistics Canada 1987a, b). Clearly, then, because it would be unreasonable to dismiss all these national expenditures as economically, morally, and politically insignificant, Treddenick's judgment is oversimplified at best.

Table 9.4 and Fig. 9.1 provide a longer and more detailed view of Canadian military exports since 1959. The bottom line of Table 9.4 shows that about 73% of our exports have gone to the United States, 14.6% to Europe, and 12% to other places, mainly in the Third World. Although we have just seen that Treddenick would be one of the last people to exaggerate the economic significance of the Canadian arms industry, he remarks that "not only have total exports consistently exceeded domestic demand by large amounts, but exports to the United States alone have done so. … This export dependence of the defence industries, and particularly the dependence on a single country, is the outstanding economic feature of the Canadian defence industrial base" (Treddenick 1987e).

Arguments Against the Production and Export of Arms

The following arguments may be offered by Canadians against the production and export of military arms broadly construed..

1. Any resources that are used for the production and export of arms cannot be used for the production and export of such necessities as food, water, clothing, shelter, medical care, and education. Because the latter are more life sustaining

Table 9.4 Canadian military exports in current millions, 1959–86[a]

Year	Exports in current millions[b]			
	United States	Europe	Other	Total
1959–69	2418.8 (78.9)	439.8 (14.3)	207.0 (6.9)	3065.6 (100.0)
1970	226.5 (67.4)	41.2 (12.3)	68.5 (20.3)	336.2 (100.0)
1971	216.3 (64.3)	67.2 (20.0)	53.0 (15.7)	336.5 (100.0)
1972	175.0 (58.3)	73.7 (24.5)	51.7 (17.2)	300.4 (100.0)
1973	198.8 (64.3)	72.8 (72.8)	37.6 (37.6)	309.2 (100.0)
1974	150.0 (53.5)	45.6 (16.3)	84.9 (30.2)	280.5 (100.0)
1975	188.5 (67.1)	58.6 (20.9)	33.7 (12.0)	280.8 (100.0)
1976	191.1 (56.9)	113.1 (33.7)	31.9 (9.4)	336.1 (100.0)
1977	314.1 (56.7)	76.0 (13.7)	163.9 (29.6)	554.0 (100.0)
1978	267.0 (55.1)	129.6 (26.7)	87.9 (18.2)	484.5 (100.0)
1979	367.7 (64.7)	145.6 (25.6)	55.0 (9.7)	568.3 (100.0)
1980	481.7 (66.7)	142.1 (19.7)	97.9 (13.6)	721.7 (100.0)
1981	826.6 (71.8)	149.4 (13.0)	174.8 (15.2)	1150.8 (100.0)
1982	1027.9 (71.7)	157.8 (11.0)	248.4 (17.3)	1434.1 (100.0)
1983	1207.4(81.5)	128.6 (8.7)	145.2 (9.8)	1481.2 (100.0)
1984	1360.5 (77.6)	243.1 (13.9)	149.8 (8.5)	1753.4 (100.0)
1985	1644.2 (86.8)	154.0 (8.1)	104.5 (5.5)	1902.7 (100.0)
1986	947.0 (68.2)	196.2 (14.1)	244.8 (17.6)	1388.0 (100.0)
Total	12,209.1 (73.2)	2434.4 (14.6)	2040.5 (12.2)	16,684.0 (100.0)

[a]Data are taken from Regehr (1987c) and Epps (1987)
[b]Percentages are shown in parentheses

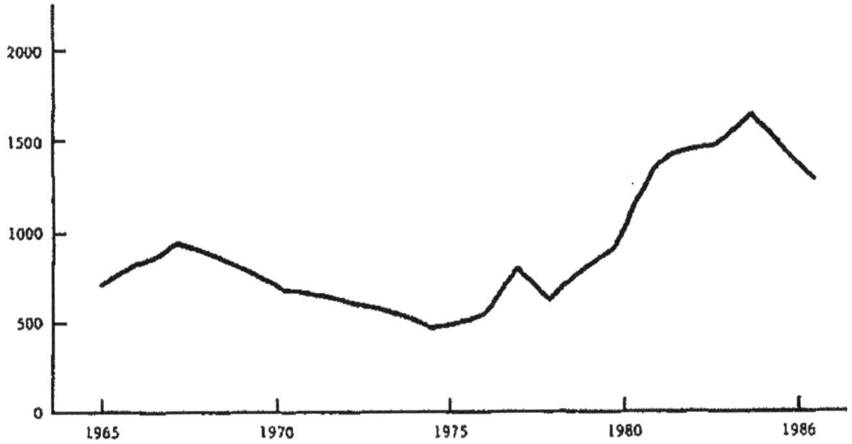

Fig. 9.1 Canadian military exports worldwide. *Vertical axis* military exports in millions of dollars. *Sources* Regehr (1987d) and Epps (1987)

than the former, they should not be traded for the former (Canada, Department of National Defense 1987; Wallace-Deering 1986).

2. Any resources that are used for the production of arms to be deployed by Canadian forces cannot be used for such necessities as food, water, clothing, shelter, medical care, education, and other social services. According to Werlin, since the Mulroney government came to office in 1984, "transfer payments from Ottawa to the provinces for health care and education have been reduced, unemployment insurance benefits have been cut back, public housing subsidies, environmental protection programs, and support for cultural activities (most importantly the Canadian Broadcasting Corporation) have all been reduced. Increases in the defence budget (averaging 6% a year for the rest of the decade) have quite simply been made by reducing the budget for public services" (Werlin 1986a). Thus, in the interest of promoting life-sustaining programs and expenditures, increases in the production of arms should at least be kept below increases in other government programs and expenditures.
3. The availability of arms increases the inclination to resort to and the ability to use violent means to make social and political changes, and decreases the inclination to resort to and the ability to use nonviolent means. Again, because the latter are more life sustaining, they should be given priority over the former (Regeher 1987a).
4. Because Canada's biggest trading partner is the United States and about half of our manufacturing industry (not merely our arms industry) consists of American subsidiaries, much of our production and export is designed to American specifications, requirements, and interests. Thus, much of what our arms industry produces and exports is designed to satisfy demands resulting from an American Cold War vision of international Soviet threats to peace. Insofar as this is a biased vision and relatively dangerous for the continued existence of life on the planet, it would be wise to reduce all activities based on this vision, including all activities related to the production and export of arms (Regehr 1987e; Deroo 1986a).
5. In order to increase Canada's "capacity to assess and pursue independent and innovative foreign policy and defence options," we ought to decrease opportunities for the United States to influence our decision-making processes. Reductions in the integration of Canadian and American arms industries would significantly decrease such opportunities, and they should therefore be undertaken (Regehr 1987i; Deroo 1986b; Werlin 1986b).
6. Because Canada and the United States agreed to have a rough balance of arms trade through the 1963 Defense Production Sharing Arrangements (DPSA), Canada cannot expect long-run economic gains from arms trade with the United States. Hence, continued increases in the production and export of arms must rely on overseas markets. Because Europeans tend to insist on exchanges similar to those of the DPSA, the most promising markets are those of the Third World. If we increase sales of arms to Third World countries, however, we will also increase the carnage of wars, economic dependence, and distorted social development. It has been estimated that as many as 20 million people have died

in the 150 wars cited by Regehr (1987h). Besides contributing to the massacre, increases in the importation of weapons create foreign exchange shortages that relatively poor countries try to alleviate through greater exploitation of their natural resources for export. Thus, they develop dependent, subsidiary economies incapable of indigenous innovation that might allow them economic independence in the long run. Distorted economies then contribute directly to distorted social development because the greatest burden of government expenditures must be devoted to international debt services rather than to social services (Regehr 1987k). In many ways, as Regehr explains, if Canadians increase their traffic in arms to Third World countries, we will inevitably reproduce some of the debilitating effects on them that trade with the United States has on us (Michalos 1982b).

7. Increases in the production and export of arms to Third World countries would increase the militarization of those countries, not only by increasing the amount of military hardware at their disposal, but by encouraging any tendencies they might have toward forming authoritarian administrations (Sivard 1986b). Thus, because increases in the militarization of Third World countries tend to undermine their democratic institutions and participative decision making, such increases ought to be resisted.
8. Increases in the production and export of arms will tend to increase the number of people in Canada whose livelihoods depend on militarization. Moreover, it is likely that most (certainly not all) people whose livelihoods depend on militarization will be relatively uncritical of militarization. Thus, because militarization is inconsistent with our democratic institutions, inclinations, and practices, the latter would be undermined by increases in the production and export of arms. Hence, increases in the production and export of arms ought to be resisted in the interest of protecting our own democratic institutions, inclinations, and practices.
9. Because the arms industry tends to be highly specialized and concentrated, labor and material costs tend to be relatively high. Besides, as indicated in argument 11 below, the arms industry tends to be characterized by relatively low productivity. Thus, the combination of these characteristics implies that increases in arms production have inflationary effects as costs outrun productivity gains. Furthermore, Werlin notes that arms production is inflationary because it generates "spendable income without at the same time enlarging the supply of goods available in the market place" (Werlin 1986c). Hence, in the interest of reducing inflation, increases in the production and export of arms ought to be resisted (Melman 1984; Sanger 1982b; Regehr 1987h).
10. It has been estimated that if 1% of the over 50,000 nuclear weapons currently stockpiled by the United States and the Soviet Union were exploded, there would be a nuclear winter of from 6 months to 3 years that most people on the planet could not survive. Because increases in the production and export of arms increases the likelihood of wars, and because any wars could accidentally initiate a global nuclear war leading to a nuclear winter, increases in the production and export of arms ought to be resisted (Pentz 1986).

11. Because some increases in the Canadian production and export of arms will be connected to the U.S. Strategic Defense Initiative (SDI), and because the latter is seriously defective technologically, militarily, and politically, we should at least resist any strengthening of such connections (Tsipis 1986; Sivard 1986a). Tsipis concluded his review of SDI with the pronouncement that it is "voodoo science." According to Nadis, "in October of 1986, a poll found that 98% of the members of the [U.S.] National Academy of Sciences in fields most relevant to SDI research believed that SDI could not provide an effective defense of the U. S. civilian population" (Nadis 1988).
12. Because Canada is a relatively small country with a relatively small military establishment and presence in the world, we have the opportunity to initiate changes in our defense policies without creating significant shocks or threats to other countries. New Zealand has denied nuclear-armed American warships the right to enter its ports and has established nuclear-weapons-free zones (NWFZs) covering over 65% of its population. Anderton suggested that a basic premise of such actions is simply that "small nations must take a stand for peace themselves, if they hope to influence big nations" (Anderton 1986).
    Thus, Canada might undertake a gradual phasing out of all arms manufacturing that is not directly connected to the particular needs of our own defense policies, assuming that the latter may be specified relatively independently of the policies of die American establishment. As of August 1987, there were over 166 NWFZs in Canada, including the cities of Toronto, Vancouver, Hamilton, and Regina, and the provinces of Manitoba, Ontario, and the Northwest Territories (Davies and Marchant 1986; Gaundun 1987). The New Democratic Party has proposed that Canada join Norway, Denmark, Sweden, Finland, Greenland, and Iceland in declaring all our countries a NWFZ, which would be an important building block for an Arctic common security system (New Democratic Party of Canada 1988a).
13. The biggest threats to international security in the future are scarcities of raw materials, environmental degradation, declining economic growth, and the severely unequal distribution of the world's wealth. Because increases in the production and export of arms contributes nothing and even decreases resources available to address these problems, in the interest of increasing international security, we ought to reduce expenditures on the former in favor of expenditures on the larger threats (Sanger 1982c; United Nations, Panel of Eminent Personalities in the Field of Disarmament and Development 1986; Creighton 1987).
14. Because the need for arms is typically largely in the eye of the beholder, one ought to be skeptical about any alleged need calling for increases in the production and export of arms. Treddenick gives about 10 reasons for defense spending tending to become a bottomless pit, but the following remarks seem to capture a main source of the problem:

> As an economic good satisfying human wants, defence, at least in peacetime, is an abstract concept, one which is technically complex and generally not well understood by the public. It cannot be measured in any objective sense, Whether defence is adequately provided for, or whether the composition of defence spending, including the equipment mix, is appropriate is a matter of perceptions about intentions and relative force sizes, training, tactics, morale and so on. It is therefore impossible to say that there is too much or too little defence spending, or to say that there are too many tanks or too many ships in the same way that it is possible to sty that there is too much of other types of goods. The relationship between spending on defence, including how it is spent, and how much defence capability is actually achieved is therefore highly ambiguous. This ambiguity can make defence planning a challenging occupation, but at the same time it provides economic policy makers with an expenditure instrument of a flexibility unmatched by other forms of government expenditure (Treddenick 1987f).

15. There is some evidence from a national opinion poll taken in October 1987 that most Canadians would prefer to see less emphasis on a militaristic approach to international security, which would imply less emphasis on the production and export of arms. The survey was sponsored by the North-South Institute (NSI) in Ottawa, and the sponsor's analysts summarized their view of their findings as follows:

> The Canadian public seems to be on a completely different wavelength from its government in what it sees as the main threats to Canadian security and what should be done about them. In 1987 the government allowed a Defence White Paper to be seen to speak for Canadian security policy, and the Department of National Defence to be seen to shape Canada's views on peace and war. In the year that ended with Mr. Gorbachev in Washington signing the INF (internuclear forces) Treaty, NSI's survey shows most Canadians implicitly rejecting both the Cold War diagnoses and prescriptions of the Defence White Paper tabled by Mr. Beatty (Minister of National Defence) in June.
>
> Canadians themselves have a different and much wider agenda for enhancing international security, including environmental, health, developmental and ethical/political goals. In the maintenance of peace, they seem likely to see Canada's best contribution in more arms control and disarmament efforts, international cooperation, conflict resolution and peacekeeping, rather than in the build-up of arms. Even among various international purposes—quite apart from needs at home—most Canadians resoundingly reject increased defence spending as a priority (North-South Institute 1988).

According to Lambert, "polls by Angus Reid and Goldfarb … show the majority of Canadians opposed to cruise testing, opposed to the purchase of nuclear submarines, and in favor of making Canada a nuclear weapons free zone" (Lambert 1987).

Conclusion

The charter of the United Nations Educational, Scientific, and Cultural Organization reminds us that "since wars begin in the minds of men, it is in the minds of men that the defense of peace must be constructed" I am enough of a feminist to believe that even if the original authors of that sentence understood the term "men" in its generic sense, it has special reference to males. We are the ones typically socialized to be competitive, aggressive, out of touch with our feelings, and all too often arrogantly defensive of our own ignorance. So, I hope that men especially will give serious consideration to this essay.

As I remarked at the beginning, insofar as my arguments are sound, a case should have been made for resisting Canada's proposed increases in the production and export of arms, and for beginning to scale down Canada's current militaristic activities. I have not recommended total disarmament or the gradual phasing out of our military establishment. On the contrary, I have suggested that the military has legitimate national and international functions: routine surveillance, disaster relief, and peacekeeping. We need a defense policy based not on military might but on wisdom, compassion, and diplomacy. As the New Democratic Party of Canada has put it: "Canadian security depends upon a stable international order that recognizes and respects Canadian sovereignty and territory, rather than on Canada's ability to defend itself militarily. Thus, Canada's primary responsibility in its own defence is to contribute to the development of a just international order. The role of the United Nations is central to this process" (New Democratic Party of Canada 1988b).

Acknowledgements I would like to thank the following people for helping me improve the final product: R.G. Good, B. Graf, L. Groake, R.R. Iyer, J. McMurtry, G. Morgan, C. Mitcham, S.S. Nagel, D.C. Poff, J.P. Roos, and J.T. Stevenson.

References

Anderton, J. P. (1986). Nuclear freedom in one country—How and why: A case study of the development of a nuclear-free policy in New Zealand. In T. L. Perry & J. G. Foulks (Eds.), *End the arms race: Fund Human Needs* (193). West Vancouver: Gordon Soules.

Canada, Department of National Defense. (1987). *Challenge and commitment: A defense policy for Canada (white paper on defense)*. Ottawa: Minister of Supply and Services.

Creighton, P. (1987). Cold war heat. *Ploughshares Monitor, 8,* 5.

Davies, L., & Marchant, F. (1986). The special role of municipalities in working for peace. In T. L. Perry & J. G. Foulks (Eds.), *End the arms race: Fund human needs* (239). West Vancouver: Gordon Soules.

Deroo, R. J. (1986a). Our war economy and conversion for peace. In T. L. Perry & J. G. Foulks (Eds.), *End the arms race: Fund human needs* (84–87). West Vancouver: Gordon Soules.

Deroo, R. J. (1986b). Our war economy (86).

Epps, K. (1987). Canadian military industrial update. *Ploughshares Monitor, 8,* 12.

Estimates of the Government of Canada. (1986–1987).

Gaundun, K. (1987). NWFZ: The Canadian scene. *Peace Magazine, 3,* 11.

Lambert, S. (1987). The Canadian peace pledge campaign. *Peace Magazine, 3,* 24.

Melman, S. (1984). Peace, employment and the economics of permanent war: 2–3. Project Ploughshares Working Paper 84–5.

Michalos, A. C. (1980a). North American social report. *Foundations, population and health* (Vol. 1). Dordrecht: D. Reidel.

Michalos, A. C. (1980b). North American social report. *Crime, justice and politics* (Vol. 2). Dordrecht: D. Reidel.

Michalos, A. C. (1980c). *Crime, justice and politics* (176).
Michalos, A. C. (1981a). North American social report. *Science, education and recreation* (Vol. 3). Dordrecht: D. Reidel.
Michalos, A. C. (1981b). North American social report. *Environment, transportation and housing* (Vol. 4). Dordrecht: D. Reidel.
Michalos, A. C. (1982a). North American social report. *Economics, religion and morality* (Vol. 5). Dordrecht: D. Reidel.
Michalos, A. C. (1982b). *Economics, religion and morality* (pp. 58–63).
Michalos, A. C. (1982c). *Economics, religion and morality* (pp. 171–174).
Nadis, S. (1988). After the boycott. *Science for the People, 20,* 23.
New Democratic Party of Canada. (1988a). *Canada's stake in common security*. Ottawa: New Democratic Party of Canada.
New Democratic Party of Canada. (1988b). Canada's Stake: 50.
North-South Institute. (1988). Fighting different wars: Canadians speak out on foreign policy. Review '87/Outlook '88: 2.
Pentz, M. (1986). To prevent nuclear war and promote nuclear disarmament: It's time for a new look. In T. L. Perry & J. G. Foulks (Eds.), *End the arms race: Fund human needs* (275, 291). West Vancouver: Gordon Soules.
Prince, M. J. (1986). The Mulroney agenda: A right turn for Ottawa? In M. J. Prince (Ed.), *How Ottawa spends, 1986–87: Tracking the Tories, Methuen, Toronto* (39).
Public Accounts of Canada, 1986, 1982, 1978.
Regehr, E. (1987a). *Arms Canada, xvii*, 194–195.
Regehr, E. (1987b). *Arms Canada*, 70.
Regehr, E. (1987c). *Arms Canada: The deadly business of military exports*. Toronto: James Lorimer & Co.
Regehr, E. (1987d). *Arms Canada*, 212.
Regehr, E. (1987e). *Arms Canada: xix, 53*(178), 181–182.
Regehr, E. (1987f). *Arms Canada*, 17.
Regehr, E. (1987g). *Aims Canada*, 18.
Regehr, E. (1987h). *Arms Canada*, 12.
Regehr, E. (1987i). *Arms Canad, xx*, 29–30, 179, 185
Regehr, E. (1987j). *Arms Canada*, 11.
Regehr, E. (1987k). *Arms Canada, 12,* 173–174.
Regehr, E. (1987l). *Arms Canada*, 164–165.
Sanger, C. (1982a). *Safe and sound: Disarmament and development in the eighties* (107). Ottawa: Deneau.
Sanger, C. (1982b). *Safe and sound, 41–43,* 73–74.
Sanger, C. (1982c). *Safe and sound* (29).
Sivard, R. L. (1986a). *World military and social expenditures 1986*. Washington, DC: World Priorities.
Sivard, R. L. (1986b). *World military and social expenditures* (25).
Sivard, R. L. (1986c). *World military and social expenditures* (18).
Statistics Canada. (1987a). Federal Government Finances 1985 (68–211): 41–42, Table 8; Finances 1982:40–41, Table 12; Finances 1979: 40–41, Table 14; Finances 1976: 44–45, Table 16. Minister of Supply and Services. Ottawa
Statistics Canada. (1987b). *Finances 1985*, 41–42.
Statistics Canada. (1987c). *Canada year book 1988* (Vols. 4–5, no. 7, pp. 11–12). Ottawa: Minister of Supply and Services.
Treddenick, J. M. (1984). *The arms race and military keynesianism. Report No. 3 for the center for studies in defense resources management* (Vol. 21). Royal Military College of Canada, Kingston.
Treddenick, J. M. (1987a). *The economic significance of the Canadian defense industrial base. Report no. 15 for the center for studies in defense resources management*. Royal Military College of Canada, Kingston.

Treddenick, J. M. (1987b). *Economic significance* (24).
Treddenick, J. M. (1987c). *Economic significance* (35–36).
Treddenick, J. M. (1987d). *Economic significance* (50–51).
Treddenick, J. M. (1987e). *Economic significance* (31).
Treddenick, J. M. (1987f). *Economic significance* (15–18).
Tsipis, K. (1986). Technical and operational consideration of space-based defensive sys tems. In T. L. Perry & J. G. Foulks (Eds.), *End the arms race: Fund human needs* (37–46). West Vancouver: Gordon Soules.
United Nations, Panel of Eminent Personalities in the Field of Disarmament and Development. (1986). *Disarmament and development.* New York, NY: United Nations.
Wallace-Deering, K. (1986). The economics of war and peace. In T. L. Perry & J. G. Foulks (Eds.), *End the arms race: Fund human needs* (78). West Vancouver: Gordon Soules.
Werlin, D. L. (1986a). Conversion to peaceful production. In T. L. Perry & J. G. Foulks (Eds.), *End the arms race: Fund human needs* (96–97). West Vancouver: Gordon Soules.
Werlin, D. L. (1986b). Conversion to peaceful production (101).
Werlin, D. L. (1986c). Conversion to peaceful production (98).

Chapter 10
The Impact of Trust on Business, International Security and the Quality of Life

Alex C. Michalos

Introduction

In this essay I am bringing together three lines of research that I have been engaged in for some years in relative isolation, namely, research on social indicators and quality of life measurement, research on international peace and security, and business ethics. The three areas overlap in many ways, but the common thread passing through all three areas that is the focus of attention here is trust. I am not going to undertake a logical analysis of the concept of trust. Bluhm (1987) claimed that trust is a "heroic concept" worthy of detailed analysis, while Baier (1985, 1986) and Govier (1989) have already begun the task in earnest. For present purposes it is enough to think of trust as a relatively informed attitude or propensity to allow oneself and perhaps others to be vulnerable to harm in the interest of some perceived greater good. As will be explained below, trust is a necessary but certainly not a sufficient condition of a high quality of life, international peace and security, and a market or exchange-based economy.

Virtually all contemporary research on subjective well-being, quality of life, happiness and satisfaction with life as a whole shows that good interpersonal relations contribute more than anything else to these desirable states. If one were to list plausible necessary conditions for good interpersonal relations, trust would certainly be included in the list. For nearly two decades there have been over 1100 tides published every year on the general topic of subjective well-being (Michalos 1987a). Much of this literature deals with the psychological dynamics of subjective well-being, including the relations between relatively objective features of the world and people's perceptions and evaluations of those features.

A.C. Michalos (✉)
University of Northern British Columbia, Prince George, BC, Canada
e-mail: michalos@brandonu.ca

A.C. Michalos, *How Good Policies and Business Ethics Enhance Good Quality of Life*, DOI 10.1007/978-3-319-50724-8_10

According to Macintosh (1985, p. 87), there are nine "serious generic problems" in the literature of Western nations' international Confidence Building and Security Measures, including the following two.

> … a failure to explicitly discuss the actual psychological processes that are assumed to (a) mediate or facilitate the creation of "confidence" and (b) overcome the "misperception" of intentions and ambiguous actions;
>
> … a general failure to appreciate the ramifications of the fact that Confidence-Building *is an intrinsically psychological process* (i.e., there is stunning disregard for the intellectual and emotional distortions that cognitive processes can wreak on perceptions of "trust", "predictability", "confidence", and "certainty" — all vital features of meaningful Confidence-Building).

When I did a computer search of the Social Science Citation Index in January 1989 on the general topics of trust and confidence, I found over 3000 titles. Macintosh was only able to scratch the surface of this research, mentioning some salient work in decision theory and cognitive psychology.

But he emphasized the need for and the potentially great benefits of a more thorough review of the literature. He did not mention the literature from the field of social indicators research and quality of life studies, but this area represents an enormous untapped resource, a resource which I am just barely going to be able to tap here. Earlier attempts to connect some aspects of social indicators/quality of life research to peace and security studies may be found in Michalos (1980a, 1989).

According to Sellerberg (1982), confidence and trust have always been necessary conditions of people living together in communities. Following insights of such sociological authorities as Georg Simmel and Max Weber, "Trade", she wrote, "needs for its existence confidence and trust" (p. 39). Then she shows how the trust and confidence based on familiarity and personal relations that was characteristic of earlier social arrangements increasingly tends to be based on non-personal information, consumer laws, technological devices and other forms of regulation.

Lewis and Weigert (1985, p. 455) claim that "society is possible only through *trust* in its members, institutions and forms", and Short (1984) takes a similar line, arguing that contemporary assessments of risk are largely assessments of the trustworthiness of institutions and institutional arrangements designed to cope with risks.

Clearly, research on trust and confidence is directly relevant to research on quality of life, peace and security, and business ethics. Although one of the aims of this essay is to review enough relevant research to provoke others to undertake their own investigations, that is not my fundamental aim. My basic theses are that the world is to some extent constructed by each of us, that it can and ought to be constructed in a more benign way, that such construction will require more trust than most people are currently willing to grant, and that most of us will be better off if most of us can manage to be more trusting in spite of our doubts.

Perception, Trust and Measurable Risk

In Michalos (1980a, p. 16) I showed that in 1973–74, although Americans were over five times as vulnerable to violent crime as Canadians,

> there was no significant difference in the proportion of people in both countries who expressed some fear of walking alone at night in their own areas. In both countries close to 40% of the respondents [in national Gallup polls] felt this way.

Clearly, there was something intervening between people's perceived security and the objectively measured risk of victimization and, with some justification, Canadians might have felt and expressed greater security than Americans.

Studies of rural residents of Ohio (Phillips and Wurschmidt 1982; Mullen and Donnermeyer 1985) and Indiana (Donnermeyer 1982) showed that concern with crime was considerably disproportionate to the probability of victimization indicated by crime rates. More importantly, for our purposes, Conklin (1976) and Mullen and Donnermeyer (1985) found that higher trust was related to less perceived crime and more perceived safety in one's neighbourhood. According to the latter two authors, trust of neighbours functioned as a mediating variable between isolation and perceived safety for the rural elderly of Ohio.

Some observers think the media create the "reality" to which people react. MacKuen (1984, p. 456) matched American concerns with crime against actual crime rates and media reports of crime in the 1966–76 period, and concluded that "the public's attention is directed by editorial judgments and not, at least in the aggregate, by awareness of the objective conditions." When he looked at concerns with Vietnam, inflation, unemployment and energy shortages, the same tidy correlation did not appear. The media do not seem to be responsible for all kinds of perceived risks.

Citrin and Green (1986) reviewed American national opinion polls regarding trust and confidence in presidential leadership and government from the early 1960s to 1984. They found that

> the so-called Misery Index (the sum of the inflation and unemployment rates) and confidence in government. … moved in tandem. Throughout the 1970s, the American economy stagnated and political cynicism increased. In the 1980s, first inflation and then unemployment abated; during this period trust in government began to rise … economic outcomes influence approval of the president's job performance, which in turn affects more generalized feelings of confidence in government (pp. 438–41).

MacKuen also found that people's judgments about the seriousness of unemployment were closely related to relatively objectively measured unemployment rates, but then judgments about inflation were more closely related to media reports.

Several studies have shown that people living relatively near to nuclear plants tend to have more confidence in the safety of nuclear power than people living relatively far from them (Manning 1982), although following the 1979 accident at the Three Mile Island Nuclear Station in Pennsylvania local residents reported levels of perceived threat considerably greater than what might have been justified on the basis of reported actual radiation levels.

Newcomb (1986) reported results of a 1980 survey of 722 young adults in Los Angeles County showing that, compared to males, females were more troubled by nuclear power and weapons, and had less nuclear denial. He ominously concluded that

> Results of this study show clearly the emotional (depression, lowered quality of life) and social (drug use and its attendant problems) concomitants of living in a world in which a nuclear atrocity is a very real danger. The consequences for emotional and psychological development are staggering because a feeling of security and trust is fundamental to healthy growth and maturation. In one way, denial and psychic numbing may be adaptive mechanisms to cope with living with the unthinkable. ... Although it relieves depression and anxiety on a temporary basis, the long-term outcome of such defenses may be nuclear war because of apathy and lack of involvement (Newcomb 1986, p. 918).

Driedger and Munton (1988, pp. 40–1) reported that Francophones found the USSR to be more of a threat than English-speaking Canadians perceived it to be, and younger Canadians expressed greater trust in the Soviets than in the Americans.

Social Construction of Perception, Knowledge and Value

I am enough of an epistemological realist or objectivist to grant that there is a world relatively independent of this or that person, containing things with more or less objectively measurable properties, which are more or less objectively comparable. But these points must be made with some care because there is a big difference between what one may grant and what one can prove.

To some extent all knowledge is relative in several respects. All human artifacts, including methods, practices, principles, and bodies of knowledge are constructed by people with a variety of interests and purposes precisely to serve those interests and purposes. The foundation of our most impressive and apparently certain empirical knowledge consists of nothing more than fallible, negotiated agreements among diverse research communities regarding what is the case and what are to count as good reasons for accepting some claims as well-warranted and rejecting others as not well-warranted. In short, assuming that one's knowledge extends precisely as far as one's good reasons and what counts as a good reason is determined by negotiations within some research community, it follows that one's knowledge is finally determined by and relative to those negotiations (Michalos 1980b).

Besides all the aspects of human artifacts that are built in by design, there are many that result from the fact that people cannot choose their biological parents or the latter's socioeconomic class; the time, place and circumstances of their birth; the events that surround them; all the people whose lives interact with theirs, such as their parents' friends and their friends' parents, relatives, school teachers, classmates, next door neighbours, neighbourhood bullies; and so on. We are creative and adaptive creatures of history and culture, and there is no way to decide once and for all time exactly which features of our world we have merely constructed and which are found. It seems highly unlikely that the whole universe has somehow been constructed out of our imagination, but there is no way, I think, to say just how much has been constructed.

An overview of the sort of symbolic interactionist point of view assumed here may be found in House (1977). Evidence for the social construction of perception, knowledge and evaluation may be found in Angel and Thoits (1987) involving the construction of illness; LaRocco (1985) regarding working conditions; O'Reilly and Caldwell (1970) for job task perceptions and job satisfaction; O'Reilly and Caldwell (1985) for job enrichment perceptions and job satisfaction; White and Mitchell (1979) for perceptions of job enrichment; Durbin (1980) for scientific knowledge; Zalesny et al. (1985) for trust in an organization's administration; Bella et al. (1988) for trust in the organizational process involved with nuclear waste disposal; Bella (1987) for trust in the professional judgment of engineers; Schlenker (1987) for self-identity; Shepelak (1987) for selfevaluations and the legitimation of socio-economic status; Lavee et al. (1987) for family crises; Short (1984) for judgments of the risk of criminal victimization; and Adams (1988) for assessments of risk on highways and in playgrounds. Generally speaking, the more ambiguous the environment and the more cohesive one's group, the more influence the latter will have on one's constructions (Hackman 1976).

O'Reilly and Caldwell (1985, p. 195) summarize some of the important dynamics in the social construction of reality in the workplace as follows:

> Within work groups, there may emerge a consensus about what are the important features of the work environment. In this manner, groups may act to make salient certain aspects of the job and downplay others. Newcomers to a group are quickly made aware of what is important, how one should feel about certain aspects of the job, and what are acceptable standards of behaviour. This may lead to identical tasks being perceived of and responded to differently across groups. Thus, in addition to the effects of informational social influence, groups may also develop a normative framework for interpreting and responding to facets of the work environment resulting in a stable social construction of reality that may vary across work groups faced with objectively similar circumstances.

If one's "workplace" happens to be an institution responsible for negotiating international peace and security, the latter may hang in a precarious socially constructed balance.

Snyder (1984, pp. 293–4) summarized his excellent review by saying that:

> Investigations of the reality-constructing consequences of social beliefs make clear just what it is that is inherently and fundamentally *social* about social beliefs. That is, these investigations sensitize us to the links between social beliefs and social reality. Social beliefs can and do create their own social reality. The very events of the social world … may be products of preconceptions about the social world … Social beliefs are *social*

beliefs precisely because of their intimate involvement in the construction and the reconstruction of social reality in ongoing and continuing social relationships. Social beliefs are *social* beliefs precisely because of the links they create between the domain of thought and the domain of action.

Personal Expectations, Bias and Constructions of Reality

Evidence for the impact of personal expectations on constructions (including perceptions, evaluations and beliefs about the world and one's own self) may be found in Miller and Turnbull (1986) and Snyder (1984). A substantial amount of evidence of personal bias in the organization of systems of cognitions, conations and affects (belief systems broadly construed) has been gathered by Schlenker and Miller (1977), Greenwald (1980, 1981), Greenwald and Pratkanis (1984, 1985).

According to Greenwald and Pratkanis (1984, pp. 139–40), most people's belief systems have a bias toward

> *egocentricity,* the tendency of judgment and memory to be focused on self, … *beneffectance,* the tendency for self to be perceived as effective in achieving desired ends, while avoiding undesired ones, and … *cognitive conservatism,* the tendency to resist cognitive change.

The second characteristic includes a

> tendency to recall successes more readily than failures … the acceptance of responsibility for successes but not for failures on individual or group tasks … denial of responsibility for harming others … [and] … the tendency to identify with victors and to disaffiliate with losers.

The third characteristic includes the tendency to adopt

> information-seeking strategies that selectively confirm initial hypotheses … selective recall of information that confirms previously established beliefs … selective generation of arguments that support opinions under attack … researchers' selective evaluation of their own data as a function of the data's agreement with their hypotheses … rewriting of memory … so as to obscure the occurrence of opinion change … believing that newly acquired facts have had lengthy residence in memory … [and] … overestimating the validity of inaccurate memories.

The tendency for people to be overconfident about their beliefs and alleged knowledge has been demonstrated in a number of studies. For example, Fischhoff and MacGregor (1982) reviewed research on groups of psychology graduate students, executives, civil engineers, bankers, clinical psychologists, untrained and professional weather forecasters, and concluded that

> Knowledge generally increases as confidence increases. However, it increases too swiftly, with a doubling of confidence being associated with perhaps a 50% increase in knowledge. With all but the easiest of tasks, people tend to be overconfident regarding how much they know (p. 155).

Faust and Ziskin (1988) reviewed several studies on the comparative accuracy of judgments of expert clinical psychologists and psychiatrists versus those of laypersons, and concluded that "Confidence and accuracy can be inversely related, and yet [a] jury may well accept the opinion of an expert who exudes confidence over that of an opposing expert who expresses appropriate caution" (p. 35).

Koriat et al. (1980, p. 117) claimed that:

> People who are interested in properly assessing how much they know should work harder in recruiting and weighing evidence. However, that extra effort is likely to be of little avail unless it is directed toward recruiting contradicting reasons.

These researchers found that the most effective way of resisting one's inclinations to consider only arguments supporting one's own position is to routinely insist on a review of arguments opposed to it. The Scholastic philosophers who typically reviewed objections to their theses before presenting arguments for them would have been pleased to see the experimental evidence uncovered by Fischhoff and his colleagues.

What actually can be recalled from one's past depends to some extent on how far away it is, how it was encoded in one's memory, and how long and hard one tries. But people's memories play tricks on them by obliterating some things and embellishing others. Sometimes they will put several events together to create an experience that never happened (Bradburn et al. 1987). If asked what particular stimulus provoked what response, they frequently will pick the wrong stimulus.

> Even when they are thoroughly cognizant of the existence of both stimulus and response, they often deny that a genuinely influential stimulus affected their response and assert that a noninfluential stimulus affect their response (Nisbett and Bellows 1977, pp. 613–4).

They seem to be more influenced by their own or generally accepted theories and rationalizations of why they behave, think and feel as they do than they are by having some privileged and private access to their own mental and behavioural processes (Nisbett and Wilson 1977).

At least since Festinger's (1957) research on cognitive dissonance, some people have wondered whether the troublesome thing about discrepancies between what one expects to happen and what actually happens is the mere fact of a perceived inconsistency in beliefs (the so-called consistency model) or the more personal fact that holding inconsistent beliefs might affect one's own selfesteem (the incentive model). Schlenker (1975) provided part of an answer. Although his research was limited to people's presentations of their own selves to themselves and to others, his results were fairly decisive in this area. "Under public performance conditions", he wrote:

> (where future public events could invalidate an unrealistically positive self-presentation), self-presentations were consistent with subjects' expectations of actual performance. However, under anonymous conditions, self-presentations were quite favourable and unaffected by expectations of actual performance. The results support an incentive model and fail to support a consistency model. Subjects seemed to desire as self-enhancing and approval gaining a public image as possible but conceded to the demands of public reality when necessary (Schlenker 1975, p. 1030).

In a later study, Schlenker and Leary (1985, p. 177) reported that:

> people with larger discrepancies between the real self and the ideal self on particular traits were prone to anxiety and self-doubt and also lacked interpersonal skills. Those with smaller discrepancies were characterised being more socially poised, confident, and adept in their dealings with the problems of everyday life.

They also found that the combination of low expectations of goal achievement and a very important goal produced not only negative affect, but also

> physical or psychological withdrawal from the situation, and self-preoccupation with one's limitations … a protective self-presentational style … a lowered level of participation in interactions (e.g., initiating fewer conversations, talking less frequently), the avoidance of topics that might reveal one's ignorance … minimal disclosure of information about the self … and a passive yet pleasant interaction style that avoids disagreement (e.g., reflective listening, agreeing with others, smiling).

On the other hand,

> high as compared to low outcome expectations prompt people to begin difficult tasks sooner rather than procrastinate or avoid the tasks, work harder on them, and persist longer in the face of obstacles (Schlenker and Leary 1985, pp. 171–6).

People's expectations are so influential that Levenson and Gottman (1985) were able to explain over 60% of the variance in a person's marital satisfaction by that person's physiological reactions (heart rates, bodily movement and skin conductance levels) to the presence of the person's partner. Experiments were designed so that participants' physiological reactions were monitored 5 min prior to and throughout some social interaction. To their surprise, physiological data from the first 5 min were highly predictive of the reported marital satisfaction of both partners. Levensen and Gottman (1985, p. 92) concluded that

> In happy marriages, there may be an expectation of pleasure and a sense of optimism that becomes associated with the anticipation of interaction, … In unhappy marriages, an expectation of displeasure, dread, and pessimism may evolve because past interactions … have been experienced as highly punishing. We believe that it is these pleasurable or unpleasurable expectations that account for the arousal differences we have observed during baseline periods when couples sit facing each other for 5 min in silence, knowing that they will soon be engaged in interaction.

According to Liebrand et al. (1986a), others have referred to egocentric biases as "self-handicapping" biases. Messick and Sentis (1983) reviewed evidence of an egocentric fairness bias, which is a tendency for people to see arrangements that favour themselves over others as fairer than arrangements that favour others.

> People will judge the efforts that they make to achieve a favourable outcome to be appropriate and proper, whereas the behaviors that the other party or parties employ to achieve their ends may be viewed as inappropriate or unfair (Leibrand et al. 1986b, p. 591).

Using samples mainly of Dutch undergraduates, these authors replicated studies undertaken by Messick and others in the United States, and concluded that

> Since the replication was conducted in a different country and different language, the results suggest that these fairness biases have transcultural generality (Liebrand et al. 1986b, p. 602).

Shepelak's (1987, p. 499) survey in Indiana led to the conclusion that "those in relatively advantaged positions believe their advantage to be fair whereas those in relatively disadvantaged positions question the fairness of their rewards". Similarly, Feather and O'Brien (1986, p. 123) claimed that "cross-sectional studies show that the unemployed tend to blame their condition on external factors while the employed are relatively more inclined to appeal to internal factors when accounting for unemployment".

Liebrand et al. (1986a) replicated other research showing that while some people think of cooperation and competition in relatively moralistic terms as good or bad, others think of these behavioural options in terms of strength or weakness; i.e., in terms of social potency. Thus, for example, behaviour that one person characterizes as cooperative and morally praiseworthy, another might characterize as weak-willed and ineffective. Add this dimension to those described above and it is easy to imagine a scenario in which I might offer you a package that I believe is fair to you but is really favourable to me; you might accept it out of generosity, and I might interpret your generosity as weakness. Indeed, since it is likely that you would recognize my interpretation and grant that there may be something in it, in time I might even get you to interpret your behaviour as I do. Of course, what one would like to see happen is that I would come to see the world as you do, in which case I might be inclined to make offers in the future that were genuinely fair.

Jones (1986) reviewed evidence indicating that people's constructions of reality have some creative impact on the latter. Thus:

> An approach orientation (for example, one involving smiles and eye contact) is the most likely behavioral reaction to the expectation of warmth, friendliness, and liking. Expectations of hostility or competitiveness tend to breed hostility or competitiveness in response. If we think someone is emotionally fragile, we will typically respond with cautious and accommodating behavior (Jones 1986, p. 43).

To make matters worse, at least from the point of view of descriptive accuracy, when people construct explanations for the constructed behaviour of others, they have a distinct bias for character-disposition accounts versus situational accounts. For example, I expect you to be untrustworthy and treat you as if you are; then, after you show some sign of untrustworthiness, I attribute it to a latent character flaw in you rather than a set up by me. Jones refers to this sort of bias as "correspondence bias" and claims that

> people almost inevitably prefer to make personal attributions for behaviors that can be fully explained by the circumstances of situational constraint … even when the constraint is extreme and even when it is induced by the perceiver himself or herself (Jones 1986, p. 44).

According to Bell et al. (1987, p. 451), Ross and Sicoly (1979), Thompson and Kelley (1981) reported that "individuals within close relationships tend to perceive themselves as more responsible than their partners for its positive aspects." Bell et al.*'s* own sample of 109 women "believed they were more responsible than their husbands for the maintenance of their marriages".

Rempel et al. (1985, p. 95) studied trusting relationships among 47 couples and claimed that "there was a tendency for people to view their own motives as less self-centered and more exclusively intrinsic in flavor than their partner's motives". For these authors, a task motivation is intrinsic for someone insofar as the latter engages in it for its own sake rather than for the sake of something else. Thus, what they observed was a tendency for people to think of themselves as doing things for their partners for their mutual satisfaction and to think of their partners as doing things for them in order to get something else, something besides mutual satisfaction.

To some extent, one's own sense of personal security and self-esteem influence one's capacity for developing intimate and trusting relationships; Barry (1970), Rempel et al. (1985). Several studies show that good communication is one of the most important influences on marital satisfaction (Michalos 1986), and among the most important things one can communicate to a loved one or friend is information about one's own self and internal states. Such communication is facilitated by trust (Gibbs 1978; Franzoi et al. 1985).

Experimental Research on Trust

Goethals (1986) reported results of several small group undergraduate studies of the following sort. Students are informed that a Red Cross blood donor clinic will be set up on campus for the next few days. They are asked if they will give blood and if they think others will do the same. Table 10.1 shows the responses from 50

Table 10.1 Red cross study

Percent who would give blood		Percent who would not give blood	
60		40	
% estimating others would give blood	% estimating others would not give blood	% estimating others would give blood	% estimating others would not give blood
39	61	30	70

60% said they would give blood but 32% thought others would
(N = 50 undergraduates)
Source Goethals (1986)

Table 10.2 Stranded senior strangers case

Percent who would stop to help				Percent who would not stop to help			
88				12			
% estimating others would stop		% estimating others would not stop		% estimating others would stop		% estimating others would not stop	
62		38		18		82	
M	F	M	F	M	F	M	F
61	39	61	39	0	100	67	33

(*N* = 93 University of Guelph undergraduates, May 1989)

undergraduates. Sixty percent of the students said they would give blood, but only 32% thought others would. Of those who said they would give, 61% thought others would not; while of those who said they would not give, 70% thought others would not. Thus, neither the givers nor the nongivers were very optimistic about the generosity of their peers, but the nongivers were more pessimistic than the givers. If we assume that the students were making honest reports about their own behaviour and judgments about that of their peers, then most students were more pessimistic about their peers than the circumstances warranted. Most students were apparently more generous with their blood than most students believed they would be.

In May 1989, I tried out a couple similar scenarios on my own students in introductory business ethics and philosophy of science courses. Results from both classes are combined and displayed in Tables 10.2 and 10.3.

Table 10.3 Lost wallet case

Percent who would return everything				Percent who would not return all			
91				9			
% estimating others would return everything		% estimating others would not return all		% estimating others would return everything		% estimating others would not return all	
51		49		29		71	
M	F	M	F	M	F	M	F
59	41	55	45	50	50	40	60

91% said they would return everything but 49% thought most would return everything
(*N* = 74 University of Guelph undergraduates, May 1989)

In the stranded seniors case, the story is that

> you and a friend are driving down a country road one night just before dusk and you see an old man and woman beside their car with its hood up. There are no homes or stores in sight, and the people are flagging passing cars in order to get someone to stop to help them out. Do you think you would probably stop to help them? (Yes or no.) Do you think most people would probably stop to help them? (Yes or no.) Are you male or female?

Table 10.2 shows that although 88% said they would stop, only 57% thought most people would stop. Unlike the Goethals study, of those who said they would stop, a minority of 38% thought most others would not stop; but 82% of the nonstoppers thought most people would not stop. So, we have a fairly clear case of what some people call a false consensus bias according to which people are inclined to estimate that the behaviour and attitudes of others are similar to their own; e.g., Fields and Schuman (1976), Ross et al. (1977), Judd and Johnson (1981), van der Pligt (1984). Nisbett and Kunda (1985, p. 309) claimed that

> … the false consensus bias is a very useful heuristic to employ in the absence of other knowledge: For most of the distributions we examined, the majority of people would be right to assume that most other people's stances are not very different from their own.

On the basis of the responses shown in Table 10.2, the false consensus bias would have been a useful heuristic for most people for the stranded seniors scenario too. More importantly, if most people would have granted that most people were like themselves, they would have found most people nicer than they imagined them to be.

Table 10.2 also provides some data regarding male and female differences. Of those who said they would stop, more males than females thought others would stop and more males than females thought others would not stop. Of those who said they would not stop, only females thought others would stop, while twice as many males as females thought others would not stop. So, the nonstopping females seemed a bit more optimistic than the nonstopping males, but the stopping females were not generally more optimistic or pessimistic than the males. Johnson- George and Swap (1982) reported that their own research and that of at least three other authors indicated that females typically scored higher on measures of "generalized trust in others".

I made up the lost wallet case after it occurred to me that some people, especially young women, as a matter of self-defence might never stop to pick up strangers on the road. The story goes as follows.

> Suppose you are walking down the street and you find a wallet containing $50, some credit cards and a driver's licence. Do you think you would probably try to return the wallet and all its contents to its owner? Do you think most people would probably try to return the wallet and its contents to its owner? Are you male or female?

Table 10.3 shows that although 91% said they would return everything, only 49% thought most people would. The false consensus bias does not appear to operate for the returners, but it does for the nonreturners. Seventy-one percent of the nonreturners thought others would not return everything. There do not seem to be any clear distinctions between male and female returners and nonreturners. Again, however, the most important message of this experiment is that most people could justifiably have more confidence in most people if they simply grant that others are probably as decent as they are themselves.

Table 10.4 reviews some of the results of a survey of 280 American marketing managers by Ferrell and Weaver (1978). There are 17 questionable kinds of business activities listed (e.g., padding expense accounts, bribing people, falsifying documents, stealing, etc.), and respondents were asked to rate each one with respect to how unethical they thought it was and how frequently they engaged in it. Then they were asked to estimate their peers' beliefs and behaviour. Every one of the 34 answers indicated that respondents thought their peers' beliefs and behaviour was not as ethical as their own.

Table 10.5 reviews results of a survey of 500 American marketing researchers, corporate planners and business librarians by Beltramini (1986). Seven questions concerning relatively unethical competitive information acquisition strategies were put to respondents, and they were asked if they themselves, their companies and other companies would use the various techniques. In every case, more respondents thought other companies were less scrupulous than their own company and themselves. Cohen and Czepier (1988) replicated these results with a sample of 451 American business personnel attending seminars on gathering competitive intelligence.

Table 10.6 lists some results of three American surveys from three different years, involving a national sample of managers and 118 executives of manufacturing firms reported by Vitell and Festervand (1987). Respondents were asked about their own behaviour and that of average executives with respect to padding expense accounts and paying fees to win contracts. For every one of the 18 comparisons, respondents judged others more harshly than themselves.

Some of the respondents may have seen some of the studies cited earlier regarding fairness biases, social and individual constructions of knowledge, and so on. If so, they would have had considerable evidence of human frailties and might have judged others harshly on the basis of extrapolating some sort of halo effect. But the same extrapolation should have extended to themselves too.

Table 10.7 gives the results of a survey of 301 members of the American Institute of Certified Public Accountants by Finn et al. (1988). Respondents were asked about the opportunities for and frequency of unethical behaviour of CPAs in

Table 10.4 Comparison of beliefs for respondents, peers and top management (*Mean Scores*)

	What I believe *X* (Note 1)	What I think my peers believe *X* (Note 1)	What I do *X* (Note 2)	What I think my peers do *X* (Note 2)
	A	B	C	D
1. Using company services for personal use	3.23	2.67	1.91	3.01
2. Padding an expense account up to 10%	4.35	3.25	1.47	2.84
3. Giving gifts/favors in exchange for preferential treatment...	3.90	3.31	1.20	2.29
4. Taking longer than necessary to do a job	3.77	2.96	1.65	2.70
5. Divulging confidential information	4.71	4.32	1.17	1.91
6. Doing personal business on company time...	3.06	2.47	2.11	3.07
7. Concealing one's errors...	3.72	3.17	1.53	2.63
8. Passing blame for errors to an innocent co-worker...	4.84	3.89	1.02	2.17
9. Claiming credit for someone else's work	4.72	3.42	1.11	2.62
10. Falsifying time/quality/quantity reports	4.73	4.06	1.08	2.17
11. Padding an expense account more than 10%	4.72	3.50	1.08	2.29
12. Calling in sick to take a day off	3.86	3.00	1.29	2.28
13. Authorizing a subordinate to violate company rules...	4.24	3.74	1.34	2.00
14. Pilfering company materials and supplies	4.50	3.56	1.59	2.50
15. Accepting gifts/favors in exchange for preferential treatment...	4.33	3.44	1.14	2.35
16. Taking extra personal time (lunch hour, breaks, early departure)...	2.60	2.29	2.22	3.15
17. Not reporting others' violations of company policies...	2.89	2.87	2.35	2.65

Note 1 A high mean score indicates that the behavior is believed to be highly unethical
Note 2 A low mean score means that the behavior is practiced infrequently
Note 3 Based on two-tailed t-tests, only where a figure appears in the "significance level" columns is the perceived difference not statistically significant at the 0.01 level
Note 4 High mean scores indicate that respondents believed that corporate policy exists and is enforced (N = 280 marketing managers)
Ferrell and Weaver (1978)

Table 10.5 Use of competitive acquisition strategies

Research strategies	Percent of affirmative responses		
1. Researcher poses as graduate student working on a thesis. Researcher tells source that dorm phones are very busy, so researcher will call back rather than have phone calls returned. This way, researcher's real identity is protected	39.6[a]	42.6[b]	75.6[c]
2. Researcher calls the V.P. while (s)he is at lunch, hoping to find the secretary who may have information but is less likely to be suspicious about researcher's motives	60.6	68.7	81.7
3. Researcher calls competitor's suppliers and distributors, pretending to do a study of the entire industry. Researcher poses as a representative of a private research firm and works at home during the project so that the company's identity is protected	46.1	54.6	81.0
4. The competitor's representative is coming to a local college to recruit employees. Researcher poses as a student job-seeker to learn recruiting practices and some other general information about competitor	30.1	35.4	62.0
5. The researcher is asked to verify rumors that the competitor is planning to open a new plant in a small southern town. The researcher poses as an agent from a manufacturer looking for a site similar to the one that the competitor supposedly would need. Researcher uses this cover to become friendly with local representatives of the Chamber of Commerce, newspapers, realtors, etc.	42.4	49.1	75.5
6. Researcher corners a competitor employee at a national conference, such as American Marketing Association, and offers to buy drinks at the hotel bar. Several drinks later, the researchers asks the hard questions	70.6	67.1	86.8
7. Researcher finds an individual who works for the competitor to serve as an informant to researcher's company	39.1	39.1	73.8

[a]Researcher's own company would use this technique
[b]Researcher would use this technique
[c]Researcher believes other companies use this technique
(N = 500 marketing researchers, corporate planners and business librarians)
Beltramini (1986)

their own and others' firms. As one would expect now, respondents thought that people in other firms had more opportunities for unethical behaviour and that they took advantage of those opportunities with more frequent unethical activities.

All of these studies are limited, perhaps outrageously so when they are compared to international peace and security negotiations with their enormous potential costs and benefits, their number and variety of stakeholders, and so on. The first three of the studies suffer the limitations of being confined to university undergraduates, and

Table 10.6 Oneself versus the average executive

Situation 1: Padding an expense account	1961[a]		1976[a]		1985	
	Oneself (%)	Average executive (%)	Oneself (%)	Average executive (%)	Oneself (%)	Average executive (%)
Unacceptable, regardless of circumstances	86	60	89	53	98	54
Acceptable, if other executives in company do the same thing	6	27	4	28	0	26
Acceptable, if the executive's superior knows about it and says nothing	11	28	9	33	2	20

Situation 2: Paying fee to get a contract	1976		1985	
	Oneself (%)	Average executive (%)	Oneself (%)	Average executive (%)
Refuse to pay, even if sale is lost	42	9	51	21
Pay the fee, feeling it was ethical in the moral climate of the foreign nation	36	45	16	27
Pay the fee, feeling it was unethical but necessary to help insure the sale	22	46	33	52

[a]Sum of percentages exceeds 100% due to multiple responses
(N = 118 executives of manufacturing firms)
Vitell and Festervand (1987)

Table 10.7 Questionnaire items for ethics

Questionnaire items	Average response[a]	Standard deviation	Percent agree[b]
A. Opportunities for unethical behavior 1. There are many opportunities for CPAs in my firm to engage in unethical activities	4.6	2.1	35
2. There are many opportunities for CPAs outside my firm to engage in unethical activities	2.7	1.6	76
B. Frequency of unethical behavior 1. CPAs in my firm often engage in behaviors that I consider to be unethical	6.2	1.2	3
2. CPAs outside my firm often engage in behaviors that I consider to be unethical	3.9	1.7	42

[a]Each respondent was asked to indicate a response on a seven point Likert scale from strongly agree (1) to strongly disagree (7)
[b]Percent responding "slightly agree", "agree", or "strongly agree"
(N = 301 members of the American Institute of Certified Public Accountants)
Finn et al. (1988)

the other four studies are constrained by the fact that all of them involve surveys of American business people of one sort or another. Still, the most remarkable fact about all the studies is their complete consistency. Every single one makes the same point: most people think most people are not as nice as they are themselves and, therefore, cannot be trusted to behave as well. Taking respondents at their words, the same studies provided clear evidence that most people were wrong about most people. A more realistic assessment of others' moral virtue would have been more optimistic.

Explaining Lack of Trust

Can the respondents be taken at their words? Of course, I don't know. They may be giving honest reports badly distorted by egocentric biases. Indeed, one might hypothesize that the egocentric biases are so strong that they virtually wipe out false consensus biases. Even though people are inclined to suppose that most others are like themselves, people may find their self-esteem threatened too much by the supposition that most others are as morally virtuous, trustworthy or nice as they are themselves. In the interest of protecting their own self-esteem, they might find it necessary to think that they are at least as good as others; i.e., others are at best equal to or less virtuous than they are themselves.

Maybe respondents just judged others on the basis of their own experiences. Insofar as egocentric biases are operative, people will be inclined to experience others as less impressive than themselves, whether or not they are. But just as the fact that one is paranoid does not imply that others are *not* out to get one, the fact that one judges others as less impressive does not imply that they are *not* less impressive than oneself. Maybe most respondents had relatively bad experiences with most people. I doubt that, because I think most people are like most people in most ways. Of course, if that is true, then most people think most people are like most people in most ways, which implies that most people expect most people to be as morally virtuous as they are. If most people ever did have such expectations, then they were either dashed by experience prior to the studies I have just reviewed, or they were not dashed. If they were dashed then respondents were simply making harsh judgments based on their harsh experiences. If they were not dashed, then we are back to square one; maybe their harsh judgments were the result of egocentric biases or intentional distortion, or something else. Again, I just don't know.

According to Headey and Wearing (1988, p. 499):

> a sense of relative superiority is the usual state for most people. To feel "above average" is normal. If events happen which cause one to feel "average" or "below average", then one has plunged below the normal baseline. To repeat: SRS [the sense of relative superiority] is a crucial mechanism accounting for high levels of SWB [subjective well-being].

As I report in detail in Michalos (1990), my own survey of over 9000 university undergraduates in 38 countries yielded results that were not quite consistent with Headey and Wearing's claim. While most of my respondents perceived their status to be "at least average" or "average or above average", it would not be true to say that most respondents perceived their status to be "above average". So, it would not be true to say that the perception of such a status "is a crucial mechanism accounting for high levels of SWB". Still, it does seem fair to say that the feeling that one is at least as good as the next person (similar other) is crucial in accounting for subjective well-being.

Both Glatzer (1987) and Davis (1984) reported social comparison results similar to mine. Glatzer (p. 44) noted that in 1980, 70% of West Germans "classified their own household income as equal to or higher than the household income of the average citizen". Davis (p. 324) looked at the period from 1972–80 covering 9297 responses to the NORC General Social Survey item asking people to compare their family incomes to "American families in general", and found that 80% of respondents thought they were average or above average.

It is likely that most respondents were taught to be nice and to not trust strangers. So, maybe most people were just reporting what they learned at their parents' knees. I guess the prescriptions are not inconsistent, but they are an odd couple because if most people obey the former, then most people can safely ignore the latter. Still, the prescriptions are not unique in this way. The same ethical codes that urge people to be self-reliant also urge them to be generous in helping their neighbours. Odd as these couples appear when given some thought, maybe most people do not give them much thought, especially in rather contrived experimental circumstances.

It is possible, though perhaps unlikely, that respondents are familiar with the economic theory of public goods and the free rider problem, and their responses are guided by theoretical considerations. A public good may be defined by either of two characteristics, namely, jointness and nonexclusiveness. Roughly speaking, something has the quality of jointness if using it does not imply using it up. For example, any number of people may use the same information or knowledge at the same time and virtually forever. Something has the quality of nonexclusiveness if nonpurchasers cannot be excluded from it. For example, if Canada is internationally secure, then all its inhabitants can enjoy that security whether every person pays for it or not. Furthermore, because everyone benefits whether they pay for it or not, self-interested people have a reason to try to avoid paying for it altogether. That is, they have a reason to try to take a free ride on other peoples' payments. This is the so-called free rider problem.

The free rider problem arises in the case before us because things like moral virtue, generosity and trustfulness are public goods. Not only does using, exercising or expressing such qualities not imply using them up, but on the contrary, they tend to grow stronger with use. The more people appeal to and display moral virtue, the more others are inclined to behave in the same way. The more people display their trustfulness, the more others are inclined to be trustworthy. Moral virtue in general and trust in particular feeds on itself (Jones 1986; Gibbs 1978). Unfortunately, what works for most people most of the time does not work for everyone always. Since most people can enjoy the benefits of most people's good behaviour even if some people do not behave well, at least some of the latter will be inclined to and will take a free ride. They will therefore enjoy the benefits of most people's good behaviour and any additional benefits they can scrounge out of their own treachery. Thus, maybe most respondents are cautious and even harsh about other people because virtually everyone knows that such free riders exist and no one wants to be taken in by them. In these cases, then, respondents' mistrust is based more on theoretical considerations than on actual experiences.

Finally, we cannot rule out the possibility that respondents do some rough and relatively unconscious calculations patterned after classic textbook decision strategies (Michalos 1969). Maybe they do a rapid minimax loss assessment, and respond in a manner that would yield the smallest of the greatest possible losses with each option. For example, if they imagine that they will give blood but that most people will not, then they can avoid any great feeling of disappointment when most people do not give blood. On the other hand, the adoption of a pessimistic attitude toward the moral virtue of most people typically would not create any great disappointment. There is some international evidence suggesting that most people are not optimistic about their future (Michalos 1988). Maybe most people are not optimistic about anything, including other people.

Addressing the Problem of Lack of Trust

So much seems to hang on trust and trustworthiness, that one ought to have some principled and well- warranted strategy for addressing the problem of what appears to be a significant lack of trust in most people by most people. Since moral reasons are generally regarded as supreme among any reasons that might be offered for intentional human action, it will be worthwhile to begin our search for a strategy in the area of moral philosophy.

Generally speaking, moral philosophers may be divided into two groups, depending on which of the following two principles they regard as the fundamental basis of morality.

1. Principle of Beneficence: One ought to try to act so that one's actions tend to impartially improve the human condition.
2. No Harm Principle: One ought to try to act so that one's actions tend not to harm anyone.

So far as I know, there is no absolutely irrefutable argument for either position. People operating on the Principle of Beneficence will try to do as much good as possible. People operating on the No Harm Principle will try to do as little harm as possible. Personally, I favour universal beneficence because I think moral goodness ought to require more of people than a life of anxious inactivity mixed with pious hopes for our common future. I have no illusions about anyone's ability to behave ideally all or even most of the time, with respect to morality or anything else. But that is not a serious objection to any ideal. Insofar as one has a choice about what sort of moral ideal one ought to be guided by, what sort one ought to recommend to family, friends and the rest of the human race, I think it is wise to aim high rather than low. So, I prefer universal beneficence.

At least one author has come out in favour of the No Harm Principle in a way that connects it directly to trust. Gewirth (1987, p. 108) claimed that

> the moral principle which is at the basis of a civilized society ... is a principle of mutual trust, of mutual respect for certain basic rights: that persons will not, in the normal course of life, knowingly inflict physical harm on one another, that they will abstain from such harms insofar as it is in their power to do so, insofar as they can informedly control their relevant conduct.

Garfinkel (1963) and Bok (1978) seem to have taken a similar line. From this point of view, then, one might say that one has a right to expect that one will not be harmed intentionally by another person, that one therefore has a right to trust people and that the latter (meaning everyone) have a duty or moral obligation to be trustworthy. Alternatively, one might say that insofar as adherence to the No Harm Principle is necessary for a civilized society or a moral community, so is trusting people and being trustworthy. Thus, although I prefer the Principle of Beneficence, even those who prefer the No Harm Principle as the fundamental basis of morality would have a good reason to take trust and trustworthiness seriously.

Baier (1985) made a provocative and persuasive case for regarding the concept of trust as central for a theory of morality that would be broad enough to include the moral insights of most male theorists concerning the importance of obligations and the moral insights of most female theorists concerning the importance of love. "To trust", she wrote:

> is to make oneself or let oneself be more vulnerable than one might have been to harm from others — to give them an opportunity to harm one, in the confidence that they will not take it, because they have no good reason to. Why should one take such a risk? ... If the best reason to take such a risk is the expected gain in security which comes from a climate of trust, then in trusting we are always giving up security to get greater security, exposing our throats so that others become accustomed to not biting. A moral theory which made proper trust its central concern could have its own categorical imperative, could replace obedience to self made laws and freely chosen restraint on freedom with security-increasing sacrifice of security, distrust in the promoters of a climate of distrust, and so on (Baier 1985, pp. 60–1).

In the famous exchange of views on the ethics of belief by William James and W.K. Clifford at the turn of the century (Michalos 1978), James (1956, pp. 25–8) wrote:

> There are . . . cases where a fact cannot come at all unless a preliminary faith exists in its coming. *And where faith in a fact can help create the fact,* that would be an insane logic which should say that faith running ahead of scientific evidence is the "lowest kind of immorality" into which a thinking being can fall. ... *a rule of thinking which would*

absolutely prevent me from acknowledging certain kinds of truth if those kinds of truth were really there, would be an irrational rule.

As I explained in Michalos (1978), James thought his line of argument was strong enough to justify his belief in God. Since the argument turns on an estimate of one's own costs and benefits of belief versus disbelief, James was probably right. That does not make it right for the rest of us, who might perceive very different costs and benefits. But it does provide a general approach to our problem. I think the following argument is consistent with James' view and reasonable in itself

From a logical point of view, there are four relevant possible worlds to consider. The world might be such that most people are actually

1. trustworthy and trusted,
2. trustworthy but not trusted,
3. not trustworthy but trusted,
4. not trustworthy and not trusted.

With some exaggeration, the first case may be regarded as Real Paradise. One's trust is completely justified by the "real" world. Assuming that there is little or nothing especially pleasing or satisfying about distrust, the second case may be regarded as a Fool's Hell. One's distrust is not justified by the world and one continues to distrust even though one gets no particular pleasure out of it. The third case may be regarded as a Fool's Paradise. One's trust is not justified by the world, although one continues to trust people anyhow. The fourth case may be regarded as Real Hell. One distrusts most people and one's distrust is completely justified.

Given these possible circumstances, if one usually does not trust most people, then the most one can usually expect to achieve is either a Real Hell or a Fool's Hell. If one usually does trust most people, then the most one can usually expect to achieve is Real Paradise or a Fool's Paradise. One can probably imagine cases in which it would be preferable to have a Real Hell rather than a Fool's Paradise, and vice versa. Still, as a long range strategy, because trust is a necessary condition of Real Paradise, which is the best of the four possibilities, one ought to try to be trustful. One ought to try to take the extra step, to risk something in order to achieve the finest human community and the highest quality of life.

It would be foolish for anyone to imagine that trust could be elevated to some sort of a supreme moral principle, the way Royce (1908) recommended loyalty to loyalty as a supreme moral principle. Neither trust nor loyalty can bear such weight (Baier 1986; Michalos 1987b). But it does seem to me that the argument in the previous paragraph has some merit, if not as the last word, at least as a first. It is both an argument from prudence and morality. It is prudential to adopt a strategy of trust because, considering the four possible worlds, that will finally lead to Real Paradise if anything will. It is morally right to adopt a strategy of trust from the point of view of the No Harm Principle, as Gewirth argued, and from the point of view of trust as a necessary condition of impartially improving the human condition, i.e., the alternative Principle of Beneficence.

The moral arguments of James, Baier and myself do not have to be taken on trust. For those who think of prudence as at least as important as, and not implied by, moral virtue, we may increase the case for adopting a strategy of trust with the following considerations.

A necessary and sufficient condition of having a world in which most people trust most people is, obviously, that most people have to trust most people. On a more personal level, is virtually impossible to have good friends if one does not trust people and is not in turn trustworthy. Furthermore, as indicated earlier, virtually all contemporary research on subjective well-being shows that without good interpersonal relations, it is virtually impossible to have high levels of subjective well-being. Hence, one would expect to find some positive association between measures of trust and subjective well-being.

Fortunately, the presumed relations between trust and subjective well-being were explored in detail by Rotter (1980) and his colleagues, using mainly university undergraduates as subjects. Among other things, Rotter (1980, pp. 3–6) reported that (l) "The high truster is less likely to be unhappy, conflicted, or maladjusted; … ." (2) "Regardless of the sex of either the subject or the target person, the high truster was seen as happier, more ethical, and more attractive to the opposite sex, as having had a happier childhood, and as more desirable as a close friend than the low-trust target." (3) "People who trust more are less likely to lie and are possibly less likely to cheat or steal. They are more likely to give others a second chance and to respect the rights of others." (4) "The low trusters of both sexes showed significantly greater feelings of being distrusted, … ." (5) "The high truster is no less capable of determining who should be trusted and who should not be trusted, … It may be true that the high truster is fooled more often by crooks, but the low truster is probably fooled equally often by distrusting honest people, thereby forfeiting the benefits that trusting others might bring." (6) "Some people, obviously low trusters, believe that high trusters are just plain dumb. … [but] … we have correlated scholastic aptitude scores with trust scores and have in each case found a non-significant relationship."

On top of all these characteristics, Williams and Barefoot (1988, p. 206) claimed that "the available evidence suggests that a cynical, mistrusting attitude toward others and a willingness to express openly the anger and contempt engendered by such an attitude lie at the heart of coronary-prone behavior". The literature on Type *A* behaviour and a variety of diseases is substantial (e.g., see Houston and Snyder 1988), but Williams (1989, p. 36) claims "Hostility and cynical mistrust are now regarded as the lethal elements of Type *A* behavior by several researchers, and driving ambition is no longer viewed as dangerous".

Inglehart and Rabier (1986, p. 53) reported

> a remarkable congruence between the levels of interpersonal trust and subjective well-being observed in given societies. … In the World Values Surveys [1981], overall life satisfaction shows a mean correlation of 0.125 with interpersonal trust, while happiness correlates with trust at the 0.109 level: A given individual is significantly more likely to be happy if he trusts those around him.

Personally, I do not find the indicated correlation coefficients as impressive as Inglehart and Rabier find them.

Finally, it is probably worthwhile to mention the fact that at least two studies showed that a promisor's credibility increased directly with the frequency with which he or she actually fulfilled promises and that subjects relied more often on the former's promises as their perceived credibility increased (Schlenker et al. 1973; Gahagan and Tedeschi 1968). This is encouraging evidence for those who are inclined to try to be trustworthy in the interest of generating others' trust.

Conclusion

I have tried to make a case for the theses that the world is to some extent constructed by each of us, that it can and ought to be constructed in a more benign way, that such construction will require more trust than most people are currently willing to grant, and that most of us will be better off if most of us can manage to be more trusting in spite of our doubts. It has not been my intention to close the subject, but to open it up for further discussion and exploration. I think Macintosh was right in his judgment that international peace and security research could profit from contributions by psychologists and sociologists of one sort or another, and I hope that this essay has established that point. The same may be said of the field of business ethics. The field of social indicators and quality of fife research is already dominated by psychologists and sociologists. So my message to people in this field is simply the central theses advocated above.

Acknowledgements Earlier versions of this paper were presented at the International Conference on Social Reporting at the Science Centre of Berlin, Federal Republic of Germany, September 18–20, 1989 and at a luncheon meeting of the Centre for Ethics and Corporate Policy, Toronto, Ontario, Canada, February 1989. I would like to thank the following people for helpful comments: Deborah C. Poff, Frank M. Andrews, Bruce Headey, Wolfgang Zapf, M. Harvey Brenner, Leo Groarke, Trudy Govier, Jean Smith and Shirley Farlinger.

References

Adams, J. G. U. (1988). Risk homeostasis and the purpose of safety regulation. *Ergonomics, 31,* 407–428.

Angel, R., & Thoits, P. (1987). The impact of culture on the cognitive structure of illness. *Culture, Medicine and Psychiatry, 11,* 465–494.

Baier, A. (1985). What do women want in a moral theory? *Nous, 19*, 53–63.

Baier, A. (1986). Trust and antitrust. *Ethics, 96*, 231–60.

Barry, W. A. (1970). Marriage research and conflict: An integrative review. *Psychological Bulletin, 73*, 41–54.

Bell, R. A., Daly, J. A., & Gonzales, M. C. (1987). Affinity—Maintenance in marriage and its relationship to women's marital satisfaction. *Journal of Marriage and the Family, 49,* 445–454.

Bella, D. A. (1987). Engineering and erosion of trust. *Journal of Professional Issues in Engineering, 113*, 117–129.
Bella, D. A., Mosher, C. D., & Calvo, S. N. (1988). Establishing trust: Nuclear waste disposal. *Journal of Professional Issues in Engineering, 114*, 40–50.
Beltramini, R. F. (1986). Ethics and the use of competitive information acquisition strategies. *Journal of Business Ethics, 5*, 307–312.
Bluhm, L. H. (1987). Trust terrorism, and technology. *Journal of Business Ethics, 6*, 333–342.
Bok, S. (1978). *Lying*. New York: Pantheon Press.
Bradburn, N. M., Rips, L. J., & Shevell, S. K. (1987). Answering autobiographical questions: The impact of memory and inference on surveys. *Science, 236*, 157–161.
Citrin, J., & Green, D. P. (1986). Presidential leadership and the resurgence of trust in government. *British Journal of Political Science, 16*, 431–453.
Cohen, W., & Czepier, H. (1988). The role of ethics in gathering corporate intelligence. *Journal of Business Ethics, 7*, 199–204.
Conklin, J. E. (1976). Robbery, the elderly, and fear: An urban problem in search of a solution. In J. Goldsmith & S. Goldsmith (Eds.), *Crime and the elderly*. Lexington, Mass: Lexington Books.
Davis, J. A. (1984). New money, an old man/lady and 'Two's Company': Subjective welfare in the NORC general social surveys, 1972–1982. *Social Indicators Research, 15*, 319–350.
Donnermeyer, J. F. (1982). Patterns of criminal victimization in a rural setting: The case of Pike County, Indiana. In T. J. Carter, G. H. Phillips, J. F. Donnermeyer, & T. N. Wurschmidt (Eds.), *Rural crime: Integrating research and prevention*. Totowa, New Jersey: Allanheld, Osmun Publication.
Driedger, M., & Munton, D. (1988). *Security, arms control and defence: Public attitudes in Canada*. Ottawa: Canadian Institute for International Peace and Security.
Durbin, P. T. (Ed.). (1980). *A guide to the culture of science, technology and medicine*. New York: The Free Press.
Faust, D., & Ziskin, J. (1988). The expert witness in psychology and psychiatry. *Science, 241*, 31–35.
Feather, N. T., & O'Brien, G. E. (1986). A longitudinal study of the effects of employment and unemployment on school-leavers. *Journal of Occupational Psychology, 59*, 121–144.
Ferrell, O. C., & Weaver, K. M. (1978). Ethical beliefs of marketing managers. *Journal of Marketing, 42*, 69–73.
Festinger, L. (1957). *A theory of cognitive dissonance*. Stanford: Stanford University Press.
Fields, J. M., & Schuman, H. (1976). Public beliefs about the beliefs of the public. *Public Opinion Quarterly, 40*, 427–448.
Finn, D. W., Chonko, L. B., & Hunt, S. D. (1988). Ethical problems in public accounting: The view from the top. *Journal of Business Ethics!*, 605–15.
Fischhoff, B., & MacGregor, D. (1982). Subjective confidence in forecasts. *Journal of Forecasting, 1*, 155–172.
Franzoi, S. L., Fi Davis, M., & Young, R. D. (1985). The effects of private self-consciousness and perspective taking on satisfaction in close relationships. *Journal of Personality and Social Psychology, 48*, 1584–1594.
Gahagan, J. P., & Tedeschi, J. T. (1968). Strategy and the credibility of promises in the prisoner's dilemma game. *Journal of Conflict Resolution, 12*, 224–234.
Garfinkel, H. (1963). A conception of, and experiments with, trust as a condition of stable concerted actions. In O. J. Harvey (Ed.), *Motivation and social interaction: Cognitive determinants* (pp. 187–238). New York: Ronald Press.
Gewirth, A. (1987). Human rights and the prevention of cancer. In D. Poff & W. Waluchow (Eds.), *Business ethics in Canada* originally published in the *American Philosophical Quarterly (1980)* (pp. 105–115). Toronto: Prentice-Hall of Canada.
Gibbs, J. R. (1978). *Trust: A new view of personal and organizational development*. Los Angeles: Guild of Tutors Press.

Glatzer, W. (1987). Income. *Social Indicators Research, 19*, 39–46. (Chapter 4 of the *German Social Report,* ed. by W. Zapf et al.)
Goethals, G. R. (1986). Fabricating and ignoring social reality: Self-serving estimates of consensus. In J. M. Olson, C. P. Herman, & M. P. Zanna (Eds.), *Relative deprivation and social comparison* (pp. 139–159). Hillsdale, New Jersey: Lawrence Erlbaum Publication.
Govier, T. (1989). Trust: Some competing accounts in social science and philosophy, unpublished manuscript.
Greenwald, A. G. (1980). The totalitarian ego: Fabrication and revision of personal history. *American Psychologist*, *35*, 603–618.
Greenwald, A. G. (1981). Self and memory. In G. H. Bower (Eds.), *The psychology of learning and motivation* (pp. 201–36). New York: Academic Press.
Greenwald, A. G., & Breckler, S. J. (1985). To whom is the self presented. In B. R. Schlenker (Ed.), *The self and social life* (pp. 126–45). New York: McGraw-Hill.
Greenwald, A. G., & Pratkanis, A. R. (1984). The self. In R. S. Wyer & T. K. Srull (Eds.), *Handbook of social cognition* (pp. 129–78). Hillsdale, New Jersey: Erlbaum.
Hackman, J. R. (1976). Group influences on individuals. In M Dunnette (Ed.) *Handbook of industrial and organizational psychology* (pp. 1455–525). Chicago: Rand-McNally.
Headey, B., & Wearing, A. (1988). The sense of relative superiority—Central to well-being. *Social Indicators Research*, *20*, 497–516.
House, J. S. (1977). The three faces of social psychology. *Sociometry*, *40*, 161–177.
Houston, B. K., & Snyder, C. R. (Eds.). (1988). *Type a behavior pattern: Research, theory and intervention.* New York: Wiley.
Inglehart, R., & Rabier, J.-R. (1986). Aspirations adapt to situations—But why are the belgians so much happier than the French? A cross-cultural analysis of the subjective quality of life. In F. M. Andrews (Ed.), *Research on the quality of life* (pp. 1–56). Ann Arbor: Institute for Social Research, University of Michigan.
James, W. (1956). *The will to believe and other essays in popular philosophy*. New York: Dover Publication.
Johnson-George, C., & Swap, W. C. (1982). Measurement of specific interpersonal trust: Construction and validation of a scale to assess trust in a specific other. *Journal of Personality and Social Psychology*, *43*, 1306–17.
Jones, E. E. (1986). Interpreting interpersonal behavior: The effects of expectancies. *Science*, *234*, 41–46.
Judd, C. M., & Johnson, J. P. (1981). Attitudes polarization, and diagnosticity: Exploring the effect of affect. *Journal of Personality and Social Psychology*, *41*, 26–36.
Koriat, A., Lichtenstein, S., & Fischhoff, B. (1980). Reasons for confidence. *Journal of Experimental Psychology: Human Learning and Memory*, *6*, 107–118.
LaRocco, J. M. (1985). Effects of job conditions on worker perceptions: Ambient stimuli vs. Group influence. *Journal of Applied Social Psychology*, *15*, 735–757.
Lavee, Y., McCubbin, H. I., & Olson, D. H. (1987). The effect of stressful life events and transitions on family functioning and well-being. *Journal of Marriage and the Family*, *49*, 857–873.
Levenson, R. W., & Gottman, J. M. (1985). Physiological and affective predictors of change in relationship satisfaction. *Journal of Personality and Social Psychology*, *49*, 85–94.
Lewis, J. D., & Weigert, A. J. (1985). Social atomism, holism, and trust. *The Sociological Quarterly*, *26*, 455–471.
Liebrand, W. B. G., Jansen, R. W. T. L., Rijken, V. M., & Suhre, C. J. M. (1986a). Might over morality: Social values and the perception of other players in experimental games. *Journal of Experimental Social Psychology*, *22*, 203–215.
Liebrand, W. B. G., Messick, D. M., & Wolters, F. J. M. (1986b). Why we are fairer than others: A cross-cultural replication and extension. *Journal of Experimental Social Psychology*, *22*, 590–604.

Macintosh, J. (1985). *Confidence (and Security) building measures in the arms control process: A Canadian perspective*. Ottawa: The Arms Control and Disarmament Division, Department of External Affairs.

MacKuen, M. B. (1984). Reality, the press and citizens political agendas. In C. F. Turner & E. Martin (Eds.), *Surveying subjective phenomena* (Vol. 2, pp. 443–74). New York: Russell Sage Foundation.

Manning, D. T. (1982). Post-TMI perceived risk from nuclear power in three communities. *Nuclear Safety*, *23*, 379–384.

Messick, D. M., & Sentis, K. P. (1983). Fairness, preference and fairness biases. In D. M. Messick & K. S. Cook (Eds.), *Equity theory: Psychological and sociological perspectives* (pp. 61–94). New York: Praeger.

Michalos, A. C. (1969). *Principles of logic*. Englewood Cliffs: Prentice-Hall.

Michalos, A. C. (1978). *Foundations of decision-making*. Ottawa: Canadian library of philosophy.

Michalos, A. C. (1980a). *North American social report,* Vol. 2: *Crime, justice and politics.* Dordrecht: D. Reidel Publication Co.

Michalos, A. C. (1980b). Philosophy of science: historical, social and value aspects. In P. T. Durbin (Ed.), *A guide to the culture of science, technology and medicine* (pp. 197–281). New York: The Free Press.

Michalos, A.C. (1986). Job satisfaction, marital satisfaction and the quality of life. In F. M. Andrews (Ed.), *Research on the Quality of Life,* (pp.57–83). Ann Arbor: University of Michigan Press.

Michalos, A. C. (1987a). What makes people happy? In *Levekarsforskning Konferanserapport* (*Proceedings of the Seminar on Welfare Research*). Oslo, Norway: Norwegian Research Council for Science and the Humanities.

Michalos, A. C. (1987b). The Loyal Agent's Argument. In D. C. Poff & W. J. Waluchow (Eds.), *Business ethics in Canada* (pp. 136–41). Toronto: Prentice-Hall Canada.

Michalos, A. C. (1988). Optimism in thirty countries over a decade. *Social Indicators Research*, *20*, 177–180.

Michalos, A. C. (1989). *Militarism and the quality of life*. Toronto: Science for Peace/Samual Stevens.

Michalos A. C. (1990). *Global report on student well-being, Vol. 1: Life satisfaction and happiness*. Dordrecht: Kluwer Academic Publication.

Miller, D. T., & Turnbull, W. (1986). Expectancies and interpersonal processes. *Annual Review of Psychology*, *37*, 233–256.

Mullen, R. E., & Donnermeyer, J. F. (1985). Age, trust, and perceived safety from crime in rural areas. *The Gerontologist*, *25*, 237–42.

Newcomb, M. D. (1986). *Journal of Personality and Social Psychology*, *50*, 906–920.

Nisbett, R. E., & Bellows, N. (1977). Verbal reports about causal influences on social judgments: Private access versus public theories. *Journal of Personality and Social Psychology*, *35*, 613–624.

Nisbett, R. E., & Kunda, Z. (1985). Perception of social distributions. *Journal of Personality and Social Psychology*, *48*, 297–311.

Nisbett, R. E., & Wilson, T. D. (1977). Telling more than we can know: Verbal reports on mental processes. *Psychological Review*, *84*, 231–259.

O'Reilly, C., & Caldwell, D. (1970). Informational influence as a determinant of perceived task characteristics. *Journal of Applied Psychology*, *64*, 157–165.

O'Reilly, C., & Caldwell, D. (1985). The impact of normative social influence and cohesiveness on task perceptions and attitudes: A social information processing approach. *Journal of Occupational Psychology*, *58*, 193–206.

Phillips, G. H., & Wurschmidt, T. N. (1982). The Ohio rural victimization study. In T. J. Carter, G. H. Phillips, J. F. Donnermeyer, & T. N. Wurschmidt (Eds.), *Rural Crime: Integrating Research and Prevention.* Totowa, New Jersey: Allanheld, Osmun Publication.

Rempel, J. K., Holmes, J. G., & Zanna, M. P. (1985). Trust in close relationships. *Journal of Personality and Social Psychology*, *49*, 95–112.

Ross, M., & Sicoly, F. (1979). Egocentric biases in availability and attrition. *Journal of Personality and Social Psychology*, *37*, 322–336.
Ross, L., Green, D., & House, P. (1977). The false consensus phenomenon: an attributional bias in self-perception and social perception processes. *Journal of Experimental Social Psychology*, *13*, 279–301.
Rotter, J. B. (1980). Interpersonal trust trustworthiness, and gullibility. *American Psychologist*, *35*, 1–7.
Royce, J. (1908). *Philosophy of loyalty*. New York: Macmillan.
Schlenker, B. R. (1975). Self-presentation: Managing the impression of consistency when reality interferes with self-enhancement. *Journal of Personality and Social Psychology*, *32*, 1030–1037.
Schlenker, B. R (1987). Threats to identity: Self-identification and social stress. In C. R. Snyder & C. E. Ford (Eds.), *Coping with negative life events: Clinical and social psychological perspectives* (pp. 273–321). New York: Plenum Press.
Schlenker, B. R., & Leary, M. R. (1985). Social anxiety and communication about the self. *Journal of Language and Social Psychology*, *4*, 171–192.
Schlenker, B. R., & Miller, R. S. (1977). Egocentrism in groups: Self-serving biases or logical information processing. *Journal of Personality and Social Psychology*, *35*, 755–764.
Schlenker, B. R., Helm, B., & Tedeschi, J. T. (1973). The effects of personality and situational variables on behavioral trust. *Journal of Personality and Social Psychology*, *25*, 419–427.
Sellerberg, A.-M. (1982). On Modem confidence. *Acta Sociologica*, *25*, 39–48.
Shepelak, N. J. (1987). The role of self-explanations and self-evaluations in legitimating inequality. *American Sociological Review*, *52*, 495–503.
Short, J. F. (1984). The social fabric at risk: Toward the social transformation of risk analysis. *American Sociological Review*, *49*, 711–725.
Snyder, M. (1984). When belief creates reality. *Advances in Experimental Social Psychology*, *18*, 247–305.
Thompson, S. C., & Kelley, H. H. (1981). Judgments of responsibility for activities in close relationships. *Journal of Personality and Social Psychology*, *41*, 469–477.
van der Pligt, J. (1984). Attributions false consensus, and valence: Two field studies. *Journal of Personality and Social Psychology*, *46*, 57–68.
Vitell, S. J., & Festervand, T. A. (1987). Business ethics: Conflicts practices and beliefs of industrial executives. *Journal of Business Ethics*, *6*, 111–122.
White, S., & Mitchell, T. (1979). Job enrichment versus social cues: A comparison and competitive test. *Journal of Applied Psychology*, *64*, 1–9.
Williams, R B. (1989). The trusting heart. *Psychology Today*, 36–42.
Williams, R. B., & Barefoot, J. C. (1988). Coronary-prone behavior: The emerging role of the hostility complex. In B. K. Houston & C. R. Snyder (Eds.), *Type a behavior pattern: Research, theory and intervention* (pp. 189–210). New York: Wiley
Zalesny, M. D., Farace, R. V., & Kurchner-Hawkins, R. (1985). Determinants of employee work perceptions and attitudes: Perceived work environment and organizational level. *Environment and Behavior*, *17*, 567–592.

Chapter 11
Ethical Considerations Regarding Public Opinion Polling During Election Campaigns

Alex C. Michalos

Introduction

This paper is divided into 8 sections. It begins with an account of my understanding of ethics and morality (section "A Moral Point of View"), and proceeds to a brief section "(Social Indicators)" on social indicators and quality-of-life measurement. The two sections are connected by the fact that I regard ethics as essentially concerned with improving the human condition or the quality of human existence.

Since one way to discover whether or not people's lives are getting better or worse is to ask them, survey research or public opinion polling has emerged as an important resource for people with my particular moral point of view. Such research is always liable to sampling and nonsampling measurement errors of various sorts, with the latter type being much less familiar to most people than the former. So, section "Survey Research" is devoted to reviewing many kinds of nonsampling errors. Although there is no simple mathematical formula that would allow one to estimate the total amount of error resulting from the variety of sampling and nonsampling problems, the 3 or 4% point sampling error margins usually mentioned in commercial polls probably represents at best only half of the total error.

Sixteen arguments in favour of banning the publication of the results of public opinion polls during election campaigns are presented in section "Arguments for Banning the Publication of Some or All Poll Results During Election Campaigns, and Replies to Them", and I try to show that each of them is defective. While some of them do have some merit, I think reasonable replies may be offered to all of them.

A.C. Michalos (✉)
University of Northern British Columbia, Prince George, BC, Canada
e-mail: michalos@brandonu.ca

A.C. Michalos, *How Good Policies and Business Ethics Enhance Good Quality of Life*, DOI 10.1007/978-3-319-50724-8_11

I then present 16 arguments against banning the publication of poll results during elections (section "Arguments Against Banning the Publication of Any Poll Results During Election Campaigns"). Insofar as my arguments (many of which are borrowed from other sources) in these two sections are sound, a case is made for not banning the publication of poll results. However, I do suggest in these sections that there is a need for some legislation regarding the disclosure of information relevant to evaluating opinion polls.

In section "Proposed Bills Banning the Publication of Poll Results During Election Campaigns" I review some Private Members's bills that have been introduced in the Canadian House of Commons with the intention of banning the publication of some or all poll results during election campaigns. Although I am opposed to such legislation, I think it is useful to document what has actually been proposed on this score in recent history.

Section "Proposed Bills Providing Disclosure Standards for the Publication of Poll Results During Election Campaigns" reviews bills that have been proposed that would require disclosure of information necessary for those interested in assessing the results of opinion polls conducted during elections. I consider each recommended requirement with a view to accepting or rejecting it. Finally, I propose a model set of disclosure requirements in section "A Model Set of Disclosure Standards for the Publication of Poll Results During Election Campaigns". Although my focus of attention throughout this paper is on public opinion polling during election campaigns and possible legislation regarding such polling, I think my model set of disclosure requirements should be voluntarily adopted by all pollsters for the publication of all poll results.

A Moral Point of View

I use the terms ethics and morality as synonyms. What is morally good or evil is ethically good or evil, and vice versa. If I say that something is morally or ethically good or evil, I mean that it is good or evil from a moral point of view. Thus, in my view nothing is inherently morally good or evil. The institution of morality, and the ideas of moral goodness and evil are human artifacts designed by human beings to serve a variety of purposes. One important purpose is the resolution of conflicts of interest without resorting to civil or criminal law. Insofar as people are willing and able to perceive, judge and act in accordance with a moral point of view, morality exists. If we stop caring, morality will cease to exist.

Since morality rests on the adoption of a moral point of view, the latter must be defined. I suppose that such a definition would be tantamount to the articulation of a principle or principles that may be used as a foundation for morality. Generally speaking, moral philosophers may be divided into two groups, depending on which of the following two principles they regard as the fundamental basis of morality.

1. Principle of Beneficence: One ought to try to act so that one's actions tend to impartially improve the quality of life.
2. No Harm Principle: One ought to try to act so that one's actions tend not to harm anyone.

The principles are not exclusive and there are other ways to express them. For example, what I call the Principle of Beneficence might be expressed in terms of the impartial maximization of utility, happiness, satisfaction or well-being. Theological ethicists might capture much of what is in this principle with their insistence on loving one's neighbour, and contemporary feminist ethicists' emphasis on care and nurturing might capture it from a slightly different point of view. Instead of a single No Harm Principle, one might capture the same idea with a list of duties, freedoms or rights. This is the moral significance of the United Nations Declaration of Human Rights and Freedoms and Canada's own Charter of Rights and Freedoms. For example, when nations or individuals grant that everyone has a right to life, they are implying that everyone else has a duty or a moral obligation to refrain from taking people's lives for the fun of it. They are creating moral codes as an immediate implication of their declarations. While everything important about duties, rights, respect for persons and so on may not be captured in my two general principles, enough can be captured for our purposes.

So far as I know, there is no absolutely irrefutable argument leading to the conclusion that one or the other of these principles must be taken as fundamental. People operating primarily on the Principle of Beneficence will try to do as much good as possible. People operating primarily on the No Harm Principle will try to do as little harm as possible. Personally, I favour universal beneficence because I think moral goodness ought to require more of people than a life of anxious inactivity mixed with pious hopes for our common future. I have no illusions about anyone's ability to behave ideally all or even most of the time, with respect to morality or anything else. But that is not a serious objection to any ideal. If one has a choice about what sort of moral ideal one ought to be guided by primarily, what sort one ought to recommend to family, friends and the rest of the human race, I think it is wise to aim high rather than low. So, I am inclined to regard universal beneficence as more fundamental than the mere avoidance of intentional harm.

Goldfarb and Axworthy (1988, pp. xiii–xiv) seem to be inclined to the opposite point of view when they write things like this:

> … ethics demand that pollsters portray the reality their research has made apparent. … There are … ethical questions that all pollsters face. Should we know? Should information gleaned from polling be made available? Should we find out what we don't want to know? These questions are crucial to the ethics of polling. Should politicians, for example, have access to the results of polls taken during election campaigns? Should polls form part of the

> context of decision-making? Indeed, the formative and abiding commitment of the pollster is to discern reality, nor to withhold or change the findings. … Pollsters, however, must be true to the portrait of reality that has emerged from their work. … Can anyone become a client?

These remarks suggest, to me at least, that the authors believe that there are some questions that are inherently ethical. On the contrary, I think that nothing is inherently ethical, whether ethically good or evil. In my view, everything is inherently neutral but subject to appraisal from a moral point of view. Ethical or moral principles in my view are constructs or artifacts designed by humans in the interest of building a good life, and everything is subject to appraisal in the light of such principles. So, every question can be regarded as an ethical question when it is considered from a moral point of view.

Social Indicators

Assuming that one is going to try to conduct one's human relations from a moral point of view as expressed in the Principle of Beneficence, again broadly speaking, there are two ways to go. One can:

1. Try to improve relatively objective circumstances that are measured by things like full employment, cleaner and safer workplaces, equitable distributions of wealth and income, longer lives free of disability and disease, elimination of poverty and homelessness, and the reduction of crime.
2. Try to improve relatively subjective circumstances that are measured by people's reported peace of mind, contentment, happiness and satisfaction.

Clearly, if one's relatively objective and subjective circumstances are improved, then the quality of one's life is improved. Since the fifth century B.C., people have haggled about what is objective, what is subjective and which is more important. But it is evidently trivially true that if one's total circumstances are improved, one is better off and the quality of one's life has improved.

Social indicators are statistics that are supposed to have some significance for the quality of life. Statistical measures of relatively objective things like death rates are referred to as objective indicators or indicators of objective well-being. Measures of relatively subjective states of affairs like personal satisfaction and happiness are referred to as subjective indicators or indicators of subjective well-being. (More detailed accounts of these terms may be found in Michalos 1980a.)

A review of *Psychological Abstracts* and *Sociological Abstracts* for the past two decades reveals that researchers around the world have been publishing articles and books on subjective well-being at a rate of over a thousand titles a year.

Survey Research

Most of the research being done on subjective wellbeing employs some sort of surveying or interviewing technique, and these techniques have some fairly notorious limitations. The research may be broad-based involving a sample of all the members of some community or country, or it may merely involve a convenience sample of students, workers, patients, consumers and so on.

In an excellent review article, Groves (1987, p. S156) summarizes the roots of survey research's problems as follows:

> Survey research is not itself an academic discipline, with a common language, a common set of principles for evaluating new ideas, and a well-organized professional reference group. Lacking such an organization, the field of survey research has evolved through the somewhat independent and uncoordinated contributions of researchers trained as statisticians, psychologists, political scientists, and sociologists. ... Such a *melange* of workers certainly breeds innovation, but it also spawns applications of the method for radically different purposes, suffers severe problems of communication, and produces disagreements about the importance of various components of quality.

One may assume that any measure taken of an individual's attitude will represent the attitude itself plus some measurement error. The latter will include both sampling and nonsampling errors. Excellent reviews of a wide variety of survey sampling and nonsampling errors may be found in Turner and Martin (1984), Frankel and Frankel (1987), Alwin and Campbell (1987), Groves (1987), and Hippler et al. (1987).

While most researchers have some familiarity with and are properly cautious about sampling errors (e.g., what size and sort of sample to draw to obtain a certain probability of error a certain percentage of the time), nonsampling errors are another matter. For the latter, there is less familiarity, less caution and much more theoretical and empirical work to be done. Turner and Martin (1984, p. 69) claimed that in their study of over 1000 newspaper reports of public opinion polls in the United States and Great Britain "less than 3% ... even vaguely refer to the possibility of nonsampling errors."

Under the rubric of nonsampling errors, there are all the problems related to interviewers, fieldwork, interviewees, questionnaire design, coding, editing, and the interview questions themselves. Regarding interviewers, for example, we know that females generally make better interviewers than males, and some interviewers will typically get more responses on more questions than others (Converse and Traugott 1986). There will therefore be predictable percentages of nonresponses and judgments will have to be made about how to count these. Nonresponses imply additional possibilities of error, error arising from the interviewers' personality, techniques, expertise and training, alone and in combination with some features of the interviewees. No one knows exactly how many percentage points of accuracy should be given up for such nonsampling errors. Sometimes all one can do is try to reduce or eliminate the errors rather than try to measure their impact (Groves 1987).

There is an enormous amount of literature on the impact of experimenter and interviewer expectancies on the performance of respondents or target populations.

Reviews may be found in Miller and Turnbull (1986), Snyder (1984) and Michalos (1990). Besides affecting respondents' behavior, an experimenter's expectations affect both his or her as well as the respondent's own perception and evaluation of that behaviour. Expectations also have a direct and indirect impact on people's self-concepts.

Even the time of day, weather, rural or urban setting, and the presence of other people have affected responses to the relatively matter-of-fact types of questions that appear in national Labour Force surveys (Bailar and Rothwell 1984).

As explained in Michalos (1990), what actually can be recalled from one's past depends to some extent on how far away it is; whether the source of one's information was perceived to be likeable, attractive or expert; whether there were arguments presented that seemed to be cogent; whether the material or event was especially relevant to one's interests or had particularly salient features; how it was encoded in one's memory, and how long and hard one tries (Ottati et al. 1988; DeBono and Harnish 1988; Holtgraves et al. 1989; Jacoby et al. 1989).

There is a general tendency for people to overreport good things and under-report bad things, the so-called social and trait desirability and undesirability effects in polls (Beggan et al. 1988; Mourn 1988). For example, there is more reported voting than actual voting, less reported drunk driving than actual drunk driving, and less reported tax evasion than officially documented evasion (Hessing et al. 1988).

Roos (1988) claimed that subjective well-being researchers face a special kind of social desirability effect, which he called "the happiness barrier." In his words, "it is an image of one's life, projected for the benefit of others: neighbours, social authorities, research workers, the society in general. ... a well- built happiness barrier becomes also an image of one's life, projected for the benefit of the subject himself: it becomes a double wall" (p. 141). Kozma and Stones (1988) demonstrated that one popular measure of social desirability, the Edwards Scale of Social Desirability, has too much content reflecting subjective well-being to be regarded as an independent, reliable and valid measure of social desirability.

There is a tendency for people to give responses that seem to be popular at the time, the so-called bandwagon effect (DeMaio 1984). From several focused samples of Norwegians, Moum (1981, 1983, 1988) found a tendency for females, people with low socio-economic status and elderly individuals to have their reported life satisfaction inflated by yea- saying and relatively high levels of resignation. Again, no one knows exactly how much of any response to most questions should be attributed to all these kinds of effects.

Whether a question allows answers in two or more categories makes a difference. Asking for approval or disapproval is not equivalent to asking for strong approval, approval, disapproval or strong disapproval. Crespi (1980, pp. 34–35) reported a study providing striking evidence of the crucial difference that numbers of response categories can make. Presidential approval scores were sought by a Gallup poll allowing one of two responses, a Harris poll allowing one of four and a Post poll allowing one of five. "The gallup method produced a favorable rating of 62% for Carter, appreciably higher than either Harris's 48% or the Post's 41%. On the other hand, the Harris method produced a 4% ‘don’t know’ compared with 10% for Gallup and 8% for the Post.”

Different pollsters prefer different question styles. Some like the take it or leave it style. Others like to creep up on a topic with a dozen or so questions and a variety of response categories (Smith 1978, 1982; Converse and Schuman 1984). According to Turner and Martin (1984, p. 82), “Any question can be considered limited from some point of view, and single questions are inherently inadequate to convey a picture of any subjective phenomenon of importance. For this reason, a range of questions should be asked and the sensitivity of measurements to wording effects should be assessed.”

Small changes in the wording of questions can radically alter responses. The simple substitution of the word job for the word work has produced differences of over 20% points in responses. Framing questions negatively rather than positively can alter responses by over 100% (Tversky and Kahneman 1986). Although some people have thought that answers to attitude questions would be less affected by wording changes among people whose attitudes are “intense, important and held with great certainty,” Krosnick and Schuman (1988) conducted 27 experiments in American national surveys designed to test this hypothesis and found no support for it.

The context of questions can make a difference (Strack and Martin 1987). If, for example, you ask someone how happy they are with life right after asking them how happy they are with their marriage, the way they feel about the latter will have an impact on the way they feel and respond about the former (Turner 1984). If you ask people how happy they are on a sunny day versus on a rainy day, the rain will depress their happiness scores (Schwarz 1984). There are seasonal effects, with reported subjective well-being in the spring being typically higher than in the fall (Andrews and Withey 1976). People’s feelings about a certain event may also change if the event is preceded or followed by a series of distinctly pleasant or unpleasant events (Wedell and Parducci 1988).

The vaguer or more ambiguous a question, the greater the variation in responses. People will just impute some particular meaning to the words uttered in order to provide some answer, some data. Many will even report reading books that do not exist and seeing movies that have not been made. Unfortunately, we have no neat way to quantify vagueness or ambiguity, and no way to know how many percentage points in confidence should be given up for people answering questions that were never asked (Turner 1984).

It is sometimes asserted that questions about life satisfaction and happiness are especially vague and that because people seldom think about such things, they are likely to avoid responding to such questions. On the contrary, in the lead article of the first issue of the journal *Social Indicators Research,* Andrews and Withey (1974) reported that four nationwide American surveys regarding satisfaction with a wide variety of life domains revealed that usually fewer than 1% of any sample chose the response “never thought about it,” and refusal rates for interviews ran about 15%. Davis and Fine-Davis (1978–79) reported a refusal rate of 3.8% for their national quality of life survey in Ireland. Inglehart and Rabier (1986) reported that for their west European surveys covering 9 countries from 1973 to 1983 and over 93,000 interviews, only 1% of respondents failed to answer a life satisfaction question and only 2% failed to answer a happiness question. The average nonresponse rate for other items in these surveys is about 10%.

Since survey research interviews tend to move along briskly and cover a wide variety of items in a relatively short space of time, results of such interviews are sometimes regarded as shallow. Some people suppose that much longer, in depth interviews might yield very different results. When Wood and Johnson (1989) compared results of relatively shallow survey research with results obtained from intensive qualitative interviews of about 12 h or more in length, they concluded that consistent assessments emerged from the two sources. As one would expect, the longer interviews uncovered nuances and suggested lines of exploration that the quantitative survey research missed. But there was substantial agreement between the findings of the qualitative and quantitative approaches.

Nobody knows exactly how much error is introduced by all of the above and other kinds of nonsampling errors. Useful work has been done and will certainly continue on the "concept of total error" (Frankel and Frankel 1987), but so far there are no generally accepted statistical formulas to take account of the great variety of nonsampling errors. Most academic, government and commercial pollsters will grant that nonsampling errors introduce at least as much error into public opinion poll results as sampling errors. But we are far from knowing what to do about it.

Lest anyone leave this section with a very pessimistic view of the "scientific status" of survey research, I offer the following quotation from Turner and Martin (1984, p. 16).

> Not only can physical measurements vary wildly, but even well-publicized "discoveries" in the physical sciences have sometimes been shown to be experimental artifacts. For example, between 1963 and 1974 more than 500 articles in journals (including *Science* and *Nature*) discussed a supposed new substance: anomalous water or polywater. Although it resembled ordinary water, polywater was alleged to have a greater density, a reduced freezing point, and an elevated boiling point, among other anomalous properties. In the end, however, it was discovered that this "new substance" was nothing more than an impure solution of ordinary water.

Obviously, pollsters seldom, if ever, get even 5 kicks at the same can, let alone 500. If they did, they would surely develop better batting averages than they have developed so far. So, at this point I would not be pessimistic. On the contrary, I would be optimistic, and urge others to be cautious and to have patience.

Arguments for Banning the Publication of Some or All Poll Results During Election Campaigns, and Replies to Them

Following are 16 arguments that might be offered by someone in favour of banning the publication of some or all poll results during election campaigns.

For each argument I have presented a reply or counter-argument that I think is sufficient to seriously undermine the original argument.

1. "The polls, and the extensive commentary on them, have no beneficial effects" (Boyer 1990, p. 33).
   Reply In the next Section I review 16 allegedly beneficial effects.
2. "Polls trivialize a parliamentary election by turning it into a horse race" (Boyer 1990, p. 33).

   Reply "Banning polls would not necessarily solve the problem. The public would be left with unreliable street surveys, self-serving leaks from political insiders, and selective canvassing of results" (*Toronto Star*, May 4, 1990, p. A26; Reid in *Hearings* for Winnipeg, p. 5).

3. Polls "displace limited newspaper space and broadcast air time that otherwise could be used for coverage of issues, candidates and party programs" (Boyer 1990, p. 33; Maureen McTeer according to Hoy 1989, p. 219; Germond 1980, p. 21; Sperling in *Hearings* for Regina, p. 1; Jones in *Hearings* for Vancouver, p. 5).
   Reply The point is well-taken, but no one knows if the trade-offs made have a net benefit or not. The critics apparently assume that most polls produce relatively trivial or useless information which ought to be replaced by something better. One can hardly argue with the view that we should have better information than we do have if it is available at a reasonable cost. I am just not persuaded that the elimination of all poll results would significantly improve our chances of getting something better. During one of the weeks while I have been writing this paper (June 1990), many of the media people in Canada have been camped on the doorsteps of the Ottawa Convention Centre gathering titbits from people involved in the constitutional discussions regarding the Meech Lake Accord. The debates are certainly important and worthy of coverage. However, there is very little useful information coming out of the secret meetings and a considerable amount of resources are being invested in broadcasting that information over and over and over. This example could be multiplied, but I think it illustrates the source of my doubts about argument number 3.
4. "They dishearten workers of parties seen to be losing, when in fact our system depends on supporters of all parties eagerly carrying their message to voters to enable an informed voting decision" (Boyer 1990, p. 33).
   Reply This objection and the couple following it suggest possibilities that are probably realized sometimes, but no one knows how often. This seems to be the view of Reid too (*Hearings* for Winnipeg, p. 4). One would suppose that in the long run such effects balance out, that we lose as much as we gain as a result of these sorts of influences. (Lemieux in *Hearings* for Quebec City takes this view, p. 4).
5. "They encourage, on the part of those trailing, a "negative" media advertising campaign to hit against whoever is leading" (Boyer 1990, p. 33).
   Reply I think my reply to argument number 4 is appropriate here too.

6. They encourage workers for frontrunners to be complacent (*Toronto Star*, May 4, 1990, p. A26; Gagne in *Hearings* for Montreal, p. 5).
   Reply Same as for number 5.
7. They "prompt people to switch their votes," perhaps for strategic reasons (*Toronto Star*, May 4, 1990, p. A26) or because they are caught up in a "bandwagon effect" (Robert Stanfield according to Hoy 1989, p. 222; Campbell in *Hearings* for Charlottetown, p. 3).
   Reply People must be allowed to change their minds as often as they like prior to and after voting. Although I already mentioned the fact that there is some evidence of some kinds of bandwagon effects for some kinds of people and some kind of surveys (in section "Survey Research"), Reid claimed (*Hearings* for Winnipeg, p. 4), "there is absolutely no evidence that there is a bandwagon effect associated with the publication of polls." Gagne made a narrower claim (*Hearings* for Montreal, p. 5), namely, that "it had not been established that polls had an impact in moving votes in a specific direction."
   Political observers have frequently complained about the bandwagon effects of polls and the compounding effects of media coverage. The more support a candidate or issue gets from the polls, it is supposed, the more media coverage there is and the more support there is likely to be, and so on. In fact, contradictory claims about such effects should be expected because interactions between media reports and poll responses are complex. As I mentioned in Michalos (1990), studies have shown that people's opinions about the seriousness of unemployment are closely correlated with objectively measured unemployment rates, regardless of the amount of media coverage. On the other hand, people's feelings about safety from violent crime are closely correlated with the amount of media coverage regardless of objectively measured crime rates (MacKuen 1984).
   Quite apart from polls, there is an enormous literature on the impact of the media on virtually every aspect of life. Good reviews may be found in Katz (1987), Beniger (1987) and Gollin (1987). Suffice it to say here that the debate about the nature and extent of media influence on what, how and why we think, feel and act remains lively.
8. Polls can be manipulated to influence and mislead voters (*Toronto Star*, May 4, 1990, p. A26; Bill Davis, Joe Clark, Robert Bourassa and Richard Hatfield according to Hoy 1989, pp. 221–223; Wilkinson and Kirwan in *Hearings* for Regina, p. 2).
   Reply The best protection against manipulators is widespread access to scientifically reliable and valid poll results (*Toronto Star*, May 4, 1990, p. A26; Lemieux in *Hearings* for Quebec City, p. 4). Regarding the issue of poll results simply influencing, but not misleading, voters, there does not seem to be any good reason for singling out such information as inappropriate, provided that it is reliable and valid. Hoy (1989, p. 227) correctly remarked that "Political advertising influences voters too, and newspaper columns, and television commentary, and front-page news stories, and the physical appearance of

candidates …" Goldforb and Axworthy (1988, p. xiii) seemed to want have their cake and eat it too when they claimed that "Pollsters do not change society's [anyone's?] behavior: this is neither their role, nor their function. They are essentially private figures who are unlikely to have any *direct* influence on the public's behavior. This is not to say, however, that a pollster's findings do not potentially influence the decisions of other individuals who do wish to affect public behavior." According to Lee (1989), during the 1988 Federal election, when polls indicated that the Tory government might be defeated by Liberals and New Democrats, the value of the Canadian dollar dropped. Noticing the relation between these events, Canadians apparently altered their opinions on election day to keep the dollar up even at the expense of keeping Liberals and New Democrats down.

9. According to Stevens (1990a, p. B3), "a majority of witnesses" before the Royal Commission on Electoral Reform and Party Financing "advocated banning the publication of opinion polls during at least the final stages of election campaigns."

   Reply At the time of the Stevens article, the hearings were still going on and briefs were still coming in. So, the majority may change by the end of the process. However, I have received and read summary transcripts from the commission's hearings in 14 of 30 (47%) projected cities, and these results confirm Stevens's comments. There were 247 speakers mentioned in these transcripts, which I suppose is fewer than actually appeared before the Commission. Twenty-five (10%) of the speakers addressed the issue of public opinion polling during elections, with 16 (64%) of these people recommending some banning of the publication of poll results and 9 (36%) recommending no banning. Six of the latter 9 people also explicitly rejected the idea of introducing some regulations or standards regarding poll data. Seven of the 9 (78%) people who opposed any sort of banning or regulations on the publication of poll results had some sort of commercial interest at stake.

   Because this sample of contributors to the Royal Commission is so small and unrepresentative of the Canadian population as a whole, one cannot extrapolate results from the former group to the latter. To do so would be to engage in the kind of pseudo sample surveys that give legitimate polling a bad name, e.g., calling a 900 phone number, buying a hamburger to endorse a candidate, etc. The best one can do is carefully weigh the arguments produced by all contributors and make a judgment. So, I have included all the arguments in my lists of those on both sides of the banning issue, and I will consider them in turn.

10. There are several democracies in which restrictions are imposed on polls and their publication through all or part of an election campaign, e.g., France, the United Kingdom, Luxembourg, Portugal, Spain, Brazil and Venezuela (Hoy 1989, pp. 219–220).

    Reply This shows that some people have thought that such restrictions are consistent with democracy and that democracies do not crumble with their introduction. It does not show that there are good reasons to introduce such restrictions in all democracies or even in Canada, or that the introduction of such restrictions always produces benefits outweighing costs for most people. There are, after all, many democracies without any specific restrictions on the publication of polls. According to Hnatyshyn (1986, pp. 25–25), from 1939 to 1982 British Columbia had a law prohibiting the conduct of opinion polls during election campaigns. On the other hand, Gollin (1987, p. S91) reported that in 1948 George Gallup claimed that "The question of government regulation of polls has come up (unsuccessfully) in nearly every Congress during the last 20 years and is certain to be raised again in the eighty-first Congress."

11. Too much of the polling undertaken for the press and broadcast media during elections is methodologically sloppy, resulting in the publication of unreliable and invalid information advertised as scientifically warranted (Hoy 1989, pp. 224–225; Roper 1980, pp. 15–16; Germond 1980, p. 23; Repo in *Hearings* for Saskatoon, p. 2). Gollin (1987, p. S90) reported results of a study of American "preelection polls that dealt with 446 state and local races (both primary and general elections) and found an appreciable difference in quality in polls carried out by independent pollsters vs. media ones, and (linked with this distinction) in polls done by interviewers in full-service polling firms versus pickup interviewers hired by the media. In both cases, the former achieved greater accuracy."
Reply In principle it seems that it should be possible to write a set of standards that pollsters and media publishers must follow in order to insure that methodologically defective polls will not be published or that defects will be adequately noted for all potential consumers. I will return to this issue below in section "Proposed Bills Providing Disclosure Standards for the Publication of Poll Results During Election Campaigns". However, a good review of American pollsters' attempts to design such standards may be found in Turner and Martin (1984, pp. 61–73). According to Gollin (1987, p. S92), "Even the guidelines for minimal disclosure of polling methods, while less contentious as an issue than were (and are) performance or procedural standards, failed to win the assent of AAPOR [American Association for Public Opinion Research] members for almost 20 years after their initial proposal in 1947. And it wasn't until 1986 that these guidelines—formulated initially to assist polling firms and news media disseminators of poll results—were revised and made an integral part of AAPOR's Code of Professional Ethics and practices, binding upon AAPOR members as individuals."
12. "In Canada, we have a polling industry with no enforceable standards and a media industry that, even if it gave a damn, is plagued by such massive ignorance of the limitations of polling that it wouldn't much matter" (Hoy 1989, p. 225).
Reply Both problems are solvable in principle, at least. The former can be solved by introducing legislation with enforceable standards. Once such legislation is in place, the media industry will be obliged to hire competent editors in order to insure compliance with the new legislation. Reid (*Hearings* for

Winnipeg, p. 5) claimed that "there were tremendous marketplace pressures on polling firms to be objective and to be accurate, so it was not necessary to address this issue by regulation." Gagne (*Hearings*, for Montreal, p. 5) took a similar line. For reasons that will become clear below (section "Proposed Bills Providing Disclosure Standards for the Publication of Poll Results During Election Campaigns"), I think these two pollsters are optimistic about the benevolent pressures of the marketplace.

13. There is a serious conflict of interest issue involved when the media conduct polls in order to generate news. According to Hoy (1989, p. 226), "No other group in society gets the relatively free ride from media scrutiny that pollsters enjoy. This surely is in part because the two crafts are sharing the same bed, a self-inflicted conflict-of-interest the media wouldn't tolerate under any other circumstances. If a newspaper or TV station hires a pollster, the results of the pollster's work, by definition, are big news for that newspaper or TV station, not subject to normal journalistic scrutiny." Roper (1980, pp. 16–18) takes a similar line.
    Reply I do not think there is any conflict-of-interest issue in the situation Hoy describes. According to Crespi (1980, p. 28), "… public opinion polling was started by the news media and has always depended upon them as the primary source of financial support. The first documented poll in the United States was conducted in 1824 by the *Harrisburg Pennsylvanian* to measure voting preferences in that year's presidential election. Today, most public opinion polls are conducted under contract to the news media or are conducted directly by them." It seems to me that what the media are doing when they hire a pollster is merely an extension of what they have always done when they hire reporters, photographers, editorialists and feature writers. Whatever their motives and however well or poorly they have accomplished their task, they have always created news. They have always and will always have to seek out events, issues, people, stories, and so on that seem relatively important and worth publishing. In the final analysis, the media make judgments about such things, and nowadays such judgments often favour the publication of poll results. While there are problems with the latter, conflict-of- interest between media sponsors and pollsters is not one of them. The question of the extreme concentration of ownership of the media is, of course, a different matter of serious concern (Michalos 1981a, b, 1982, 1988a).
14. There is a tendency for people to regard poll results as an indication of "the collective will of Canadians," but survey research is not designed to and cannot serve that purpose. Vague as the idea is, one would suppose that a "collective will" would be the sort of thing that might be reflected by an election in which there is a fair and public debate over some issue. Since pollsters usually do not attempt to present a balanced set of relevant considerations to a respondent prior to asking any questions, it is likely that a typical respondent is not giving

answers in the light of such considerations. So, those who regard poll results as an indication of a "collective will" are misleading themselves and perhaps others (Hoy 1989, p. 226).

Reply I think this is a fair criticism of some people's views about the significance of public opinion polls, but I do not think the problem should be addressed by banning the publication of poll results. Granted that most people are not very sophisticated about polling, it must also be granted that there is considerable disagreement about the requirements of democratic decision-making. I have personally shed an embarrassingly large amount of ink trying to specify necessary and sufficient conditions for good individual and group decision-making in democracies, e.g., in Michalos (1970a, b, 1971, 1972, 1978, 1980b, 1981c, 1985, 1987, 1988b).

According to Converse (1987, p. Si5), "… virtually all of the major figures before 1940—including George Gallup, Elmo Roper, and Archibald Crossley in the private sector, or Henry Wallace and Rensis Likert in the government at the [U.S.] Department of Argiculture—were strong on democratic principles and pleased to provide a means that the voice of the people might be more clearly heard to compete with the few voices in the ears of power. …" Furthermore, I am sure that these pioneers recognized the danger in their becoming and reproducing a new elite group of technicians who might stifle and distort the very populist voices they were trying to amplify. That danger is still with us, and I hope my proposals in section "A Model Set of Disclosure Standards for the Publication of Poll Results During Election Campaigns" will significantly address it.

15. Polls "invade the privacy of respondents" (Hoy 1989, p. 227).

    Reply This is a fairly old but pointless complaint about all survey research. People who feel that their privacy is invaded by pollsters usually just refuse to respond. There is some evidence indicating that in the United States refusal rates are increasing, e.g., in Groves (1987), Gollin (1987) and Frankel and Frankel (1987). Indeed, the problem was perceived to be so serious there that in 1977 the Committee on National Statistics of the Commission on Behavioral and Social Sciences and Education of the U.S. National Academy of Sciences established a Panel on Incomplete Data. The Panel published a three-volume report in 1983. As I mentioned above (section "Survey Research"), nonresponse does create problems for pollsters and for anyone interested in correctly interpreting poll results. But none of these problems involves citizens' privacy. The latter is easily protected by the citizens themselves.

16. The publication of poll results can "make cowards of politicians, generating a reluctance for decision-making on issues that does not serve us well" (Hoy 1989, p. 227).

    Reply If any politicians are disposed to abandon their principles or their own best judgment about what must be done in the interests of the good of the country as a result of hostile polls, it would be helpful to be able to identify and replace them.

Arguments Against Banning the Publication of Any Poll Results During Election Campaigns

Following are 16 arguments that might be offered by someone opposed to banning the publication of any poll results during election campaigns.

1. "Voters are entitled to as much information as they care to digest when making their decision" (*Toronto Star*, May 4, 1990, p. A26; Reid in *Hearings* for Winnipeg, p. 5).
2. Favourable poll results can encourage workers to continue their efforts.
3. Candidates and other key players will always want to have polls for their internal use. So restricting publication of polls would make voters significantly disadvantaged compared to political elites regarding relevant information (*Toronto Star*, May 4, 1990, p. A26).
4. Any attempt to restrict publication of poll results might be challenged as a violation of the 1982 Charter of Rights and Freedoms (Hoy 1989, p. 220; Reid in *Hearings* for Winnipeg, p. 4). The prohibition of third-party advertising that was built into the 1974 Election Expenses Act was struck down as a violation of freedom of expression by the Alberta Supreme Court in 1984 and was not appealed.
   Stevens (1990a, p. B3) suggested that Section 33 of the Charter (the "notwithstanding" clause) might be invoked to override the freedom of expression clause, and in a later article, he indicated clearly that what would be at stake in such a move would be an assessment of the value of fair elections versus the right to free expression (Stevens 1990b, p. B3). I will have more to say about free expression and the pursuit of truth in the next section.
5. For all its limitations and disadvantages, polling may produce better information about what people think, feel and want than any of the standard alternatives. That seems to be the view of academic and commercial pollsters, and their sponsors and clients. Converse (1987, p. S16) was surely right when he wrote that "… the political impact of public opinion data would be quite muffled indeed if politicians themselves gave such data no credence." But politicians are hardly alone. According to Sudman and Bradburn (1987, pp. S67–S78), in the United States alone "The number of firms conducting either public opinion polls or market research surveys now numbers in the thousands, with an annual dollar volume of over two billion dollars, … [and] … there are approximately 50 organizations conducting surveys in a university setting." As well, Turner and Martin (1984, pp. 43–44) noted that "survey research presently provides one of the prime sources of courtroom testimony as to community prejudice" in the United States.
6. A national Gallup Poll taken in 1977 found that 57% of sampled Canadians opposed the banning of pre-election polls, while 32% favoured such banning (Hoy 1989, p. 222).

7. The issue of restricting publication of poll results might never have arisen and might be disposed of easily "if the media practised the social responsibility they claim to treasure" (Hoy 1989, p. 224).
8. Polls can help citizens "understand where their opinions and values fit in the range of attitudes about issues that affect their lives and their country" (Goldfarb and Axworthy 1988, p. xi).
9. According to Goldfarb and Axworthy (1988, p. xi), "Polls are not plebiscites, … [but] … they provide instant feedback on the most important issue." Although it is certainly an exaggeration to claim that they provide "instant feedback" and, as I have already shown, many critics believe that during elections polls on "the most important issues" are neglected in favour of polls on who is winning for whatever reason (i.e., candidate popularity polls), it does seem fair to say that polls can provide timely information for average citizens and inside operators prior to election day.
10. Goldfarb and Axworthy (1988, p. xi) also claim that "Polls create an involved citizenry. For the voter, polls may make the political process more gratifying, challenging and thought-provoking." (Whidden in *Hearings* for Thompson, p. 2 takes a similar line.) I think there is a heavy dose of optimism in this assertion, but the optimism would have a good chance of being justified if pollsters would undertake more of the issue-oriented polling that critics charge they typically neglect.
11. We have seen that some people would restrict polls because poll results might frighten politicians. On the contrary, Goldfarb and Axworthy (1988, p. xi) advocate polling during elections precisely because "Polls put pressure on politicians. In the shadow of public opinion and public accountability, politicians cannot lead blindly." While one might argue that there is so much information overload and confusion created by having so many polls that politicians really are not faced with any constraints as a result of any particular poll results, I think that on particular issues the results of diverse polls frequently point fairly dramatically in one direction and do create some pressure. Francis Fox and Serge Joyal recommended banning the publication of poll results for the last ten days prior to an election because of the "pollution" resulting from too many polls (*Hearings* for Montreal, p. 4). Steeves (*Hearings* for Moncton, p. 6) took a similar line.

    Going a step farther, Goldfarb and Axworthy (1988, p. xvii) claim that "Today's politicians have access to very little information that is not also available to the public. … No longer do we see ourselves electing, or hiring, politicians as wiser, more knowledgeable sages to protect us with their deeper insight into the means of attaining the public good. … What one knows, the other knows. What one wants, the other one can engineer." I am sure these optimistic remarks would be regarded as incredible to the Commissioner of Information for the federal Access to Information Act (Vienneau 1989, p. A14). While I would agree that today's citizens are probably better informed than their predecessors, I would doubt that the publication of public opinion polls is especially responsible for our advantages. After all, besides having more polls, we also have an expanded educational system and more media outlets reaching more people than ever before.

12. Poll results can be useful in the generation of ideas regarding new policies and programs (Goldfarb and Axworthy 1988, p. xi; Crespi 1980, pp. 43–44). Presumably this applies primarily to issue-oriented polls rather than to candidate preference polls, though results that are very positive or negative for candidates can generate plenty of ideas too.
13. Such results can be used for setting agendas for public discussion of important issues and "engineering" consent in the best sense of this term (Goldfarb and Axworthy 1988, pp. xi–xii). Although these possibilities present opportunities for abuse along the lines suggested above, it cannot be denied that they also provide opportunities for significant benefits. Because there are many other ways to obtain such benefits, one must weigh the likely consequences of using polls versus other instruments in particular cases. But that seems to grant no more than any reasonable person would insist upon regarding any course of action (Michalos 1978).
14. Poll results may be used to obtain a balanced assessment of social conditions against mere economic assessments. Like the two previous points, this applies primarily to issue-oriented polls.
15. They might be used to facilitate comparisons among the attitudes and beliefs of different regions, cities and other groups.
16. Given our proximity to American media, "no prohibition can be completely effective, … no statute to that effect would have any force outside Canada's boundaries" (Hnatyshyn 1986, p. 27).

Proposed Bills Banning the Publication of Poll Results During Election Campaigns

According to the *White Paper on Election Law Reform* published in June 1986, "More than 20 Private Members' bills have been introduced in the Canadian House of Commons with the purpose of either prohibiting the publication of polls or to control the methodology of polls published in newspapers during campaigns. Several debates on this issue were held in the House in recent years" (p. 26).

I was able to track down eight bills, including several duplicates, from the House and only one extensive debate. I also found one bill from the Ontario Legislature. Most of the bills that I found are little more than a paragraph long. So it will be easy to review them.

Bill C-213, "An Act to amend the Canada Elections Act" was introduced by Robert C. Coates on October 15, 1974. It is virtually identical to Bill C-361 introduced by Harold T. Herbert on October 22, 1976.

According to Bill C-213, Section 105 of the Canada Elections Act would be amended by inserting after subsection (l), "(2a) No person, company or corporation shall, in any province after the issue of the writ for an election, or after the dissolution of Parliament or the occurrence of a vacancy in consequence of which a writ for an election is eventually issued, and before the hour of closing of the polls in such province, publish the result or purported result of a poll of the political opinions of the electors or any of them in any electoral district or districts in Canada, whether such publication is by radio or television, broadcast, or by newspaper, news-sheet, poster, bill-board, handbill, or in any other manner."

The explanatory note following the text says that "The purpose of this amendment is to prohibit, and to make punishable as an illegal practice, the publication in any manner before an election day of the results of a poll of the political opinions of the electors. The proposed amendment does not prohibit the taking of such a poll for private purposes."

Bill C-266 introduced by Harold T. Herbert on October 31, 1977 is very similar to C-213. Bill C-266 bans what C-213 bans, but the former explicitly mentions opinion polls related to referenda and candidates in federal elections.

Two points should be emphasized about C-213 and C-266. First, they would ban publishing poll results concerning all political opinions during an election, including opinions about issues as well as candidates. Second, because they are quite general prohibitions in terms of their temporal scope and types of polls, all of the arguments listed above against banning the publication of poll results would be applicable to them.

Bill C-364 introduced by Benno Friesen on October 31, 1977 would ban the publication of polls throughout election campaigns provided that the polls are about "any candidate or registered party." Although the explanatory notes for this bill are virtually identical to those for the previous bills, the test of this bill represents a significant departure from the others. This bill is apparently designed to eliminate the publication of the results of candidate and party popularity/preferences polls. If that is the correct reading of the bill, then it would directly address the second listed objection that critics raise against the publication of poll results during elections (i.e., section "Arguments for Banning the Publication of Some or All Poll Results During Election Campaigns, and Replies to Them", no. 2). The only bill on polling that I found in the Ontario Legislature had the same prohibition as C-364. It was numbered C-79 and was introduced by George Samis in 1979.

The only extensive debate I found in the House of Commons concerned Bill C-213 (*Commons Debates,* pp. 1816–1823, November 29, 1974). Coates defended his bill by mentioning some version of arguments listed in section "Arguments for Banning the Publication of Some or All Poll Results During Election Campaigns, and Replies to Them" above, namely numbers 2 (turning elections into horse races), 7 (bandwagon effects), 8 (misleading polls) and 12 (absence of publication standards). Although the debate took place prior to the introduction of the 1982 Charter, he addressed a version of the freedom of expression argument (no. 4, section "Arguments Against Banning the Publication of Any Poll Results During Election Campaigns") as follows. "I do not know about the radio and television stations, but many of the newspapers in this nation become very upset by any suggestion that they should be prevented from using polls. They say this would be curtailment of freedom of speech. I say in answer to that that any time the press does not provide accurate information to the public, based on sound facts, that information should not appear in the newspapers. I say there is no curtailment of freedom involved if the newspapers are prevented from using information which, in the first instance, is not authentic. All too often newspapers have neither the staff, the time nor the capability to produce accurate information in respect of what they endeavour to place before the public about an event that is taking place." (Recall section "Arguments for Banning the Publication of Some or All Poll Results During Election Campaigns, and Replies to Them", nos. 11 and 12).

There is, of course, an enormous literature on freedom of speech or more generally of expression. Without pretending to address all of the important issues related to this freedom, I would like to present a brief overview based on one of my earlier writings. Interested readers can consult the longer an earlier discussion at their leisure.

> People have traditionally defended free speech or expression on two grounds. For some it has been a matter of moral principle that people ought to be allowed to express their views without fear of reprisals. While it may be a defeasible moral right, it is nevertheless a fundamental moral right, like the right to life, for example. For others, free expression has been defended as a matter of epistemological good sense. These people are more interested in the pursuit of truth and the avoidance of falsehood than they are in moral principles, and they see the free expression of ideas as a necessary condition of their epistemic aims.
>
> Of course, no one has to choose between these two different grounds for defending free expression, but historically I think people have tended to lean toward one or the other as especially weighty. If one is primarily interested in the free expression of fictional or visual material (stories, films, paintings, sculptures) then one's defence might run more smoothly from moral grounds, while if one is primarily interested in the free expression of nonfictional or descriptively accurate material, then one's defence might run more smoothly from epistemic grounds. The point I want to emphasize here, however, is that the two grounds often coalesce. Indeed, I suspect that this is typically the case (Michalos 1987, p. 353).

I suppose that people opposed to banning the publication of poll results during elections would be inclined to use the epistemic defence of free expression more than the moral defence, but in either case freedom of expression cannot be taken as a licence to intentionally publish misleading or false reports. From an epistemic point of view, the publication of misleading or false reports would be objectionable because such reports directly undermine the epistemic grounds for free expression. So, insisting on allowing such reports would be inconsistent with the very goal that freedom of expression is supposed to be pursuing. From a moral point of view, the publication of misleading or false reports would be objectionable because such reports would undermine our pursuit of human well-being indirectly as a result of people believing and acting in accordance with an inaccurate view of reality.

Philosophic niceties aside, virtually everyone thinks that lying or intentionally spreading falsehoods is morally wrong and, in some circumstances, it is also illegal, e.g., in cases of false advertising, libel and slander. So, anyone inclined to argue for the moral supremacy of free expression over telling the truth would have an uphill battle at best. Indeed, insofar as free expression is regarded as taking precedence over telling the truth, the latter is significantly undermined. What good could it do to urge people to tell the truth, and then to allow that it is more important to say anything they like?

As a matter of fact, at the beginning of this century two great philosophers, the American William James and the Englishman W.K. Clifford, carried out a somewhat famous exchange of views over what is called the ethics of belief (Michalos 1978, pp. 204–218). This is not the place to review that exchange, but I merely want to indicate that several of the arguments used by both James and Clifford were designed to establish that one has a moral obligation not only to tell the truth as one sees it, which everyone will grant, but also to make a reasonable attempt to pursue the truth and avoid falsehood. In general they argued as I did in the preceding paragraph. That is, it would be epistemologically and morally wrong to urge people to take truth-telling seriously but to allow them to be frivolous regarding the pursuit of truth and the avoidance of falsehood. In short, freedom of expression cannot be a licence to express anything that takes one's fancy, under any and every possible circumstance.

Following Coate's remarks in favor of C-213, C.-A. Gauthier offered his support using some versions of arguments no. 8 (misleading polls) and no. 13 (media sponsored polls) in section "Arguments for Banning the Publication of Some or All Poll Results During Election Campaigns, and Replies to Them". Serge Joyal spoke against the bill. Although he granted that the publication of poll results could and probably did influence some voters, he thought the influence was exaggerated. In effect he rejected arguments 4–8 in section "Arguments for Banning the Publication of Some or All Poll Results During Election Campaigns, and Replies to Them". Interestingly enough, he cited some survey research indicating that polls had no affect on voter turn-out or switches between one party or another. (Recall the comments of Reid and others above, section "Arguments for Banning the Publication of Some or All Poll Results During Election Campaigns, and Replies to Them", Reply to no. 7). In defence of polling, he mentioned a version of argument 5 (section "Arguments Against Banning the Publication of Any Poll Results During Election Campaigns", scientific status of polls) and the high credibility of survey research undertaken by reputable agencies like Statistics Canada, e.g., regarding the measurement of unemployment rates. Rather than a ban on polls during elections, he recommended careful consideration of appropriate regulations and standards of good practice. In particular, he mentioned the importance of having surveys undertaken by agencies "famous" as specialists, with "a proven method", a "representative" sample and a clearly articulated time period for any surveys.

Joyal's bottom line seemed fairly close to that of Coates as the latter concluded his remarks. "At the same time," Coates said, "so that members of Parliament cannot be charged with limiting freedom of the press in any way, I would accept as an alternative guidelines established by Parliament that would tell the media that if they are to produce the results of polls during an election campaign, and place these results before the public as accurate and authentic information on which the public should be able to rely, then the media will have to follow a set of rules and regulations to the effect that it must be shown how many people were encompassed by a poll, that the poll was national in its investigative function, or provincial if the poll being placed before the public purports to give a reading on the trends in a given province. … There are many other considerations, but I believe there should be a substantial contact with the people in the nation, that all parts of the nation must be involved, and that there should be a minimal doubt factor" (*Commons Debates,* pp. 1817–1818, November 29, 1974).

The reference to surveying "all parts of the nation" is included because Coates believed that "Far too often, especially in respect of Gallup polls produced in this country, there is no mention of the attitudes of the people who live in the four eastern provinces." Typical Gallup polls draw such small samples from the Atlantic provinces ($N < 150$) that any comments made about the attitudes of people in those provinces have error margins too wide to make them useful. Unfortunately, instead of drawing larger samples in order to justify making reliable and valid comments about those provinces, usually pollsters have just gone ahead and made the comments anyhow.

Two other Members of Parliament made substantive comments on C-213. Jack Pearsall objected to the bill mainly on the grounds of argument 3 (denying information to voters that is available to insiders) in section "Arguments Against Banning the Publication of Any Poll Results During Election Campaigns", while Stanley Knowles challenged it as a limitation of free expression or of a free press (i.e., no. 4, section "Arguments Against Banning the Publication of Any Poll Results During Election Campaigns"). The following remarks by Knowles are especially relevant to the moral point of view outlined above in section "A Moral Point of View".

> A concern that is really hitting us in our society today is the extent to which freedom of thought and freedom of decision as to the kind of people we want to be is terribly thwarted by commercial interests. I am glad there is some legislation on the books regarding misleading advertising. I think we have to go a lot further. I hope that one day we will have media, print and electronic, educational forces, religious forces and all the rest, the aim of which will not be some particular axe to be ground and not some particular profit to be made, but the real enrichment of human life.

I suppose many of us share Knowles's hope, and I think some appropriate legislation can make a positive contribution toward realizing it.

Proposed Bills Providing Disclosure Standards for the Publication of Poll Results During Election Campaigns

While banning the publication of poll results during an election would effectively eliminate many or all of the costs cited by critics, depending on how severe a blackout is legislated, many or all of the benefits cited by the other side would also be eliminated. Therefore, as I have already suggested, I think it would be preferable to provide standards for the publication of poll results. This strategy would allow Canadians to maintain and even increase the benefits of public opinion polling while significantly reducing the costs.

Although the bills that have been introduced have been intended to apply only to polls undertaken during elections, I think that any good reasons for insisting on quality standards at such periods would be applicable to the publication of poll results at any time. In the long run it would be self-defeating to insist on a certain quality for a 6 week period every 4 or 5 years, and to allow sub-standard material to be published the rest of the time.

I suppose that once Canadians get a clear idea of the difference between a quality product and the quick and dirty imitations that are frequently published these days, there will be a dechne in the marketability of the latter. So, it might be sufficient to legislate standards only for election periods and let nature take its course for non-election periods. At any rate, I will proceed on the premise that legislation for election periods is sufficient.

Dean Whiteway introduced Bill C-265, "An Act respecting public opinion polls," on October 30, 1978. I believe it is substantially the same as Bill C-455 and Bill C-459, which he introduced on May 15, 1978 and June 7, 1978, respectively.

Bill C-265 would amend the Canada Elections Act so that immediately after Section 105, there would be inserted

105.1 (1) Where, during an election, a person publishes by radio or television broadcast or by newspaper or periodical publication in a result or purported result of a survey of the political preferences of electors with respect to a candidate, registered party or election issue, he shall also publish the following additional data:

(a) who commissioned the survey, who paid for it, and who carried it out;
(b) when the survey was carried out;
(c) a description of the target population of the survey;
(d) a description of the procedure followed to select a sample of the target population;
(e) the size of the sample selected;
(f) a description of the procedure followed to collect the survey data;
(g) the amount of non-response to each survey question for which a result is published; and
(h) an estimate of the sampling error for each numerical result published.

Any violation of the provisions of the bill would be "punishable on summary conviction and liable to a fine of up to ten thousand dollars." Commenting on Bill C-455, Whiteway said, "Mr. Speaker, my bill would not disallow public opinion polls during the time of a writ period, but simply make certain requirements, namely, stating who took a poll, the sampling and the results of the poll, in order that Canadians are able to ascertain whether the poll was an adequate one and not simply one done by a political party with no real basis of sampling."

To get some idea of how demanding the eight items of C-265 are compared to current practice, one might consider the information provided in typical commercial polls published in a daily newspaper, e.g., the *Toronto Star*. Usually we are given (a) who did it, (b) when, (c) the target population, (e) the sample size and some of (h) the sampling error. That is, typically less than half of the information required by the items in C-265 is provided.

Item by item, what difference would the additional material make?

(a) If we knew who commissioned and paid for all or part of a survey, would that allow us to judge the results any better? It often happens that a single survey is constructed of questions paid for by different people. We might discover exactly who paid for a survey or some of the questions, which would certainly be additional information. But it would not allow us to judge the results any better. Even if we found that whoever paid for the poll really wanted to mislead us somehow with the results of the poll, it is not clear that this information should have any affect on our judgment of the poll results. We would be able to make a harsh judgment about the purchaser and the pollster on the grounds of their intention to mislead us, but that is irrelevant to the reliability and validity of the poll results (Michalos 1969, 1970c). The latter has to be assessed on the basis of the methodology employed, not on anyone's intentions.

    On the other hand, the identification of the pollster is relevant to our judgment of the likely reliability and validity of poll results. After all, as we saw in section "Arguments for Banning the Publication of Some or All Poll Results During Election Campaigns, and Replies to Them", no. 12, neither commercial, government nor academic pollsters work in a vacuum. They have peers, competitors and concerned critics. Their peers and competitors frequently survey the same populations regarding the same issues. They develop relatively visible track records that allow us to assess their long term reliability and validity compared to that of their peers and competitors. In polling as in other areas of life, a good reputation is not a guarantee of quality, but it is relevant. In the absence of specific data and the expertise to analyze it oneself, one may have little else to go on but the good name of the pollster. In short, regarding (a) I would keep the pollster's name and not require the other two names.

(b) Since people's opinions may change with the passage of time and the occurrence of events, the dates of polls are certainly relevant to our judgments regarding their results. So, this requirement is uncontroversial.

(c) Unless we know what population was supposed to be surveyed, either in part or as a whole, we cannot make any useful judgments about poll results. To be informed that certain percentages of anonymous respondents some place in the world answered some questions some way is simply worthless. So, the target population requirement must stay.

(d) At some level of analysis, the procedure used to draw the sample (i.e., the sampling design) must be known. Different sampling procedures have different advantages and disadvantages, yielding different estimated reliabilities and validities for poll results. The problem I have with this requirement is knowing how much of this sort of information to insist upon. For statisticians it is enough to say, for example, that a simple random probability sample was drawn from a list of all households in some area. They will know that means every household in the area had an equal chance or probability of being drawn. But for a variety of reasons related to the actual distributions of populations in different areas of our country and the costs of surveying them, simple random samples are virtually never drawn. Pollsters stratify, cluster and weigh samples in various ways to accommodate geography, settlement patterns, costs and so on. Descriptions of their sampling designs that are precise enough to be useful to experts interested in double-checking their calculations would be useless noise for most people. One might require that such information should be available to anyone who wants to contact the pollster directly, but it would be pointless to require the popular media to publish such information. I am not even sure that it would be fair to require pollsters to make such information available to everyone who asks for it. While the fundamentals of sampling theory have been around for over 40 years, there may be cost-effective competitive advantages to some procedures involving fieldwork and computers that ought to be enjoyed by their inventors. There may be proprietary rights involved similar to those for copyrights and patents. Still, the fact that academic and government pollsters are expected to provide complete information on sampling designs as requested by anyone inclines me to expect the same from commercial pollsters. So, while I would not endorse item (d) as it stands, I would recommend that pollsters should be required to disclose their sampling designs on demand.

(e) I suppose no one questions the requirement regarding disclosure of total sample sizes. Pollsters routinely provide such information. However, the fact that the same pollsters routinely fail to provide sub-sample sizes indicates a serious problem, and a serious moral problem at that. Pollsters know that the error margins applicable to their total samples usually do not apply to their sub-samples, but they seldom say so. While some people are aware of the need for greater caution in judging poll results for sub-samples, most people probably are not. Most people probably just assume that the error margins mentioned at the end of the reports are roughly applicable to all the statistics mentioned in the report.

Insofar as all of these facts are as clear to commercial pollsters as they are to me, I concluded long ago that pollsters intentionally mislead the public on this score. Since I find it incredible to believe that the editors of our major media are any less informed than I am about this issue, I believe they also are guilty of intentionally misleading the public. It seems to me that the behavior of pollsters and media editors on this score is patently immoral and it ought to be illegal. So, in item (e) I would insist upon full disclosure of every sample and sub-sample size about which any reports are made.

(f) There are basically only three alternatives here, namely, face-to-face interviews, telephone interviews and mail-out surveys, and most of the evidence indicates that very similar returns can be obtained from the three procedures. I would accept the requirement because it is very easy to satisfy, not because satisfying it provides especially useful information.
(g) As suggested above in section "Survey Research", nonresponse figures are as important as response figures because originally specified sample and sub-sample sizes can be significantly distorted by nonresponse rates, resulting in very misleading percentages being reported. For all public opinion polls, it is highly unlikely that everyone is home when called, willing and able, and in fact answers all the questions. Typically, there must be some nonresponse and it must be accommodated somehow, with additional calls on other people, special weighting by quotas, substitution of mean values for missing values or something. In the absence of information on nonresponse and its treatment, one cannot judge the percentages that pollsters report. Therefore, I would not only insist on the publication of nonresponse rates for each question reported, I would also want some indication of how nonresponses are treated. Since most pollsters will have preferred ways of dealing with nonresponse, most of them will only have to formulate a single sentence or phrase to be included with all their releases.
(h) Perhaps enough has been said regarding the necessity of providing the sampling error margins for each question under (e) above. Since part of the point of publishing sample sizes is to allow one to estimate error margins, most people might be better served by simply publishing the latter. However, I think that the publication of sample sizes probably makes people a bit more cautious about poll results and that is probably beneficial. If there is one thing about which all pollsters agree, it is that while all information-gathering methods are subject to a variety of errors, public opinion polls based on probability sampling are subject to measurable errors. Thus, there can be no excuse for not requiring the publication of measurable error margins with all poll results. Insofar as error margins are not strictly measurable, appropriate cautionary remarks should be required.

The federal government's *White Paper on Election Law Reform* included most of the eight items of C-265, arranged in a different order. The list in the former (p. 27) runs as follows:

(A) The name and address of the organization which conducted the inquiry;
(B) The population polled, the size of the sample and the percentage of completed interviews;
(C) The dates of the first and last completed interviews;
(D) The name and address of the person or organization who paid for the conduct of the inquiry;
(E) A summary description of any normalization procedure used in order to account for the under- or over-representation of some strata of the population in the sample.

The omitted items are those regarding (f) survey method and (h) error margins. I suppose (E) would cover the issues I discussed in relation to the treatment of non-response, and I suppose addresses are unnecessary.

The last bill introduced that I am aware of is Bill C-79, introduced for the government by Ray Hnatyshyn on June 30, 1987. It applies to polls concerning candidates and registered parties, and would require disclosure of:

(a) the name and address of the person or organization that conducted the inquiry;
(b) the size of the sample;
(c) the dates of the first and last completed interviews;
(d) the name and address of the person or organization who paid for the conduct of the opinion poll;
(e) the margin of error if calculable; and
(f) the exact wording of each question the answers to which led to the results so printed and broadcast.

Fines for individual violators of any of these provisions have a maximum value of $5 000 and for corporate violators $10 000.

The requirements of C-79 are similar to those of the *White Paper,* with the important addition of item (f) regarding the exact wording of questions. The latter is obviously absolutely necessary.

A Model Set of Disclosure Standards for the Publication of Poll Results During Election Campaigns

The results of my consideration of alternative disclosure standards to be met in the publication of poll results during election campaigns may be summarized as follows. There should be routine disclosure of the:

(a) name of the person or organization that conducted the inquiry;
(b) name or description of the target population;
(c) size of the total sample and any sub-samples used;
(d) dates of the first and last completed interviews;
(e) margins of sampling and (if calculable) nonsampling errors for any reported percentage results;
(f) exact wording of each question about which results are reported.
(g) non-response rates and method of treating non-responses;
(h) data collection procedures.

While routine disclosure of sampling designs is not required, such disclosure should be available on request by interested persons.

As suggested earlier, although these requirements are specifically intended for polls conducted during elections and I would recommend legislation to that end (including appropriate fines for violators), I can see no good reason not to place such disclosure requirements on the publication of all polls. Indeed, I think such requirements would yield significant net benefits (as described in section "Arguments Against Banning the Publication of Any Poll Results During Election Campaigns") for Canadians and the development of democracy in our country.

Probably one consequence of the introduction of the recommended legislation would be a reduction in the amount of published poll results. Relatively incomplete passing references to such results would be effectively prohibited. Editors would either have to provide enough information in their stories to satisfy the requirements of the legislation or pick another story. While some people will claim this is unnecessary and unwarranted interference with free expression or a free market, I have already explained why I think such claims are unreasonable. Communities have as much right to protect themselves against intellectual pollution as they do against environmental pollution.

References

Alwin, D. F., & Campbell, R. T. (1987). Continuity and change in methods of survey data analysis. *Public Opinion Quarterly, 51,* S139–S155.

Andrews, F. M., & Withey, S. B. (1974). Developing measures of perceived life quality: Results from several national surveys. *Social Indicators Research, 1,* 1–26.

Andrews, F. M., & Withey, S. B. (1976). *Social indicators of well-being*. New York: Plenum Press.

Bailar, B. A., & Rothwell, N. D. (1984). Measuring employment and unemployment. In C. F. Turner & E. Martin (Eds.), *Surveying subjective phenomena* (Vol. 2, pp. 129–142). New York: Russell Sage Foundation.

Beggan, J. K,, Messick, D. M., & Allison, S. T. (1988). Social values and egocentric bias: Two tests of the might over morality hypothesis. *Journal of Personality and Social Psychology, 55,* 606–611.

Beniger, J. R. (1987). Toward and old new paradigm: The half-century flirtation with mass society'. *Public Opinion Quarterly, 51,* S46–S66.

Boyer, P. (1990). 10 steps to a better election law. *Policy Options Politiques, 11,* 32–34.

Converse, P. E. (1987). Changing conceptions of public opinion in the political process. *Public Opinion Quarterly, 51,* S12–S25.

Converse, J. M., & Schuman, H. (1984). The manner of inquiry: An analysis of survey question form across organizations and over time. In C. F. Turner & E. Martin (Eds.), *Surveying subjective phenomena* (Vol. 2, pp. 283–316). New York: Russell Sage Foundation.

Converse, P. E., & Traugott, M. W. (1986). Assessing the accuracy of polls and surveys. *Science, 234,* 1094–1098.

Crespi, I. (1980). The case of presidential popularity. In A. H. Cantril (Ed.), *Polling on the issues* (pp. 28–45). Cabin John, Maryland: Seven Locks Press.

Davis, E. E., & Fine-Davis, M. (1978–79). On the relationship between objective and subjective social indicators: Implications for social planning in Ireland. *Journal of the Statistical and Social Inquiry Society of Ireland, 24*, 91–131.

DeBono, K. G., & Harnish, R. J. (1988). Source expertise, source attractiveness, and the processing of persuasive information: A functional approach. *Journal of Personality and Social Psychology, 55,* 541–546.

DeMaio, T. J. (1984). Social desirability and survey measurement: A review. In C. F. Turner & E. Martin (Eds.), *Surveying subjective phenomena* (Vol. 2, pp. 257–282). New York: Russell Sage Foundation.
Frankel, M. R., & Frankel, L. R. (1987). Fifty years of survey sampling in the United States. *Public Opinion Quarterly, 51*, S127–S138.
Germond, J. W. (1980). The impact of polling on journalism. In A. H. Cantril (Ed.), *Polling on the issues* (pp. 20–27). Cabin john, Maryland: Seven Locks Press.
Goldfarb, M., & Axworthy, T. (1988). *Marching to a different drummer: An essay on the liberals and conservatives in convention*. Toronto: Stoddart Pub. Co., Ltd.
Gollin, A. E. (1987). Polling and the news media. *Public Opinion Quarterly, 51,* S86–S94.
Groves, R. M. (1987). Research on survey data quality. *Public Opinion Quarterly, 51,* S156–S172.
Hessing, D. J., Elffers, H., & Weigel, R. H. (1988). Exploring the limit of self-reports and reasoned action: an investigation of the psychology of tax evasion behavior. *Journal of Personality and Social Psychology, 54,* 405–413.
Hippler, H.-J., Schwarz, N., & Sudman, S. (Eds.). (1987). *Social information processing and survey methodology*. New York: Springer.
Hnatyshyn, R. (1986). *White Paper on Election Law Reform,* Released in June by the Honourable Ray Hnatyshyn, President of the Queen's Privy Council for Canada and Government House Leader.
Holtgraves, T., Srull, T. K., & Socall, D. (1989). Conversation memory: The effects of speaker status on memory for the assertiveness of conversation remarks. *Journal of Personality and Social Psychology, 56,* 149–160.
Hoy, C. (1989). *Margin of error: Pollsters and the manipulation of Canadian politics*. Toronto: Key Porter Books Ltd.
Inglehart, R., & Rabier J.-R. (1986). Aspirations adapt to situations—But why are the Belgians so much happier than the French? A cross-cultural analysis of the subjective quality of life. In F. M. Andrews (Ed.), *Research on the quality of life* (pp. 1–56). Ann Arbor: Institute for Social Research, University of Michigan.
Jacoby, L. L., Kelley, C., Brown, J., & Jasechko, J. (1989). Becoming famous overnight: Limits on the ability to avoid unconscious influences of the past. *Journal of Personality and Social Psychology, 56,* 326–338.
Katz, E. (1987). Communications research since Lazarsfeld. *Public Opinion Quarterly, 51,* S25–S46.
Kozma, A., & Stones, M. J. (1988). Social desirability in measures of subjective well-being: Age comparison. *Social Indicators Research, 20,* 1–14.
Krosnick, J. A., & Schuman, H. (1988). Attitude intensity importance, and certainty and susceptibility to response effects. *Journal of Personality and Social Psychology, 54,* 940–952.
Lee, R. M. (1989). *One hundred monkeys: The triumph of popular wisdom in Canadian politics*. Toronto: Macfarlane Walter and Ross.
MacKuen, M. B. (1984). Reality, the press and citizens' political agendas. In C. F. Turner & E. Martin (Eds.), *Surveying subjective phenomena* (Vol. 2, pp. 443–474). New York: Russell Sage Foundation.
Michalos, A. C. (1969). *Principles of logic*. Englewood Cliffs: Prentice-Hall Inc.
Michalos, A. C. (1970a). Cost-benefit versus expected utility acceptance rules. *Theory and Decision, 1,* 61–88.
Michalos, A. C. (1970b). The costs of decision-making. *Public Choice, 4,* 39–51.
Michalos, A. C. (1970c). *Improving your reasoning*. Englewood Cliffs: Prentice-Hall Inc.
Michalos, A. C. (1971). *The Popper-Carnap controversy*. The Hague: Martinus Nijhoff.
Michalos, A. C. (1972). Efficiency and morality. *The Journal of Value Inquiry, 6,* 137–143.
Michalos, A. C. (1978). *Foundations of decision-making*. Ottawa: Canadian Library of Philosophy.
Michalos, A. C. (1980a). North American social report In *Foundations, population and health* (Vol. 1). Dordrecht: D. Reidel Pub. Co.

Michalos, A. C. (1980b). A reconsideration of the idea of a science court. *Philosophy and Technology, 3,* 10–28.
Michalos, A. C. (1981a). North American social report. In *Science, education and recreation* (Vol. 3). Dordrecht: D. Reidel Pub. Co.
Michalos, A. C. (1981b). North American social report. In *Environment, transportation and housing* (Vol. 4). Dordrecht: D. Reidel Pub. Co.
Michalos, A. C. (1981c). Technology assessment, facts and values. *Research in Philosophy and Technology, 4,* 59–81.
Michalos, A. C. (1982). North American social report. In *Economics, religion and morality* (Vol. 5). Dordrecht: D. Reidel Pub. Co.
Michalos, A. C. (1985). Multiple discrepancies theory (MDT). *Social Indicators Research, 16,* 347–413.
Michalos, A. C. (1987). What makes people happy? In *Levekarsforskning Konferanserapport (Proceedings of the Seminar on Welfare Research)* (pp. 12–93). Oslo, Norway: Norwegian Research Council for Science and the Humanities.
Michalos, A. C. (1988a). A case for a progressive annual net wealth tax. *Public Affairs Quarterly, 2,* 105–140.
Michalos, A. C. (1988b). Integrated development planning using socio-economic and quality-of-life indicators. In *Innovative approaches to development planning* (pp. 113–216). Paris: Unesco.
Michalos, A. C. (1990). The impact of trust on business international security and the quality of life. *Journal of Business Ethics, 9,* 619–638.
Miller, D. T., & Turnbull, W. (1986). Expectancies and interpersonal process. *Annual Review of Psychology, 37,* 233–256.
Moum, T. (1981). Social inequality, social status, and quality of life. *Psychiatry and Social Science, 1,* 177–195.
Moum, T. (1983, July 11–15). *Resignation and quality of life: On the self-regulatory nature of subjective well-being.* Paper presented at the World Conference on Systems, Caracas, Venezuela.
Moum, T. (1988). Yea-saying and mood-of-the-day effects in self-reported quality of life. *Social Indicators Research, 20,* 117–139.
Nisbett, R. E., & Bellows, N. (1977). Verbal reports about causal influences on social judgments: Private access versus public theories. *Journal of Personality and Social Psychology, 35,* 613–624.
Nisbett, R. E., & Wilson, T. D. (1977). Telling more than we can know: Verbal reports on mental process. *Psychological Review, 84,* 231–259.
Ottati, V., Fishbein, M., & Middlestadt, S. E. (1988). Determinants of voter's beliefs about the candidates' stands on the issues: The role of evaluative bias heuristics and the candidates' expressed message. *Journal of Personality and Social Psychology, 55,* 517–529.
Roos, J. P. (1988). Behind the happiness barrier. *Social Indicators Research, 20,* 141–163.
Roper, B. W. (1980). The impact of journalism on polling. In A. H. Cantril (Ed.), *Polling on the issues* (pp. 15–19). Cabin john, Maryland: Seven Locks Press.
Royal Commission on Electoral Reform and Party Financing (1990). *Hearings* from various cities.
Schwarz, N. (1984, September). *Informative and directive functions of affective states in information processing.* Paper presented at the 23rd International Congress of Psychology, Acapulco, Mexico.
Smith, T. W. (1978). In search of house effects: A comparison of responses to various questions by different survey organizations. *Public Opinion Quarterly, 42,* 443–463.
Smith, T. W. (1982). House effects and the reproducibility of survey measurements: A comparison of the 1980 GSS and the 1980 American national election study. *Public Opinion Quarterly, 46,* 54–68.
Snyder, M. (1984). When belief creates reality. *Advances in Experimental Social Psychology, 18,* 247–305.
Stevens, G. (1990a, March 18). *Money's ruining electoral system* (p. B3). Toronto Star.

Stevens, G. (1990b, May 6). *Sorting out bugs in voting system* (p. B3). Toronto Star.

Strack, F., & Martin, L. L. (1987). Thinking, judging, and communicating: A process account of context effects in attitude surveys. In H.-J. Hippler, N. Schwarz & S. Sudman (Eds.), *Social information processing and survey methodology* (pp. 123–148). New York: Springer.

Sudman, S., & Bradburn, N. M. (1987). The organizational growth of public opinion research in the United States. *Public Opinion Quarterly, 51,* S67–S78.

Toronto Star (1990, May 4). Banning polls a big mistake (p. A26).

Turner, C. F. (1984). Why do surveys disagree? Some preliminary hypotheses and some disagreeable examples. In C. F. Turner & E. Martin (Eds.), *Surveying subjective phenomena* (Vol. 2, pp. 159–214). New York: Russell Sage Foundation.

Turner, C. F. & Martin, E. (Eds.). (1984). *Surveying subjective phenomena* (Vols. 1 and 2). New York: Russell Sage Foundation.

Tversky, A., & Kahneman, D. (1986). Rational choice and the framing of decisions. *Journal of Business, 59,* s251–s278.

Vienneau, D. (1989, June 28). *Information chief criticizes ministers.* Toronto Star.

Wedell, D. H., & Parducci, A. (1988). The category effect in social judgment: Experimental ratings of happiness. *Journal of Personality and Social Psychology, 55,* 341–356.

Wood, L. A., & Johnson, J. (1989). Life satisfaction among the rural elderly: What do the numbers mean? *Social Indicators Research, 21,* 379–408.

Chapter 12
Brief to the Ontario Cabinet Committee on North American Free Trade

Alex C. Michalos

Introduction

I would like to express my appreciation to the Government of Ontario, through its representatives in the Cabinet Committee, for holding these Public Hearings. They not only provide an opportunity for citizens to speak directly to their government on an issue of vital importance, but they also act as a catalyst to transform apathy into action. They draw our attention to the fact that once again the worst federal government in Canada's history is imposing its neoconservative agenda, its backward blueprint for irresistible underdevelopment, on an unwilling electorate today and on the unfortunate electorate of tomorrow. Most importantly, they call upon each of us to get informed and get involved. Democracy works exactly to the extent that individuals make it work by investing their private resources in the interest of the public good. For what it is worth, then, what follows is my personal contribution to this noble ideal.

My remarks are presented as answers to some fundamental questions regarding the Canada-US Free Trade Agreement (FTA) and the North American Free Trade Agreement (NAFTA). They are the result of my own reading of the texts of both Agreements, of critical reports by nonpartisan interest groups and of research produced by the federal New Democratic Party. They are partisan because, all things considered, I believe the positions articulated by the NDP, federally and provincially, are the right ones for Canada. At the very end of the paper, I briefly outline an alternative agenda for economic and political development. It is con-

Michalos, A.C.: 1993. Brief to the Ontario Cabinet Committee on North American, Free Trade. April 2, 1993, Kitchener, Ontario Copyright.

A.C. Michalos (✉)
University of Northern British Columbia, Prince George, BC, Canada
e-mail: michalos@brandonu.ca

A.C. Michalos, *How Good Policies and Business Ethics Enhance Good Quality of Life*, DOI 10.1007/978-3-319-50724-8_12

sistent with the federal NDP's recently released Strategy for a Full-Employment Economy, but has some different emphases.

Question 1: The NDP's position on the Canada/US trade deal (FTA) is abrogation rather than renegotiation. What's wrong with renegotiation?

Answer: Those who talk about renegotiating the FTA have not read NAFTA. If they had, they would realize that NAFTA is the renegotiation of FTA, and we lost even more.

For example, one reason Liberals call for renegotiation is to revise the subsidies code of the FTA. FTA recognizes only 2 kinds of subsidies as acceptable, namely, for oil and gas exploration and exploitation, and for military purposes. In effect, FTA recognizes US style development insofar as the US uses military industry as its chief development tool. However, in FTA we agreed to take 7 years to work out a new subsidies code, while in NAFTA we agreed to abandon that commitment. New codes might be developed through GATT, but in NAFTA we agreed to let the current US style code continue indefinitely. So, the Liberal issue of renegotiating the FTA subsidies code was addressed in NAFTA and settled in favour of the status quo.

A second example concerns the Liberals' claim to want to renegotiate to get more control over our energy and other resources. Again, a renegotiation took place with NAFTA, and again we gave up still more to the Americans. The detailed investment chapter in NAFTA puts more limits on our ability to manage our resource development, prohibiting performance requirements, content requirements, processing requirements, export/import balancing, and so on. This chapter guarantees there can be no managed trade in, for example, land transportation; there can be no more auto-pacts, which has been so successful for us. So, again the Liberal issue of renegotiating the FTA energy provisions was addressed in NAFTA and settled in favour of the status quo.

Question 2: Since NAFTA represents a renegotiation of the FTA, why can't we also renegotiate NAFTA? Apparently Bill Clinton is undertaking the negotiation of parallel agreements or side deals. Why is the NDP opposed to such side deals?

Answer: To answer this question, one must know exactly what is being proposed. Michael Wilson has been the clearest proponent of side deals, and his position is that such deals are in principle acceptable only if they are completely consistent with NAFTA. Put another way, Wilson is willing to add things to NAFTA that are consistent with its provisions, but he is not willing to consider anything that is inconsistent with NAFTA. In other words, in his view NAFTA may have some errors of omission, but there is nothing already included in NAFTA that ought to be excluded.

Thus, people who think (as I do) that NAFTA includes provisions that are anti-democratic, anti-labour and anti-environment/conservation cannot be expected to undertake a renegotiation of NAFTA based on the premise that all of these objectional provisions must be accepted precisely as they are, without any revisions or deletions. To enter into negotiations under such constraints would be either foolish or deceptive, or both.

Supposing there was some willingness on the part of those who signed the original deal to have wide-open discussions about trade among the three countries, then it might be worthwhile to enter into such discussions. No one in the NDP is opposed to increasing incomes through increased trade.

Question 3: Some critics of the NDP's position say that it is basically selfish because, by their own admission, Mexico will be a major beneficiary of NAFTA. That is, there seems to be a moral case in favour of supporting NAFTA in the interest of the poorest member of the agreement. What is the NDP's response to that?

Answer: There are a few considerations here. Although Mexico may well be the major beneficiary of NAFTA, there are good reasons for thinking that most Mexicans will probably be worse off with than without NAFTA.

First, one must realize that most of the investment being attracted to Mexico is going into the maquiladora region, as a result of the relatively lax rules regarding taxation, environmental pollution and labour standards.

Second, since this region has existed for about 20 years already without significant improvements in the working environment without NAFTA, it would be reasonable to predict that there would be no improvement in the future.

With NAFTA, however, it certain that the maquiladora conditions will spread to all of Mexico and create enormous pressures to drag down the working conditions of Canadians and Americans to very similar levels. This certainty is the result of a little-known provision in the NAFTA, on page I-M-42, which says that after 8 years from signing the deal, maquiladora producers can sell their products anywhere in Mexico. Therefore, anyone interested in competing with these producers for the Mexican market, will have to drive down their costs to the same level, presumably largely by the same means. Thus, the long run consequences of NAFTA will certainly be, on balance, devastating for Mexican as well as other North American workers.

Sometimes people recall passages from introductory economics texts that tell us that increases in trade will increase Mexicans' standard of living. In fact, increases in trade do not guarantee increases in standard of living. Mexican trade with the rest of the world has increased in the past decade, but the real wages of Mexicans have decreased.

Sometimes the same books are cited telling us that increases in productivity will lead to increases in Mexicans' standard of living. Again, however, increases in productivity do not guarantee increases in standard of living. Louisiana has higher levels of productivity than Michigan, but Michigan workers have a higher standard of living. Workers at the Ford plant at Hermosillo, Mexico are at least as productive as Ford workers in Ontario, but the Mexicans still make one seventh of what the Ontarions make.

As we have seen in Canada following implementation of the FTA, it is possible for exports to rise along with a rise in unemployment and a decline in overall output. It is also possible for overall output to rise along with rising unemployment, as it has, for example, when capital intensive manufacturing and farming are substituted for labour intensive alternatives. In fact, many Mexican critics of

NAFTA claim that its aim is precisely to implement a model of development that includes relatively high unemployment as a necessary consequence. Critics of the econometric models of such development correctly point out that the alleged net benefits to working people predicted by such models are the result of assuming full employment following implementation of the deal, i.e., assuming that every job lost will be matched by a job gained elsewhere. Empirical analyses of the performance of OECD countries over the past 20 years shows that almost never happens.

Addressing the issue of Canadians' moral obligations to the relatively poorer Mexicans, one would have to take some account of the alleged political abuses and violations of human rights, including the unjustified arrest, imprisonment, torture and murder of critics of current federal government policies like NAFTA. The problems involved in such accounting are familiar and substantial. Whatever one finally concludes regarding one's moral obligations in the light of such alleged abuses, it will probably remain controversial.

It is perhaps worthwhile to mention here that one of the motives for American and Canadian governments wanting to open up the Mexican market is to "help" the Mexican government continue to make payments on its debts to the former governments and commercial banks. At least part of the solution to the Mexican government's defaulting on its international loans in the early 1980s was to roll them over with new payment schedules that require increased exports to pay the additional interest costs, presumably without end. The fact that the defaults were mainly the result of the tight money policies of the U.S. Federal Reserve addressing the incoherent fiscal policies of the Reagan Administration is neglected in this solution. Instead of relieving the victims of their misery by cancelling the debts, the preferred solution merely alters the form of the misery. The moral implications of participating in this solution through NAFTA are considerable.

Question 4: Michael Wilson claims the FTA has been a success already because exports to the US have gone up since January 1989. So we may expect NAFTA to make things even better. If that is true, where is the problem?

Answer: First, if you examine the Canada to USA export statistics over the past 100 years, you will only find 10 years in which annual exports to the USA from Canada did not increase. Thus, since our exports to the USA have increased in 9 out of every 10 years for the past hundred years and we have only had the FTA for 4 years, it is preposterous to attribute export growth to the FTA. Export growth to the USA is the natural state of affairs.

Second, if you compare the growth in exports to the US for the 3 years prior to the FTA with those of the 3 years following the FTA, you will find that the growth in the prior years was nearly double the growth in the following years.

Third, Wilson never mentions the fact that our imports from the USA have gone up even faster than our exports south. More importantly, an important consequence of this net increase in imports is a loss of our domestic market share for Canadian producers, requiring a further loss of Canadian jobs and tax revenue. In fact, we have lost 4 times as many jobs permanently as the Americans have had in this recession.

Fourth, Wilson never mentions that the joint effect of the new export and import picture is that we now have the biggest deficits in our current account balance that we have ever had.

Fifth, Wilson never mentions that the recent export increases have been in crude petroleum, motor vehicles and wheat. In fact, one Stats Canada report on exports to the USA from Canada in the 1988–91 period had exported raw materials growing at 23% compared to manufactured goods growing at 2%. The increased export of raw materials like crude petroleum was to be expected, since we abandoned the opportunity to require any sort of processing of raw crude prior to export, leaving increased exports of the raw material as the only means of oil companies increasing their incomes. Again, selling unprocessed raw materials instead of high value added materials is part of the root cause of Canada's underdevelopment, and both FTA and NAFTA exacerbate this problem.

Motor vehicle exports are to some extent still managed by the auto pact agreement, though NAFTA will weaken the benefits for Canada. Still any use of motor vehicle trade statistics to make a case for our competitiveness or free trade is simply propaganda disguising the fact that such trade is managed by a cooperative agreement.

Sixth, Wilson never mentions the fact that since the implementation of the Canada-US deal, the share of Canada's total exports going to the USA has increased from 73 to 76%. That means that one effect of the deal was to make us even more dependent on the US market than we were before, which is exactly the opposite of the sort of trade development we should be encouraging.

Another way to look at this problem of over concentration on one market is to compare before and after figures for the growth in our exports to two other important markets, Japan and the European Community (EC). In the 3 years prior to the FTA, Canadian exports to Japan grew nearly 300%, compared to a net loss of 18% after the deal. In the 3 years prior to the FTA, Canadian exports to the EC grew nearly 60%, compared to 4% after the deal.

Seventh, since the deal was implemented, Canadian investments in the US have been twice as big as US investments in Canada. Besides, about 97% of the American investments here have been buyouts of Canadian businesses, not the creation of new businesses and jobs. Given the clause in NAFTA preventing buy-backs based on nationality, the original deal is making an impressive contribution to the permanent foreign ownership of our country.

While we are at it, it is worthwhile to mention that although Wilson claims we have had great success through the Dispute Settlement Panel decisions, the fact is that Canada won 4 out of 12 cases and the US won 7.

Question 5: The NDP claims NAFTA is anti-democratic, that it subverts democracy in general and Canadian sovereignty in particular. How is that?

Answer: NAFTA is anti-democratic and subverts democracy in several ways.

1. It prevents Canadians from buying back key industries to put their ownership in Canadian hands, specifically from requiring "an investor of another party, by

reason of its nationality, to sell or otherwise dispose of an investment in the territory of the Party" (1102.4).

2. It forces provincial and local governments to abide by rules that it had no part in designing.
3. It establishes a Free Trade Commission to supervise further developments, but the Commission is not elected and provinces have no standing before it.
4. Environmental, citizen and labour groups have no standing before the Commission while federal governments and corporate investors do have standing.
5. It allows provincial standards and Crown corporations to be challenged, though provinces can't challenge the Commission or its rulings.
6. It does not allow benefits to any country not having diplomatic relations with the US, which subverts Canadian sovereignty.
7. It locks in the status quo of Crown corporations, and public service provisions.
8. By eroding the tax base, it erodes the capacity to have social programs.
   The previous two points merit a few more comments. By preventing or limiting our use' of Crown corporations and social programs, NAFTA severely limits our capacity to compensate for unacceptable market anomalies, systemic discrimination, and accidents of birth, geography or demography. It must be remembered that the point of introducing Crown corporations and social programs is usually to empower relatively powerless people and strengthen our democratic institutions. Public institutions like the National Research Council, CBC, medicare, our system of schools and universities, and so on create and redistribute new wealth and a better quality of life for all Canadians. The fact that public institutions often create public, rather than merely private, goods and services must be emphasized over and over in the presence of contemporary right-wing propaganda. Constraints on the development of public institutions designed to serve public purposes are fundamentally constraints on the development of democracy in Canada.
9. By eroding control of government procurement provisions, it is more limiting to Canadians than Americans because we use such provisions more than Americans for development.
10. When there are disputes over international agreements, e.g., on the environment, NAFTA panels have the last word and these panels are unelected, operate in secret, have their own bias for trade and get to select their own evidential sources.

Question 6: The NDP claims NAFTA is anti-environment and anti-conservation, while Wilson says it's the greenest trade deal ever cut. What is the basis of the New Democrats' position?

Answer: There are several reasons for saying that the NAFTA is an anti-environmental and anti-conservationist document.

1. The treaty has no environmental standards and no conservationist standards, such as energy efficiency standards.

2. What standards it appeals to first are those provided in international treaties, which typically represent the least common denominator or most modest standards about which there is international agreement. While the NAFTA says that other more stringent standards may be accepted, the burden of proof or justification for such standards falls on those proposing them.
3. Those who propose more stringent standards must somehow get their case heard before an unelected panel of experts on international law and trade, meeting in secret, operating in the context of a treaty giving precedence to trade, although "the least trade restrictive enforcement policy may well be the least effective". Neither provinces, local governments, environmental groups, conservationist groups, labour groups nor individuals have standing before such panels, and experts from such groups need not be consulted by the panels. So it is unclear how new more stringent standards would be established.
4. Some state, provincial and local laws are initiated to prevent potential harm in the absence of actual harms having already occurred. In such cases, the NAFTA requirement to demonstrate actual harms before establishing more stringent standards would pre-empt such preventive measures.
5. Having no environmental and conservationist standards, the treaty is understandably void of enforcement mechanisms.
6. The treaty allows no subsidies for environmental cleansing, conservation or renewable energy.
7. The treaty does allow subsidies for increased exploration and exploitation of fossil fuels, oil and gas.
8. The proportionality clauses carried forward from the FTA encourage the continuous flow of natural resources without restrictions. The elimination of energy conservation rules (e.g., the requirement to have 25 years' supply remaining before exports would be approved) as a side-deal to the main treaties has the same effect.
9. The prohibition of export taxes on natural resources implies for example that our oil and gas will be sold at world prices which are below their local replacement costs.
10. The prohibition against requiring certain levels of processing of our resources before they can be exported will encourage more rapid exploitation of raw material as producers try to keep up their incomes by moving more product.
11. The global trade envisioned by NAFTA is based on an unsustainable supply of cheap fossil fuel.
12. NAFTA creates a catch 22 situation for conservationists. Conservation must be paid for by governments or industries. If Canadian governments pay, then US industries claim we are giving unfair subsidies. If we ask our industries to pay, then they claim we are giving them an unfair handicap unless the Americans also make their industries pay. The likely result is that no conservationist measures will be introduced, requiring no payments and guaranteeing an impoverished future for those who come after us.

13. It should be remembered that

    (a) the US refused to follow up its own EPA policy of having an Environmental Impact Assessment of NAFTA, and also refused to sign the Rio accords;
    (b) the Canadian government failed to keep its promise to have an environmental assessment made of NAFTA;
    (c) the Canadian government used the FTA to prevent EPA restrictions on the use of asbestos;
    (d) GATT rules were used to block a US law prohibiting the sale of tuna fish captured with driftnets that were killing dolphins;
    (e) the B.C. government backed away from its reforestation subsidies in the face of US complaints that they were unfair.
    (f) An example of an accepted international regime is that of the Codex Alimentarius food standards, which were designed with the participation of chemical companies and agribusinesses and which allow DDT residues far in excess of Canadian standards.

Question 7: Why do New Democrats and labour groups claim NAFTA is anti-labour?

Answer: There are several reasons for saying NAFTA is anti-labour.

1. It has no minimum labour standards, nothing like a minimum wage requirement, occupational health and safety regulations.
2. It has no labour rights: no rights regarding organizing, collective bargaining, child labour, forced labour, racial or sexual harassment prohibitions.
3. Neither labour unions nor individual workers have any standing in dispute settlement procedures.
4. There are no mechanisms for labour complaints, no rules of procedure or regulatory codes to be enforced.
5. Because the prescribed risk assessment procedure includes balancing economic benefits and costs against those of health and safety, worker safety may be traded off against high profits.
6. Because greater freedom is given to corporations in the investment chapter to move jobs at will, there is less job security for workers, more pressure to depress wages, more pressure to reduce benefits and taxes, and therefore less social security available for workers.
7. NAFTA rules punish people in definite ways who deny expected trade profits to corporations, but there are no rules punishing corporations for violating worker rights. The only recognized unfair trade practices are those that destroy expected or real profits, not those that destroy people's lives, the quality of people's lives or even whole communities. For example, governments must compensate corporations for trade profits lost if Crown corporations are established, but there are no required compensations to workers or communities for runaway corporations.

8. NAFTA's rules of origin provisions for duty free goods practically throw away our clothing industry by requiring that Canadian clothing exports must be made from North American textiles and yarns. While American manufacturers typically use yarns made in the USA, Canadian manufacturers use yarns made abroad. So the deal just gives preference to American over Canadian clothing manufacturers.

   Again, by moving to a relatively high North American content instead of Canadian content, the deal gives away Canadian jobs in the auto industry. Allowing a high percentage of imports of car parts and cars may be good for profits, but a low percentage of such imports would be better for local jobs.
9. Wilson and Mulroney talk about adjustment programs for workers losing jobs, but a progressive deal would have protected worker rights and prevented job losses resulting from exploiting the most vulnerable people. It would encourage upward harmonizing labour standards instead of NAFTA's downward approach.
10. If one thinks of family farms as relatively labour intensive enterprises, then the anti-family farm and rural development provisions of NAFTA may also be regarded as anti-labour. For examples, such provisions include those (1) Allowing the phasing out supply management programs which have been essential for Canadian dairy, poultry and eggs farmers, US dairy, sugar, peanuts and cotton farmers, and Mexican corn farmers, and (2) extending patent protection to life forms, so relatively small farmers will be at greater risk in developing and purchasing seed, which will increase pressure on the continued existence of such farms.

    As the relatively small farms disappear, we have increased loss of control of Canadian food security and production.

    The NAFTA econometric model for agriculture is based on cheap prices for farmers, partly on the assumption that cheaper prices for consumers will lead to increases in consumer spending. However, cheaper prices for consumers do not guarantee increases in consumer spending. When Canadian producers moved their operations south to enjoy the benefits of the FTA, they left many Canadians behind without jobs and with a decreased capacity to consume anything. When relatively small farms are replaced by relatively big ones and many farmers are bankrupt, they are hardly in a position to take advantage of cheap prices.
11. Many of the arguments used to show that NAFTA subverts democracy and Canadian sovereignty also show that the deal is anti labour because it subverts our capacity to design and implement an industrial strategy. For example, virtually everyone insists that we must develop secondary, high-value-added, high-wage industries based on our natural resources and that the main beneficiaries of such developments would be the people working in those industries. Thus, because NAFTA's investment chapter severely limits our capacity to develop such industries, it effectively destroys the possibility of having such beneficiaries.
12. The FTA and NAFTA provisions that allow American producers of films, records, books, tapes and magazines ("cultural industries") to demand compensation if Canadians move to take back their own markets may also be

regarded as anti-labour. For example, the fact that only 4% of screen time in Canadian theatres is devoted to Canadian films means that nearly all of the money made in such theatres is made by foreign producers, mainly American. Under such circumstances, it is practically impossible to develop a strong film industry generating great wealth and jobs. By agreeing to the provisions of the "cultural industries" of these deals we simply agreed to refrain from creating wealth and jobs in these industries. In effect, we capped the satisfaction of our labour needs and industrial growth potential to benefit the American industries. Interestingly enough, in NAFTA the Mexicans were guaranteed 30% of the screen time in their theatres (I-M-15).

13. The NAFTA provisions regarding telecommunications give American long-distance carriers like AT & T access to the Canadian telecommunications network but prevents us from requiring the American firms to cross-subsidize local domestic service. Thus, while Canadian firms must make their long distance service pay part of the cost for their local service, American firms are free of such costs. So, the latter will be able to capture more of the Canadian long-distance market, effectively eliminating Canadian jobs in this industry.

Question 8: Wilson claims NAFTA is about liberalizing trade, but the NDP claims the deal is fundamentally a protectionist treaty, protecting American transnational corporations and investors in Fortress North America. What is the basis of the New Democrats claim?

Answer: First, the trilateral deal NAFTA is explicitly given precedence over the multilateral deal GATT (Article 103), unless there is specific notice to the contrary. That is one reason why Europeans and Asians correctly regard the deal as creating a trading bloc, Fortress North America,

The chapters on investment and intellectual property give more protection to investors and transnational corporations than any other international treaty in existence. The real winners in this deal, besides the oil and gas industry, are the pharmaceutical manufacturers, biotechnologists and computer software makers. The big losers are consumers, inventors and the poor.

The aim of these chapters is to prevent communities from controlling their own economic development in the interests of those communities.

The Structural Adjustment Policies of the World Bank are designed into NAFTA so that adherence to those policies is a necessary condition of admission to Fortress North America. Giving additional protection to transnational patent holders, insisting on shifting from sustainable agriculture or manufacturing to cash cropping and other export-oriented production, reduction of real wages, reducing government services are all good means of protecting bankers' loans above everything else.

Strong patent protection prevents dissemination of technology and more rapid development of Third World countries. Eliminating compulsory licensing prevents countries from insisting that patented products be marketed in the interests of community development.

By protecting transnational corporations from special taxes and community development while allowing them to have market shares, NAFTA allows these corporations to take a free ride on indigenous people's needs to develop their own regions.

The Tory agenda involves 3 main tactics. First, privatise as many Crown corporations as possible. Second, with FTA, prevent the social control of all private corporations. Third, with NAFTA, force any remaining or new Crown corporations to behave like private corporations, effectively removing any rationale for having Crown corporations. In short, the aim is to have no public service Crown corporations at all or, failing that, to have no corporations fulfilling a public service mandate. The treaties effectively eliminate the possibility of having Crown corporations established for the sole purpose of serving the public interest above any private interests. In this sense, the treaties protect private power and interests against any incompatible public interest.

Notes on an Alternative Agenda

Our aim should be to create an environmentally sustainable and compassionate system of producing and distributing a good quality of life for all Canadians.

A good quality of life includes financial security, a clean environment, compassionate communities, loving families and friends, healthy bodies and generous spirits, understanding and wisdom, peace of mind and happiness.

Six specific goals are implied by our overall aim: full- employment, fiscal and monetary integrity, fair taxation, environmental viability, gender equity and electoral reform.

Full-employment requires abrogation of the job-exporting Canada-US Trade Deal and rejection of the North American Trade Deal; government investments to build social capital (e.g., low-cost and co-operative housing, sewage systems, hospitals and clinics, educational institutions, mass transit systems), to build private capital (e.g., development councils coordinating efforts of business, labour and government), and to build human capital (e.g., education and training, family assistance, research and development).

Fiscal and monetary integrity requires understanding that our federal debt, annual deficits and battered economy are the direct results of mismanagement of the public's business, including mismanagement of the Bank of Canada; a more balanced approach to development, including the creation of private, social and human capital; new priorities in government spending (e.g., less for military and more for civilian purposes, less for fossil and nuclear energy and more for conservation, renewable and alternative energy); international regulation of short-term financial capital flows; improving public asset and liability accounting, and supplementing the National Income and Product Accounts with Natural Resources and Environment Accounts, and social Accounts.

Fair taxation requires understanding that 10% of the population owns 51% of the private wealth in Canada; eliminating the regressive Goods and Services Tax that is increasing wealth concentration; making income taxes more progressive by increasing the number and spread of tax brackets; treating all income the same for tax purposes; eliminating business entertainment and lobbying tax deductions; reintroducing some estate and gift taxes, and introducing an annual net wealth tax.

Environmental viability requires understanding that globalized production structures have unsustainable needs for cheap fossil fuel; legislation with targets, timetables and penalties to increase energy efficiency, reduce waste and pollution, and to conserve soil and subsoil minerals, forests, fisheries, wetlands, wilderness, wildlife and biodiversity; amendments to the Access to Information Act so people can monitor and take action against polluters; a clean water act demanding zero discharge of toxics into all waters; mandatory recovery and recycling of ozone-depleting chemicals; reduction of solid waste generation by 50% by 2000; reduction of carbon dioxide emissions by 20% by 2005.

Gender equity requires understanding that, besides their paid labour, women do most of the unpaid labour of caring for men as well as for the very young, old, sick and disabled, and that family assistance programs are the main mechanism of redistributing this unpaid labour and equalizing women's opportunities for full participation in paid work and public life. Therefore justice for women requires government initiatives in family assistance with a national child care program, increased support for elder and disabled care, birth control and family planning, and women's health clinics; in the workplace with pay equity and stronger employment equity legislation, sexual harassment legislation, parental and maternity leave benefits; in efforts to eliminate violence against women and children through education and training of police, lawyers, judges, social workers, educators and health care workers, public awareness campaigns, increased support for transition houses and sexual assault centres.

Electoral reform requires a reduction in disparities between constituency sizes to get a more even representation by population; proportionate representation to eliminate the anomaly of parties forming governments with a minority of popular support; limiting contributions to $1000 by individuals and organizations; banning contributions from foreign sources.

Chapter 13
Issues for Business Ethics in the Nineties and Beyond

Alex C. Michalos

Introduction

In response to Bob Cookes invitation to write a paper about important issues for business ethics in the nineties and beyond, I listed as briefly as I could some topics that seemed to me to be enormously important for the quality of most peoples lives. Unfortunately, most of these topics have been relatively ignored by writers in the field of business ethics. To be more precise, these topics have rarely been considered in papers submitted to the *Journal of Business Ethics* (*JOBE*). To be more provocative, as Editor-in-Chief of the *Journal*, I would certainly welcome research studies related to them. (Some of the topics discussed below are examined in more detail in Michalos 1995.)

The paper that follows is basically the one presented at the conference with some additions and subtractions that resulted from three days of discussions with participants.

Organized Labour

When Deborah Poff and I were getting *JOBE* off the ground a dozen years ago, some friends urged us to include "labour" in the title somehow. Otherwise, they claimed, the journal would be both ignored by people with an interest and/or

---

Michalos, A.C.: 1997. Issues for business ethics in the nineties and beyond. Journal of Business Ethics, 16(3), pp. 219–230.

A.C. Michalos (✉)
University of Northern British Columbia, Prince George, BC, Canada
e-mail: michalos@brandonu.ca

A.C. Michalos, *How Good Policies and Business Ethics Enhance Good Quality of Life*, DOI 10.1007/978-3-319-50724-8_13

expertise in the issues particularly important to organized labour as well as quickly dominated by people with an interest and/or expertise in business as seen from the point of view of owners and managers, who are not particularly sympathetic to the views of labour people. In reply, I argued that since there could be no business without labour, working people and employees, it would be redundant to include "labour" in our title.

Well, today I must admit that although I think I was conceptually right, my friends were practically right. *JOBE* gets relatively few submissions dealing with issues of special interest to organized labour, and that is a pity because organized labour is still the best friend most ordinary workers have in our market economies. Weak as the trade union movement currently is in North America, the history of the movement and its current concerns show that it is a progressive voice for the improvement of occupational health and safety, universal health care and education, healthy physical environments and sound conservation, equality of opportunity for disadvantaged groups (women, visible minorities, First Nations and disabled people), job security, fair treatment of workers versus owners and managers, and resistance to the globalized downward harmonization of working conditions and the quality of life.

Obviously, there are often serious conflicts of interest among all these things. As a member of Canadas New Democratic Party and a candidate for our federal Parliament in 1988 and 1993, I participated in heated, painful and divisive debates within the Ontario Party between unionized bottle producers joined with environmentalists pressing for special environmental taxes on cans and can producers fearful for the loss of their jobs. In Nova Scotia we had internal debates between out-of-work coal miners and environmentalists resisting strip mining, and in British Columbia our debates among loggers and environmentalists are apparently interminable.

Since practically every national study ever done on life satisfaction and happiness of ordinary people around the world has shown that the most miserable people everywhere are those who are in the labour force but unemployed, job security must be close to the top of the list of important issues for practically everyone. Unemployment trends in both developed and undeveloped countries since the end of the Second World War have shown a steady increase (e.g., see Cornwall 1990). So, it is not surprising that organized labour would be a leader in pressing for job security. What is surprising is that academic researchers with an interest in business ethics seem to find so little to say about such a crucial issue. Indeed, reflecting on the short list of issues mentioned in the previous paragraph, it is remarkable that there has been so little attention paid to all of them in *JOBE*.

Social Dumping

Besides the issues already listed as of special concern to organized labour, I would like to mention the relatively unfamiliar problem called "social dumping". Generally speaking, a company is said to be dumping its products on foreign markets if its prices in those markets are lower than the costs of production. The aim of such predatory pricing is at least to capture greater market shares in competitive markets or at best to drive competitors out of the markets altogether. Government subsidies may be used in the same way in the interests of domestic producers, as in the case of North American wheat subsidies. The main differences between the two kinds of predatory pricing practices are that in the subsidies case governments are acting as the agents of businesses and tax payers are covering the costs not covered by market prices, while in the ordinary dumping case (in principle anyhow) businesses are covering their own costs from other business sources, perhaps including higher consumer costs in their home markets.

Social dumping, then, occurs when companies are able to sell their products in foreign markets with prices below the costs of production at home because employees of the company or local residents have been forced to absorb the losses themselves. The local costs to employees and residents for environmental pollution provide perhaps the simplest example of social dumping. When a paper and pulp company is able to sell its products abroad at a profit because it is allowed to treat the destruction of a river, animal habitat and human health as someone elses problem (economists' "externalities"), a common species of social dumping has occurred. Similar reasoning may be applied to companies that are able to sell their products abroad because they operate with relatively lower than average occupational health and safety standards. Governments can also be the agents of social dumping by passing "right to work" laws that undermine labour unions' ability to organize workers in order to collectively press for greater shares of company profits that may have been the result of labour-productivity increases.

Whether one shares my bias in favour of organized labour or not, one must grant that social dumping presents an increasingly important aspect of our globalized market place, about which business ethicists should have something to say. [Good places to begin looking at this problem may be found in Stanford et al. (1993) and Stanford (1991).]

International Finance and Third World Debt

There are a variety of ethical issues related to international finance that have been relatively untouched by actual or potential *JOBE* writers. For example, with the breakdown of the Bretton Woods system following Richard Nixon's announcement in August 1971 that U.S. dollars would no longer be automatically convertible into gold, the value of international currencies began to float freely in international markets. According to the Ecumenical Coalition for Economic Justice (1994, p. 2), today an estimated "US$900 billion worth of currencies are traded every day. Only one of every seventy dollars that changes hands on world currency markets actually pays for trade in goods or services." Among other things, these numbers imply that wealth-creating real or industrial economies are being relatively starved compared to wealth- distributing financial economies. In other words, money that might be used for long-term investment in research and development that might create new wealth in the form of new goods and services to improve the quality of life of more people today and in the future is being diverted into short-term speculation fattening the purses of a relatively few privileged wealth holders. What is worse, democratically elected governments around the world have their domestic socio-economic agendas increasingly distorted because of their inability to control the practically instantaneous shifts of massive funds from one country to another at the whim of fund managers/owners. Thus, the absence of an adequate international monetary regulatory system threatens the quality of people's lives, ordinary industrial development and even democracy itself, but so far business ethicists have been relatively silent about these issues. (A good review of these issues may be found in Guttman 1989.)

Another important financial issue concerns the problem of Third World debt, which might be more appropriately called the problem of First World usury. The Ecumenical Coalition for Economic Justice (1994, p. 7) pointed out that "Total less developed country debt has doubled from approximately US$819 billion in 1982 to US$1,712 billion in 1993 despite their having repaid over US$14 trillion in debt service. The reasons for such massive payments include the compounding effect of high real interest rates and the need to take on new debt just to service old loans." In a scathing attack on IMF and World Bank policies, Susan George wrote that "The economic policies imposed on debtors . . . have cured nothing at all. They have, rather, caused untold human suffering, and widespread environmental destruction, emptying debtor countries of their resources, rendering them each year less able to service their debts, let alone invest in economic and human recovery" (quote taken from Hotson 1994, p. 7).

Although the First World commercial banking and finance industry is not solely responsible for Third World debt and the degradation connected with it, the industry is largely responsible. To be sure, First World governments are also responsible for encouraging reckless lending by private companies protected by Federal Deposit Insurance whose bills are finally laid at the doorsteps of taxpayers. But my main purpose here is not to accuse financiers or government officials of irresponsibility. Rather, my point is that business ethicists should apply their investigative resources to these issues. (Good places to begin studying these issues include Greider 1987; George 1992; Hixon 1991.)

Tobacco Promotion

The evidence for the harmful effects of tobacco use is beyond reasonable doubt. Lifetime smokers who do not use the product in any particularly extreme way, who are not negligent and do not have accidents with the product still have a much higher risk than nonsmokers of horrible diseases and deaths as a result of using the product. So far as I know, there is no other product that is sold legally about which this can be said, which makes tobacco quite unique.

Although the tobacco industry produces great benefits in the form of pleasure for its consumers, jobs, wages and salaries for its workers, dividends for its stockholders, taxes for governments and social goods and services paid for out of such taxes, and incomes for the variety of others engaged in some sort of economic exchange with members of the industry, it still seems fair to say that the expected long-run costs to the human community for continuing its addiction to and dependence on tobacco are greater than the expected long-run benefits. So, as a matter of long-term policy, we should be finding ways to end that addiction and dependence. Furthermore, since our (Canadian and American) governments are clearly trying to phase in their restrictions of tobacco sales to allow a relatively less painful transition to a tobacco-free society, anything ordinary citizens can do to help them would be worthwhile. In particular, business ethicists should be encouraging people connected to the tobacco industry to increase investments in retraining its workers so they have a better chance of finding alternative employment, in pension plans for those who will be too old to change jobs, in research and development to find some harmless uses for tobacco products, and in ways to convert their expertise and other resources to sustainable and even growing industries. (A more detailed analysis of this issue may be found in Michalos 1995.)

Arms Trade

I have already published a monograph defending the thesis that the Canadian government should arrest its activities designed to promote the manufacture and export of armaments (Michalos 1989). Modest as our arms industry is in comparison with that of other industrialized countries and especially with the world's leader, the United States, there is no excuse for complacency. If our best estimates are accurate, then about half of 1% of the Canadian GNP is involved in arms production. In 1992 that would have been half of 1% of at least $664 billion or roughly $3.3 billion dollars. Three and a third billion dollars that year would have matched Ontario's capital spending on roads, sewers, public buildings, etc. and supported 67,000 jobs. It would have built over 30,000 non-profit housing units, supporting 3,600 jobs, or provided jobs and training for over 300,000 long-term unemployed people.

Clearly, these figures show that significant choices have been made regarding the best way to spend government revenues, and these choices have serious consequences for business and the quality of peoples lives. So it is remarkable that business ethicists in my country have not had more to say about these issues. Given the vast sums spent on armaments in the United States and the high percentage of *JOBE* authors living there, the relative silence from that source is even more remarkable. There has certainly been no lack of unofficial and official American critics of their domestic arms industry, but the relative silence of such voices in a journal devoted to business ethics strikes me as odd.

Wealth Concentration and Taxation

Moral problems related to the concentration and taxation of wealth may be traced back to mythical stories regarding hard-hearted rich people taxing good-hearted poor people, and a variety of avenging Robin Hoods restoring the ill-gotten gains of the former back to the latter. Since, in theory at least, one of the virtues of a free enterprise economy is its ability to create and distribute wealth on the basis of millions of individual decisions of sovereign consumers and producers, such an economy has some economic and moral respectability. In practice, of course, the historical examples we have of societies that approached the *laissez-faire* model relatively closely have not been as attractive or virtuous as one might have hoped, from economic and moral points of view. Nevertheless, it seems fair to say that the ideal of a free enterprise economy has some economic and moral virtue and the fact that the real world has failed to live up to the promise of the ideal, for free enterprise or anything else, is not surprising.

One of the main disadvantages of a free enterprise economy and apparently even of our mixed market economies is that they allow dangerously large concentrations of wealth. This disadvantage is a case of "what you win on, you lose on". The promise of commanding great wealth as a result of hard work and good luck is one of the most attractive features of free enterprise. The fact that the promise may happen to be kept for only a few people, none of whom has much interest in the well-being of others, is one of its most unattractive features. For example, after people around the world have made Steven Spielberg rich by their individually modest but collectively huge purchases of his products, they might well have second thoughts about putting all that power into the possession of one person. After all, ignoring luck, the virtue that allowed Speilberg to accumulate his vast fortune may be far out of proportion to his virtue in spending it.

For all I know, Spielberg is a saint and every dime he spends is well-spent, and there certainly are many others with more money and perhaps less virtue of any kind than he has. But my point is that an economic and political system that would allow such people to spend all their money, say, buying and levelling large chunks of the remaining forests of cash-starved Third World countries or promoting North American football around the world is a dangerous system. It seems to me that the world would be a better place for more people if no one were allowed to have such power. Since twenty of the twenty-two countries in the OECD have some sort of wealth taxation, modest as it is in every country, other people apparently have shared some of my intuitions about these things.

In another paper (Michalos 1988) I made a detailed case for the introduction of a progressive annual net wealth tax in Canada. Here I only want to insist that problems related to the concentration and taxation of wealth, especially of wealth resulting from successful business activity, are problems that ought to engage the attention of business ethicists. Among other things, there is an assumption made in all industrialized countries that there is a legitimate role for corporate philanthropy. Indeed, it is usually assumed that measures of corporate philanthropy may be used as measures of good corporate citizenship. However, this assumption should be carefully scrutinized. When businesses lobby governments for favourable tax treatment, their expenses are tax-deductible, which means they are tax- expenditures in government accounts. When businesses' lobbying efforts are successful, then other taxpapers are beaten a second time because they must cover any shortfalls resulting from the new tax regime. Since favourable tax treatment effectively subsidizes the total cost of bringing a product to market, social dumping occurs, the market price gives a misleading signal to potential purchasers and consumer sovereignty is undermined. Insofar as a community funds important public services through corporate philanthropy instead of through fair taxation, it is allowing its services to be designed by an unelected group of relatively privileged people, with no mandate or promise to serve the public interest. Besides buying public services, corporate philanthropists are buying private acquiescence to corporate mischief in the form of trade in cigarettes, war machines and usurious interest rates. The purpose of public services in education, health care, family assistance and housing is to empower relatively under-privileged people, to strengthen their voices, and to help them become full participants in civil society. To make such services depend on the whims of corporate philanthropists, as we are increasingly doing in Canada, is a moral outrage. When businesses make tax-deductible contributions to their favourite charities (creating more government tax-expenditures), they usually ask for and get special recognition as generous benefactors, even though the sums involved are typically lower than the sums they would have had to pay in a system of taxation that was not biased in their favour as a result of their lobbying.

In the light of all these considerations, it is ironic that corporate philanthropists get special recognition as benefactors. It would be more accurate to recognize such businesses as successful self-serving subverters of our mixed market economy and egalitarian democracy. All things considered, from the point of view of strengthening democracy, it would be preferable to increase corporate taxes and prohibit all forms of corporate philanthropy. Similarly, I suspect that it would be preferable to eliminate most, if not all, foundations and levy fair taxes on accumulated wealth. [A good place to begin thinking about tax fairness is in Curran (1974). For a good analysis of the impact of Canada's business community on our tax system, see McQuaig (1987, 1993), and for a good overview of our tax system with special emphasis on Ontario, see the Ontario Fair Tax Commission (1993). Regarding the impact of foundations, see Arnove (1982).]

Pollution and Resource Depletion

The struggles to reduce waste and pollution, and conserve our natural resources must become increasingly important as the earth's population continues to expand. It is no secret that most of the world's waste is produced in and by First World consumer societies, many of the world's remaining natural resources are in Third World countries, and most of the producers of the products creating the waste, pollution and resource depletion are transnational businesses.

Because there are several scholarly journals devoted to environmental issues more or less broadly construed, there may be many more attractive outlets than *JOBE* for research on such issues related to business ethics. For a few years, *JOBE* had the services of Mark Stevenson on issues we advertised simply as Energy and Ethics, and Mark wrote a series of useful and provocative review essays through which we hoped to encourage business ethicists to become engaged in the discussions. When we began our initiatives, Mark worked for Ontario Hydro, which produces over half the province's energy from CANDU reactors. Although Mark was basically pro-nuke and I was basically anti-nuke, we both thought that there ought to be a public forum for the debate to continue, and it seemed virtually impossible to get the conflicting parties together for face-to-face exchanges. As it turned out, for *JOBE* at least, it was even impossible to get paper-to-paper exchanges. Indeed, nuclear energy aside, it has proven to be impossible to get more than a small handful of publishable papers on any ethical issues related to the production of waste and pollution, and the depletion of natural resources resulting from business practices.

International Trading Blocks

From 1987 to 1994 nothing got more attention from the Canadian news media and the Canadian public than the Canada-United States Trade Agreement (CUSTA) and the North American Free Trade Agreement, involving the United States, Mexico and Canada. (Most of the remaining paragraphs in this section are taken from a long essay on the NAFTA in Michalos 1995.)

Ethical considerations were at the heart of many of the debates over the two agreements. For example, some proponents of the NAFTA claimed that Canadians (like me) who opposed it were basically selfish because the poorest of the three countries, Mexico, would be a major beneficiary of the agreement. In response, opponents claimed that there were good reasons for thinking that most Mexicans would probably be worse off with than without the NAFTA. In particular, we pointed out that most of the investment being attracted to Mexico was going into the maquiladora region bordering on the United States, and the evils of this region and others like it around the world were well-documented.

Characteristically, such zones offer prospective investors relief from restrictions on their right to transfer profits and capital to a head office outside the host country, from duties on equipment and raw materials used in production, from direct and indirect taxes, from environmental pollution laws and special labour-relations provisions (bans on trade unions, weaker occupational health and safety regulations, relief from labour laws, including minimum wage and maximum working time laws). Employees are typically females aged 17 and 24 from rural areas, with at best a high school education. They are given minimum training, paid minimum wages, and have relatively short periods of employment with no job security.

Opponents also pointed out that the NAFTA included provisions clearly implying that the working environment characterizing the maquiladora region would become the standard for not only all Mexicans but anyone else determined to compete in the Mexican market.

In response to theoreticians who claimed that increases in trade would necessarily lead to increases in living standards, we reported that Mexican trade with the rest of the world had increased in the past decade, but the real wages of Mexicans had decreased. We also reminded the theoreticians that increases in productivity do not guarantee increases in living standards. For example, Louisiana has higher levels of productivity than Michigan, but Michigan workers have a higher standard of living.

There were also serious ethical considerations related to the alleged Mexican political abuses and violations of human rights, including the unjustified arrest, imprisonment, torture and murder of critics of current federal government policies like the NAFTA.

Finally, there were problems related to American and Canadian governments wanting to open up the Mexican market in order to "help" the Mexican government continue to make payments on its debts to the former governments and commercial banks, about which enough has been said here already.

Throughout the seven years of heated debates in many places in North America, *JOBE* attracted only one paper (unpublished at this writing) dealing with issues closely connected to the NAFTA, and this paper did not focus on the specific provisions of the agreement. Since most of the trade between Canada and the United States, at least, will be governed for the foreseeable future by the provisions of the NAFTA and the CUSTA, which are supposed to be consistent with but more extensive than the General Agreement on Tariffs and Trade (GATT), there will be ample opportunity for business ethicists to become engaged in a wide variety of moral issues related to these agreements. Obviously, I hope they will take up the challenges.

The Business Council on National Issues

Some people have argued that business people have no right, expertise or even competence to become involved in the world's social and political issues. This was Friedman's (1970) view.

In the worst case scenario, such people argue that the power wielded by the world's corporate elite is so great and their basic values are so perverse that they are bound to destroy the very ideals that moralists and other reformers want to preserve.

In Michalos (1987) I argued against these views on several grounds, e.g., that business people certainly had a right to attempt to make their firms good corporate citizens, that morally good action did not require special expertise or competence, that the fundamental values of business people were as diverse as other people's and that there would be more danger in having them apathetic or alienated than engaged in trying to take their moral and social responsibilities seriously. Although I still think I was right about these four points, I also think Friedman's fears were more credible than I realized. I have come to this conclusion after several years of observing the behaviour of Canada's Business Council on National Issues (BCNI).

The BCNI explicitly opposes Friedman's view. According to the Winter/Spring 1991 brochure of the Council, it was founded in 1976 based on "a progressive idea —that corporations and their leaders have a responsibility not merely to their traditional constituents but to society as a whole".

The brochure describes the Council as "the senior voice of Canadian business on public policy issues in Canada and abroad", "a nonpartisan and not-for-profit organization ... composed of the chief executive officers of the 150 leading Canadian corporations", and "its focus nationally is to help build a strong economy, progressive social policies, and healthy political institutions".

Unfortunately, the Council is precisely the sort of Frankenstein monster that Friedman and others feared, with a white collar to be sure.

Contrary to its stated purposes, it is not socially progressive, nor non-partisan and not- for-profit. Rather than helping to build a strong Canadian economy and healthy political institutions, it is destroying the economy and subverting democracy.

Consider the record. In the 1991 brochure, 143 officers (all men) and companies were listed, with about a third of the latter foreign-owned. While one might say that it is not extraordinary to have a Canadian business organization with a third of its members representing foreign interests because that just happens to reflect the structure of Canadian business, there is good evidence that such interests are at best a mixed blessing for the Canadian national interest (e.g., Hurtig 1991; National Advisory Board on Science and Technology 1991; Michalos 1982).

More importantly, since the American companies are also represented in lobby groups like the Business Roundtable in the United States, on which our Council is modeled, those companies get to make their case in both countries.

Again, it is not extraordinary to have big transnational companies wielding more power than relatively smaller national companies. But it is extraordinary to imagine that an organization ruled by economic power might somehow become a legitimate model for governing an egalitarian democracy.

Just as transnational companies have more than one voice across national boundaries, some Canadian companies and families have more than one voice at the Council's table. For example, the Bronfman family interests may be expressed through the C.E.O. of Brascan Ltd., John Labatt Ltd., Noranda Inc., Noranda Forest Inc., MacMillan Bloedel Ltd., Norcen Energy Resources Group, or Joseph E. Seagram and Sons.

Granted that the seven voices may not always sing in harmony, it is still the case that seven different Bronfman interests are given a voice instead of seven different interests of some other families. It might be expected and accepted in an economic forum, but it can hardly be accepted from a Council purporting to help us design a healthy democracy.

The Council's membership is as notable for those absent as for those present. The most glaring absentee is a representative from the Canadian Federation of Independent Business. So it would be more accurate for the Council to describe itself as the "voice of big business".

Notwithstanding the fact that the Council is not democratically constituted, or mandated, for that matter, to provide unbiased representation of all business interests, it might still function as a progressive, democratic force. In fact it does not.

On February 12, 1991 the *Toronto Star* published an article by Ontario's former Fair Tax Commissioner, Neil Brooks, challenging the Council and other business organizations to speak out against cost-inefficient subsidies to business and the notoriously regressive Goods and Services Tax. Although the President of the Council, Tom d'Aquino, informed me that the Council had "repeatedly endorsed the elimination of government subsidies to business", it was one of the first advocates of the GST and remains one of its most ardent supporters.

Researchers at Statistics Canada have shown that our corporate income tax structure favours the biggest companies over the smallest, and that government policy is therefore contributing to the disadvantages that relatively smaller sized companies have in the economic marketplace. But such research has never emerged from the Council, or even received recognition and endorsement, let alone a call for appropriate remedial action.

Many people have remarked on the fact that some big companies frequently pay no income tax (e.g., Michalos 1991), but the Council has never suggested that there is anything wrong with a tax system that allows such free riders.

Nor has the Council protested against a system that makes lobbying expenses in the private interests of businesses tax-deductible although lobbying expenses in the public interests of antipoverty groups are not tax-deductible.

The Council qualifies as a "not-for-profit" organization according to Canadian law. However, in the light of the clearly self-serving positions the Council takes on tax structures that favour its members over others, it is simply incredible to suggest that the Council is free of bias in favour of its members' own profits.

Although the Council was an early advocate of the CUSTA and the NAFTA, it has never insisted on a European style social charter of rights as a prior condition of such deals in order to protect Canadians from being drawn down to American and Mexican levels of social security. (During the discussion of John Abbarnos paper on corporations' responsibilities toward the homeless, I remarked that contrary to most Americans' impressions, the United States has traditionally been one of the most mean-spirited of all industrialized countries when it comes to social spending. Using OECD statistics from 1990, McQuaig (1993, pp. 15–16) wrote that "... West Germany, France, Austria, Belgium, the Netherlands, Denmark, Sweden and Norway spend far more on social programs than we do in North America—*and do as well or better than we do in economic growth and international competitiveness.* These European nations spend a large percentage—between 18 and 30%—of their Gross Domestic Product on social security and other transfer payments, while Canada spends only 12.8%, and the U.S. only 11.5%.")

Regardless of the fact that excellent studies for Statistics Canada showed that social spending is not responsible for our annual deficits and national debt, the Council continues to complain about extravagant Canadian spending and the need for further cuts to social spending (*CCPA Monitor* 1994). Similarly, the Canadian Chamber of Commerce, which is a member of the BCNI, continues to hammer away at social spending in spite of the evidence, e.g. see Beauchesne (1994). For the record, I quote from the definitive study by Mimoto and Cross (1991, pp. 3.1–3.9):

> Broadly speaking, government spending as a share of GDP did not rise significantly over the whole period from 1975 [to 1990]; in fact, it moderated compared to the preceding ten years, when social programs proliferated. ... Excluding the cost of unemployment insurance, which is intended to be self-financing over the business cycle, social program spending has not increased relative to GDP over the last 16 years. ... Deficits became steadily larger after 1975–76 initially more from a shortfall of revenues than higher spending. Much of this shortfall originated in numerous changes designed to reduce taxes and in the transfer of tax points to the provinces. ... higher debt charges accounted for the bulk (70%) of the increase in spending relative to GDP from the base period [1974–75].

In fact, every year since 1986 the federal government has had an operating surplus for all government programs and administration, and the higher debt charges are primarily the direct result of the Bank of Canada's tight monetary policy (Cohen 1994; Biddell 1993). Consequently, the solution of Canada's debt problem must begin with the Banks policy. According to Bradfield (1994), among others, the Bank must at least return to its practice (abandoned in the early 1970s) of holding roughly 20% of federal debt, compared to its current holdings of 6%. (The U.S. Federal Reserve holds about 30% of U.S. federal debt.) To prevent inflation, the Bank would also have to raise the reserve requirements for commercial banks, which only this year [1994] were reduced to zero.

Clearly, the Business Council on National Issues is committed to a worldview that favours the privileged few over the less privileged many. And that, I suppose, is precisely the sort of aberration that Milton Friedman and others feared. Although one ought to be cautious about inferring too much on the basis of a single case, the BCNI is a very important case. At a minimum, business ethicists reflecting on this case should be provoked into examining this case and others like it more carefully. What does the Business Roundtable do? What do Chambers of Commerce do around the world? Who benefits, at whose expense? (Chorney 1989, showed that during the great depression of the 1930s, the business press and big business leaders were apparently committed to the same worldview as the BCNI is today.)

A Quantitative Overview

I have briefly reviewed several issues that I think should have occupied the attention of business ethicists in the recent past and that I hope will occupy them in the future. In order to supplement my overall impressions with a rough quantitative measure of *JOBE*'s output regarding these issues, I reviewed all our titles, some abstracts and some papers covering the period from Volume 1, Number 1 (February 1982) through Volume 13, Number 8 (August 1994). In that period we published 946 articles, including about 74 or 8% of which involved some of my preferred issues fairly directly. Because my criteria for identifying relevant papers were not rigorous, the following allocations should be regarded as merely suggestive. Roughly speaking, then, the picture looks like this.

Issue	N	%
Labour	35	4
Environment	14	2
Finance/Third World	15	2
Arms trade	7	1
Tobacco	3	0
Subtotal	74	8[a]
All other issues	872	92
Total	946	100

[a]The actual subtotal is 9 because the figures for the environment and finance/Third World are both rounded upward

Even if my rough assessment were 100% short of the real figure, less than a fifth of *JOBE*'s total output would have been on the issues I identified as especially important. So, I suppose my overall impressions were fairly accurate.

Concluding Remarks

Before closing, I want to make some comments about some ideas that occurred to me during and since the DePaul conference, and to raise the question: Why have most of these problems received so little attention from people interested in business ethics? Beginning with the latter question, I suppose my first and most unbiased answer would be that business ethicists have not attended to these issues because they were busy considering other, equally important issues. And why not? There are certainly enough problems to occupy all kinds of moralists for several lifetimes. Personally, I hope this is the main reason for their lack of attention to the issues raised here.

However, I suspect that there is a more serious bias responsible for the relative inattention to my set of problems. In particular, I think that most of the contributors to *JOBE* are Americans working in American business schools, sharing a relatively strong bias in favour of free enterprise, and that from their point of view my list of issues are at best relatively unimportant and at worst subversive.

The democratic ideals of liberty, equality and community are practically infinitely plastic. American democratic capitalists have traditionally emphasized liberty, apparently even at the expense of equality and community. Canadian democratic socialists have traditionally emphasized equality and community, apparently even at the expense of liberty. Since there is no rule book to appeal to in order to determine what emphasis is right, all one can do is construct a clear vision of a good society and work to realize the vision in fact. Although I am a democratic socialist and an atheist, I am deeply impressed by the similarities of the vision of a good society that the Vincentian sponsors of the DePaul conference and I share. Responding to Dennis McCann's presentation, one of the conference participants said that he thought the spectrum of Christian beliefs was too broad to produce effective guidance for business ethicists. I think this is correct. Indeed, I remember one of my professors of Christian Theology at the Divinity School of the University of Chicago telling our class (around 1959) that when he was a student at the Divinity School in the 1930s all of his professors of Christian Theology were atheists. When I asked him how that was possible, he said, "After you have been around here longer, you will see how". Over 30 years later, it still looks logically incoherent to me.

The main reason I have always identified myself as a pragmatist is that writers in the pragmatic tradition typically downplay theory of all sorts in the interests of practice aimed at achieving apparently good results. I do not believe that we can and hence do not believe that we should try to avoid theory, metaphysics, unprovable assumptions and many other things that disturb positivists. But I do think, with people like Braybrooke and Lindblom (1963), that progress can often be made by pursuing sharing goals with a minimum of theoretic substantiation.

Although Wes Cragg did not use the word "heuristics" in his presentation, he did emphasize, among other things, the heuristic value of having a moral agenda. It seems to me that this is an aspect of the moral enterprise that cannot be over-emphasized. Those of us who are teaching business ethics cannot hope to transform many of today's business practitioners, including labour and management. As usual, the impact of today's teachers will be felt in tomorrow's graduates. If the importance of the moral point of view for the quality of human existence can be impressed upon our students, I am confident that our labours will not have been in vain.

In the break after my presentation, a friend asked me why I did not just start a journal devoted to politics. Presumably this was a response to my talk and his knowledge that besides the *Journal of Business Ethics*, I have edited *Social Indicators Research* since 1974, a journal devoted to measuring aspects of the quality of life. For ethicists working in the consequentialist/utilitarian/pragmatic tradition, politics is inseparable from ethics, as Benthams life and work clearly illustrated. Our commitment to egalitarian democracy is both moral and political. The main reason my list of important issues for business ethics includes topics related to the strengthening or weakening of democratic institutions and democracy itself is because my vision of a morally good society is also that of a democratic society maximizing liberty, equality and community. Thus, my approach to the identification of important issues is nearly the opposite of those business ethicists who see moral issues almost exclusively in terms of criminal law- breaking.

While most ethicists regard legal issues as a subset of morality, many business ethicists seem to identify the spheres of morality and legality. For people with such views, my insistence on the immorality of subverting democracy by disempowering the relatively poor through continued assaults on our modest social security safety nets must sound strange indeed. After all, there is no criminal law against destroying democracy by allowing dangerous concentrations of economic power and massive numbers of disillusioned, alienated and apathetic citizens to withdraw from all forms of legitimate democratic participation. There is no criminal law against these things, but to me they are a moral outrage that should not be tolerated.

References

Arnove, R. F. (Ed.). (1982). *Philanthropy and cultural imperialism: The foundations at home and abroad.* Bloomington: Indiana University Press. Reviewed by Michalos, A. C. in the *Journal of Business Ethics, 3,* 69–89.

Beauchesne, E. (1994). Business leaders say, "Cut, Cut, Cut". *The Prince George Citizen, 7.*

Biddell, J. L. (1993). *A self-reliant future for Canada.* Thornhill, Ontario: LNC Publications.

Bradfield, M. (1994). Bank of Canada should hold more federal debt. *CCPA Monitor, 1*(4), 10.

Braybrooke, D., & Lindblom, C. E. (1963). *A strategy of decision.* New York: Macmillan Co.

CCPA Monitor. (1994). Business leaders demand more cuts in social programs *1*(6), 11.

Chorney, H. (1989). *The deficit and debt management: An alternative to monetarism.* Ottawa: Canadian Centre for Policy Alternatives.

Cohen, M. G. (1994). *Debt and deficit: A problem or the problem.* Ottawa: New Democratic Party of Canada.

Cornwall, J. (1990). *The theory of economic breakdown: An institutional analysis.* Oxford: Basil Blackwell.

Curran, D. J. (Ed.). (1974). Harold M. Groves: Tax philosophers; two hundred years of thought in Great Britain and the United States. Madison: University of Wisconsin Press.

Ecumenical Coalition for Economic Justice. (1994). Cooling hot money. *Economic Justice Report, 5*(2), 1–12.

Friedman, M. (1970, September 13). The social responsibility of business is to increase profits. *The New York Times Magazine.*

George, S. (1992). *The debt boomerang: How the third world debt harms us all*. London: Pluto Press.
Greider, W. (1987). *Secrets of the temple: How the federal reserve runs the country*. New York: Simon and Schuster.
Guttman, R. (Ed.). (1989). *Reforming money and finance: Institutions and markets in flux*. Armonk, New York: M. E. Sharpe.
Hixon, W. F. (1991). *A matter of interest: Reexamining money, debt, and real economic growth*. New York: Praeger.
Hotson, J. H. (1994). Book review of Susan George, the debt boomerang. *Economic Reform, 6*(9), 7.
Hurtig, M. (1991). *The betrayal of Canada*. Toronto: Soddart Publishing Co.
McQuaig, L. (1987). *Behind closed doors: How the rich won control of Canada's tax system . . . and ended up richer*. Markham: Penguin Books Canada.
McQuaig, L. (1993). *The wealthy banker's wife: The assault on equality in Canada*. Toronto: Penguin Books Canada.
Michalos, A. C. (1982). Economics, religion and morality. In *North American social report* (Vol. 5). Dordrecht: D. Reidel.
Michalos, A. C. (1987). Moral responsibility in business, or fourteen unsuccessful ways to pass the buck. In D. C. Poff & W. Waluchow (Eds.), *Business ethics in Canada* (pp. 12–25). Toronto: Prentice-Hall Canada, Inc., reprinted in Michalos (1995).
Michalos, A. C. (1988). A case for a progressive net wealth tax. *Public Affairs Quarterly, 2*, 105–140, reprinted in Michalos (1995).
Michalos, A. C. (1989). *Militarism and the quality of life*. Toronto: Science for Peace, reprinted in Michalos (1995).
Michalos, A. C. (1991, May 16). Corporations must pay their fair share of taxes. *The Mercury, 4*.
Michalos, A. C. (1995). *A pragmatic approach to business ethics*. Thousand Oaks: Sage Publications.
Mimoto, H., & Cross, P. (1991). The growth of the federal debt. *Canadian Economic Observer*, 3.1–3.18.
National Advisory Board on Science and Technology. (1991). *Science and technology, innovation and national prosperity: The need for Canada to change course*. Ottawa: Committee on National Science and Technology Priorities.
Ontario Fair Tax Commission. (1993). *Fair taxation in a changing world: Report of the Ontario fair tax commission*. Toronto: University of Toronto Press.
Stanford, J. (1991). *Going south: Cheap labour as an unfair subsidy in North American free trade*. Ottawa: Canadian Centre for Policy Alternatives.
Stanford, J., Elwell, C., & Sinclair, S. (1993). *Social dumping under North American free trade*. Ottawa: Canadian Centre for Policy Alternatives.

Chapter 14
Observations on Performance Indicators and Performance-Based Management in Public Administration

Alex C. Michalos

Introduction

The aim of this essay is to respond to Professor Guglielmo Negri's invitation to

(1) comment on the background paper written by Professor Franco Archibugi for the symposium (Archibugi 1997, p. 4; hereafter referred to as the Background Paper) and
(2) present some of my own "ideas and experience" about the subject. In this section, I want to indicate some of my biases and assumptions, and briefly outline the structure of the essay.

First, I think performance-based management is a new name for an old idea. The idea is that of a pragmatic, consequentialist or utilitarian approach to management. I am a strong proponent of pragmatism, with all its disadvantages and advantages. In Michalos (1995, p. 1) I wrote:

> The trouble with pragmatists is that they will get in bed with anyone. At least that has been the main complaint against them since the beginning of the 20th century. From a moral point of view, it is difficult to imagine a more devastating criticism. After all, although politics, prudence, or one's own self-interest narrowly defined might lead one to bunk down with strange bedfellows, human decency or morality requires considerably more. There must be some lines that a morally good person should not cross.

Michalos, A.C.: 1997. Observations on performance indicators and performance-based management in public administration. Paper presented at the International Symposium on Performance-Based Management in Public Administration at the Royal Palace of Caserta, Naples, Italy, September 24–26, 1997.

A.C. Michalos (✉)
University of Northern British Columbia, Prince George, BC, Canada
e-mail: michalos@brandonu.ca

A.C. Michalos, *How Good Policies and Business Ethics Enhance Good Quality of Life*, DOI 10.1007/978-3-319-50724-8_14

> The defining characteristic of any sort of pragmatic philosophy is its emphasis on evaluating actions and beliefs on the basis of their consequences. But there is no generally accepted rule book to tell pragmatists which consequences are good and which are bad. So, pragmatism provides, at best, necessary but not sufficient guides to behaviour. The bank robber, Willie Sutton, illustrated the moral bankruptcy of pragmatism when he said that he robbed banks because that is where we keep our money. The great American pragmatist, William James, would have been appalled by such a perversion of his philosophy. James was a relatively decent but apolitical human being who evaluated his actions and beliefs according to their contributions to sustaining other decent human beings. Some American pragmatists, like Sidney Hook, for example, leaned to the right or conservative side of the political spectrum. Some, like John Dewey, espoused relatively left of center or liberal political views. Still others, like myself and Deborah Poff, press pragmatism into the service of feminist and democratic socialist egalitarian ideals.

(A detailed examination of the insufficiency of the pragmatist's prescription for action may be found in Michalos 1992.)

Second, as we accept Professor Negri's invitation to reflect on and help prepare a new curriculum for "a *new and different type of manageriality in public administration*" (Background Paper, p. 4), it is worthwhile to remember those who have gone before us. Accordingly, it seems especially appropriate that here in Italy we should hear again from one who might be regarded as the founder of modem political science, the much misunderstood Niccolo Machiavelli. (Without going into detail, I think he was misunderstood because his brand of pragmatism was roughly what contemporary philosophers would call 'act utilitarianism', which prescribes always acting in particular situations so as to do as much good as possible for as many people as possible even if the action requires violating some moral rules.) Here is Machiavelli's view.

> …what should be the methods and procedures of a prince in dealing with his subjects and friends? Because I know that many have written about this, I am afraid that by writing about it again I shall be thought of as presumptuous, since in discussing this material I depart radically from the procedures of others. But since my intention is to write something useful for anyone who understands it, it seemed more suitable to me to search after the effectual truth of the matter rather than its imagined one. And many writers have imagined for themselves republics and principalities that have never been seen nor known to exist in reality; for there is such a gap between how one lives and how one ought to live that anyone who abandons what is done for what ought to be done learns his ruin rather than his preservation: for a man who wishes to make a vocation of being good at all times will come to ruin among so many who are not good. (Machiavelli 1513, p. 519)

For me it was impossible to read the Background Paper with its pragmatic focus on performance-based management without recalling the handbook written nearly 500 years earlier. While there are of course many differences between the two works, the main difference is that Machiavelli wrote for aspiring princes while Archibugi writes for aspiring civil servants. Since the Florentine Secretary was himself a high level civil servant, maybe we should think of our task as writing *The Upper Level Public Manager* for the Machiavellis of the future.

Third, social indicators are essentially statistics that may be used to measure aspects of the quality of life (Michalos 1980a, pp. 1–10). Since the quality of people's lives is affected by the quality of the performance of public administrators and other government officials, performance indicators may be regarded as a species of social indicators. There are a variety of ways in which apparent measuring instruments are or can be politically and socially substantively biased. In other words, there are a variety of ways in which apparently neutral measuring devices are really windows that allow a certain point of view of reality, and therefore constrain all evaluations and moral choices. In Michalos (1980a, pp. 11–17) I reviewed 15 "uses and abuses of social indicators". The following Citizens' Guide is adapted from that earlier list. Above all else, Performance-Based Managers should remember these things when they think about or use performance indicators (PI).

Citizen's Guide to Performance Indicators

Performance indicators:

(1) encourage commission of The Number-Crunchers' Fallacy, which is this: Anything that cannot be counted is unimportant and anything that can be counted is important.
(2) can be used to predict and alter future behavior, for better or worse depending on the nature of the alterations.
(3) can give visibility to problems, and also create them by focusing attention on them, or by hiding some in the interest of emphasizing others.
(4) can help obtain balanced assessments of conditions against mere economic assessments, and can distort appropriate assessments by assuming that everything valuable can be given a price in monetary terms.
(5) can help in the evaluation of current public policy and programs, and also contribute to perverse evaluations because the statistics routinely collected may not allow decision-makers to control for important contaminating variables when they are trying to decide what has caused what.
(6) can help determine alternatives and priorities, but also allow an elite corps of statisticians to unduly influence the public agenda by providing the "official version" of the state of the world.
(7) can facilitate comparisons among nations, regions, cities, other groups and service-providers, but also encourage invidious comparisons, raising aspirations and hopes too high or not high enough.
(8) can suggest areas for research to produce new scientific theories and more knowledge about the structures and functions of systems, but also retard action because people may be unwilling to act in the absence of a perfect theory or model.
(9) can provide an orderly and common framework for thinking about social systems and social change, perhaps so orderly and common that alternatives from different points of view might be perceived as unrealistic, unthinkable, totally radical and incredible merely because they are different.
(10) can stimulate thinking about new polices and programs, or stifle such thought as a result of massive "group-thinking".

Politics in the "New Professionalism"

There is a saying that generals are always preparing for the last war in which they participated, and I suspect that the remark may be relevant here. From the summer of 1997, following a modest renaissance of moderately centre-left political parties in Europe and North America, there is much in the agenda of the "new professionalism" that is a child of the more right-wing governed late 1970s, 1980s and earlier 1990s. The market-oriented calls from the business community and international investors around the world for privatization, deregulation, decentralization and the general liberalization of trade found sympathetic listeners in high places. By any reasonable measure of success, those who advocated the market-oriented agenda have been spectacularly successful in realizing their dreams. In roughly the past 20 years, in most industrialized countries, we have seen the shredding not only of social safety nets or welfare states, but of the very idea of providing the kinds of services that many of us talked about providing and made significant real steps toward providing in many countries in the previous 30 years. In Canada today I think it is fair to say that most people, most voters anyhow, seem to be unable to even imagine public services delivered on the level and at the price in taxes that they are delivered in the Scandinavian countries. Of course there has been downsizing in the latter countries too, but they still deliver much more than we deliver in Canada.

Kettl's observations about downsizing are worth repeating here.

> The federal government's downsizing movement derives heavily from private-sector initiatives of the late 1980s and early 1990s. The private sector, however, is already beginning to learn painful lessons from its own downsizing experiences; the federal government is on the verge of stumbling into the movement's worse problems. …
>
> Research is now beginning to demonstrate that the initial advantages of corporate downsizing have often produced higher long-run costs. Stressed workers burn out, leave, or remain with lower morale. Large cuts in staff tend to 'penalize departments that are slim and reward those that are oversized,' management analyst Eileen Appelbaum concludes. The biggest performance differences, in fact, appeared due more to the quality of management than strategic downsizing (or upsizing). Indeed, a study of 531 American corporations revealed that private-sector downsizing rarely helped companies achieve the goals of higher profits and lower costs. Moreover, employee morale and motivation among surviving employees suffered. More successful efforts, on the other hand, began from a clear vision for the future coupled with a fundamental restructuring of the organization, from top managers to front-line employees. The biggest private-sector successes came when people came to see change as an ongoing process instead of a short-term event. …
>
> The biggest temptation in reinventing government is to reach for quick success by embracing downsizing without doing the hard work of improving performance, or to seek performance improvement while resisting the powerful political pressures to reduce the size of government. The single most important reality of American public management for the coming decade is the need to solve the paradox these two movements present. Big-politics downsizers will have to reckon with the fact that, without careful planning, they could 'dumbsize' the federal government, worsen performance, and even further enrage voters. Little-politics performance improvers will have to reckon with the fact that expectations will increase as resources shrink (Kettl 1995, pp. 77–79).

To one who has been teaching business ethics and editing the *Journal of Business Ethics* over this period, and who still gets cute cracks about "business ethics" being an oxymoron like "military intelligence", it is incredible that government officials of all people would want to be seen to be modeling their behaviour after business people. It is really depressing to think that as bad as the reputation of business people is from a moral point of view, the reputation of government officials might be improved by becoming more like business people! (For an overview of contemporary and likely future issues related to interactions between business and governments, see Michalos 1995, 1997d, e, and for a review of some arguments against privatization see Hardin 1990 or Michalos 1990b). I suppose that from the point of view of the government officials making these judgments, morality may be irrelevant. According to Berry and Wechsler (1995), about 76% of their national sample of 307 U.S. state civil service personnel reported that a "desire to emulate good business practices" was an "important" objective in the introduction of strategic planning in their organizations, though only 14% claimed it was "most important". In their minds, the definition of "good business practices" may have been relatively technical, amoral and apolitical.

In Canada, 20 years of governments pursuing the market-oriented agenda along with many other countries has left us with higher rates of unemployment, bankruptcies, poverty, student debt loads and taxes, a wider gap between the income and wealth of the richest and poorest quintiles, fewer public services and more personally perceived, reality based, feelings of insecurity. While there is plenty of room for debate regarding causal connections, I believe that most of these consequences could have been and were predicted by many people prior to and during the last 20 years. I also believe that while many have suffered and continue to suffer, a few have profited and continue to profit greatly from the revolution. On this score, the following remarks from Stanford (1996, p. A20) comparing the *Economic Freedom of the World 1975–1995* (Gwartney et al. 1996) with the *Human Development Report 1995* (United Nations Development Programme) are worth noting.

> The Fraser Institute, together with other right-wing think-tanks, have ranked the countries of the world according to their economic 'freedom'. ...it is interesting to compare the Fraser Institute list with the UN ranking of nations according to their human development... . Countries ranked at the top of the Fraser Institute list (Hong Kong, New Zealand, Singapore) are ranked well down on the UN list (24th, 17th and 35th, respectively). On the other hand, the Scandinavian countries which dominate the UN's top 10 are ranked no higher than 41st on the Fraser list.
>
> Indeed, there is no reliable correlation whatsoever between economic 'freedom' and human development. In statistical terms, the correlation coefficient between the top 20 countries on the UN's 1995 list and their corresponding Fraser Institute rankings for 1993–95 is almost exactly zero – in fact, the coefficient is slightly *negative*, implying a weak inverse relation between the two lists. Since the various rules and policies which are held to interfere with so-called economic 'freedom' were motivated precisely by the desire to ensure that economic activity is better translated into social progress, this result should not be surprising.

Regardless of the evidence indicating that the market-oriented agenda is more harmful than beneficial for most people in my country, I think the mind set of most Canadians is still fixed on the rightness (no pun intended) of that agenda. Thus, keeping Machiavelli's wise counsel in mind, it is imperative that high level public administrators here, and I gather in Italy and elsewhere, be prepared to manage the public's business in such a world. Nevertheless, while we prepare our students to manage and thus survive in today's world, we must also prepare them to appreciate and help create an even better world for tomorrow. According to Machiavelli's biographer, Villari (1892), one of the reasons Machiavelli had so much difficulty with public officials above and around him was precisely that he could not practice what he preached and was continually overestimating the generosity of mind and spirit of the wrong people, and continually trying to make the world better than he found it. So, our students should study not only the teachings of the masters, but also their lives, and learn from what they did as well as from what they said (which was also Machiavelli's recommendation to his students).

On p. 9 of the Background Paper we are told that "society's needs for PA services" have been greatly increased, leading to "an unbearable *overload* (exacerbated moreover by the existence of a 'democratic' regime, i.e., by a 'vote market') that

> has placed the PA system (both from the financing and organizational point of view) in a crisis situation in which there is an objective need for transformation and transition. Rather than increase its role of provider of services, it [i.e., the PA system] must increase its role in the 'management', regulation, programming and encouragement of the substitution of the public sector with the private one, wherever possible: …
>
> We may wonder whether these different effects of societal transformation underway may determine that the needs for transformation within PA with regard to the 'workforce' justify…a requalification of the *management,* and *upper management.* …Therefore we can ask whether there has matured today in PA…the need for a new specific *managerial professionally* independent from the specific competence of this or that branch of administration… .

As I explained in Michalos (1997a), so far as Canada and I think the United States are concerned, the "unbearable *overload"* was deliberately manufactured in the interest of serving the right-wing, market-oriented political agenda. Furthermore, insofar as the overload was manufactured, it can be recrafted to suit a different political agenda, provided of course that there are alternatives and sufficient political will pursue them. Alternatives have been sketched for changes in the national political agenda in Canada, but so far there is not sufficient political will to make the changes. (For one alternative, see Canadian Centre for Policy Alternatives and Choices 1997).

The "New Professionalism" Without Politics (Almost)

Suppose I am wrong and it is true that in Canada and other industrialized countries our PA systems collapsed under their own weight. Would that warrant the development of "a new specific *managerial professionally*"? I doubt it. Although I believe there is much that is admirable in intent and even in recognized achievements already resulting from the introduction of performance-based management in public administration, I think what is required is not a whole new curriculum but some marginal changes. Again, however, let's suppose I am wrong and assume the ambitious task of developing a whole new curriculum. From this point of view, it will be useful to work through the Background Paper step by step, making whatever critical and constructive comments seem to be appropriate.

To begin with, judging from the absence of any explicit requirement for research in the new curriculum, I suppose it is not designed to produce research scientists. I think that is reasonable because the upper level new managers are probably not going to be called upon to conduct research. At any rate, perhaps we should address this question briefly at least in our curriculum discussions.

I agree that there should be greater efforts at "transnational collaboration in the field of public administration" (p. 3) and greater efforts in the conceptualization and "measurement of output in PA" (p. 8).

The principle *of flexibility,* "that this training [for new professionals] must be aimed at forming a manager who can be used in *any* operational sector of PA" (p. 12) and its corollary of ignoring the specific "operational destinations" of graduates (p. 13) seem worthwhile. However, on p. 43 a question is raised about the possible need for different kinds of training for upper level managers working in international, national, regional and municipal jurisdictions. As I reflected on this question, it seemed to me that the principle of *flexibility* would have to be interpreted with some flexibility because some specialization of training for the various jurisdictions would probably be desirable, especially for upper level managers.

The problem I see here is that appropriate training for an upper level manager in some field would vary depending on whether the manager (1) had been in that field a long time and planned to stay in it, (2) had been in that field a short time and planned to stay in it, (3) had been in that field a long time and planned to leave it, or (4) had been in that field a short time and planned to leave it.

In case (1), some sort of generic training or skill development might be appropriate, assuming that the manager would be well-informed in the specifics of his or her field. In case (2), some sort of training specific to the new field might be more appropriate. In case (3), generic training might increase the manager's options as he or she looked for other fields to work in. In case (4), generic training might be the most appropriate sort because the manager is planning to leave, but specific training for his or her current field might be more appropriate because it might eliminate the need or desire to leave by increasing competence in the current field. About all I can conclude from reviewing these scenarios is that maybe we should give some thought to having more than one curriculum stream for managers in different situations.

The ideas of instruction in "the functionality of the public system" from the *institutional, economic* and *socio-cultural"* points of view (pp. 16–26) seem to me to be necessary.

Regarding legal matters (p. 18), the assumption must be that the "new professionals" are not being trained to be lawyers, but to understand law, its role and rules. It will be impossible to function without access to good legal counsel. So what the public manager needs is some training in how to access the right sort of legal aid in a variety of areas over a variety of political/administrative jurisdictions. I guess some of this is standard material in most of our public administration curricula.

Regarding problems of "*community income*" and "*outgoings*" (p. 20), the new public managers should be familiar with and willing to undertake meaningful consultations with various stakeholders in order to discover citizens' preferred methods of delivering and paying for services. Presumably this is at least part of the motivation for Osborne and Gaebler's (1992) recommendation to put "citizens in the position to take control away from bureaucracy and bring it into the community" (p. 28). Anyone who has tried to elicit *reliable and valid* input from citizen-stakeholders about any public policy matter knows how difficult it is. There is no difficulty getting input. Any radio talk show host can do that. The trick is to get information that reliably and validly reflects the considered views of relatively well-informed people. In classical terms, one might say that the trick is to determine exactly the "general will" of a population (Michalos 1991a). The real danger is that because a well-organized, well-funded group can monopolize a public debate about practically any issue, if "control" is taken away from a "bureaucracy" that is in principle answerable to democratically elected officials and given to a "community", the latter may be a very specialized interest group and most people may be net losers.

There are two studies directly related to the issue of eliciting citizens' views that I would like briefly mention here, one from my own work and one from Gauthier (1987). A few years ago I undertook a survey of the residents of Prince George in order to find out, among other things, how their use of 23 public services was related to their levels of satisfaction with them and how their satisfaction levels were related to their willingness to pay more or less taxes for those services. The results were not entirely surprising, but they are instructive. To begin with, I found that the zero-order correlations among the scores for usage of public services, spending preferences and levels of satisfaction were on average fairly small.

> The average correlation between use and spending scores was $r = .12$, between spending and satisfaction $r = .21$, and between use and satisfaction $r = .08$. Even in the strongest case, then, only about 4% of the variance in spending preferences can be explained by satisfaction with the service. If this relationship is so weak, one wonders what exactly does motivate spending preferences for public service.
>
> While the average correlations are modest, they are often interesting. For example, while only 16% of respondents reported any use of hospitals and clinics, 28% were very or

> somewhat dissatisfied with them and 82% thought more tax money should be spent on them. The spending and satisfaction figures were negatively associated ($r = -.28$), indicating that as respondents' levels of satisfaction went down, their willingness to spend more on the service went up. The spending and use figures were positively associated ($r = .16$), indicating that their willingness to spend more increased slightly with increased usage of the service.
>
> Considering provincial government officials, only 5% of respondents reported that they contacted them often, 62% reported that less tax money should be spent on them and 36% were very or somewhat dissatisfied with them. The spending and use figures were slightly positively correlated ($r = .07$), indicating that willingness to spend more on such officials was only slightly related to the actual experience of making use of them. However, the spending and satisfaction figures were more strongly positively associated ($r = .35$), indicating that the more satisfied respondents were with their provincial officials, the more they were inclined to favour spending more tax money on them. Still, since only about 12% of the variance in spending preferences could be explained by satisfaction with the 'officials,' that means that 88% has to be accounted for by something other than satisfaction with officials' performance. Exactly what that "something" might be would be worth exploring in the future. (Michalos 1996, p. 53)

City administrators in Prince George thought the results of the survey were interesting enough and potentially useful enough for planning purposes that they have now made a commitment to have a broad based survey of community services and quality of life every spring at least for the next three years.

The following quotation is from Michalos (1993a, p. 18).

> Gauthier (1987) reported the results of a survey of nearly one thousand clients who received some assistance from the Canada Mortgage and Housing Corporation Residential Rehabilitation Assistance Program (RRAP) in 1981. The basic aims of the program are to improve substandard housing units, extend the useful lives of buildings and generally aid residents in maintenance. Objective and subjective indicators of program success were used and, among other things, Gauthier claimed that "The most conclusive finding of this analysis and of the literature in general is that the level of client satisfaction for a particular program is only indirectly related to his/her objective conditions and to real results of the program's actions. ...Moreover, the lack of stability in the measurement of satisfaction over time makes its use difficult; a particular measurement taken at the time of program activity will be more positive than a measurement taken later" (p. 250).

In Michalos (1997b) I reviewed several studies involving research on associations among levels of taxation, the provision of public services, and migration or residential mobility. This sort of material ought to be very useful for public administrators, and I suppose Archibugi had some of these issues in mind when he wrote about studying "the behaviour of the citizen in their various roles as (a) user-consumer; (b) elector," and so on, and he posed the question of "whether the public manager should be taught to face those problems of behaviour with direct enquiries aimed at pointing out, in concrete, what behaviour could result in particular decisions…" (pp. 24–25). My view would be that managers must be able to appreciate good survey research and program evaluation, but they do not have to be able to carry out the research. I think the same point would apply to many of the technical subjects listed on p. 40 too; e.g., multi-linear programming and optimisation, the use of "software programmes for the graphical and cartographical representation of territorial and environmental phenomena". So, managers are rather more like art critics than artists in this respect.

A program of study for managers, at any level, ought to include a heavy dose of practice-based training in "people skills", not only conflict resolution techniques involving managers as mediators or arbitrators, but skills for identifying and managing difficult people and one's own weaknesses and strengths, and collective bargaining skills (Michalos 1990a). Perhaps such issues can be addressed in or around the "sociocultural behavioural" module of the curriculum, and perhaps it would be worthwhile to emphasize here that although I think upper level managers are primarily managers of people, the curriculum outlined in the Background Paper seems to be designed to train fairly technical people, not to say technocrats. Maybe that is just my impression because I have not thoroughly digested the rich array of issues introduced in the Paper, but maybe it is real and intended, and therefore worth some discussion.

Regarding "reflection on the efficiency of policies for the *allocation* of public means…*stabilisation…redistribution..,* and…*regulation"* (p. 21), I agree that this is necessary, but I do not know "to what extent" the reflection should be carried out. Upper level managers may be spared the burden of detailed instruction in abstract axiomatic analysis, as Archibugi suggests on p. 21. Many of "the points which should be the object of teaching" listed on pp. 36–37 can quickly become mired in formal analysis that is not only practically useless but probably bewildering to the sort of people-oriented managers one tends to find at higher levels of management. Although I do not recall the assumption being made in the Background Paper that most upper level public managers will not be technicians, I think that is a fair assumption. At any rate, if one thinks of the three broad skills of literacy, numeracy and diplomacy, my guess would be that upper level managers would be especially strong in the third category and would manage others tending to be stronger in one or the other two categories.

The idea that we need whole new programs "*exclusively* aimed at the training of the new professional figure of public administration manager, and nothing else" (p. 12) strikes me as a luxury that most governments cannot afford, especially in the market-oriented ethos of today.

It is unclear to me how the principle of *peculiarity* implies that "the study programme should not be able to count on any basic propaedeutic training…unless that which is common to all accesses to higher education" (p. 13), but I think I would accept the alleged implication as a fair assumption.

If the principle of *post-scholasticism* implies that there should be a master's degree for upper level PA managers on top of an ordinary master's degree in PA, I doubt it because I doubt that there are enough new ideas to make a whole new degree program for the managers of managers. I suppose this issue must be given some major time for reflection and discussion.

The idea of *"homogeneity"* applied to the proposed curriculum is unclear to me, and in particular I do not know how we might measure the "internal coherence" of a program (p. 13).

The alleged "fact [for public administrators] that the final decision is that of the political decision-taker" (p. 14) strikes me as unrealistic for managers at the municipal, provincial, national or international levels. At all levels of administration there are more or less significant areas of discretionary authority and responsibility (judged by the potential costs and benefits of various kinds of decisions) for which administrators have "the final decision". Perhaps more importantly from the point of view of a discussion of a "new professionalism", I think the more we admit, encourage and hold administrators and elected officials accountable for their decisions and actions, the better our administration and governments will be.

On p. 29 of the Background Paper we are given a list of topics covering material consistent with the principles of the Osbome-Gaebler decalogue (See next section.), e.g., "Introduction of elements of competitivity" and "market-oriented government". Then the question is raised about starting "the debate on the new teaching relative to the managerial capacities of the new manager from these classifications". I think that is one good point of departure for initiating the debate and I would offer my critical comments in the next section on the principles of the decalogue as representing some opposition to including some of the suggested topics.

I agree that the educational program should include the "*operations of general planning*", including "*techniques for the management of information flows relative to the construction of scenarios and balance sheets for socio-economic development* (*cf.* Michalos 1970a, 1997c)...*techniques for the evaluation of alternative decision-making scenarios*...[and] *techniques for the evaluation of the public use of national resources*" (p. 31) (*cf.* Michalos 1970b, 1978, 1980b, 1981).

The "techniques of evaluation of regulation" and "techniques for procedural management of regulation" (p. 33) are quite basic to the aims of "performance-oriented professionalism". So they should certainly be part of the curriculum.

Some "Knowledge of the Main Public Policies" (pp. 37–38) is essential, but it is difficult to say how much. Indeed, in most of the 13 policy areas listed in the footnote it is often difficult to determine what counts as a policy or part of a policy with which administrators at various levels should be familiar. Sometimes there are explicit documents indicating specific policies and sometimes not. Because specific programs exist at various levels of action in a bureaucracy, what is essential policy for people working with programs at one level may be irrelevant for people working at a different level. I do not know of a good way to sort out the issues here, but I agree with the negative answer to the two questions cited from Jan-Erik Lane in the footnote on p. 38.

I am sympathetic to the motives behind the comments on p. 39 that "The informing principles...postulate the radical abandonment of any form of instruction which is repetitive in some way of university disciplines and grouping in disciplinary 'areas'" and "the possibility should be anticipated...of 'complementary' or 'integrative that are parallel to the 'institutional' ones...". My problem is that I cannot imagine developing courses dealing with, for example, monetary or fiscal policy that would not in some way involve repetition of basic knowledge. Partly this is a result of the strength of disciplinary instruction in universities and partly it is a result of our assumption of the "principle of peculiarity". Because we presuppose nothing in particular about knowledge of monetary and fiscal policy, we seem to be obliged to repeat disciplinary fundamentals in order to guarantee that all students have the appropriate background information to deal with advanced subjects. Perhaps the specification of "alignment courses" is intended to address this issue.

Remarks on the Osborne-Gaebler Decalogue

A long footnote on p. 28 summarizes "a 'decalogue' proposed by David Osborne and Ted Gaebler' which has been recognized as inspiring principles for the NPR [National Performance Review]; a decalogue of 'entrepreneurial' requirements for the new public management, addressed to the reinventing of public administration". The second principle was mentioned earlier, including the danger in helping citizens "take control away from bureaucracy". It seems to me that some of the other principles are also questionable on many different grounds and that, therefore, our "period of reflection, study and experimentation" (p. 11) should include at least some mention of these. If we had the time and other resources, we should make a broad based benefit/cost analysis of each of the principles with an aim to deciding if, all things considered, it is likely that the long run benefits are at least as valuable as the long run costs of accepting the various principles and their implications. Needless to say, we do not have such time or resources. So, my strategy will be mainly to play devil's advocate and to indicate some of the most salient costs, disadvantages or dangers of uncritically accepting the various principles. This seems like a particularly useful approach to take in the light of all the ink that has been shed by the advocates of change that were cited in the Background Paper.

Consider, then, the assumption behind the first principle, namely, that "the promotion of competition between services" would produce a long run net benefit for the general public. Everyone knows that, while competition can be invigorating and productive, it can also be wasteful, debilitating and counter-productive. One of the least controversial claims of Plato's *Republic* (c.380 B.C.) was that an individual or group living in conflict with himself, herself or itself would be weaker and less happy than one living in cooperative harmony. After 2400 years, there is plenty of evidence showing that cooperation often has better long term results than competition. So, it is remarkable that the decalogue's first principle calls for competition and the word "cooperation" is never mentioned in the decalogue at all. (The idea of cooperation does seem to come out in the tenth principle). Personally, I find it hard to believe that setting civil servants in different services against each other competing for funds, personnel or anything else will always or usually produce better service (though it might reduce expenditures) than getting them to work cooperatively to provide a coherent network of public services at the lowest cost. Does anyone think that having the U.S. Department of Agriculture aiding tobacco companies to sell cigarettes overseas at the same time the Department of Health is trying to get people to stop smoking is an optimal solution of the labour, health and tax revenue problems connected to this industry?

While the competitive spirit is advocated in the decalogue, the U.S. Vice President's overview of "the new job of the federal executive" strongly advocates a cooperative spirit (Gore 1994). In fact, the word "competition" does not appear at all in his overview (unlike Gore 1993, as indicated below). Here is a sample of his description of some of the "seven characteristics" of the "new job".

> In the new way, federal executives need to involve all employees in developing a clear vision and a shared sense of mission. …This approach results in the empowerment of all employees… .It ensures that everyone 'buys into' the vision and is part of the process for creating it, so that the goals can be developed together. …
>
> In the new way, federal executives will need to help staff cross boundaries to work effectively with other organizations. …teamwork is now the other hallmark of success. …In intelligent organizations, teams and their members must reach out through voluntary collaboration to create a more integrated organization. …
>
> In the new way, federal executives will need to work to satisfy their customers. In the past… .The idea of a customer survey would have seemed ridiculous to federal executives. …
>
> If…a manager asks all of the employees to think about the part of [a] problem that he or she is most familiar with, and participate collectively in an organization wide effort to solve that problem, and then assemble all of the answers to change the organization, then an organization can change much more rapidly and learn much more quickly. …
>
> In the new way, federal executives will be expected to concentrate on performance and carefully measure results–outcomes and outputs, not just inputs. …
>
> Specifically, our challenge is to create a work environment that: (1) promotes and rewards innovation, (2) preserves accountability and respect for the law, (3) puts customers first, and (4) provides employees with a feeling of security, recognition, and personal accomplishment (Gore 1994, pp. 318–320).

If there is a problem with Gore's view of the new management in his overview, it is in his neglect of what public choice theorists call "the aggregation problem" and moral philosophers call "conflicts of interest". Reading Gore's paper I couldn't help thinking that he was really talking about politics without tears. In his world or the world that will be created by his new managers, people put their heads and hearts together' and joyfully "promote innovation and quality". As Garvey (1995, p. 103) put it, "With the kind of cultural transformation that Gore professes to envisage, thousands of innovations by members of an energized federal work force would integrate to create constructive change across the bureaucracy at large". Of course we all know better. Kettl (1995, p. 68) remarked that "Practical management … suggests that it is unlikely that the accumulated decisions of millions of empowered workers will be consistent with each other, the law, or the public interest". The very fact that Gore only explicitly recognizes two "hurdles in accepting the challenge of change", namely, "cynicism" and "the existing work culture" makes him and other advocates of his views liable to be quickly disillusioned when there are conflicts among thoroughly good ends or means (Gore 1994,

p. 320). On this score, it is worthwhile to recall Berry and Wechsler's (1995, p. 165) comments.

> The history of public administration provides many examples of new management tools that have been hailed for their promise to improve government performance. PPBS, MBO, and Quality Circles, for example, were all greeted initially with great (and largely uncritical) enthusiasm by politicians and administrators looking for answers to an array of public sector woes. Unfortunately, as in the cases cited, disillusionment with the latest management innovation can set in very quickly when reports from the field describe poor results or unanticipated negative consequences.

In his *Report of the National Performance Review* (1993), the Vice President has a great deal to say about competition. There one finds such remarks as the following.

> Not all federal operations should be forced to compete, of course. Competition between regulatory agencies is a terrible idea. …Nor should policy agencies compete.
>
> In the development of policy, cooperation between different units of government is essential. Competition creates turf wars, which get in the way of creating rational policies and programs. It is in *service delivery* that competition yields results–because competition is the one force that gives public agencies *no choice* but to improve. …
>
> Every federal agency needs 'support services'–accounting, property management, payroll processing, legal advice, and so on. Currently, most managers have little choice about where to get them; they must use what's available in-house. But no manager should be confined to an agency monopoly. Nor should agencies provide services in-house unless the services can compete with those of other agencies and private companies. …
>
> *The administration should encourage operations of one agency to compete for work in other agencies. …*
>
> Not all public activities should be subject to competition, … . In some cases, even service delivery operations are better off as monopolies. In the private sector, we call these utilities and regulate them to protect the consumer. …Many governments, including our federal government, do something very similar. They create government-owned corporations to undertake specific tasks. The Postal Service and Tennesee Valley Authority are two such examples. …
>
> As we reinvent the federal government, we, too, must rely more on market incentives and less on new programs. …Government should assume a more appropriate and effective role: setting standards and imposing penalties on workplaces that don't comply. …
>
> By creating competition between public organizations, contracting services out to private organizations, listening to our customers, and embracing market incentives wherever appropriate, we can transform the quality of services delivered to the American people (Gore 1993, pp. 54–64).

The third principle of the decalogue calls for "a concentration of attention not on inputs but rather on outcomes". (See also the discussion on pp. 35–37.) This was a fundamental tenet of the pioneers in the social indicators movement in the 1960s (Michalos 1980a) and remains a key feature of much social indicators research. However, by now I would insist that the focus of attention must be on outcome indicators related to inputs, or benefits related to costs, because either kind of indicator without the other gives an incomplete database for the assessment of efficiency and action. Although it is often difficult or practically impossible to get cardinal measures of outputs and inputs, as well as agreement about all the other variables that have to be taken into account for a rigorous benefit/cost analysis (Michalos 1992), our long term attention has to be directed to both inputs and outcomes.

The fourth principle advises us to be "guided by goals—or missions—and not by rules and regulations", which would have impressed me more in 1994 than it does today. In 1994 I left the University of Guelph, where I had been teaching for 28 years, and joined the University of Northern British Columbia, which officially opened its doors in a brand new facility one month before I arrived. What often bothered me about my old university was that we had rules and regulations that seemed too often unrelated or even antithetical to the goals of the institution. It was difficult to get things done because we had too many rules and regulations. At my new institution we had an abundance of goals and very few rules and regulations, and we were often paralysed by both. Because we were a new institution, people inside and outside the university expected us to and sometimes committed us to doing all kinds of things, many more things than a tiny faculty of 150 people could do. What was worse, because we had few rules and regulations, people just did whatever they thought was reasonable or they did nothing at all. In the latter case, of course, things just did not get done that should have been done. In the former case, people too frequently discovered that what was reasonable to them was unreasonable to someone else. So, different people, and often this meant students, were sent off in several different directions to accomplish similar tasks and it was impossible to hold anyone accountable or responsible precisely because there were no generally accepted rules and regulations specifying appropriate behaviour. I suppose it was simple observations like this that led people like Hobbes and Locke to accept the truism that where there is no law, there can be no justice or injustice. On this score, Marcus Tullius Cicero (c. 50 B.C.) was particularly eloquent. "Whence comes our sense of duty?", he wrote.

> From whom do we obtain the principles of religion? Whence comes the law of nations, or even that law of ours which is called 'civil'? Whence justice, honour, fair-dealing? Whence decency, self-restraint, fear of disgrace, eagerness for praise and honour? Whence comes endurance amid toils and dangers? I say, from those men who, when these things had been inculcated by a system of training, either confirmed them by custom or else enforced them by statutes (Cicero c.50, p. 145).

The fifth principle recommends "redefining the users as customers and offering them alternative choices (between schools, training programmes, housing options)". It seems to me that this recommendation could only be made and accepted by people who, at a minimum, do not understand what schools are or what they are supposed to do. In brief, schools are places where people without some sort of knowledge go in order to acquire it. To suppose that students can or ought to be able to pick and choose curricula, texts and teachers' with the same freedom that people pick and choose food and drink, clothes or other consumer goods is to suppose that the former and latter kinds of choices are equally matters of mere taste. But this is quite wrong, and if we believed it was true then we would be wasting our time at this gathering. If the fifth principle were reasonable, we would be making better use of our resources to just do a survey of our likely student population (our potential market) and offer any old courses, with any old texts and any old instructors or even "none of the above" if that is what the market would bear. That would be genuinely entrepreneurial but counter productive if our aim is to have excellent schools training excellent public managers and not just excellent money-making institutions.

Nobody has captured the essence of the "conflicts between the principles of education and the market" better than McMurtry (1991). In his words,

> The overriding goal of corporate agents in the marketplace is to maximize private money profits. The overriding goal of educational agents in schools, colleges and universities is to advance and disseminate shared knowledge. …
>
> The determining motivation of the market is to satisfy the wants of whoever has the money to purchase the goods that are wanted. The determining motivation of education is to develop sound understanding whether it is wanted or not. …
>
> What is the best policy for buying a product–to assert the customer's claim as 'always right'–is the worst possible policy for a learner. What is the best policy for selling a product–to offend no-one and no vested interest–may be the worst possible policy for an educator (McMurtry 1991, pp. 211–214).

More generally, Garvey (1995, pp. 104–105) asserted that

> The case for the customer-oriented approach to federal bureaucratic restructuring may be as empirically weak as critics charge it is normatively. Donald Kettl has described the evolution of the national government's role as a transition from retail to wholesale governance. Well into the twentieth century, federal officials provided direct–often face-to-face–services. But such 'retail' functions constitute a diminishing share of the activities of federal bureaucrats. Although federal spending has mushroomed, the federal civilian labor force is now about the same size as it was in the 1950s. Increasingly, Kettl has documented, federal workers act as check writers, service packagers, and program overseers. Federal employees 'wholesale' programs to a vast network of state and local officials or private contractors: the retailers, as Kettl terms them, who actually deliver the products or programs that the federal government funds. The authors of the NPR fail to explain how customers are going to influence federal bureaucrats, most of whose activities they experience only as mediated by multiple layers of intervening state, local, and frequently private actors working on contract. …
>
> Vis-a-vis state, local, and private-sector retailers, federal bureaucrats are mainly supervisors–not service providers. Vis-a-vis many of those whom the proponents of the bottom-up theory describe as 'customers,' federal bureaucrats have no direct relationship at all.

The sixth principle recommends "anticipating problems before they emerge" and it strikes me as eminently reasonable. I would only have added, "and then taking action to avert danger".

The seventh principle advises public managers to use their "energy to make money, rather than to spend it". It seems to me that a literal interpretation of this principle would have the implication that the aim of public administration is either to make money or to spend it. This involves a false dichotomy in the first place, and a mistaken view of the ultimate aim of civil service in the second place. It involves a false dichotomy insofar as it neglects the options of saving and investment.

Another way to look at the second error is to see it as a confusion between the means and end of public service. The end is excellent service in the interest of a good quality of life for citizens and the means should be the most cost effective available.

The eighth principle calls for "decentralising authority by introducing participatory management". There is quite a bit of evidence in support of participatory management as a good means to increasing job satisfaction, which is certainly a worthwhile aim (Michalos 1993a). Unfortunately, when Iaffaldano and Muchinsky (1985) did a meta-analysis of 217 studies of the relationship of job satisfaction to job performance, they found an average zero-order correlation of $r = 0.17$ between these two variables. So, only about 3% of the variance in either variable can be explained by the other. This was a remarkable finding because most people seem to assume that if they really enjoy what they are doing, they are doing a good job, and if they hate what they are doing, they are doing a poor job. The fact seems to be that on average, for a wide variety of jobs and people, people's level of job performance has very little to do with their level of job satisfaction. This is not a good reason to ignore people's feelings about their work, but it is a good reason not to confuse such good feelings with good work. (There is an enormous literature on personal satisfaction, happiness and subjective well-being in general. The investigation of the causal antecedents and complex structure of such feelings and attitudes have generated a rich mine of new questions about the foundations of rational and moral decision making; e.g., see Michalos 1985, 1991b, c, 1993a, b.)

The ninth principle recommends "preferring market mechanisms to bureaucracy mechanisms". I am not sure about the authors' definition of "bureaucracy mechanisms", but I have a pretty good idea of the meaning of "market mechanisms". In a way, the idea of "preferring market mechanisms" has been the commanding notion of most governments in industrialized countries for the past 20 years. The fact that governments have enthusiastically espoused such a notion is evidence of the success of the mixed market economies of these countries. The trouble is that too many people forget the word "mixed" in the phrase "mixed market economies" and they imagine that the success has been that of some virtually pure sort of market economies that one reads about in introductory economics texts. While this is wonderful for teachers and advocates of neo-classical economics, it is a serious mistake with very dangerous consequences for most people and democracy itself.

The danger arises from the fact that economists traditionally use a person's willingness to pay for a good or service as a measure of its value to that person, and the sum total of such payments as the measure of its value to society, in the absence of externalities. This is perhaps the single greatest defect of economics, because one's willingness to pay is a function of one's ability to pay and the latter may have little or no relation to what one needs or deserves. Since there is certainly value in satisfying people's legitimate needs and giving them their just desserts, it is a serious mistake to believe that commercial markets will somehow be able to put reasonable prices on such values when such markets are restricted by people's ability to pay. A relatively poor person may need at least as much medical care and education, and deserve at least as much justice in our courts of law as a relatively rich person, but the difference in their ability to pay in our democratic capitalist societies implies that the former person will typically be relatively less willing than the latter person to pay. A poor person's revealed preferences are necessarily constrained by his or her income. In such circumstances, to use a poor person's relative unwillingness to pay as a measure of the value of medical care, education and justice to that person is to demonstrate a severe lack of common sense and moral sensitivity. Unfortunately, that is the traditional state of much (not all) economic analysis and that is why it is so dangerous for governments and/or public managers to give preference to market mechanisms.

In roughly other words, one might say that since the fundamental organizing principle of free market capitalism is that a person's voice and influence should be proportionate to the size of a person's purse, and the fundamental organizing principle of democracy is that each person's voice and influence should be equal to that of every other person, there is a basic inconsistency between free market capitalism and democracy. Our major industrialized countries have addressed this inconsistency by developing a variety of fairly successful mixed market economies. While no one would argue that the particular "mixes" existing in diverse countries are necessarily the best and beyond improvement, it is naive to suppose that the quality of human existence will be improved by simply eliminating the "mixes" in favour of a purer market economy as the nineth principle suggests.

The tenth principle strikes me as the best of the lot. It recommends that public managers act as "catalyzing" agents to get "all sectors—public, private and voluntary—[to act] to resolve the problems of the community". Contrary to the first principle, it seems to prescribe cooperation over the broadest set of actors without ever using the word. If that is its intention, it is a welcome behavioural guide for the "new professionals".

Conclusion

In the preceding sections, I have tried to respond to the two requests put to conference participants by Professor Negri about Professor Archibugi's proposals in the Background Paper. I have tried to provide brief criticisms and comments directly here and indirectly by citing other things that I or others have written. I think a fair summary of my position would consist of the following four points.

1. Performance-based management in public administration is a welcome articulation of the philosophy of pragmatism.
2. The spread of this idea can lead to significant improvements in the quality of public administration and in the quality of life of ordinary citizens provided that it is combined with progressive substantive political, economic, social and environmental theory.

3. I doubt that a purely or even a primarily market-oriented theory would be progressive enough to be sustainable or worth sustaining in the long run.
4. I doubt that what is worthwhile about the introduction of performance-based management into public administration and government in general requires a whole "new and different type of manageriality in public administration".

Finally, I would emphasize that my position regarding the previous point is not based on any survey of contemporary public administration programs anywhere. So, in general it may well be true that many or most contemporary programs are in need of extensive and serious revision, and in particular it may be possible to make the case for a special new Master's level degree in public administration in Italy on grounds outside of those provided in the Background Paper. Lane's (1995, p. vii) view of the general state of things was similar to Archibugi's "Public administration", he wrote, "as an academic discipline has more or less crumbled during the recent decades of research into the public sector. It has become outdated, losing its status as the main approach to the interpretation of the state or government."

References

Archibugi, F. (1997). *Performance-based management in public administration and its training implications*. Paper prepared for the International Symposium on Performance Based Management in Public Administration, Royal Palace in Caserta, Italy, September 24–26, 1997.

Berry, F. S., & Wechsler, B. (1995). State agencies' experience with strategic planning: Findings from a national survey. *Public Administration Review, 55,* 159–168.

Canadian Centre for Policy Alternatives and Choices. (1997). *Alternative federal budget 1997*. Ottawa and Winnipeg: CCPA and Choices.

Cicero, M. T. (c.50). *The Republic* (parts Reprinted in W. Ebenstein & A. O. Ebenstein (Eds.), *Great political thinkers: Plato to the present* (pp 144–154). Fort Worth: Harcourt Brace College Publishers, 1991).

Garvey, G. (1995). False promises: The NPR in historical perspective. In D. F. Kettl & J. J. Dilulio, Jr. (Eds.), *Inside the reinvention machine: Appraising governmental reform* (pp. 87–106). Washington: Brookings Institution.

Gauthier, B. (1987). Client satisfaction in program evaluation. *Social Indicators Research, 19,* 174–201.

Gore, A. (1993). *From red tape to results: Creating a government that works better and costs less: Report of the national performance review*. Washington: USGPO.

Gore, A. (1994). The new job of the federal executive. *Public Administration Review, 54,* 317–321.

Gwartney, J., Lawson, R., & Block, W. (1996). *Economic freedom of the world: 1975–1995*. Vancouver: Fraser Institute.

Hardin, H. (1990). *The privatization putsch*. Halifax: Institute for Research on Public Policy.

Iaffaldano, M. T., & Muchinsky, P. M. (1985). Job satisfaction and job performance: A meta-analysis. *Psychological Bulletin, 97,* 251–273.

Kettl, D. F. (1995). Building lasting reform: Enduring questions, missing answers. In D. F. Kettl & J. J. Dilulio, Jr. (Eds.), *Inside the reinvention machine: Appraising governmental reform* (pp. 9–83). Washington: Brookings Institution.

Lane, J.-E. (1995). *The public sector: Concepts, models and approaches*. London: SAGE Publications.
Machiavelli, N. (1513). *The Prince* (Reprinted in M. L. Morgan (Ed.) *Classics of moral and political theory* (pp. 493–542). Indianapolis: Hackett Publishing Co., 1992).
McMurtry, J. (1991). Education and the market model. *Journal of the Philosophy of Education, 25,* 209–217.
Michalos, A. C. (1970a). Cost-benefit versus expected utility acceptance rules. *Theory and Decision, 1*, 61–88.
Michalos, A. C. (1970b). Decision making in committees. *American Philosophical Quarterly, 7*, 91–106.
Michalos, A. C. (1978). *Foundations of decision-making*. Ottawa: Canadian Library of Philosophy.
Michalos, A. C. (1980a). North American social report. In *Foundations, population and health* (Vol. 1). Dordrecht: D.Reidel Publishing Co.
Michalos, A. C. (1980b). A reconsideration of the idea of a science court. In P. T. Durbin (Ed.), *Philosophy and technology: An annual compilation of research* (Vol. 3, pp. 10–28). JAI Press.
Michalos, A. C. (1981). Technology assessment, facts and values. In P. T. Durbin (Ed.), *Research in philosophy and technology* (Vol. 4, pp. 59–81). JAI Press.
Michalos, A. C. (1985). Multiple discrepancies theory (MDT). *Social Indicators Research, 16,* 347–413.
Michalos, A. C. (1990a). The impact of trust on business, international security and the quality of life. *Journal of Business Ethics, 9,* 619–638.
Michalos, A. C. (1990b). Review of the privatization putsch. *Journal of Business Ethics*, *9*, 206–214.
Michalos, A.C. (1991a). Ethical considerations regarding public opinion polling during election campaigns. *Journal of Business Ethics, 10*, 403–422.
Michalos, A. C. (1991b). *Global report on student well-being, vol. 1, life satisfaction and happiness*. New York: Springer.
Michalos, A. C. (1991c). *Global report on student well-being, vol. 2, family, friends, living partner and self-esteem*. New York: Springer.
Michalos, A. C. (1992). Ethical considerations in evaluation. *Canadian Journal of Program Evaluation, 7,* 61–75.
Michalos, A. C. (1993a). *Global report on student well-being, vol. 3, employment, finances, housing and transportation*. New York: Springer.
Michalos, A. C. (1993b). *Global report on student well-being, vol. 4, religion, education, recreation and health*. New York: Springer.
Michalos, A. C. (1995). *A pragmatic approach to business ethics*. Thousand Oaks: SAGE Publications.
Michalos, A. C. (1996). Aspects of the quality of life in Prince George. *South Asian Journal of Psychology, 1,* 45–70.
Michalos, A. C. (1997a). *Good taxes: The case for taxing foreign currency exchange and other financial transactions*. Toronto: Science for Peace and Dundurn Press.
Michalos, A. C. (1997b). Migration and the quality of life: A review essay. *Social Indicators Research, 39,* 121–166.
Michalos, A. C. (1997c). Combining social, economic and environmental indicators to measure sustainable human well-being. *Social Indicators Research, 40,* 221–258.
Michalos, A. C. (1997d). Issues for business ethics in the nineties and beyond. *Journal of Business Ethics, 16,* 219–230.
Michalos, A. C. (1997e). Non-academic critics of business ethics in Canada. *Journal of Business Ethics, 16,* 611–619.

Osborne, D., & Gaebler, T. (1992). *Reinventing government: How the entrepreneurial spirit is transforming the public sector*. Reading: Addison-Wesley.

Stanford, J. (1996). Economic freedom. *Globe and Mail*, A20.

United Nations Development Programme. (1995). *Human development report 1995*. New York: UNDP.

Villari, P. (1892). *The life and times of Niccolo Machiavelli, Volumes I and II*. (Reprinted by New York: Haskell House, 1969).

Chapter 15
The Integration of Public Policy-Making with Outcomes Measurement

Alex C. Michalos

Introduction

I appreciate the opportunity to share my thoughts on the use of outcomes measurement in public policy-making, and especially on the idea that focussing on such measurement might lead to more integrated, coherent processes of policy-making. The idea struck me like a lightning rod, sending off sparks in every direction. When the so-called social indicators movement took off in the late 1960s, there were four things that captured our imagination.

First, most of us were pragmatists. So we had a natural inclination to focus on outcomes, results and consequences, and we thought of social indicators primarily as measures of such things. When we talked about measuring the quality of life, we meant the quality as lived or experienced, not as dreamed of, hoped for or planned for. (I recall a luncheon meeting in Washington of the US Social Science Research Council's Center for the Co-ordination of Social Indicators in the early 1970s in which Silvia Ostry said she thought Statistics Canada's proposed compendium of social indicators should have only output measures. I was on the other side of the table, literally, arguing that a compendium would be relatively useless unless it included measures of costs (inputs) as well as benefits (outputs and outcomes).).

Second, most of us were tired of economists dominating discussions of public policy-making with their limited focus on things that could only be measured in dollars. We thought, for example, that measures of lives lost or debilitated by disease or malnutrition were important in themselves, whatever their dollar value.

Michalos, A.C.: 1998. The integration of public policy-making with outcomes Measurement. Paper presented at a Conference at Queen's University, Institute on Social Policy, August 1998.

A.C. Michalos (✉)
University of Northern British Columbia, Prince George, BC, Canada
e-mail: michalos@brandonu.ca

A.C. Michalos, *How Good Policies and Business Ethics Enhance Good Quality of Life*, DOI 10.1007/978-3-319-50724-8_15

We thought that it was important to know how many people in our country were functionally illiterate, how many were abused at home or likely to be criminally assaulted on our streets, whether that mattered to anyone's pocket book or not.

Third, most of us were number crunchers. In this respect, we were like the economists, only we thought our numbers could beat their numbers. (I think it was guy thing.)

Finally, most of us knew we were painfully short on theory and even lacked a coherent reporting system in which we might plug in all our numbers. There was and still is no generally accepted theory of a good society, a good life or a good quality of life. More importantly, there was and is no apolitical means to discovering such a theory or such a life. Anyone who believes we can find such a theory or life without patient, careful research and endless negotiation with people who often hold seriously incompatible views believes in politics without tears, and is mistaken. There is no politics without tears, and in there is no public policy-making without tears. Betty Davis said growing old is not for the timid. Neither is public policy-making.

Ursula Franklin said some place that she was shocked to discover that people who are quite well-informed might be uninterested in doing anything. More directly, knowledge is not sufficient or even necessary for action. People can know what should be done but be unwilling to do anything, and what is required to improve the quality of people's lives is the willingness to act.

Gloria Steinem always says she is for anything that will get people off their asses.

Aristotle was not one of my favourite authors but he had some bright ideas. One was that the observation of good moral character can motivate people to act accordingly. The only way to observe good moral character is to observe its effects in good moral action. In short, the real point is that when people see someone do something morally good or noble, they are inclined to replicate it.

Well, we must not get carried away. Some people are inclined to replicate it. I don't know how many. It depends on the issues and the people, but often enough many Spartacuses (Spartacae?) do come forward given the proper leadership.

Finally, in these introductory remarks, I would like to share the following long quotation from Cole's (1961) book *The Story of Fabian Socialism*. Deborah Poff and I are editing a volume of the correspondence between George Bernard Shaw and Beatrice and Sidney Webb, and I found Cole's comments just when I began thinking about this conference. She wrote:

> …the Fabians were answering the question asked in their first Tract, *Why Are the Many Poor?* [1884] with the assertion that they need not be, and that concerted action by society as a whole could prevent it. They began their propaganda at a time when it was the general opinion that poverty was an inescapable fact of society, destitution a reasonable consequence of a person's own faulty character, and unemployment, for the most part, a form of malingering which could be stopped if the penalties were made sufficiently deterrent. Today nobody–or hardly anybody–believes that any longer; and the disappearance of the belief can without hesitation be ascribed in great part to the persistent propaganda of Fabians over the years. It is, as Tawney said, the Acquisitive Society, and not the laws of nature, which prescribe poverty. But to disclose evil is not to cure it; and the merit of Fabian reformers is

that they went on to press for the abolition of great tracts of poverty by specific action–through a system of social security above all, but also through such lesser measures as provision of dinners and milk for school children and of public housing of reasonable standard, through reduction of hours of work and improvement of factory conditions, through wage regulation for the underpaid and fair wages clauses in local authority and government employment. All these today are commonplaces, and the phrase used by the Webbs to sum them up, 'A National Minimum of Civilised Life', seems sometimes to irritate young Socialists who feel (not unreasonably) that a society calling itself 'affluent' ought to have something rather more inspiring to offer as an end; nevertheless, that irritation is largely due to the change brought about in social consciousness, the belief that primary poverty–in Britain, at all events–need no longer exist, and a great reluctance to admit, on the evidence of eyes and ears, that it still does....

Beatrice Webb's *Minority Report* to the Poor Law Commission, which had been preceded, be it remembered, by earlier Fabian Tracts, was itself a fully worked out and cogently argued scheme of social security. It appeared in 1909. Two years later, Lloyd George appropriated a small piece of it in the first Insurance Acts; eighteen years after that, Neville Chamberlain took a further step by abolishing the Guardians of the Poor, though not the Poor Law; in the middle of the war, so long after the *Minority Report* that its very name had been all but forgotten, its proposals, with inevitable modifications, reappeared in the Beveridge Report; by 1948 the Poor Law had finally ceased to exist, and universal insurance and a national medical service were a reality. Sidney Webb, in a moment of pessimistic realism, said that it took the British public twenty or thirty years after a reform was first proposed to accept it; in the case of the *Minority Report* it took forty. (Cole 1961, pp. 330–333)

Forty years is a long time in the life of an individual, but not in the life of the human race itself. When one thinks about significant social change, I think it is vitally important to think of the human community as a whole and to think of one's efforts as contributions to the creation of a good quality of life for all the members of that community, most of whom have not even been born.

Outcome Measures as Unifying Instruments

Suppose we take seriously the idea that outcome measures might serve as unifying instruments to improve public policy-making. What empirical evidence is there that might make the idea more or less attractive? Below I will describe six cases that seem to me to shed diverse lights on this question. However, after some weeks of thinking about this paper and the six cases, I recalled some additional useful history. The fact is that when the people in the U.S. Office of Management and Budget decided to produce their volumes on social indicators in the early 1970s, there was an interdepartmental committee chaired, I believe, by Dan Tunstall. At any rate, Tunstall was responsible for putting the first collection (*Social Indicators 1973*, I think). Denis Johnston produced one or two more reports in the series, again using a mixed committee. Both men told me how dependent they were on various other people in various departments. In Canada, Statistics Canada's *Perspectives Canada* series was the result of work by an interdepartmental committee, chaired I believe by Hans Adler when Sylvia Ostry was Chief Statistician. I do not know how much provincial and state personnel got involved in the federal efforts in Canada and the USA, but there was certainly cooperation across departments around the selection and use of appropriate outcomes measures.

I was on the Advisory Committee of British Columbia's *Report on Sustainability,* which was sponsored by the Commission on Resources and the Environment. The people who actually wrote the document drew on work from several departments and several departments were represented on the Advisory Committee. Besides, several of us on the Committee drew on work of federal agencies like Statistics Canada, other provinces, municipal level research and even international research.

Currently I am on the B.C. Advisory Committee on Health.

Case 1. Sustainable Development

The term 'sustainable development' has had a rough ride since the Report of the World Commission on Environment and Development (*Our Common Future* 1987). However, for our purposes it is worthwhile to begin with the clearest case available of the construction and good use of outcomes measures for public policy-making. It is a good news fish story.

Pacific herring are a small silver-coloured fish that flourish on Canada's Pacific coast. The importance of these fish to other species may be appreciated by noting that they make up 62% of the diet of Chinook salmon, 58% of the diet of Coho salmon and 53% of the diet of Pacific halibut (Environment Canada 1994, p. 2).

In 1967 the commercial fishery collapsed and the federal government's policy response was to ban commercial herring fishing for four years. By 1972 the fish stock was rebuilt to 100,000–200,000 tonnes and a new commercial fishery was developed based on sales of about 35,000 tonnes of Pacific herring roe (eggs). The most remarkable thing about this fish story is this.

> Since 1983, catches have not been permitted to exceed 20% of each stock's spawning biomass, as forecasted annually.... Since 1982, the value [of the fishery] has generally been well above $40 million although the current 'roe' fishery harvests only about one-tenth the herring caught during the 'reduction' fishery of the 1960s. (Environment Canada 1994, p. 4)

Figure 15.1 shows the commercial catch and spawning biomass trends from 1951 to 1994, clearly indicating a commercial fishery that is sustainable in the long run.

Figure 15.2 shows the forty year trends in commercial catch and landed values, clearly indicating that we are now making more money and using fewer assets than ever before.

In 1993, the wholesale market value of herring roe was $180 million and about 6,000 people were employed annually in the fishery. While average earnings for fishery workers were not available,

> In 1991, on average, herring contributed $214,500 to gross income of a herring boat, while other species, mainly salmon, accounted for $146,500 per boat. (Environment Canada 1994, p. 4)

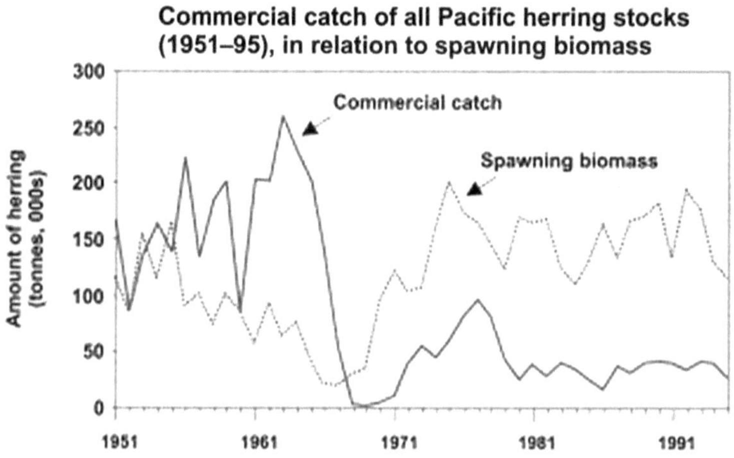

Fig. 15.1 *Source* Environment Canada, SOE Bulletin No. 98-2, Winter 1998

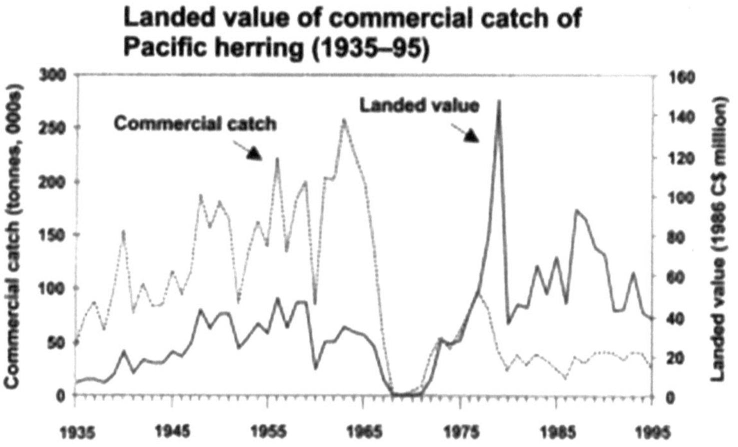

Fig. 15.2 *Source* Environment Canada, SOE Bulletin No. 98-2, Winter 1998

To the extent that human well-being is directly and indirectly connected to these figures, one must conclude that our condition appears to be both better than it was and sustainable in the long run.

The policy outcomes measures involved in this story include measures of

1. a usable stock of physical resources, measured in tonnes of spawning biomass and commercial catch;
2. the asset value of these resources, measured in landed value dollars;
3. the jobs based on these resources, measured by total numbers of people employed annually in the fishery;

4. the income value based on the resources and jobs, measured roughly by the total landed value dollars divided by the total numbers of workers;
5. the consumptive value (not measured but could be measured by the personal satisfaction of producers and consumers).

If one were looking for a clear case in which public policy-making could be focused around a set of outcomes measures, it would be difficult to find a better example than this one. We had a fishery that had collapsed under a public policy regime of unregulated free enterprise, a regulated response leading to the rebuilding of the fishery, and the subsequent development of a resource market that was more profitable and sustainable than ever before.

While this is certainly a good news fish story, we have yet to notice one other necessary condition of success. We were lucky to find a very lucrative market for the roe in Japan. That market is not as lucrative today as it was when the Japanese economy was booming, but it is still far superior to what it was throughout the 1960s.

Case 2. Alternative Measures of Poverty

Figure 15.3 shows nine different poverty lines constructed by different individuals and agencies with different criteria and aims. We need not consider the various sources. It is enough to understand that there were nine different proposed income thresholds for families of four living in large cities in 1995, beneath which such families would be regarded as living in poverty (National Council of Welfare 1997, pp. 6–7). Consequently, even if agreement was reached on the size of a poverty rate that might be acceptable at some future date, it might be difficult to get agreement on when that rate is achieved because of the 9 different ways to measure who is poor. So, in this case we have agreement on a target figure but no agreement on how to measure progress toward it. Still, if we could negotiate agreement on appropriate low income thresholds for families in different census areas then presumably all interested agencies (if not individuals) would be able to measure progress toward it in the same way. Such agreement would not guarantee that any new *will to action* would be generated, but it would remove potential barriers whenever and wherever such *will* occurred.

Although it is not entirely clear that recognizing the usefulness of removing such barriers is itself very useful, I think it is useful and I think it is strategically important to appreciate how useful it is. To see my point, imagine two scenarios. In the first, we all agree that we want to eliminate poverty and we have 9 different ways to measure progress toward achieving our goal. In the second, we all agree that we want to eliminate poverty and we also agree on one reliable and valid measure of progress. In which case are we most likely to be able to design policies and programs for the elimination of poverty? It seems to me that we are much better off in the second case because in the first we will have key players disagreeing about the nature of our problem, the general public's normal apathy increased by confusion driven by controversies among alleged experts, and elected officials unable to determine what the problem is and therefore unwilling to devote much effort to finding solutions. Thus, in the light of these considerations, I think the

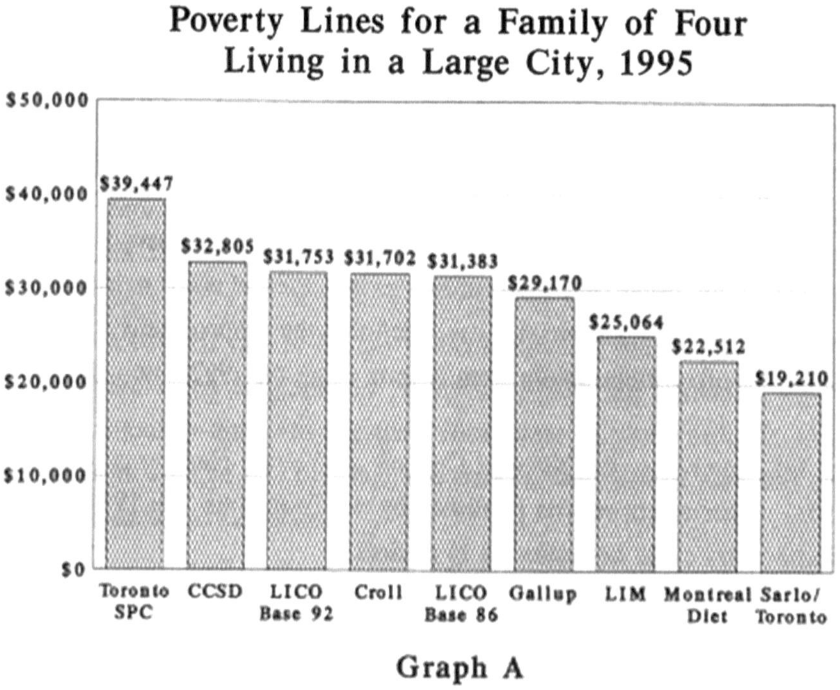

Fig. 15.3 *Source* National Council of Welfare 1997, p. 6

importance of trying to reach agreement on appropriate measures of low income thresholds should not underestimated.

Case 3. Transportation, Energy and Incomes

Figure 15.4 shows the trend in four modes of passenger transportation for the period from 1950 to 1995. A passenger-kilometre is simply the product of numbers of passengers traveling *times* the numbers of kilometres traveled. The figure clearly indicates the relative importance of the four modes, with automobile travel dominating the other modes by a wide margin. As indicated in Michalos (1997a), the rank-ordering illustrated in this figure is pretty well duplicated for all OECD countries. In most industrialized countries of the world, then, the most environmentally hostile mode of passenger transportation is most frequently used and the most environmentally friendly mode is least frequently used.

While it is true that we were making more money using less energy in 1995 than we were in 1950 (Michalos 1997a), it is also true that each of us was using nearly twice as much energy at the end of the period as at the beginning which, because of its concomitant emission effects and the limits of our resources, indicates that our situation deteriorated. That's the bad news. The good news is that in Canada transportation services contribute between three and four percent of GDP, and most of the activity is related to automobiles. Hopefully, over time it would be possible to

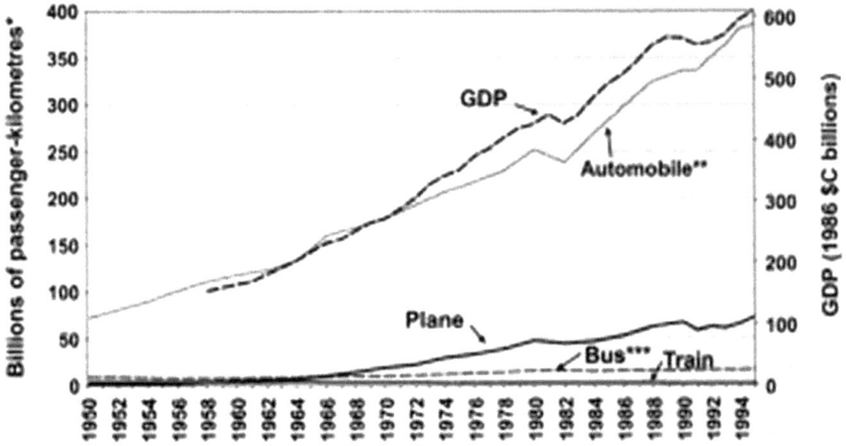

Fig. 15.4 *Source* Environment Canada, SOE Bulletin No. 98-5, Spring 1998

shift a considerable amount of the activity from automobiles to urban transit systems while sustaining roughly the same levels of employment and income, but I have no evidence that this is so. Since Canada is notorious for its wasted energy, I suppose there is much progressive work that might be done in this area if the political *will* existed.

Our question is: Could a focus on outcomes measurement contribute anything useful in solving the apparent dilemma of having a population hooked on a mode of transport that is disastrous for our environment and our physical well-being but essential for our economic well-being? Maybe. At least with good outcomes measurement we could measure the size of our problem in terms of relevant benefits and costs. If we could do that then we could assess the reasonableness or rationality of our actions. If the benefits were at least as good as the costs, then our actions would reasonable, otherwise they would not be. Of course this is not much of a triumph. It is a long shot at best to actually get such tidy information, and it is almost certain that there would be serious disagreements among the key stakeholders about how to count which benefits and costs, among other things. But in principle a focus on outcomes measurement could help.

Case 4. Federal Government Debt

There is overwhelming evidence that our federal government debt is primarily the result of government policies and actions designed to decrease tax revenues and to increase real interest rates (pursuing a zero inflation rate), rather than the result of excessive spending on social programs. Excellent and much more detailed accounts may be found in McQuaig (1995), Workman (1996), Klein (1996) and Michalos (1997b). Unfortunately, most of Canada's political leaders and the popular press continue to repeat the false story that excessive spending has driven governments into such deep holes that they can no longer afford further social spending on anything like a reasonable social safety net or, to use a more traditional phrase, on a reasonable welfare state.

In fact, the size of the social safety nets in the relatively wealthy OECD (Organization for Economic Cooperation and Development) countries like Canada has, at least since the 1950s, been mainly a matter of politics rather than economics (McQuaig 1993). Poverty statistics regarding lone parent families may be used to illustrate my point. In 1987 45% of lone parent families with children under age 18 in Canada were classified as low income families and 53% of such lone parent families were classified that way in the United States in 1986, while only 6% were classified that way in Sweden and 8% in the Netherlands in 1987 (Smeeding and Rainwater 1991, p. 67). Although Sweden and the Netherlands were certainly not six or eight times as wealthy as Canada and the United States, the former countries apparently cared more than the latter countries about the elimination of poverty through state welfare programs. (The 1991 public debt as a percent of GDP in Sweden was 46%, compared to 78% in Canada; United Nations Development Program 1994, p. 198.) While I do not imagine that everything that is possible in Sweden and the Netherlands is possible (or even desirable) in Canada and the United States, I do think that with appropriate education, political action and taxation, governments could do much more to improve the quality of people's lives at much lower costs, all things considered.

The question for us is this: Given the number of independent analyses of this issue that have reached the same conclusion, why has there been no change in policy? Why does the federal government continue to say that it was overspending on our social safety net that created and sustains the federal debt in spite of all the evidence that it was and is the result of restrictive monetary and tax policies leading to outrageously high real interest rates, high unemployment and low government revenues? Here we have a case in which everyone seems to be using the same outcomes measures, the same regression equations based on those measures and seeing the same results, but government rhetoric and policies do not change. Why is that the case? In my view, which is certainly not new or unique, our federal government and policies have not changed on these issues since the Mulroney government because those with great wealth and power have been spectacularly successful in getting first Tory and then Liberal governments to adopt policies that serve the interests of the privileged few at the expense of the less privileged many. I think federal economic policies are fundamentally political policies designed specifically to solve the political problem of getting the support of those with the greatest wealth and power, which is essential to political sustainability. If I am anywhere near right in this fairly leftist vision of what is happening, the making of some public policies will not be greatly affected by agreement on reliable and valid outcomes measures.

Case 5. Provincial Government Deficits

Table 15.1 lists 9 forecasts for the percent of GDP growth in British Columbia for 1996/97, along with the actual growth based on 1992 prices. Without going into all the details, charges and counter-charges, there was some evidence that the provincial government of Glen Clark obtained information during the election indicating that its original forecasts should probably have been revised downward, and the government waited until after the election to announce the revisions. There was quite an ugly public debate about whether the government intentionally lied to the electorate, and I am not going to rehash any of it here.

If you compare the most and least optimistic estimates in the exhibit, you will find that the former is almost twice the size of the latter. Imagine being promised a raise of X dollars, plus or minus about X dollars! Whatever X is does not matter. That is roughly the situation in which the B.C. government found itself and in which other governments find themselves at budget time.

Public policy made in the context of such great uncertainty with such undesirable costs for failing to get it right is bound to be extremely cautious. Besides, precisely because the costs of failure are so very different for the various forecasters, one would expect the latter to produce forecasts that are sensitive to those costs. Consequently, one would expect some difficulty in reducing the size of the range of variation in economic forecasts. Perhaps more importantly, one would expect that a government once burned by optimistic forecasts would prefer pessimistic forecasts in the future. While they might be inaccurate, misleading, demoralizing and even self-serving in a roundabout way, if they turn out to be wrong in the most likely direction, the worst critics can say is that the government's forecasts were overly cautious, which is not such a bad thing after all.

So, what does this case tell us about the usefulness of outcome measures for improving public policy-making? I suppose a budget deficit is a legitimate outcome measure and that there is some flexibility about exactly what to count and how to count expenditures and revenues. Given this flexibility and the different costs of inaccurate forecasts of deficits for different stakeholders, one should probably expect limited agreement about forecasts. I don't know if one should go as far as Ken Galbraith, who once said that all economic forecasts are propaganda, but there might be a lot less exaggeration in his remark than one might imagine.

Table 15.1 B.C. Budget Forecasted Economic Growth in 1996/97 by 9 Forecasters

	Percent
Conference Board of Canada	3.2
Canadian Imperial Bank of Commerce	3
Government of B.C.	2.7
Bank of Montreal	2.5
Royal Bank	2.5
Scotia Bank	2.3
Toronto Dominion	2.3
B.C. Central Credit Union	1.7
Actual Increase	2.2

Sources B.C. Ministry of Finance, B.C. Stats

Case 6. Efficient Market Hypothesis

A basic assumption of free market enthusiasts since Adam Smith is that if rational agents are allowed to buy and sell goods and services without any interference from state regulation, there will be efficient allocations of productive resources and consumers' economic well-being (at least) will be maximized.

Regarding the buying and selling of securities (stocks, bonds, foreign currency), the basic assumption became the so-called efficient market hypothesis (EMH), which asserts that securities prices are accurate estimates of the present value of future cash flows from the securities.

To the extent that the EMH is true, government regulation of securities markets would be at best unnecessary and at worst distortionary and harmful, and to the extent that the EMH is false, some sort of regulation would be necessary to achieve maximization of economic well-being.

For the past couple of decades, most governments of industrialized countries have behaved as if the EMH is true and have taken significant steps to not only remove existing regulations in securities market trading but also to prevent new regulations from being imposed in the future.

However, there are four good reasons for thinking that the EMH is false.

First, if EMH were true, then actual market prices would give good estimates of the actual cash flows from securities. But market prices do not give good estimates of the actual cash flows from securities; rather, market speculation makes market prices much more variable than earnings (cash flows).

Second, if EMH were true, then there would be no speculative booms and busts, no cyclical fluctuations in securities market prices. But there are such fluctuations.

Third, if EMH were true, then irrational investing, noise trading, fads, herd behaviour and over-speculation would tend to disappear in favour of rational trading based on fundamental values. But securities trading is notorious for its signs of irrational investing.

Fourth, if EMH were true, then there would be some relatively objective basis on which the future value of securities rests. But there is no such objective basis because the future value of securities rests on diverse and transient human assumptions, perceptions, judgments, expectations and behaviour.

Since in every case the implied predictions from the EMH are known to be false, it is unreasonable for governments and others to continue to believe and behave as if the EMH is true.

Again, our questions are the same. Given the number of independent analyses of this issue, why has there been no change in policy? What more has to be done to move from accurate analysis to policy change? Like the early Fabians, my answer would be to continue to analyze, publicize and develop an educated electorate which will elect representatives willing and able to change policies in the light of evidence. I can appreciate that some people find such a gradualist approach less than satisfactory, and I would be glad to consider more reasonable alternatives if there are any.

Critical Issues

Having reviewed half a dozen different cases that reveal different issues related to the use of outcomes measures for integrating public policy-making, it will be worthwhile to mention some of the most salient critical issues. Anyone constructing social indicators with the aim of integrating them into a social reporting or accounting system to monitor changes in the quality of people's lives and develop public policies to alter events will have to address these issues. The success or failure of one's efforts will be determined by how well or poorly one carries out this set of tasks.

1. *Settlement/Aggregation Area Sizes*. The size of the community, settlement or aggregation area to be used in social accounting systems is crucial. Roughly in descending order of size, there are international communities (e.g., member countries of the United Nations, OECD, Latin America, Africa), countries, regions within countries, provinces/states, counties, Census Metropolitan Areas (CMAs)/Standard Metropolitan Statistical Areas (SMSAs), cities/municipalities, suburbs, central cities, neighbourhoods, dwelling units (single family detached houses, condominiums, apartments). The dynamics of change within aggregations of various sizes can affect comparative studies across space and time. Further, very often one has some sorts of data for certain aggregations but not for others. For example, one might want to examine municipality water or air pollution but the only relevant data applies to broad watersheds or air catchment areas. Even if one ignores international applications, there are 10 possibilities left. How many of these should be considered?
2. *Time Frames*. Some data are only collected at 10 year census intervals, some at five, some yearly, some monthly and some only sporadically. The selection of some time frames may be a matter of convenience, while others may have important substantive consequences. For examples, in developed countries one can usually count on a broad array of Vital Statistics (e.g., births, deaths, life expectancy figures) and National Income and Product Accounts statistics (e.g., Gross National Products, balance of trade, government expenditures) on an annual basis. However, one cannot usually count on seeing annual health status reports (e.g., levels of bed disability, obesity, chronic disease) or natural resource reports (e.g., depletion of forests, fisheries, fossil fuels). One's ability to perceive significant changes and to intervene in any particular system may be increased or decreased by how timely one's information is. How frequently should data of a certain duration be collected to be included in a social accounting system?
3. *Population Composition*. Supposing one picks some particular settlement areas, one then has to decide how, if at all, to classify the population in the area. One often wants population statistics by age, sex, education, language, occupation, employment, incomes, marital status, family status and religion. Except for sex, which has two categories, the other groups may be divided on average at least five times. Which divisions should be used?

4. *Domains of Life Composition*. Having fixed the area and characterized a population demographically, one must then decide which domains of life are important for public policy-making in general or in particular circumstances. In general, at least a dozen possibilities immediately come to mind: health, finances, job, family, friends, living partner, education, recreation, housing, transportation, human-made and natural environments. Research has shown that some of these domains have typically greater impact on well-being than others, and of course each domain may be usefully subdivided. For example, the domain of natural environments includes air, land and aquatic environments. Each of the latter have stocks and flows of assets and liabilities. What should be the focus?
5. *Indicator Selection*. The issue of objective and subjective indicators has not been considered here. Briefly, objective indicators measure things that are relatively easily observable by researchers, like numbers of graduates from primary schools, hospital admissions and trips abroad. Subjective indicators measure people's attitudes or feelings by getting verbal reports about their levels of satisfaction or happiness. The issue here concerns exactly which set of which kinds of indicators should be used for a general or particular system of social accounts? Gauthier (1987) reported the results of a survey of nearly one thousand clients who received some assistance from the Canada Mortgage and Housing Corporation Residential Rehabilitation Assistance Program (RRAP) in 1981. The basic aims of the program are to improve substandard housing units, extend the useful lives of buildings and generally aid residents in maintenance. Objective and subjective indicators of program success were used and, among other things, Gauthier claimed that "The most conclusive finding of this analysis and of the literature in general is that the level of client satisfaction for a particular program is only indirectly related to his/her objective conditions and to real results of the program's actions.... Moreover, the lack of stability in the measurement of satisfaction over time makes its use difficult; a particular measurement taken at the time of program activity will be more positive than a measurement taken later" (p. 250). How, then, should subjective and objective indicators be selected?
6. *Measurement Scales*. Objective and subjective indicators can be constructed with ordinal, interval and ratio scales, with single item scales or multi-item indexes, with standardized or relatively ad hoc scales. If one operationalizes subjective well-being or quality-of-life as life satisfaction or happiness, there are at least two dozen standardized tests that might be used (Michalos 1991). Which scales should be used in a social accounting system?
7. *Decision Makers*. Different decision makers often make very different decisions about what domains of life are most important to monitor, for which people, with what indicators, scaled in what way, over what period of time, and so on. At a minimum a planner or planning consultant must work closely with his or her management team in order to reach agreement on the basic building blocks of one's system. It is, of course, possible to construct focus groups with different sorts of people represented. The crucial point here is that there must be

agreement on who is to be in the decisive set of decision makers to approve the final research product before a thorough search is launched to identify relevant available indicators. Who should be in this set?

8. *Appropriate Working Model.* Whatever indicators are selected to be used in some operational model, decisions still have to be made about the functional form or aggregation function of the model. Most researchers use multiple regression techniques, with single equations or simultaneous equations. Alternatively, many researchers do not aggregate statistics at all, and work with profiles of the quality of people's lives. What model or models should be used?
9. *Distributions.* While most researchers work with some measures of central tendency (means, medians or modes), measures of distribution, variation and inequalities are very important. At a minimum, one would want to know how evenly distributed the good and bad things in life are for visible minorities, handicapped people and women. What other groups should be given special attention?
10. *Distance Impacts.* The last critical issue I would mention for anyone interested in developing a social accounting system arises from this question: Where does a person live? Unfortunately, there is no simple answer. There is an abundance of evidence indicating that people live primarily in their own heads. The gaps between virtually all features of what researchers might call their "objective circumstances" and their perceived circumstances are usually quite substantial. But ignoring this familiar problem, there is the more subtle and much less researched problem regarding the fact that people's living space is usually much greater than the town, suburb, city or even metropolitan area containing their home. For example, living in Guelph, Ontario, one enjoys the theatres at Stratford (30 miles from Guelph), Niagara on the Lake (80 miles from Guelph), Hamilton (26 miles) and Toronto (50 miles). For serious health problems, one uses the MacMaster University hospitals in Hamilton, or those of London (130 miles) or Toronto. Toronto's zoo, science museum, arena, art and history museums, restaurants and shopping areas are frequently used by Guelphites. The provincial parks at Elora (12 miles) and Rockwood (7 miles) are also used by people in Guelph. There are a dozen universities within a 90 min drive, with interlibrary loan systems connecting most of them.

So far as I know, no one has been able to adequately address this problem. How should one define place of residence so that it captures the real living space of a population?

Finally, then, if one simply multiplies some of the options mentioned above by others, one can get a rough idea of the magnitude of the problem facing people interested in designing social accounting systems for public policy-making. Consider: 10 size options, 5 time options, 11 population categories, 12 life domains, 2 indicator types, 7 scale types, 2 model types = 184,800 combinations!

Thus, to make a very long story short, long before anyone gets to the notoriously difficult evaluative decisions regarding what is good or bad about this or that phenomena or statistic, one must make many evaluative decisions about the best (most useful, important, cost-effective, policy-relevant, etc.) data to gather. Decisions regarding the latter may be regarded by some analysts as descriptive and technical, but since there is no rule book about how to make them, it would be more accurate to say that they require negotiation among many individuals with diverse evaluative judgments. A considerable amount of confusion exists in the research literature simply because many people make many different judgments about basic building blocks.

Concluding Remarks on Performance Indicators

So far I have said nothing about performance indicators, but there is so much talk and work related to such things going on these days that it may be worthwhile to make a few remarks on this subject. Since the quality of people's lives is affected by the quality of the performance of public administrators and other government officials, performance indicators may be regarded as a species of social indicators. As our six cases illustrate, there are a variety of ways in which measuring instruments are or can be politically and socially substantively biased. In other words, there are a variety of ways in which apparently neutral measuring devices are really windows that allow a certain point of view of reality, and therefore constrain all evaluations and moral choices. In Michalos (1980, pp. 11–17) I reviewed 15 "uses and abuses of social indicators". The following Citizens' Guide is adapted from that earlier list. Above all else, Performance-Based Managers should remember these things when they think about or use performance indicators (PI).

Citizen's Guide to Performance Indicators

Performance indicators:

(1) Encourage commission of The Number-Crunchers' Fallacy, which is this: Anything that cannot be counted is unimportant and anything that can be counted is important.
(2) Can be used to predict and alter future behaviour, for better or worse depending on the nature of the alterations.
(3) Can give visibility to problems, and also create them by focusing attention on them, or by hiding some in the interest of emphasizing others.
(4) Can help obtain balanced assessments of conditions against mere economic assessments, and can distort appropriate assessments by assuming that everything valuable can be given a price in monetary terms.
(5) Can help in the evaluation of current public policy and programs, and also contribute to perverse evaluations because the statistics routinely collected may not allow decision-makers to control for important contaminating variables when they are trying to decide what has caused what.

(6) Can help determine alternatives and priorities, but also allow an elite corps of statisticians to unduly influence the public agenda by providing the "official version" of the state of the world.
(7) Can facilitate comparisons among nations, regions, cities, other groups and service-providers, but also encourage invidious comparisons, raising aspirations and hopes too high or not high enough.
(8) Can suggest areas for research to produce new scientific theories and more knowledge about the structures and functions of systems, but also retard action because people may be unwilling to act in the absence of a perfect theory or model.
(9) Can provide an orderly and common framework for thinking about social systems and social change, perhaps so orderly and common that alternatives from different points of view might be perceived as unrealistic, unthinkable, totally radical and incredible merely because they are different.
(10) Can stimulate thinking about new polices and programs, or stifle such thought as a result of massive "group-thinking".

References

Cole, M. (1961). *The story of Fabian socialism*. London: Heineman.

Environment Canada (1994). Sustaining marine resources: *Pacific herring fish stocks*. SOE Bulletin No. 94–5 (September): 1–6.

Gauthier, B. (1987). Client satisfaction in program evaluation. *Social Indicators Research, 19,* 229–254.

Klein, S. (1996). *Good sense versus common sense: Canada's debt debate and competing hegemonic projects* (Master's Thesis, Simon Fraser University, Burnaby, B.C.).

McQuaig, L. (1993). *The wealthy banker's wife: The assault on equality in Canada*. Toronto: Penguin Books Canada.

McQuaig, L. (1995). *Shooting the hippo: Death by deficit and other Canadian myths*. Toronto: Penguin Books Canada.

Michalos, A. C. (1980). *North American social report, Vol. 1, Foundations, population and health*. Dordrecht: D. Reidel Pub. Co.

Michalos, A. C. (1991). *Global report on student well-being, Vol. 1, Life satisfaction and happiness*. New York: Springer.

Michalos, A. C. (1997a). Combining social, economic and environmental indicators to measure sustainable human development. *Social Indicators Research* (to be published).

Michalos, A. C. (1997b). *Good taxes: The case for taxing foreign currency exchange and other financial transactions*. Toronto: Science for Peace and Dundurn Press.

National Council of Welfare (1997). *Poverty Profile 1995*, Ottawa: Minister of Supply and Services.

Smeeding, T. M., & Rainwater, L. (1991, September 20–21). *Cross-national trends in income poverty and dependency: The evidence for young adults in the eighties*. Prepared for the JCPS Conference, Washington, D.C.

United Nations Development Programme. (1994). *Human development report 1994*. New York: UNDP.

Workman, T. (1996). *Banking on deception: The discourse of fiscal crisis*. Halifax: Fernwood.

Chapter 16
A Handful of Sand in the Wheels of Financial Speculation

Alex C. Michalos

Introduction

The aim of this essay is to briefly review some of the broadly financial and narrowly currency crises of the 1990s, consider their causal antecedents and consequences, and finally examine in some detail one plausible remedial policy initiative that might be undertaken by key players in the international game of financial trading. (An interesting review of similarities between banking and currency crises may be found in Marion (1999).) The next section "The Risks of Financial Crises" is a review of the crises drawn from several contemporary researchers and deliberately expressed largely in their own words. This is followed by a section "Financial Transactions" giving an overview of the foreign currency market, and then a section "Taxing Financial Transactions and Tobin's Tax" describing some of the current tax regimes applying to securities trading within countries and a proposed international tax regime, the Tobin tax. Arguments in support of the latter sort of taxes are listed in the section following that "Arguments for Tobin Taxes" and arguments against such taxes are presented in section "Arguments Against Tobin Taxes, with Refutations". The sixth section is the longest part of the paper because an attempt is made to demonstrate that the arguments against Tobin taxes are refutable. Most of the material for sections "Financial Transactions" to "Arguments Against Tobin Taxes, with Refutations" of this paper was drawn from Michalos (1997) and readers who are interested in more detailed and documented arguments on both sides of the issue should consult that monograph.

Michalos, A.C.: 2000. A handful of sand in the wheels of financial speculation. Paper presented at a Conference on New Rules for the New Millennium, sponsored by Mani Tese in Florence, Italy, March 2000.

A.C. Michalos (✉)
University of Northern British Columbia, Prince George, BC, Canada
e-mail: michalos@brandonu.ca

A.C. Michalos, *How Good Policies and Business Ethics Enhance Good Quality of Life*, DOI 10.1007/978-3-319-50724-8_16

The Risks of Financial Crises

In his excellent review article, Krugman (1998) noted that major currency crises occurred in the 1990s on average about every 19 months. In fact, there were crises in Europe in the summers of 1992 and 1993, Latin America in 1994–5, Southeast Asia in the summer of 1997, Russia in the summer of 1998 and Brazil in January 1999. According to Felix (1998a, p. 164),

> Nearly three-fourths of the 181 members of the IMF suffered one or more periods of banking crises or 'significant banking problems' during 1980–95. Banking crises, defined as 'cases where there were runs or other substantial portfolio shifts, collapses of financial firms or massive government intervention' afflicted 36 countries. 'Significant banking problems' defined as 'extensive unsoundness short of crisis' afflicted another 108 countries….

Once a few important currency traders begin to sell a substantial amount of a certain currency, others suspect a devaluation may be coming and rush to sell their own holdings before it occurs. The greater the rush, the sooner and deeper the crisis.

So far economists have not reached agreement on all the causally necessary conditions and consequences of currency crises. Regarding causes, Krugman claimed that there is some support for the views that such crises are often the result of governments pursuing the inconsistent policies of trying to maintain fixed exchange rates in order to attract and keep foreign investors while also printing more money to cover budget deficits (so-called "first-generation models") or trying to maintain fixed exchange rates while also initiating an expansionary monetary policy to stimulate domestic industrial growth and employment ("second-generation models"). Supposing these policy configurations are unsustainable in the long run, currency traders act sooner to prevent losses later, making the long run shorter than it might otherwise have been. For our purposes, it is worthwhile to quote him at length here.

> One can think of a range of fundamentals in which a crisis cannot happen, and a range of fundamentals in which it must happen; at most, self-fulfilling crisis models say that there is an intermediate range in which a crisis can happen, but need not. It is an empirical question (though not an easy one) how wide this range is. …A situation in which a crisis could happen but need not presents speculators with a 'one-way option': they will reap a capital gain (or, if you measure it in foreign currency, avoid a capital loss) by selling domestic currency if the exchange regime collapses, but will not suffer an equivalent loss if it does not. What, then, prevents them from fleeing the currency at even a hint of trouble? My conjecture is that microeconomic frictions - transaction costs, the difficulty of arranging credit lines, and so on - play an important role. Ordinarily we think of these frictions as being of trivial importance for macroeconomic issues, on the grounds that they are only a small fraction of a percentage point of the value transacted. However, currency crises unfold over very short periods, in which even small transaction costs can offset very large annualized rates of return. It may be small frictions that prevent a subjectively low-probability crisis from ballooning into a full-fledged speculative attack. If this is true, then the improving technical efficiency of markets may actually be a contributory factor to the frequency of currency crises in the 1990s" (Krugman 1998, p. 6).

Granted that it is only a conjecture, it is precisely such a conjecture that led Keynes and later Tobin and others (Michalos 1997) to recommend a small transaction tax that would have the effect of throwing sand into the wheels of currency trading which would create enough friction to prevent the eruption of full-fledged crises.

Regarding the consequences of currency crises, Krugman claimed that there were significant differences among the countries in the crises in Europe, Latin America and Asia.

> The quick review of the main episodes in the decade to date indicates pretty clearly that crises in the 90s are best described by 'second-generation' models - that is, the motives for devaluation lie in the perceived need for more expansionary monetary policies rather than in budget deficits and inflation. One might therefore suppose that when a country gives into temptation it would receive a reward - that whatever the cost in political capital or long-term inflation credibility, there would at least be a payoff in terms of short-run economic expansion. And this was exactly what happened in the European crises; indeed, those countries that abandoned their principles seem to have gone completely unpunished.
>
> In the Latin crisis, however, and at least as far as we can tell in the Asian crises, the decision to devalue seems to have led to serious adverse short-run consequences on all fronts. Instead of permitting reflation, the devaluations seem to have led to even more severe contraction (Krugman 1998, p. 14).

While he had no certain answer to the question of why there were different consequences in the different regions, Krugman guessed that investors never lost confidence in "British institutions" but did lose confidence in "the political and institutional environment" in Asia and Latin America. When he addressed the question "Can currency crises be prevented?" in the final section of his paper, he did not return to his conjecture about the likely benefits of some sand in the wheels, but mentioned only short-term capital controls, "sound and consistent policies", floating exchange rates and finally, "The only absolutely sure-fire way not to have one's currency speculated against…is not to have an independent currency" (Krugman 1998, p. 15). In a later paper Krugman (1999) considered some "third-generation" models and as prevention measures he recommended "that countries need to take much greater care with their banking systems–that they need 'transparency,' better capital standards, more careful regulation of risk-taking, and end to cronyism, etc. (p. 470)".

Writing late in 1998, Cassimon (1999, p. 7) summarized the Asian crisis that was unfolding when Krugman was writing.

> Open unemployment has increased significantly relative to the pre-crisis year 1996. In Indonesia, the projected official unemployment rate will increase from about 4% in 1996 to between 9 and 12% at the end of 1998. In the Republic of Korea, it grew from 2% in 1996 to 4.7% in February 1998 and a projected 6.2% at the end of 1998. In Thailand, an increase from 1.5% in 1996 to about 6% at the end of 1998 is projected. …The strong increase in real wages of the past few years was abruptly halted in 1997 and turned negative in 1998. As an example, in the Republic of Korea, real wage growth which was on average 6.5% during 1995–96, was reduced to 2.7% during the third quarter of 1997, and −2.3% during the last quarter of 1997. …In Indonesia, it is estimated that real wage levels will decrease by more than 15%. …in a report to its Development Committee, the World Bank estimates

> that an average drop of economic activity by about 10 per cent in Indonesia, Thailand, Malaysia and the Philippines will result in a doubling of the number of poor people to more than 90 million.
>
> Quite generally, U.S. Congressman Peter DeFazio indicated in his Tobin tax resolution that "...such crises have not only economic impact, including exacerbation of global economic inequality; but also social impact including increased unemployment, price increases and disruptions, plant closures, poverty, human rights violations, diversion of resources from sustainable development, and social upheaval; which burden poor, indigenous, and middle-income populations most heavily" (Sand in the Wheels, ATTAC Weekly Newsletter, Feb. 2, 2000).

In an interview with James Tobin published February 1, 1999, the economist was asked "Would the so-called Tobin tax have actually prevented an Asian crisis?" Here is Tobin's reply.

> Certainly you would need other things as well. You need reforms in your own banking system and stock markets. The other big mistake, perhaps a bigger mistake than some of the things we have been discussing, is the practice of having a fixed exchange rate. You wouldn't have the currency crisis if you didn't have a fixed exchange rate. A fixed exchange rate is a promise by the central bank of the country to pay a fixed amount of dollars, yen, euros or a basket of several currencies. If the central bank doesn't have a reserve of hard currency, it has to default on this promise. It's like the failure of an ordinary bank. If depositors come and ask for cash for their deposits and the bank doesn't have them, then the bank has to close and there is a crisis. ...Financial crises are not inevitable. I think we will probably learn from mistakes and we won't go back - at least in the case of these countries - to trying to defend a fixed rate of exchange, against dollars or yen, and that will certainly make crises less frequent. The whole of history is peppered with international financial crises. I am not sure it's right that they are more frequent now (http://www.globalpolicy.org/socecon/glotax/currtax/cur7_2.ht, p. 4).

Concluding their excellent review of recent currency crisis literature, Flood and Marion (1998, pp. 42–43) wrote

> The currency crises of the 1990s have made us appreciate the fragility of fixed exchange-rate regimes. Responsibility for these crises cannot be placed entirely on the shoulders of poorly-behaved governments who pursue excessively expansionary policies. While some governments make policy mistakes and are disciplined eventually, others face hard policy choices not entirely of their own making. When speculators sense that a fixed parity is tightly constrained by other policy goals, that parity may be prone to attack.
>
> Evidence to date reinforces the view that currency crises are not all alike.... Some crises, particularly those in developing countries, have a significant predictable component. Others may have a predictable component only in hindsight, once we broaden our notion of the fundamentals affecting the strategic interactions of governments and speculators. Still other crises are difficult to interpret exclusively on the basis of fundamentals and have led to new explanations based on informational frictions and herding behavior. *We note, however, that the speculative attacks we understand least well occur in foreign-exchange markets that we understand equally poorly.* (*Emphasis added.*)

Chang and Velasco (1998) reviewed financial crises in emerging markets and provided the following summary statement.

> Both casual observation of recent crises and formal econometric work suggest the existence of important links between financial liberalization and crises. In particular, Kaminsky and Reinhart (1996) examined a number of bank crises and balance of payments crises and found that:
>
> (a) Of the 26 banking crises they studied, 18 were preceded by financial sector liberalization within a five year interval.
> (b) Financial liberalizations accurately signalled 71% of all balance of payments crises and 67% of all banking crises.
> (c) The M2 multiplier rose steadily in the periods leading to the banking crises. Its growth rate was 20% higher than in tranquil times.
> (d) Growth in the ratio of domestic credit to nominal GDP was high and increasing as crises approached, peaking when crises erupted at about 15 above the growth rates observed during tranquil periods.
>
> These 'stylized facts' have been also verified in many notorious crisis episodes, including Chile in 1982, Sweden and Finland in 1992, Mexico in 1994, and Asia today. Clearly, explaining why and how this is so has become crucial for the design of public policy (p. 20).

In what is perhaps the shortest, and likely tautological, account of crises written by anyone, Chang and Velasco (1998, p. 1) claimed that "Illiquid banks are a necessary and a sufficient condition for financial crises to occur".

According to Felix (1998a, b, p. 2), currency crises are partly the result of an operational crisis at the IMF which is itself largely driven by a U.S. policy crisis.

> The IMF's current policy line stands the original Bretton Woods position on its head, contending that free international capital mobility advances (rather than undermines) the basic Bretton Woods goals. The claim is that by globally integrating financial markets, capital flows reduce the cost of capital and bring about both an international converging of real interest rates and a more accurate pricing of capital assets. This should raise the global rate of investment and improve its efficient allocation. …All this should raise productivity and global output - most dramatically in the capital-short, technology-dependent third world, where the return on investment should be highest. …
>
> But this claim is an assertion with negligible support from economic theory and is refuted by the actual trends since the 1970s. Removing capital controls has opened the gates to an accelerating volume of financial flows. This has been paralleled, however, by slackened growth of investment, savings, output, trade volume, and productivity in both the third world and the OECD countries, with the main exceptions - the East Asian 'miracle' economies - now joining the pack.
>
> *The explosive growth of cross-currency financial flows has also been paralleled by increasing volatility of both nominal and real exchange rates and by sharply rising real interest rates. This identifies one of the causal links between increased capital mobility and its attendant growth slowdown. Higher volatility raises the risks of investing long-term, while higher real interest rates boost the cost of capital. Each deters long-term investment.* Thus, private investment has been tilted toward projects with short-term payoffs, which contribute less to productivity growth than did the long-term investments dominating the less volatile Bretton Woods decades. An extreme example is the upsurge since the 1980s of investments in mergers, acquisitions, and exchange and interest rate speculation, none of which adds to productive capacity. (Emphasis added.)

In testimony given to the Canadian House of Commons Standing Committee on Finance on April 21, 1998, the former Deputy Prime Minister of Canada, Paul Hellyer, also laid the blame for currency crises partly at the feet of IMF policies.

> A system under which mega-banks print money willy-nilly to lend to almost anyone in the world who will line up for it is inherently unstable. The IMF bailouts only exacerbate the situation. The 1995 Mexican bailout sowed the seeds of the current Asian crisis [with a bailout cost nearly three times as great as the cost of the Mexican bailout]. The assurance that the IMF will ride to the rescue encourages international bankers and speculators to make still riskier loans. They escape the consequences of their actions while the costs of their excesses are socialized and picked up by taxpayers at large.
>
> In the face of all the evidence it is more than astounding that the IMF is now pushing to have its articles amended. …The IMF is seeking global authority over national governments' ability to control capital inflows and outflows including the power to require member countries to commit to full capital account liberalization.
>
> This move should be recognized for what it is. It would mean the end of national sovereignty in economic matters. No country would be master in its own house. The IMF seeks the power to control the world economy. …
>
> The world should view the prospect with fear and trembling. It should be obvious to all except the most encrusted ideologue that *the world financial system has been completely disconnected from the real economy*. Wall Street (or Bay Street) is in cyberspace and programmed to ignore the real needs of the vast majority of the world's population still in need of food, clothing and shelter. Only the holders of financial assets - a tiny fraction of the world's population and the ones whose needs have already been met - have anything to gain from perpetuating the global mythology (http://attac.org/fra/part/doc/cancap.htr). (Emphasis added.)

In his Perdana Lecture in Kuala Lumpur, April 2, 1999, Jonathan Michie raised the question "Is it really true that currency speculation is a problem about which nothing can be done?" and gave the following reply.

> The answer must be an emphatic no. There is nothing inevitable or natural about current international financial arrangements. Indeed, financial speculation introduces 'systemic' risk which is the duty of governments and others to tackle. …Individual speculators (or financial institutions) will calculate the costs and benefits to themselves from the various speculative choices they face.
>
> They will not factor in the wider costs to society, to the system as a whole, of their activities. These costs to the system as a whole include the resulting exchange rate instability and the periodic financial crises, with all the real economic hardship that inevitably follows in the wake of such financial crises. …
>
> *Few activities have proved more anti-social than international currency speculation. If ever there was an activity crying out for taxation and control, this is it. Indeed, it is bordering on the bizarre that when such a high proportion of goods and services, and of economic activity generally, is taxed, currency speculation remains one of the few activities to demand, and get, total exemption from taxation and control.* Instead of wringing our hands at the loss of power of national governments, we should therefore be setting in place new controls and new regional and global structures to give us the ability to control our economic environment.

> Turning to what specific steps might be taken to manage these problems…the three main categories [of actions], all of which should be pursued together, are firstly a tax on speculation, secondly, exchange controls and thirdly, reforming the international institutions, particularly the IMF.
>
> …A proposal for the adoption of [a Tobin tax] internationally was published last December by a network of European Economists, of which I am a member. …It is certainly true that attempts should be made to adopt such a tax internationally. And if the European Union, the US and Japan all agreed, the chances are they could ensure its success (http://www.globalpolicy.org/socecon/glotax/currtax/michie99.ht, pp. 2–3). (Emphasis added.)

Without using the word ‘crisis’, Crotty and Goldstein (1993, p. 275) claimed that the neo-liberal deregulation policies of the 1980s (Felix’s ‘U.S. policy crisis’) had disastrous consequences for the United States economy.

> We conclude, based on an evaluation of both theoretical and empirical evidence, that the allocation of credit by the deregulated, speculative financial markets of the 1980s was not only inequitable in its distributional effects, but also grossly inefficient. The costs of this misallocation in the form of high default and bankruptcy rates, constrained investment and R & D spending, slow economic growth, high unemployment, low productivity, stagnant wages, and shattered communities have hit hard already and will continue to plague the [American] economy for some time to come. The economic stagnation we experienced beginning in early 1989 may represent only the first downpayment on our mortgaged future.

Comparing the shares of GDP generated by finance, insurance, and real estate (FIRE) on the one hand to real growth of goods and nonfinancial services on the other hand for each of the G-7 countries over the period from 1959 to 1994, Felix (1998a) was able to show that after the early 1970s “the increasing absorption of resources in FIRE activities has become counterproductive”. That is, in the G-7 countries since the early 1970s, growth of the financial services sector came at the expense of growth in the sector of real goods and nonfinancial services. Along with the growth in asset trading involving foreign currency exchanges, there has been an increase in exchange rate volatility. In Felix’s (1998a, pp. 181–83) words,

> Higher volatility increases liquidity and other risks of investing long term, tilting private investors toward investments with faster payoffs. …‘What’s happened in the past 25 years,’ the head of IBM’s global securities and capital markets operations observes, ‘is that enormous risk has been added to the financial markets. There’s liquidity risk, interest-rate risk, exchange-rate risk, portfolio-composition risk.’ That the heightened volatility has been partly responsible for the slackened growth of the volume of world trade seems incontrovertible, although empirical studies disagree on how much.

Stanford (1999) made detailed analyses of several aspects of the real and paper economies of Canada that clearly indicated differences in their development. Among other things, he showed that in the 1990–97 period there was a growth in financial assets per Canadian of 47%, compared to a growth in real GDP per Canadian of 4%. The growth in after-tax profits of the five largest banks was 101%, compared to growth in real disposable income per Canadian of −7%. The separate paths taken by real and financial wealth since 1980 may be measured by the fact that

> Prior to 1980, there was roughly one dollar in real wealth for every dollar of financial wealth in this country. In other words, it was safe to conclude that each financial asset had something 'real' underlying it: a house, a factory, or a parcel of land. Since that time, however, the link between real wealth and financial wealth has been broken. By 1997, there were only 58 cents of real wealth underlying each dollar of financial wealth (Stanford 1999, p. 30).

For ten OECD countries Stanford examined the relationship between financial intermediation and economic growth.

> The degree of financial intermediation is measured by the value of trading on the major stock market of each country in 1994, expressed as a proportion of each country's GDP. Real investment is captured by the average proportion of GDP that was allocated to gross real fixed capital formation between 1990 and 1995. The correlation…is actually *negative*: that is, the larger and busier a country's stock market, the less successful its record of actually putting money into motion in the real economy. The more attention and resources a country devotes to paper trading in corporate equities, the less attention and resources it is likely to devote to the accumulation of real capital in the real economy (Stanford 1999, pp. 60–70).

Reflecting on all these remarks by contemporary economists, then, it is fair to say that there are serious risks involved in the excessive growth of the world's financial economy relative to the world's real economy and it will be worthwhile to examine proposals and policies that seem to have some promise of reducing those risks. Tobin taxes are regarded by many people as one sort of policy instrument that will not only reduce the risk of financial crises but will also raise revenue on a global scale to press into service to solve global problems.

Financial Transactions

Foreign currency exchange transactions are a species of financial transactions. More precisely, they are financial transactions in which by means of some sort of financial instrument (coins, currency, securities, etc.) the value of the asset in the currency of one country is exchanged for the value of the asset in the currency of some other country.

According to Frankel (1996, p. 46), the Bank for International Settlements's 1995 estimated daily foreign currency exchange trading figure of $1,300 billion included derivative contracts (i.e., contracts involving assets 'derived' from others, as for example, financial futures and options contracts to buy or sell foreign currency at a future time). When derivatives are excluded, the trading figure drops slightly to $1,230 billion a day. Multiplying the $1,300 billion daily figure by 240 business days yields a yearly figure of $312 trillion (Tobin 1996, p. xvi).

Summarizing the scope of foreign currency exchange (Forex) activity in the 1977 to 1992 period, Felix (1995, pp. 1 5–17) claimed that by the latter year annual net global trading was worth "an astonishing $220 trillion, whereas global exports as a percent of Forex trading declined from a sizeable 28.5% in 1977 to a minuscule

1.7% in 1992". Furthermore, he estimated that "In 1992,...over 81% of global Forex transactions were for round-trips of 7 days or less", and nearly 80% of foreign exchange transactions were handled in 7 countries (UK, USA, Japan, Singapore, Switzerland, Hong Kong, Germany).

In 1992 in the United States, $114 in stock trades took place for every dollar raised to finance new corporate investments (Baker et al. 1994). According to Kodres (1996, pp. 23–23),

> A typical dealing institution writes between 3,000 and 4,000 trading tickets for foreign exchange transactions during an average 24 h day, and about 50 percent more than that on a busy day. Quoted prices can change 20 times a minute for major currencies, with the dollar-deutsche mark rate changing up to 18,000 times during a single day. During periods of extreme stress, a single dealer may execute a trade every two to four minutes. Single transactions worth between $200 million and $500 million are not uncommon in the foreign exchange market and, at most times, do not affect prices.

Taxing Financial Transactions and Tobin's Tax

Today there are no taxes on foreign currency exchange transactions, but the Nobel Laureate, James Tobin, recommended their introduction in 1972. Besides such international financial transactions across national boundaries, there are intranational financial transactions within national boundaries. There are also many countries with excise taxes on intranational financial transactions; e.g., taxes on the sale and/or purchase of stocks and/or bonds within a country. These include Argentina, Australia, Austria, Belgium, Brazil, Chile, China, Colombia, Denmark, Finland, France, Hong Kong, India, Italy, Japan, Malaysia, New Zealand, Portugal, Singapore, South Korea, Spain, Sweden, Switzerland, Taiwan, Thailand, and the United Kingdom (Spahn 1995, pp. 51–54). Some other countries have had such taxes and phased them out (e.g., Germany and the United States).

The wide variety of intranational financial transactions taxes is remarkable in itself and shows that different policy-makers have selected different instruments to suit the special conditions of their own countries. For examples, some countries have maximum tax levels (Australia, France) and some do not (Japan); some countries tax only new security issues (Sweden), some tax no new issues (Denmark) and some tax both new security issues and transfers (Austria); some tax only transfers of shares (Argentina) while others tax transfers of shares, bonds and securities (Belgium); some tax only banks and financial institutions (Australia) but some tax no financial institutions (Denmark); some tax their own citizens anywhere (Austria), some tax their own citizens trading outside their country (Italy, Japan); some tax borrowers and buyers of securities or foreign currency (Brazil) but some tax only stock transactions (China); some tax all banking transactions (Brazil (temporary)), some tax all checks (New Zealand) and some tax all financial transactions (Portugal); some tax only resident sellers of shares (Denmark) while some tax only resident buyers and sellers of stocks (France, Malaysia); some tax buyers of their own securities lower than foreign securities (Switzerland); some tax the sale of government bonds lower than the sale of shares and have no tax on government money market securities (Japan) (Spahn 1995).

What was novel about Tobin's tax was its focus on international transactions. What is complicated about this whole area of research, among other things, is the fact that a tax on such transactions inevitably raises questions about "foreign currency exchange equivalents" and exactly what sorts of financial instruments and assets are to be covered by the tax. The pursuit of satisfactory answers to these questions draws one into discussions of a wide variety of financial or securities transactions excise taxes. Studies of the advantages and disadvantages of financial transactions excise taxes typically have direct implications for Tobin taxes, and vice versa.

For countries such as Canada and the United States, which currently have no financial transactions excise taxes, the idea of introducing a Tobin tax may seem very whimsical indeed. Nevertheless, from the point of view of most other industrialized countries which have some form of financial transactions excise taxes, the idea of a Tobin tax is considerably less whimsical. Whatever apparent whimsy there is in the idea of introducing a Tobin tax in Canada and the United States, there really are some live options here which finally require political will more than anything else to bring them to fruition.

The latest version of Tobin's proposal is more sophisticated than his first version. In the latest version, Eichengreen et al. (1995, pp. 165–166) explain its essential elements as follows.

> A transactions tax on purchases and sales of foreign exchange would have to be [1] universal and [2] uniform: it would [3] have to apply to all jurisdictions, and [4] the rate would have to be equalized across markets. Were it imposed unilaterally by one country, that country's forex market would simply move offshore.... [5] Enforcement of the universal tax would depend principally on major banks and on the jurisdictions that regulate them. [6] The surveillance of national regulatory authorities could be the responsibility of a multilateral agency like the Bank for International Settlements or the International Monetary Fund. It might be authorised to set the size of the tax within limits. [7] It would have to possess sanctions that could be levied on countries that fail to comply with the measure.

A review of the literature surrounding the Tobin tax since 1978 in the light of the seven enumerated features in the preceding paragraph clearly reveals that the current advocates of the tax have taken their critics seriously. Although some of Tobin's remarks about his tax (e.g., Canadian Centre for Policy Alternatives 1995) suggest that the Tobin tax is a species of financial transactions tax which is levied on only one of many kinds of financial instruments, he clearly intended a much broader tax at least since 1978. Near the end of that paper, he wrote: "The tax would apply to all purchases of financial instruments denominated in another currency–from currency and coin to equity securities. It would have to apply, I think, to all payments in one currency for goods, services, and real assets sold by a resident of another currency area. I don't intend to add even a small barrier to trade. But I see offhand no other way to prevent financial transactions disguised as trade" (p. 159).

Presumably, all or most of the tax would be paid for by purchasers of financial instruments, either directly and explicitly or indirectly as part of sellers' fees.

Felix and Sau (1996, pp. 238–240) estimated global revenues running from about $302 billion to $393 billion in 1995 from a 0.25% tax, from about $148 billion to $ 180 billion from a 0.1% tax, and from about $90 billion to $97 billion from a 0.0 5%. Using Felix and Sau's estimates for the annual revenue from a 0.05% tax applied to 1995 foreign currency exchange volumes, the distribution in billions of U.S. dollars would have been as follows: (Industrial Countries) United Kingdom 28.7 billion, United States 15.1, Japan 9.9, Switzerland 5.3, Germany 4.5, France 3.6, Australia 2.4, Denmark 1.8, Canada 1.7, Netherlands 1.4, Sweden 1.2, Other OECD countries 8.1, (Developing Countries) Singapore 6.4, Hong Kong 5.5, South Africa 0.3, Bahrain 0.1, Other LDCs 1.1. The total for all countries, then, would be 97.1 billion. Clearly, we are talking about potentially huge *annual* revenues, so huge that it is incredible that there has yet been no focused, high-level and serious official discussions about Tobin taxes.

Addressing the perceived problem that "a small charge on international financial transactions would not create distortions but would also fail to inhibit speculative behavior in foreign exchange markets", Spahn (1996, pp. 26–27) suggested that

> A possible compromise would be a two-tier structure: a minimal-rate transaction tax and an exchange surcharge that, as an antispeculation device, would be triggered only during periods of exchange rate turbulence and on the basis of well-established quantitative criteria. …
>
> A minimal nominal charge of, for example, 2 basis points [i.e., 0.02%] on foreign exchange transactions would raise the cost of capital insignificantly and would probably have no effect on the volume of transactions involving currency conversions. A transaction tax could also be imposed on derivative trades at half the standard rate, or 1 basis point. This would allow the derivatives markets to continue functioning at low cost while preventing the use of derivatives to evade taxes. …
>
> The exchange surcharge would be administered in conjunction with the underlying transaction tax, but its aim and implementation would be different. The aim would be to tax negative externalities associated with excessive volatility. For normal operations, the fixed-rate surcharge would be zero because the tax base is zero, which assures market liquidity and allows efficient trading. The surcharge would be levied only during periods of speculative trading when the tax base becomes positive. It could be confined to cash transactions or, if necessary, could easily be extended to the derivative market. Ideally, if the exchange surcharge achieves its objective, it would generate no revenues. …
>
> Ideally, the two-tier scheme would work on a global scale, as would the tax originally proposed by Tobin, but, initially, it could be implemented unilaterally by one or a few countries.

As a matter of fact, I believe that at this point in time some sort of a two-tier version of the tax probably has the greatest amount of support. At an international meeting at the University of Antwerp in October 1999 several key researchers came together sponsored by the International Cooperation for Development and Solidarity Task Group on Social Justice. In his report summarizing the meeting, Ross (1999) made the following important points, among others.

> ...An impressive, but not fully tested, case has been made for saying that (i) a CTT (Currency Transactions Tax) could be easily and reliably applied to the whole foreign-exchange market given general international consent or even the cooperation of only four or five main currency authorities; and that (ii) most countries could apply a CTT unilaterally to transactions in their own currencies, without significantly diverting the activities taxed to other jurisdictions.
>
> A two-tier CTT has the potential for providing a watertight defence against speculative currency crises without impairing desirable market-adjustment or national autonomy in policy (pp. 9–13).

The group at Antwerp regarded Spahn's two-tier idea and Schmidt's (1999) idea of levying the tax through settlement systems (explained below) as major break-throughs and turning points in the development of Keynes's and Tobin's idea.

Arguments for Tobin Taxes

In support of some sort of Tobin tax, it may be argued that such a tax would:

1. Give Central Banks an added advantage against currency speculators;
2. Give governments greater control over their own monetary policies;
3. Generate world-wide revenues four times bigger than what is required to eliminate the worst forms of world poverty;
4. Take advantage of interest in and support for the tax at the United Nations and in many countries;
5. Take advantage of a currently untaxed international tax base;
6. Be attractive as a kind of "sin tax" against speculators, similar to taxes on tobacco;
7. Be an appropriate tax to get revenue to pay for a particular public good, namely, a viable international financial system;
8. Be more progressive than consumption taxes like the hated GST;
9. Be relatively popular with most people compared to other kinds of taxes;
10. Encourage longer term investment in the production of real goods;
11. Encourage shareholders to pay more attention to longer-term development;
12. Provide opportunities for international cooperation focused on a type of globalized activity that would serve the public interest rather than merely the interests of private wealth holders;
13. Demonstrate that such cooperative activity in the public interest is still possible.

Arguments Against Tobin Taxes, with Refutations

Several arguments have been raised against any sort of Tobin tax, but each argument is refutable. For examples, it has been claimed that:

1. Such a tax would distort the efficient operation of international capital markets. According to Raffer (1998, p. 530), who supports Tobin taxes, "Due to their virtual independence of physical location and their speed, financial markets are seen as the closest approximation to the textbook ideal of perfectly competitive markets."

   Replies Regarding the buying and selling of securities (stocks, bonds, foreign currency), the so-called efficient market hypothesis (EMH) asserts that securities prices are accurate estimates of the present value of future cash flows from the securities. To the extent that the EMH is true, government regulation of securities markets would be at best unnecessary and at worst distortionary and harmful, and to the extent that the EMH is false, some sort of regulation would be necessary to achieve maximization of economic well-being. There are four good reasons for thinking that the EMH is false.

   (1) If EMH were true, then actual market prices would give good estimates of the actual cash flows from securities. But market prices do not give good estimates of the actual cash flows from securities; rather, market speculation makes market prices much more variable than earnings (cash flows).
   (2) If EMH were true, then there would be no speculative booms and busts, no cyclical fluctuations in securities market prices. But there are such fluctuations.
   (3) If EMH were true, then irrational investing, noise trading, fads, herd behaviour and over-speculation would tend to disappear in favour of rational trading based on fundamental values. But securities trading is notorious for its signs of irrational investing.
   (4) If EMH were true, then there would be some relatively objective basis on which the future value of securities rests. But there is no such objective basis because the future value of securities rests on diverse and transient human assumptions, perceptions, judgments, expectations and behaviour.

   Since in every case the implied predictions from the EMH are known to be false, it is unreasonable for governments and others to continue to believe and behave as if the EMH is true. On the contrary, the only reasonable course now is to consider some appropriate sorts of regulation for securities markets and, in the case of foreign currency exchange markets, the most promising instrument is some sort of Tobin tax. (See Crotty and Goldstein (1993) for details regarding the four arguments.)

2. Speculators would use off shore tax havens to evade the tax.

   Replies (1) Since about 80% of global Forex trading is carried out in seven financial center countries, an agreement among the seven on a uniform Tobin tax would capture most of the taxable activity.

   (2) Another factor reducing the scope of required regulatory arrangements is the fact that nearly three quarters of global spot transactions tend to be inter-dealer exchanges. Clearly, the relatively small numbers of significant

players implies that relatively small numbers of regulating authorities would be required to ensure acceptable levels of compliance.

(3) This problem could also be addressed by making collection of the tax a condition for membership in the IMF and

(4) By allowing small countries to keep all the revenues raised by the tax within their territories.

(5) Schmidt (1999) argued that because foreign exchange transactions are exchanges of bank balances in different currencies made by banks issuing interbank transfer orders to central clearinghouses which determine the *net amounts* of various currencies that actually have to be transferred, Tobin taxes can be levied on the netting systems. In Schmidt's (1999, p. 4) view,

> When payments are accepted for netting, the original foreign exchange payment obligations between the two parties to the trade are replaced by payment obligations between each party and the netting system. …Thus, gross foreign exchange payments can be identified and taxed as part of the netting process. …[Besides] central banks or their supervisory bodies regulate offshore netting systems and can enforce those regulations. The same mechanisms can be used to enforce a foreign exchange payments tax. The right of central banks to individually and collectively regulate offshore netting systems was codified by the BIS *Committee on Interbank Netting Schemes of the Central Banks of the Group of Ten Countries* in the Lamfalussy Minimum Standards in 1990, and re-affirmed by the same Committee in 1998. …Also, most netting services, whether in formal systems or informally between pairs of banks, are delivered by a single third party, the Society for Worldwide Interbank Financial Telecommunications (SWIFT).

3. Another frequently mentioned objection to a Tobin tax concerns the problem of traders shifting to other financial instruments or assets.

   Replies (1) I would remind the critics that given the hypothesized sort of comprehensive agreement among the most powerful countries in the world that dangerously rampant capital mobility cannot be tolerated, it would be difficult for rogue speculators to hop blithely from one financial instrument to another.

   (2) Apart from any real or threatened sanctions, there would be significant operational costs to anyone inclined to enter into and sustain the game of keeping ahead of an international community determined to lengthen the turn-around time of foreign currency exchange transactions with a Tobin tax.

4. Besides shifts to other jurisdictions and instruments, critics have suggested that there would be shifts from banks and other financial institutions to other institutions.

   Replies (1) Presumably the critics suppose that as the number and variety of institutions and/or intermediaries involved in currency exchanges expands for whatever reason, there would be a need for some expansion of the world's surveillance and enforcement mechanisms. This seems like a plausible assumption to me, and I suppose that the opponents and proponents of a Tobin tax would make different estimates of the likely benefits and costs of expanding these mechanisms.

5. The tax would increase exchange rate volatility by reducing the liquidity of Forex markets.
   Replies (1) On the contrary, proponents of the tax claim that the reduction of liquidity must lead to a decrease in exchange rate volatility.
   (2) Stiglitz (1989, p. 111) offered some indirect empirical evidence by noticing that "Closing a market can be viewed as an extreme case of a prohibitive tax. [and]…French and Roll (1987) provide convincing evidence that during the period in 1968 when the market was closed on Wednesday (because of the inability of the back rooms to keep up with the increasing volume of trade), volatility was greatly reduced—by a factor of 1/2!"
6. Successful implementation of a Tobin tax would require much more international cooperation on tax policy, tax administration and the sharing of tax revenues than can probably be achieved, and therefore efforts to achieve it are probably a waste of time and other resources.
   Replies (1) On this score, I think Langmore (1995, p. 191) has provided the most reasonable response one could give. Granted that there are "technical and political difficulties" with proposals like the Tobin tax, he said, "Yet the issues are quite pragmatic: does the proposed policy have greater potential net benefits for a nation or the globe than the net effect of leaving the problem unaddressed?". It is hardly asking too much for politicians to give careful consideration to such proposals and to support or reject them on the basis of their overall merits.
   (2) Langmore also reminded us that "…in the late 1980s the BIS [Bank of International Settlements] succeeded in achieving agreement between countries to set increased prudential reserve ratios for commercial banks. Since [a Tobin tax] would be of benefit to everyone except foreign exchange dealers and the companies for which they work, such agreement could well be possible" (p. 192).
7. The implementation of a global tax would require some sort of a supranational taxation authority, and no national government would be prepared to submit to such a power.
   Replies (1) Although some people have recommended the establishment of some sort of a supranational authority, I think there are more people who think such a novel institution would not be required; e.g., Tobin (1996, p. xvii), Eichengreen et al. (1995b, pp. 165–166), Kaul et al. (1996, p. 9).
8. The people who would suffer most under such a tax probably have more political clout than any other group in the world, and they are bound to offer considerable resistance. One way to illustrate the potential clout that such people have in Canada is to review recent contributions to the federal Liberal Party. According to Cleroux (1996, p. 16),

> Last year the five largest banks made an unprecedented $5 billion in profits….According to 1994 figures from Elections Canada, the latest year for which they are available, the banks

and their investment companies were the Liberals most generous political contributors. The four top donors to the Liberals for 1994 are four banks. The CIBC and Wood Gundy donated a total of $115,237.66, while second-place Bank of Nova Scotia and Scotia McLeod gave the Liberals $110,825.65. The Royal Bank of Canada and RBC Dominion Securities gave $89,291.79. The Toronto Dominion Bank and TD Securities gave $82,180.81.

Even if all elected Liberals were saints, which they certainly are not, they could hardly be oblivious to the wishes of people providing such material support. Besides, it is likely that many of these elected officials have precisely the same sorts of wishes that their financial supporters have.

Another illustration of the strength of the opposition to such taxes may be taken from the Prohibition on United Nations Taxation Act of 1996 (S.1519) which was introduced in the United States Senate on January 22, 1996 by Senators Bob Dole, Jesse Helms and others. (An identical Act was introduced in the House of Representatives (H.R. 2867) at the same time by Congressman Gerald Solomon and others.) In their preliminary remarks about the Act, the sponsors noted that *only eight days earlier* "On January 14, 1996, United Nations General Secretary Boutros Boutros-Ghali stated that an international tax would mean that '[he would] not be under the daily financial will of the Member States'" and that "The 1994 *Human Development Report* of the United Nations Development Program stated that '[i]t is appropriate that the proceeds of an international tax be devoted to international purposes and be placed at the disposal of international institutions" (Tax Analysts, Tax Notes Today, January 31, 1996, p. 5). In the final version of the proposal that was passed in the Omnibus Appropriations Act 1997 (Public Law 104–208, Section 581.b) it was asserted that

None of the funds appropriated or otherwise made available by this Act may be made available to pay any voluntary contribution of the United States to the United Nations (including the United Nations Development Program) unless the President certifies to the Congress 15 days in advance of such payment that the United Nations is not engaged in *any effort to implement or impose any taxation on United States persons* in order to raise revenue for the United Nations or any of its specialized agencies. (Emphasis added.)

Since the italicized part of the preceding sentence could be interpreted as a prohibition against United Nations personnel recommending or promoting Tobin taxes even though they would be levied and collected by Member States rather than by the United Nations or its agencies themselves, the legislation was bound to have a dampening effect on any such activities by such personnel. It is ironic to say the least that such a prohibition should be legislated in a country in which people boast of free speech and for which, according to the U.S. General Accounting Office (October 8, 1999), it was estimated that "the United States will need to pay about $111 million in addition to anticipated payments of $548 million before the end of 1999 to reduce its arrears sufficiently to avoid losing its right to vote in the U.N. General Assembly on January 1, 2000". Raffer (1998, p. 532) remarked that having such a large unpaid bill meant that "to some extent [the United States is] enjoying a status of representation without taxation" at the same time it is opposing "other ways of raising revenue most strongly."

Lest anyone imagines that the will to resist was exhausted in 1996, Congressman John E. Sweeney introduced the original Dole bill again on January 6, 1999 (H.R. 280). Sweeney's bill even included a prohibition against United States payments to the United Nations if the latter engaged in any "attempts to borrow funds", a prohibition that was in the original Dole bill but deleted before it was passed (http://thomas.loc.gov).

Replies: I suppose the most useful thing one should say about such warnings is that there is hardly anything new in the fact that the relatively few powerful privileged people always have and always will resist giving up their privileges, and that the relatively many less privileged people still occasionally manage to prevail in spite of the incredible odds against them. Until we try, we cannot know if the odds against Tobin taxes are overwhelming or not.

9. Summers and Summers (1990, p. 170) noted that opponents of such taxes claim that many of the people who would be hurt by such taxes would be "workers by reducing the return on their pension investments".

   Replies (1) Responding to this suggestion, Summers and Summers (1990, p. 170) claimed that "Given that most pension funds that trade actively underperform the market, a tax which discourages active trading might actually improve performance. Furthermore, for the majority of workers who are in defined-benefit pension plans, changes in pension tax rules would have no impact on the size of benefit checks".

   (2) More importantly, however, since it is beyond doubt that some countries which have some forms of financial transaction taxes (e.g., Sweden) also have much more generous social safety nets than some countries without such taxes (e.g., Canada), it is unlikely that the mere presence of such taxes would make any significant difference to the level of pension benefits.

10. Shome and Stotsky (1995, p. 7) claimed that "a strong case can be made that short-term capital flows (and long-term capital flows) have benefits, among others, in forcing governments into credible and consistent policies". Thus, a tax on such flows would undermine the ability of markets to discipline governments.

    Reply Unfortunately, Shome and Stotsky did not try to make the "strong case". Presumably, such a case would consist of examples in which governments introduced "incredible" policies which were immediately met with massive capital outflows. I suppose such examples would not be very hard to find, e.g., in Folkerts-Landau and Ito (1995), and Mathieson and Rojas-Suarez (1993).

    (1) However, the fact that governments can make mistakes is not an argument against having governments, government regulation or taxation. If it were, then the fact that investors or markets in general can be mistaken would have to be accepted as a good reason to eliminate them.

    (2) While Eichengreen et al. (1995a, p. 252) apparently endorsed the government-discipline argument, they went on to show that many "governments whose currencies are attacked do not clearly bring their exchange

market difficulties on themselves through the reckless pursuit of expansionary policies. Virtuous behaviour, in other words, is no guarantee of immunity from exchange market pressures" (p. 294). Thus, insofar as capital flows punish saints as well as sinners, it cannot be assumed that the impact of such flows on government practices is always beneficial.

11. Canadians, like the citizens of most countries, are already overtaxed. Even if a Tobin tax were initiated worldwide through international agreements, it would be unfair and unpopular.
Replies (1) My educated guess is that it is true that most citizens of most countries are overtaxed compared to the privileged few who are notoriously undertaxed. Regarding Canadians and Americans, in particular, I addressed this problem in some detail in a paper recommending an annual net wealth tax (Michalos 1988). As indicated above, part of the virtue of a Tobin tax is precisely that it would be relatively progressive, and it would therefore shift the burden of taxes away from those with relatively less to those with relatively greater ability to pay. Such a shift would certainly be fair and ought to be popular.

(2) One must also remember that taxes are essentially prices and that, like other prices, their fairness has to be judged in relation to the value of the things purchased. "In return for their taxes," Brooks (1995 pp. 14–21) wrote, "citizens receive goods and services from government. Like prices, the only sensible question to ask about taxes is whether people are getting good value for their money. [The]…question is whether we want services like education, health and child care to be provided through the public sector and pay for it in the form of taxes, or through the private sector and pay for it in the form of prices". Presumably, people are not simply going to stop buying things like health, education and child care services. In the worst case scenario, what may happen is that there will be a massive swing backward to a time when women performed virtually all of the unpaid labour required to socialize, civilize and care for the young, the old and the infirm, and people went without benefits such as health care.

12. Even if most Canadians and the current federal government were persuaded of the reasonableness and justice of introducing some sort of financial transactions tax, nothing would come of it because, since the beginning of Confederation, successive Finance Ministers from all parties have demonstrated a reluctance to levy taxes that are very different from American taxes (Gillespie 1991).
Replies (1) It should be remembered that our federal governments have shown no particular reluctance to have tax and other financial policies which are quite different from those in the United States, so long as they are favourable to their relatively privileged main constituencies. For examples, we have a Goods and Services Tax, no wealth taxes, our commercial banks have no reserve requirements and the Bank of Canada carries only 6% of government debt, while the Americans have a Minimum Corporate Income Tax, taxes on inherited wealth, their banks have reserve requirements and the U.S. Federal

Reserve carries 30% of government debt. Regarding wealth and financial transactions taxes, it seems to me that Canada is an international free rider. While Canadians whine about the possibilities of losing revenue to other countries by driving away potential wealthy investors with taxes directed primarily at them, most other industrialized countries simply levy the taxes and, with the exception of the United States, most of them manage to provide a more generous social safety net than Canada provides.

Conclusion

Good taxes should generate enough revenue to pay for public goods and services that not only provide a social safety net for relatively underprivileged or unlucky people but also provide the resources to create sustainable human communities with a good quality of life. Good taxes should be levied roughly in proportion to people's ability to pay, and should be administratively manageable and cost effective, but these features of any tax regime must be examined in relation to the benefits mentioned in the previous sentence. In other words, in this area as in most other areas of life, one can only decide what is good or bad, right or wrong, pragmatically by carefully weighing all the likely benefits and costs involved (Michalos 1995). As I tried to explain in the work just cited, rational and moral decision making is not a logically tidy activity, but one cannot abandon such activity without abandoning one's own humanity. Accordingly, what I have tried to do here is construct a reasonable sort of benefit-cost analysis of some taxes which, I am convinced, are indeed good taxes.

It would not be useful to revisit all the arguments I have just presented. I know my analyses have left many unanswered questions. That is also true of everyone else's analyses. However, it was not my intention to provide the reader with a relatively complete description of a new tax regime which could just be accepted or rejected on its merits. We have elected officials and plenty of professional public servants whose job it is to do just that. It was my intention to persuade such people finally but many more people initially to take a very serious and careful look at the issues surrounding financial transactions taxes.

For the past few years we have had daily reminders that we have entered the age of globalization. Although it is far from clear what that means, nobody can doubt that people living in diverse parts of the globe in the twenty-first century will be more interdependent than people have been in any previous century. Sooner or later people will realize that mindless Darwinian competitiveness must finally give way to compassionate cooperation in the common cause of a sustainable good quality of life for all the planet's inhabitants. When that time comes, it will be comforting to know that some kinds of financial transactions taxes can help provide the revenue to fund many of the initiatives and institutions that will be required in that more perfect world.

References

Baker, D., Pollin, R., & Schaberg, M. (1994). Taxing the big casino. The Nation, May 9 (pp. 622–624).

Brooks, N. (1995). *Left vs right: Why the left is right and the right is wrong*. Ottawa: Canadian Centre for Policy Alternatives.

Canadian Centre for Policy Alternatives. (1995). *Transcript of CCPA Luncheon Seminar, Guest Speaker: James Tobin, on his proposed tax on international monetary transactions*, May 29.

Cassimon, D. (1999). *Taxing excessive currency speculation to prevent social crisis and finance global challenges* (CIDSE (International Cooperation for Development and Solidarity), Caritas Internationalis, and Justice and Peace Europe).

Chang, R., & Velasco, A. (1998). Financial crises in emerging markets. NBER Working Paper No. W6606.

Cleroux, R. (1996). The party of corporate Canada. *The Canadian Forum, 74*(847), 15–18.

Crotty, J. R., & Goldstein, D. (1993). Do U.S. financial markets allocate credit efficiently? The case of corporate restructuring in the 1980s. In G. A. Dymski, G. Epstein & R. Pollin (Eds.), *Transforming the U.S. financial system: Equity and efficiency for the 21st century*. (pp. 253–286). Armonk, New York: M.E. Sharpe.

Eichengreen, B., Rose, A. K., & Wyplosz, C. (1995a). Exchange market mayhem: the antecedents and aftermath of speculative attacks. *Economic Policy, 21,* 250–312.

Eichengreen, B., Tobin, J., & Wyplosz, C. (1995b). Two cases for sand in the wheels of international finance. *The Economic Journal, 105,* 162–172.

Felix, D. (1995) *Financial globalization versus free trade: The case for the Tobin tax*. Discussion Paper No. 108 (United Nations Conference on Trade and Development, Geneva).

Felix, D. (1998a, April). IMF bailouts and global financial flows. *Foreign Policy in Focus*, *3*(5), 1–4.

Felix, D. (1998b). Asia and the crisis of financial globalization. In D. Baker, G. Epstein & R. Pollin *Globalization and progressive economic policy* (pp. 163–191). Cambridge: Cambridge University Press.

Felix, D., & Sau, R. (1996). On the revenue potential and phasing in of the Tobin tax. In M. ul Haq, I. Kaul & I. Grunberg (Eds.), *The Tobin tax: Coping with financial volatility* (pp. 223–254). New York: Oxford University Press.

Flood, R., & Marion, N. (1998). *Perspectives on the recent currency crisis literature*. NBER Working Paper No. 6380.

Folkerts-Landau, D., & Ito, T. (1995). *International capital markets: Developments, prospects, and policy issues*. Washington: International Monetary Fund.

Frankel, J. A. (1996) How well do foreign exchange markets work: Might a Tobin tax help? In M. ul Haq, I. Kaul & I. Grunberg (Eds.), *The Tobin tax: Coping with financial volatility* (p. 4181). New York: Oxford University Press.

French, K., & Roll, R. (1987). Stock return variances: The arrival of information and the reaction of traders. *Journal of Financial Economics, 15,* 5–26.

Gillespie, W. I. (1991). *Tax, borrow and spend: Financing federal spending in Canada, 1867-1990*. Ottawa: Carleton University Press.

Kaminsky, G., & Reinhart, C. (1996, March). The twin crises: The causes of banking and balance of payments problems. International Finance Discussion Paper No. 544, Board of Governors of the Federal Reserve System.

Kaul, I., Grunberg, I., & ul Haq, M. (1996). Overview. In M. ul Haq, I. Kaul & I. Grunberg (Eds.), *The Tobin tax: Coping with financial volatility* (pp. 1–12). New York: Oxford University Press.

Kodres, L. E. (1996). Foreign exchange markets: Structure and systemic risks. *Finance and Development, 33*(4), 22–25.

Krugman, P. (1998). *Currency crises*. http://web.mit.edu/krugman/www/crises.html.

Krugman, P. (1999). Balance sheets, the transfer problem, and financial crises. *International Tax and Public Finance, 6,* 459–472.

Langmore, J. (1995). Restructuring economic and financial power. *Futures, 27,* 189–194.
Marion, N. P. (1999). Some parallels between currency and banking crises. *International Tax and Public Finance, 6,* 473–490.
Mathieson, D. J., & Rojas-Suarez, L. (1993). *Liberalization of the capital account: Experiences and issues.* Occasional Paper 103. Washington, D.C.: International Monetary Fund.
Michalos, A. C. (1988). A case for a progressive annual net wealth tax. *Public Affairs Quarterly, 2,* 105–140. Reprinted in Michalos 1995.
Michalos, A. C. (1995). *A pragmatic approach to business ethics.* Thousand Oaks, California: Sage Pub.
Michalos, A. C. (1997). *Good taxes: The case for taxing foreign currency exchange and other financial transactions.* Science for Peace and Dundurn Press.
Michie, J. (1999). Factors to consider in effecting global financial system reforms. http://www.globalpolicy.org/socecon/glotax/currtax/michie99.ht.
Raffer, K. (1998). The Tobin tax: Reviving a discussion. *World Development, 26*(3), 529–538.
Ross, A. C. (1999, October 22). *A tax on foreign-exchange transactions.* Report of a Consultation held by CIDSE in collaboration with the University of Antwerp (UFSIA).
Schmidt, R. (1999). *A feasible foreign exchange transactions tax.* http://www.sierraclub.ca/national/halifax/Tobin/schmidt.htn.
Shome, P., & Stotsky, J. G. (1995). *Financial transactions taxes.* IMF Fiscal Affairs Department, Working Paper 77, August, Washington, D.C.
Spahn, P. B. (1995). *International financial flows and transactions taxes: Survey and options.* IMF Working Paper 60, June, Washington, D.C.
Spahn, P. B. (1996). The Tobin tax and exchange rate stability. *Finance and Development, 33,* 24–27.
Stanford, J. (1999). *Paper boom: Why real prosperity requires a new approach to Canada's economy.* Ottawa and Toronto: Canadian Centre for Policy Alternatives and James Lorimer and Co., Ltd.
Stiglitz, J. E. (1989). Using tax policy to curb speculative short-term trading. *Journal of Financial Services Research, 3,* 101–115.
Summers, L. H., & Summers, V. P. (1990). The case for a securities transactions excise tax. *48 Tax Notes, 879,* 161–171.
Tobin, J. (1996). Prologue. In M. ul Haq, I. Kaul & I. Grunburg (Eds), *The Tobin tax: Coping with financial volatility* (pp. x–xviii). New York Oxford University Press.

Chapter 17
Ethics Counselors as a New Priesthood

Alex C. Michalos

Introduction

A few years ago I saw a film called *Out of Africa* in which the heroine, played by Meryl Streep, said "When the gods want to punish you, they let you have what you have been praying for". I am not a religious or a praying person, but if I were, I would have prayed for something like the practice of ethics counseling and I think I would regard the current practice of ethics counseling as something like punishment. The trouble is, for me at least, there are so many things for which I might justifiably be punished that I could never be sure that any particular evil happening to me was the direct consequence of anything in particular. I might have a whole array of character flaws and misdeeds meriting a wide variety of punishments. Indeed, if the gods follow Sam Levinson's mother's principle of punishment before the crime, I might be reasonably punished for anticipated as well as actual moral failures.

I am going to use the term "ethics counseling" to cover all kinds of decision making regarding relatively institutionalized ethical appraisal (for profit or not), including, for examples, group decision making in various reviewing committees of universities and hospitals for research on human subjects, individual decision making in private and public institutions for Harassment and Discrimination Officers and Human Rights Officers, and distinctly for-profit decision making on behalf of business clients of one sort or another. I am not going to talk about people

---

Alex Michalos is Editor-in-Chief of the Journal of Business Ethics.

Michalos, A.C.: 2001. Ethics counselors as a new priesthood. Journal of Business Ethics, 29, pp. 3–17. © 2001 Kluwer Academic Publishers. Printed in the Netherlands.

A.C. Michalos (✉)
University of Northern British Columbia, Prince George, BC, Canada
e-mail: michalos@brandonu.ca

A.C. Michalos, *How Good Policies and Business Ethics Enhance Good Quality of Life*, DOI 10.1007/978-3-319-50724-8_17

discussing moral problems, giving and taking advice from friends and colleagues, although much of what I have to say clearly applies to such communication.

There is a long and stupid tradition among would-be reformers of various sorts of beating up the home team. It's a natural extension of the useless tradition of preaching to the converted. Activists in the women's movement, labour unions, environmental groups, political parties and church groups will be familiar with the phenomena. For example, no one cares more deeply than feminists about social justice issues for women but feminists are often more critical of each other than outsiders are of them. And no one has been more critical of church groups than members of those same groups. Since I have done and most likely will continue to do some ethics counseling, I regard myself as an insider in the trade and my criticisms are to some extent self-criticisms of my own behaviour and that of my peers. So my remarks today are a bit like stones thrown from a man in a glass house, which makes them a bit self-destructive. In my more optimistic moments I would simply blast the internal critics with "Ok. We're doing it wrong, but who is doing it better? More to the point, are you prepared to lay down and let the world go to hell in a handbasket just because you can't quite get it right?" Well, no, of course not, at least not in my more optimistic moments.

To make matters worse, the negative case I will present will not be based on any systematically collected data. I am the Director of the Institute for Social Research and Evaluation at my university and I do a lot of survey research and number crunching. So as I write this paper the survey researcher in me is shaking his head and mumbling things like "You have no data. You are taking cheap shots based on your own experience. You are behaving like an academic whiner with enough nerve to complain but not enough to undertake the research that might demonstrate that your complaints are well or ill-founded. Shame on you".

Fortunately, or unfortunately, the philosopher in me says "Piffle" to such complaints. My experience is limited but not zero or totally useless. Even if it were, I might be able to construct an a priori analysis that would be useful. Great fiction writers sometimes reveal truths about people and the human condition that they have not had any experience with themselves. For that matter, great survey researchers sometimes reveal nothing but their own inability to construct questions whose answers might shed some light on the human condition. So, I think the philosopher need not be put off by the social scientist in me.

Priests and Other Do-Gooders

When one thinks about the idea of ethics counselors as a new priesthood, one quickly realizes that the intended sense of "priesthood" is negative and that many kinds of practitioners could be substituted for "ethics counselors" to make the same sort of point. For example, panels of experts judging research proposals for funding might be similarly accused. The minimal point is, of course, that the priesthood's office takes on a negative character to the extent that priests occupying that office misbehave. The maximum point would be, I suppose, that the priesthood's office is inherently negative or evil because it is built on superstition and fear. I think the maximum point is a gross oversimplification and would not give it serious consideration. I spent four years at the Divinity School of the University of Chicago giving it serious consideration and would recommend that to anyone who has questions or doubts about such things, but for me it's a matter of "been there and done that".

The minimal point captures the sense I intended in my title. The office of ethics counselor seems to me to be inherently respectable, but people who occupy the office seem to be doomed to fail to measure up to what the office demands of them and promises to others. What does the office of ethics counselor demand and promise?

I once asked a friend trained in moral philosophy who does quite a bit of ethics counseling for private and public agencies "What do you think people are buying when they hire you? Do you think they think they are buying an ethically good person? Are you selling your moral niceness or what?"

"Definitely not my moral niceness" he said. (My friend appreciated Groucho Marx's quip that he wouldn't belong to any organization that would allow people like him in it.)

What my friend thought he was selling was some expertise in logical and moral analysis, expertise developed after years of study combined with some practical experience dealing with ethical issues. At the time I nodded and said "I see", but I am here to tell you that in a fairly troublesome way I don't see. For openers I doubt that anyone would hire an ethics counselor if they had doubts about the likelihood of the counselor's expertise to produce something like moral goodness or virtue. As is the case with many other kinds of agents, if an ethics counselor were ever tainted in any way with ethical misconduct, that would be the kiss of death for him or her. But I think ethics counselors are under a special obligation to practice and to appear to practice what they preach, as clerics are for that matter. Even though ethics counselors do not wear the special collars and other symbols of their trade, they are expected to behave as one would behave if one actually believed and tried to live by the moral codes they represent and verbally endorse. They may be painfully aware of the great gap between what they preach and what they practice, and they may not be intending to sell their moral virtue, but I would bet that purchasers of their services are intending to buy precisely that virtue plus the expertise at analysis.

Moral/Ethical Classification

One of the first things I explain to my students of business ethics is the necessity of distinguishing the classificatory from the evaluative sense of the terms "ethical" and "moral", which I treat as synonyms. Just as a judge in a dog show must first classify the animals as beagles, collies and so on in order to know what criteria are appropriate to evaluate them, anyone interested in making a moral appraisal of an issue must first classify it as moral rather than, say, mathematical, chemical and so on in order to know what criteria are appropriate to evaluate it as morally good or morally evil. In other words, one must be able to distinguish things that are moral and properly subject to moral appraisal (e.g., some human action) from things that are nonmoral and not properly subject to moral appraisal (e.g., rose bushes and mathematical equations) in order to be able to decide which of the former are morally good or evil, granting that the latter cannot be either morally good or evil because they have no moral status at all.

Having explained this distinction, the question naturally arises "Exactly what is an ethical issue?" Or, "How can one decide (first) which issues are appropriately classified as 'ethical' or 'moral' in order to decide (second) which ones are ethically/morally good or bad?"

In general, I think there is a narrow and a broad answer to these questions, but I have no idea how many or what percentage of all ethicists would accept my view. The narrow answer is that an ethical issue is any issue covered by an ethical or moral maxim or rule. For example, if you accept a maxim in the imperative "Do not lie" or in the declarative "It is morally wrong to lie", then all issues involving lying are moral issues. The broad answer is that any issue is an ethical issue when it is considered from a moral point of view, i.e., from the view of its likely contribution to impartially improving the human condition or impartially maximizing happiness for the greatest number or some such thing. According to the narrow answer some issues are inherently moral or ethical according to accepted moral maxims, and according to the broad answer all issues are inherently neutral but may be subject to moral appraisal by examining them from a moral point of view.

Given these two different ways to determine moral issues in preparation for a moral evaluation, different people might select different issues to evaluate and might consequently give different evaluations of the issues. That is why I said it was not clear to me what my friend meant when he said he had some experience dealing with ethical issues. If I had asked him how he decided which issues had moral relevance and which did not, I might have gotten some clarification. Of course, "clarification" is not synonymous with "agreement" and once I got clarification we might have found it impossible to reach agreement.

Principled Moral/Ethical Evaluation

Let's suppose we, you and I, or some people reach agreement about which issues are properly subject to moral appraisal, and we then want to go on to appraise the issues. How are we going to do that? At a minimum I think we would like our moral appraisals to be principled, rule governed or rationally defensible rather than ad hoc or arbitrary. This is easier said than done. People working in philosophy of science spent and probably still do spend a lot of time writing about the structure of scientific explanations (e.g., Michalos 1980a, b, c). Such writings are intended partly to describe the structure of explanations actually used in science and partly to evaluate those explanations by providing normative criteria for them. As a rough generalization, one might say that historians and sociologists of science tend to emphasize the need for descriptive accuracy while philosophers of science tend to emphasize the need to satisfy criteria prescribed as acceptable or good according to some other criteria. Regarding the results of such writings from the point of view of philosophers, we have a spectrum of proposals ranging from the classic hard-line positivists calling for highly structured Covering Law Models of Explanation to the classic soft-line verstehen theorists calling for understanding regardless of any structure at all. Whether philosophers defend one of the extreme views or some view between the extremes, they all believe that the view they are defending is the right one. Typically, they could be expected to say that using this or that model is tantamount to providing principled, rule governed or rationally defensible kinds of explanations rather than mere ad hoc or arbitrary ones. That's fair enough, but the point of the story here is that because the kinds are so different, it is not at all clear what one is committed to when one is committed to a principled explanation except an intention not to be arbitrary or ad hoc.

I know there is a vast literature on the structure of rational and moral decision making (e.g., Michalos 1978). Is there any agreement on the correct or even best structure for decision procedures for making moral decisions? I doubt it. If we return to the history of research on the structure of scientific explanations, we find that for some models it was and is impossible to provide a complete account of the nature of good explanations without first knowing the nature of laws and theories. The literature on the structure of scientific laws and theories, of course, is at least as extensive as the literature on explanations. There must be much more written on moral theories and laws (rules, maxims) since philosophers and theologians have been writing on such things for a longer time than they have been writing on scientific theories and laws. Is there any agreement on the correct or even best account of the nature of a good moral theory or moral law? I doubt that too. And what does "good" mean in this context?

Adequacy Conditions for an Acceptable Moral Theory

Let's pursue the last question a bit. Suppose we ask: What adequacy conditions should be posited for any acceptable moral theory? In other words, what criteria should one use to determine which proposed moral theories are acceptable and which are not? In another place I argued that finally there can only be one acceptable moral theory (Michalos 1995, pp. 41–43). So, our question is really: What are the adequacy conditions for our single acceptable moral theory? I do not think I have a mutually exclusive and exhaustive set of conditions, but I would propose the following. The acceptable moral theory should,

1. be true;
2. enable one to distinguish moral issues from nonmoral issues;
3. enable one to distinguish morally good from morally bad things;
4. provide a reasonable motive for one to make moral appraisals;
5. provide a reasonable motive for one to engage in moral rather than immoral action;
6. enable one to resolve conflicts of interest;
7. be internally and externally coherent.

These are not entirely clear or uncontroversial conditions, but the most casual inspection of them in connection with some well-known moral theories immediately reveals the severity of our problem. For example, consider the theory sketches listed in Exhibit 1 from the point of view of the seven conditions. I offer only *sketches* because a full account of the theories would require much more space than I have here.

Without fully developed accounts of the various theories and much more controversial argumentation than I can produce here, I think it is fair to say that depending on who is making the assessment, each theory would fail to satisfy one or more of the adequacy conditions. If it were not so, we would have a generally accepted moral theory according to at least one set of adequacy conditions. In the absence of even a generally accepted set of adequacy conditions for a moral theory, much less a generally accepted moral theory itself, what good does it do to insist that one's moral appraisals should be principled or rule governed? My principled or rule governed moral decisions may be ad hoc and arbitrary according to yours (Table 17.1).

I think that lurking behind the insistence that moral decisions should be principled or rule governed is something like the insistence that in order to have knowledge, versus mere opinion that happens to be true, one must have good reasons for one's opinions. Virtue theorists are perhaps the most articulate about the nature of the supporting reasons and dispositions required for morally good actions, but all theorists are sensitive to the need for some such requirement. If they were not, they would not have bothered with theories at all. At any rate, I believe the requirement is epistemologically appropriate to knowledge claims generally and to moral claims and moral action in particular. The fact that it is extremely difficult if not impossible to satisfy the requirement in a thoroughly satisfactory way is, to say the least, regrettable. The frequent absence of concern about this state of affairs is even more regrettable.

Some Negative Consequences of Unprincipled Moral/Ethical Decision-Making

The fact that our fundamental demand for principled moral decision-making is usually not met in a thoroughly satisfactory way has important implications for ethics counseling, besides the obvious one that such counseling as we are able to offer is not going to be thoroughly satisfactory. Typically, I am afraid, we really do

Table 17.1 Sketches of some moral theories

1.	*Theism*: Assume there is a God. God wants people to accept this or that moral maxim or set of maxims; e.g., the Ten Commandments. Whatever God wants people to do, they should do. So people should accept this or that moral maxim
2.	*Secular Authority*: People live in communities that recognize some people as authorities for the good of each member of the community. Such authorities construct rules of good conduct or moral behaviour, and if people break the rules they will be punished. Assuming you want to live in communities without being punished, you should follow the rules. The moral lawmaker is not supernatural but powerful enough to enforce the laws
3.	*Functionalism/Implicit Contract*: Communities cannot exist unless people follow a minimal set of moral maxims (e.g., Don't kill people for fun. Speak the truth.). Individuals cannot exist unless they live in communities. If individuals do not follow the rules they will undermine their community's existence and their own. Assuming you want to live in communities without undermining their and your own existence, you should follow the rules
4.	*Moral Sense/Natural Law*: Just as there are laws of nature whether or not people are aware of them, there are moral laws. Just as most people are able but some people are not able to see the difference between the colours red and blue, most people have a moral sense that allows them to see the difference between what is morally good or bad, right or wrong. People should follow the rules because they are natural or normal and those who disobey the rules are violating nature, behaving unnaturally. Examples typically include things like duties of fair sharing of burdens and benefits, duties not to injure others (non-maleficence), duties of gratitude for favours, duties to improve the condition of those in need (beneficence), and duties of reparation or compensation for our own wrongful conduct
5.	*Golden Rule*: People ought to treat others as they would like others to treat them. You would like others to follow moral rules in their treatment of you. So you should follow moral rules in your treatment of others
6.	*Act Utilitarianism*: On any given occasion, people ought to act so as to produce the greatest good for the greatest number, impartially considered. This moral rule supercedes all other rules
7.	*Rule Utilitarianism*: On any given occasion, people ought to act in accordance with moral rules which, if everyone follows, will produce the greatest good for the greatest number, impartially considered
8.	*Kantianism/Deontology*: A moral maxim for Kant is a specification of conduct *plus* a sufficient reason for the conduct. Such maxims are supposed to be universally generalizable in the sense that if they are acceptable for anyone then they are acceptable for everyone in exactly similar circumstances. For example, suppose you can avoid unpleasant consequences by breaking a promise to someone and you wonder if that is morally good or bad. If you broke a promise in such circumstances, the maxim of your behaviour would be: "It is ok to break promises whenever breaking promises helps to avoid unpleasant circumstances". If this maxim were universally generalized so that everyone followed it (everyone broke promises whenever that helped them to avoid unpleasant circumstances), then the institution of making promises would be severely undermined. Assuming you want to be able to make promises and to have others make promises to you with the assurance that the promises will be kept, it would be self-contradictory and self-destructive for you to accept that maxim of behaviour. In effect, you would be asserting "I want to have and destroy the institution of promise-making', which is logically and practically (prudentially) absurd. Thus, you

(continued)

Table 17.1 (continued)

	ought to follow acceptable moral rules because it is literally reasonable or rational to do so, while unacceptable moral rules are literally unreasonable, irrational or incoherent
9.	*Virtue Ethics*: Ethics is primarily about being a good or virtuous person or a person of good/virtuous character rather than merely having good behaviour. A good or virtuous person has developed a disposition to deliberate and choose to do the right thing in the right way, from the right motive, in the right circumstances to get good consequences. Ultimately "good consequences' consists of happiness or well-being broadly construed. Assuming that you want the quality of your life to be good, to enjoy overall well-being or happiness, then you ought to be a virtuous or good person because such a person has the greatest chance of having such a life
10.	*Egoism*: On any given occasion, one ought to act to produce the greatest good for oneself

just muddle through. Practically, that is to say, in practice, that means that those who engage in or provide ethics counseling may, more or less unwittingly, create illusion, confusion, anxiety and conflict resulting from their own, their colleagues and/or clients,

1. making ad hoc or arbitrary decisions;
2. making shallow or perfunctory ethical evaluations;
3. providing advice on a volunteer/part-time basis or for profit;
4. not having the opportunity to help construct the theories, principles or rules applied in particular cases;
5. not having education and training programs regarding the theories, principles or rules, or their application;
6. having different understanding of basic terms;
7. accepting different ethical theories, principles and rules;
8. having different life experiences, expectations, aims and motives;
9. being afraid of violating principles and rules unclearly understood;
10. failing to act rather than acting in the wrong way;
11. applying theories, principles and rules that give visibility to some kinds of activities and neglect others;
12. applying theories, principles and rules that are mutually incompatible;
13. following theories, principles and rules in unreflective, conventional or robotic ways;
14. assuming that the status quo provides acceptable moral standards;
15. inviting invidious comparisons of other people's behaviour;
16. failing to monitor anyone's behaviour or compliance following judgments about it;
17. failing to create reward/punishment systems for behaviour judged to be morally praiseworthy or blameworthy;
18. failing to actually reward and punish behaviour according to the established systems.

These are potentially serious problems for ethics counseling and counselors. One would like to know how often counselors and clients suffer from illusions, confusion, anxiety and conflict as a result of such problems, but that is an empirical question to be examined some other time. For present purposes, the question is: Does the existence of all these deficiencies inherent in ethics counseling imply that ethics counselors are indeed doomed to being a new priesthood in the pejorative sense of this term?

Now a chorus of voices from the cheaper seats should be shouting "Say it ain't so Joe!" Alas, I think it is so, but I will try to rescue at least some of the baby while the bath water disappears down the drain.

More Problems for Principled Moral/Ethical Decision-Making

Let's think positive. What, after all, can be said for the home team, for ethics counseling and counselors? All things considered, is the world a better place, morally speaking, for all our activity? In a few places (e.g., Michalos 1978, 1992) I explained the great difficulties contained in the apparently reasonable idea of *considering all things,* namely, specification of an appropriate recipient population presumably affected by all the things, temporal and spatial coordinates, benefit and cost composition, specific measures, confidence levels, research procedures and personnel, aggregation functions and discount rates. Each of these ten essential aspects of a decision situation requires some evaluative decision as complicated as the original decision. Laying all of these formidable problems aside, can we begin to satisfactorily answer the question about the world being a better place without some general agreement about the most appropriate measure of the moral goodness of the world? I think not. To make matters worse, besides having a variety of moral theories to contend with, there are several theories of value and not every moral theory is compatible or even comparable with every theory of value. If one seriously sets out to measure the net moral goodness in the world or in some part of the world, one really has to have some fairly clear ideas about other kinds of goodness or value and some clear ideas about how to aggregate distinct kinds to calculate net goodness or value. Table 17.2 lists some theories about the nature of values, just to provide more food for thought about such things. Some of the theories are species of others listed in the table; e.g., Naturalism is a species of Cognitivism.

Table 17.2 Sketches of some theories of value

1.	*Cognitivism*: The terms "value" or "good" designate something which is identifiable and namable, but not necessarily describable in other terms. Value claims have the logical status of declarative sentences; if they are meaningful, they must be true or false, though we might not know which
2.	*Non-cognitivism*: The terms "value" or "good" do not designate anything at all. Value claims have the logical status of exclamatory and/or imperative sentences; if they are meaningful, they still cannot be true or false
3.	*Naturalism*: Value or goodness is a natural property inherent in things, similar to other physical properties like weight and mass
4.	*Non-naturalism*: Value or goodness is some sort of supernatural property inherent in things, similar to things like souls or spirits
5.	*Naturalistic Objectivism*: The value or goodness of things is natural and lies within the things themselves, not in people's perceptions of them
6.	*Naturalistic Subjectivism*: The value or goodness of things is natural and lies within people's perceptions of things, not in the things themselves
7.	*Non-naturalistic Objectivism*: The value or goodness of things is supernatural and lies within the things themselves, not in people's perceptions of them
8.	*Non-naturalistic Subjectivism*: The value or goodness of things is supernatural and lies within people's perceptions of things, not in the things themselves
9.	*Emotivism*: Value claims are expressions of emotion, similar to "Ouch!" or "Hurrah!", and cannot be true or false
10.	*Prescriptivism*: Value claims are prescriptions for behaviour, similar to "Close the door." or "Walk this way.", and cannot be true or false (Michalos 1981a, b)

A Thought Experiment

We might try a thought experiment. Is there any good reason to suppose that if we did not have the expansion of ethical appraisals in medicine, engineering and business that we have had over the past twenty years the world would have been any worse off than it is? Did we stem an evil tide or have we merely been engaged in sweeping the ocean out of our living rooms? Worse, as people continue to ask me about business ethics in particular, "Don't you think a lot of the activity around business ethics is just window dressing?" In the United States in particular people say that since the courts have agreed to go relatively lighter on companies caught up in illegalities if they have undertaken some activities in the interests of raising ethical consciousness, such activities are most likely motivated by an interest in securing lighter treatment than by an interest in doing the morally right thing, in the right way, from the right motive, and so on.

Well, yes, I do think a lot of the activity around business ethics is window dressing, but that does not answer our question. My impression, based on quite a bit of empirical research published in the *Journal of Business Ethics*, is that business people and business students are not any less ethical than the rest of the population. I do not even think there is any clear evidence that they are more materialistic, whatever that means exactly, than other people. It is an empirical question, but supposing my impression is true, the extra bit of effort made to get business people to do the morally right thing may not have made any difference. It is possible that all our efforts resulted only in net changes in window dressing, but that seems improbable apriori and in fact.

Regarding the apriori argument, suppose the disposition (if there is or could be such) and the opportunities to engage in immoral activity are normally distributed in the population. That is, like brains, height and weight, most people (roughly 68%) are like most people, and the probability of meeting a very good or very bad person decreases as their degree of goodness or badness increases. Then suppose we take two samples at random from this population, "treat" one to a heavy dose of moral indoctrination and leave the other group alone. Does it seem apriori likely that both groups would act the same morally speaking? I don't think so. That is probably why in every society reasonable people at least give their own offspring some moral training. They assume that if no one tries to teach the kids right from wrong, they will certainly and probably increasingly get into trouble, and end up miserable. There is a considerable body of evidence connecting criminal behaviour to the absence of proper training or to the presence of learning experiences reinforcing the wrong sort of behaviour (Michalos 1980a). So we know that training can make a difference. Unfortunately, we also know that a lot of training seems to make no difference, especially the sort of training a student might get in a 13 week course in business ethics, an employee might get in a four hour course designed to familiarize him or her with a company's ethics policies, or a researcher might get by correctly answering the sorts of questions asked by research ethics approval boards. We know that the promise of education is often unfulfilled (Michalos 1981a, b), but we cannot give up on it, and this includes the promise of moral education.

Is that it? Is that our best shot, the best we can do for the home team? Does it come down to Reichenbach's (1949) remark that "It is preferable to try even in uncertainty than not to try and be certain of getting nothing?" Shaw (1931, p. 101) said,

> All Governments are open to Shakespear's (sic) description of them as playing such fantastic tricks before high heaven as make the angels weep, just as all men who undertake the direction of other men are open to William Morris's objection that no man is good enough to be another man's master. But when a job has to be done, it is no use saying that no man is good enough to do it. Somebody must try, and do the best he can. If war were declared against us we could not surrender at discretion merely because the best general we could lay hands on might as likely as not be rather a doubtful bargain as a sergeant.

Are these comments going to be our answer to the question "Is there any good reason to suppose that if we did not have the expansion of ethical appraisals in medicine, engineering and business that we have had over the past twenty years the world would have been any worse off than it is?" We better think some more.

A Step Backward and a New Assessment

Suppose we ask: What good *could* all the extra effort devoted to ethical appraisals over the past twenty years have done? Lakatos (1968) became famous for characterizing research programs as regressive when they began with difficult important questions and continually redefined the questions so they became relatively easier to answer and less important. I suppose by switching to this hypothetical question Lakatos might regard this investigation as regressive at this point. Nevertheless, its seems to me that the extra effort devoted to ethical appraisals over the past twenty years *could have produced*, whether or not it *did*, such benefits as providing

1. encouragement for people to make moral assessments of their own and other people's actions;
2. some guidance regarding assessment criteria;
3. support for people interested in such assessments;
4. official voices and bases of power to initiate changes in the interest of ethics;
5. some deterrence for people inclined to fare poorly in the light of such assessments;
6. greater understanding of ethical theories and maxims;
7. more visibility through public forums for debate about ethical theories and maxims;
8. a more positive public image for people, private and public institutions taking such things seriously;
9. greater autonomy and freedom from external surveillance;
10. reduced costs resulting from fewer morally questionable practices, including possibly reduced externalities;
11. increased self-confidence and increased trust and confidence received from others;
12. increased self-esteem;
13. improved overall quality of life as a consequence of previous benefits;
14. encouraging the development of appropriate sanctions for those who behave unethically.

This is not an insignificant list of possible benefits from our labours. It is a pity we are not able to provide some empirical evidence showing that such benefits have actually been obtained. But it is still useful, I think, to have such a list, especially since most of the things listed would be empirically measurable. Living in the highly interdependent and complicated world that we have today, it is difficult to isolate the precise impact of this or that event or set of events or actions on others. But it is not impossible and over time I do think we have made and will make more progress at monitoring the consequences of specific actions, designing remedial actions and generally improving the human condition.

In an essay on the misuse of history, Skidelsky (1993, pp. 431–432) remarked that "the assertion of basic values is necessary for their survival". In particular, "Commitment to freedom can direct attention and energy to those solutions to problems which do least damage to it". He had no more evidence for his claims than I do, but it is pretty clear that he had similar sympathies.

In an essay on psychohistory, Skidelsky (1993, p. 414) reviewed the case of a man who repeatedly made speeches with slim chances of producing changes in anyone's behaviour and quoted him responding to an enquiring spectator who had asked why he continued, "has it ever occurred to you that I enjoy making speeches?" As I read about this case, I recalled the feminist saying that "the personal is political". The more I thought about it, the more I realized that there are really four cases to consider, each of which may be illustrated with real experiences. There are cases in which:

1. What is political in effect can be personal in its cause; e.g., fighting back (or merely making speeches) feels good to the fighter and occasionally helps produce intended political changes.
2. What is personal in effect can be political in its cause; e.g., structural or systemic oppression of women can be personally devastating for individual women.
3. What is political in effect can be political in its cause; e.g., electoral victory can help produce intended political changes.
4. What is personal in effect can be personal in its cause; e.g., a person's personal need for self-esteem can help make a person hardworking, honest, loyal and relatively self-sufficient.

When we think about and search for the benefits of action intended to improve the human condition, it is probably worthwhile to keep one eye on the personal and the other on the political.

So there. There may be something close to a happy ending after all.

Troublesome Second Thoughts

1. In an essay subtitled "Fourteen Unsuccessful Ways to Pass the Buck" (Michalos 1987) I presented and allegedly refuted a "level of competence" argument. Briefly the argument was based on the claim that because businesspeople had no special interest or competence in moral action, they should not be urged to perform such action. My reply was that moral action did not require any kind of special expertise and becoming a good person, morally speaking, was not like becoming, say, a good dentist. Morally good behaviour is a kind of public good in the sense that "nonpurchasers" (i.e., people who don't buy into the game by at least trying to behave in morally appropriate ways) usually cannot be excluded from its benefits, while good dentistry is a kind of private good in the sense that nonpurchasers usually can be excluded from its benefits. Morally good behaviour is the sort of behaviour that is required of and is specific to human beings,

whether they are dentists, football players or acrobats. Thus, a person's innate or learned competence for morally good behaviour is irrelevant to its being demanded of them.

That is roughly how I saw things a dozen years ago when that essay was first published in Poff and Waluchow (1987). Here I have been arguing that competence *is* relevant, and that a person's behaviour can be so uninformed, ill-intentioned, poorly timed and poorly executed that it may be unwise and immoral to demand any action from such a person. On the contrary, the wise and morally right thing to do might well be to prevent such a person from acting at all. In effect, one would be saying to such a person, "You are such a klutz that, all things considered, the world would be a better place if you did nothing at all, at least nothing about this or that in some situation". That's a pretty heavy load to drop on someone, but don't we all know such people? I think so. So, I suspect my earlier position was wrong. I still think it would be a mistake to give any class of people, businesspeople, baseball players or any other group a permanent moral holiday and free ride on the rest of us on the grounds of their having some sort of class deficiency or incompetence. But that is a weaker claim than the one I made in 1987. It would certainly be unreasonable to single out ethics counselors of all people as a group to be prevented from engaging in ethical analysis and action.

One of the unfortunate implications of my current position is that the door has been opened for anyone to claim that he or she is such a klutz, morally speaking, that he or she should be allowed a relatively permanent moral holiday or free ride on the rest of us. That is, someone might say, "Alex, at last you are right. I really don't know what all this talk about ethics and morality is about. I doubt that you or anyone else does either, but I am willing to let you or anyone else tote your red wagon any way you want as long as you leave me alone".

Until our free-riding friend got to the "leave me alone" part, I might have gone along. Unfortunately, again, in the interest of livable human communities, in which we all have a stake, we can't just leave people alone because they claim they have no interest or competence in moral behaviour. We have to insist that everyone plays by the rules and that means someone has to agree to monitor the players, to keep score, praise, blame, reward and punish with good reasons, at the right time, with the right motive, in the right way and so on. And that, as I have tried to show, seems to require some expertise and to open the door for some priestly perversions.

2. The first long essay I ever published was called "Decision making in committees" (Michalos 1970). It had two aims, namely, (1) to provide a basis for logical and empirical investigations of voting procedures allowing inequalities in the "weight" of individual voters and their votes, and (2) to evaluate some apparently plausible solutions to the problem of selecting an acceptable group-decision procedure. I introduced some necessary conditions of adequacy for acceptable solutions to the problem, evaluated the apparently plausible solutions according to those conditions and reached the startling conclusion that

> Perhaps the most appropriate summary of our results. ... would be a loose paraphrase of a remark made by Sir Winston Churchill: "The usual (democratic) procedure is a very bad form of government, but it is every bit as good as all the others." (p. 106)

In other words, my investigation convinced me that group decision procedures requiring *equal* voices for all participants were at least as good as those allowing *unequal* voices, although all of the procedures seemed to have serious defects.

Some weeks after I finished an earlier draft of this paper I had the shocking and depressing discovery that it took me 30 years to drop the other shoe. In the 1970 paper I was primarily concerned with formal issues. In this paper I have argued that decision-making involving ethical appraisals, especially group decision-making, must be seriously defective because there is such a diversity (a mess) of opinion about so many fundamental and primarily substantive issues.

Thirty years is a long time to wait for a second shoe to drop. If all my bright ideas come at this rate, I guess we have seen the last of them. The only bright side I can see in all of this is that having decided that my decision procedures are defective, there is not much point in worrying about the fact that I have decided that my decision procedures are defective. If I am right about their defects, maybe I am wrong about how bad I think they are, and if I am wrong about their defects, then maybe I am right more often than I think I am. So whether I am right or wrong maybe things are not as bad I think they are.

3. One of my friends (Hodgson in correspondence) suggested that some of the apparent diversity in the sketches of moral theories might be alleviated by noticing some commonalities among them. In particular, he thought that there were "two basic normative considerations" involved in most of the theories. In his words, "a good deal of moral deliberation and reasoning is directed towards constructing imperatives which, if followed, would bring about general human "well-being", and which do so with practical consistency—most critically, the imperatives do not permit the agent to make an exception in his own favour". Granting that people often disagree about "good consequences", he thought that they at least as often reach agreement.

I would agree that proponents of all the theories sketched in Table 17.1 would probably grant the importance of the sort of impartiality indicated above for moral appraisal. Egoists present an odd case, but they might claim that they endorse impartiality insofar as they think everyone should regard everyone else's interests as equally subordinate to their own and they might believe that if everyone held such a view general human well-being might be maximized. I doubt that all theistic theories or theorists would grant that the aim of moral reasoning is the production of general human well-being. It seems to me that some theists assert that one ought to do what God commands because it pleases God, whether or not it improves human well-being in general. Still, I would be willing to grant that lots of theists would insist that universal obedience to God's commands would improve human well-being. Unfortunately, there is not universal agreement among theists about which commands do or do not come from God, but that is a different problem.

Granting all this, it still seems to me that there is much more nominal and apparent than real agreement, and that is the problem with which I began. If the determination of real agreement among a set of moral judgments is contingent upon real agreement on the estimated consequences for human well-being in general, then the former probably never occurs because the latter probably never occurs. That is to say, consequentialist appraisal is probably never rigorously carried out by anyone, and if it were no one would be able to certify it as such because there is no general agreement or rule book about its exact requirements. Again, the main argument for this assertion is in Michalos (1992), and I make this assertion as a committed pragmatist and consequentialist. To those who think that the simple solution to my problem would be to abandon consequentialism I would say that as a matter of fact some sort of consequentialist analysis is practically unavoidable in moral assessments because of the frequency of conflicts of interests, rights and rules.

4. Hodgson also suggested that diversity of opinion might as often lead to "well-considered" and "deep, reflective disagreement" rather than to shallow agreement. I agree that that is logically possible, but I think that as a matter of fact usually shallow nominal agreements are reached instead of deep disagreements because the latter are more costly for group members. Deep disagreements about moral appraisals make people uncomfortable, require more time, attention and work, threaten individual belief systems and selfesteem, and put group solidarity and sustainability at risk.
5. Another one of my friends (Durbin in correspondence) suggested that I should have a look at an article by William James called "The moral philosopher and the moral life", originally published in 1891. Although James' language is a bit different from mine, his problem was virtually identical and his solution differed from mine in a familiar way. He wanted to avoid moral scepticism in the presence of a bewildering variety of competing views and in the light of his own brand of consequentialism. In his first paragraph he asserted

> The main purpose of this paper is to show that there is no such thing possible as an ethical philosophy dogmatically made up in advance. We all help to determine the content of ethical philosophy so far as we contribute to the race's moral life. In other words, there can be no final truth in ethics any more than in physics, until the last man has had his experience and said his say. In the one case as in the other, however, the hypotheses which we now make while waiting, and the acts to which they prompt us, are among the indispensable conditions which determine what that "say" shall be (James 1977, pp. 610–611).

His view of moral goodness and evil is essentially that which I defined as "Naturalistic Subjectivism" in Table 17.2. The most thorough account of this view was written by his student and biographer, Perry (1926), but the particular emphasis on the absence of "final truth in ethics" was expressed most cogently in Lewis (1946). According to Lewis, because people evaluate things in different ways as they have different experiences, it is impossible for anyone to know exactly what their most appropriate or correct evaluation of anything is, all things considered, until all their experiences are completed. Unfortunately, since at that point they are dead, they can't know then either. In fact, James' remark about "the last man" introduced a very serious additional complication, namely, the importance of *every individual's* view to the final most appropriate or correct evaluation of anything from a Naturalistic Subjectivist point of view. Here is a summary of his position.

> Since everything which is demanded is by that fact a good, must not the guiding principle for ethical philosophy (since all demands conjointly cannot be satisfied in this poor world) be simply to satisfy at all times *as many demands as we can*? That act must be the best act, accordingly, which makes for the *best whole*, in the sense of awakening the least sum of dissatisfactions. In the casuistic scale, therefore, those ideals must be written highest which *prevail at the least cost*, or by whose realization the least possible number of other ideals are destroyed. Since victory and defeat there must be, the victory to be philosophically prayed for is that of the more inclusive side, — of the side which even in the hour of triumph will to some degree do justice to the ideals in which the vanquished party's interests lay. The course of history is nothing but the story of men's struggles from generation to generation to find the more and more inclusive order. … All this amounts to saying that, so far as the casuistic question goes, ethical science is just like physical science, and instead of being deducible all at once from abstract principles, must simply bide its time, and be ready to revise its conclusions from day to day. The presumption, of course, in both sciences, always is that the vulgarly accepted opinions are true, and the right casuistic order that which public opinion believes in; and surely it would be folly quite as great, in most of us, to strike out independently and to aim at originality in ethics as in physics. Every now and then, however, some one is born with the right to be original, and his revolutionary thought or action may bear prosperous fruit. He may replace old "laws of nature" by better ones; he may, by breaking old moral rules in a certain place, bring in a total condition of things more ideal than would have followed had the rules been kept. … There is but one unconditional commandment, which is that we should seek incessantly, with fear and trembling, so to vote and to act as to bring about the very largest total universe of good which we can see. … The philosopher, then, *qua* philosopher, is no better able to determine the best universe in the concrete emergency than other men (James 1977, pp. 623–626).

Although this position has problems with the ontological, axiological and epistemological status of basic "demands" (or "interests" in Perry's language) and "public opinion", on the whole I accept the position. I should note, however, that while I agree with James' view that philosophers *qua* philosophers are not "better able to determine the best universe", I do believe that some people are better able than others. In fact, James seems to have believed it too in the light of his remarks about people "born with the right to be original". I should also add that although I don't recall reading this essay by James before my friend called my attention to it, I tried to become an expert in voting theory and survey research precisely because I accepted naturalistic subjectivism as a plausible theory of value, and voting theory and survey research as important methods for the application of that theory. In Michalos (1980b) I tried to salvage a decision procedure (the so-called "Science Court") designed to resolve conflicts among experts. Granting all this, it seems to me that the admission and clarification of the limitations of one's proposed solution is not necessarily and not in this particular case a happy solution. James certainly felt this way. Just as he pulled Almighty God out of his "will to believe" hat in his more famous essay of 1896, he did it again at the end of this essay. This time he said,

> It would seem, too - and this is my final conclusion, - that the stable and systematic moral universe for which the ethical philosopher asks is fully possible only in a world where there is a divine thinker with all-enveloping demands. … In the interests of our own ideal of systematically unified moral truth, therefore, we, as would-be philosophers, must postulate a divine thinker, and pray for the victory of the religious cause (James 1977, p. 628).

Here, of course, James and "once born atheists" like myself must part company. When I said earlier that our solutions differed in a familiar way, what I meant was that once before in his dispute with W.K. Clifford over the "ethics of belief" I was with James right up to the same point, and then parted company (Michalos 1978).

6. Besides sending me to James, Durbin gave me the benefit of his personal reflections based on, among other things, ten years or more experience on medical ethics committees. He wrote,

> In my view - which I have persuaded others to accept - even ethics committees should not think of themselves as expert decision makers, but only as consultants to the real decision makers [e.g., patients, doctors, judges]. However, I recognize that some ethics committees do think they should make authoritative decisions - thus setting themselves up in the "priestly" role, bad sense. One example: in the U.S.A. many people (including those writing on bioethics issues) take the Supreme Court as the final arbiter. But immediately people on all sides challenge the SC's decisions as unethical - and they have every right to if a given SC decision is inconsistent with their moral theories. …
>
> So what about your central conundrum, how to provide useful ethics counseling in the absence of general agreement about the basic principles of ethics - and without taking on a despised "priestly" role? I think I'd say (along with Mead and Dewey) you have been gulled by academic ethics into thinking there ought to be ethics expertise - even a single set of universally acceptable ethics criteria. I also think Mead and Dewey have the (a?) solution to your problem: that we should step down off our pedestals and join as equals (no "priestly" role here) with those who are trying to solve our social problems (so often created by people trying to impose their ethical theories on others) progressively.

I am not so sure I have been gulled and I very much like Durbin's last sentence. I think we do have to do precisely what he says. In spite of the fact that we know people have different kinds and degrees of abilities, different levels of interest and effort, different motives and opportunities, we have to interact or negotiate with people on some sort of a level playing field. For ethics counselors especially to assume special privileges would be counter-productive and priestly in the pejorative sense. Nevertheless, I also think that one of the unfortunate consequences of doing what he says and assuming we have a level playing field is that it is probably not true and we still have to deal with all the individual diversity of abilities, interests, views, etc. and the essential incompleteness of analyses that we started with. Then, insofar as we stipulate this or that proposition for the sake of reaching agreement about what is the case or what ought to be done, we find ourselves occupying a "priestly role" in spite of our good intentions.

7. Following our symposium, Durbin, Hodgson and I talked about the issues over a pleasant lunch. We all agreed that my main problem seems to be that I forgot Aristotle's warning about not expecting more of a field of inquiry than the subject matter would allow. Maybe I expect too much of ethical decision making. I have always known that I was a teen-aged logical positivist. Maybe more of the boy remains in the man than I have imagined.

Conclusion

The aim of this paper was to critically evaluate the thesis that ethics counselors constitute a new priesthood in the pejorative sense of this term. In defense of the thesis, an account was given of the diverse variety of fundamental ideas about ethics or morality. The underlying argument was simply that there is such a diversity of opinion about so many fundamental issues that most ethical appraisals, especially in committees, are probably very shallow and barely warranted. There is probably something like Gresham's Law operating in the area of moral/ethical appraisal. That is, relatively cheap appraisal tends to drive out relatively competent appraisal, and there is a general debasing of our moral/ethical currency. A similar phenomenon occurs in the political area, with relatively cheap one-liners, short sound-bites and "fluff" driving out carefully thought-out policies, clearly articulated and subjected to public debate. Following this negative assault on the home team, an attempt was made to try to find some positive benefits from the work of ethics counselors. Some potential benefits were identified, but there is a need for empirical research in order to construct a more persuasive case for such work. In the penultimate section of the paper I addressed some of my own second thoughts about the discussion and some provocative suggestions that friends gave me about earlier drafts. As usual, I hope that someone reading this paper will undertake the needed research.

Acknowledgements An earlier version of this paper was written for presentation at the Fifth Annual International Conference on Business Ethics at Niagara University, October 21–23, 1999. I would like to thank Edmund Byrne, Russell Cornett, Harold Coward, Paul Durbin, Bernard Hodgson, Deborah Poff and Lloyd Spurrell for their helpful suggestions. Of course none of these people should be held responsible for the final product.

References

James, W. (1977, originally published 1891). The moral philosopher and the moral life. In J. J. McDermott (Ed.), *The writings of William James: A comprehensive edition* (pp. 610–629). Chicago: University of Chicago Press.

Lakatos, I. (1968). Changes in the problem of inductive logic. In I. Lakatos (Ed.), *The problem of inductive logic* (pp. 315–417). Amsterdam: North-Holland Pub. Co.

Lewis, C. I. (1946). *An analysis of knowledge and valuation*. LaSalle: Open Court Publishing Co.

Michalos, A. C. (1970). Decision-making in committees. *American Philosophical Quarterly, 7*(2), 91–106.
Michalos, A. C. (1978). *Foundations of decision-making*. Ottawa: Canadian Library of Philosophy.
Michalos, A. C. (1980a). Philosophy of science: Historical, social and value aspects. In P. T. Durbin (Ed.), *The culture of science, technology and medicine* (pp. 197–281). New York: The Free Press.
Michalos, A. C. (1980b). *North American social report* (Vol. 2, Crime, Justice and Politics). Dordrecht: D. Reidel.
Michalos, A. C. (1980c). A reconsideration of the idea of a science court. In P. T. Durbin (Ed.), *Research in philosophy and technology* (Vol. 3, pp. 10–28). Boston: JAI Press.
Michalos, A. C. (1981a). Technology assessment, facts and values. In P. T. Durbin (Ed.), *Research in philosophy and technology* (Vol. 4, pp. 59–81). Boston: JAI Press.
Michalos, A. C. (1981b). *North American social report* (Vol. 3, Science, Education and Recreation). Dordrecht: D. Reidel.
Michalos, A. C. (1987). Moral responsibility in business, or, fourteen unsuccessful ways to pass the buck. In D. C. Poff & W. J. Waluchow (Eds.), *Business ethics in Canada* (pp. 12–25). Scarborough: Prentice-Hall Canada. Reprinted in Michalos, 1995.
Michalos, A. C. (1992). Ethical considerations in evaluation. *Canadian Journal of Program Evaluation, 7*, 61–75. Reprinted in Michalos, 1995.
Michalos, A. C. (1995). *A pragmatic approach to business ethics*. Thousand Oaks: Sage Publications.
Perry, R. B. (1926). *General theory of value*. Cambridge: Harvard University Press.
Poff, D. C., & Waluchow, W. (Eds.). (1987). *Business ethics in Canada*. Toronto: Prentice-Hall of Canada.
Reichenbach, H. (1949). *The theory of probability*. Berkeley: University of California Press.
Shaw, B. (1931). *Pen portraits and reviews*. London: Constable and Co.
Skidelsky, R. (1993). *Interests and obsessions*. London: Macmillan.

Chapter 18
Observations on the Proposed BC—STV Voting System

Alex C. Michalos

In systems of representative government, (among other ways) one might divide the whole territory into roughly equal constituencies and elect governments on the basis of which party wins the most or a majority of constituencies, or on the basis of which party wins the most or a majority of votes across the whole country. In Canada we use the former alternative, but we also routinely count and advertise the popular vote. Within each constituency and for the country as a whole, we use a plurality system (PS) to elect our representatives. The candidate in the constituency and the party in the country getting the most votes wins. We often call this a First Past the Post (FPTP) system, but in fact there is no post, no threshold or set quota of votes to be secured in order to win.

We know that it is practically impossible to make every constituency have exactly the same number of people. So, of course it is possible that when we count the total votes in diverse sized constituencies, one party might carry a majority of constituencies and another party might carry a majority of votes when results of all constituencies are amalgamated. Some people find this discrepancy troublesome and some don't. I find it troublesome, but I don't think I have a good argument to change the minds of people who don't. However, I do think that in democracies governments would have greater legitimacy and perceived legitimacy if there were greater proportionality between the percentages of seats in a legislature and total voter support. It would be hard to prove the 'legitimacy' or the 'perceived legitimacy' part of this claim. So, I will not try. I will merely say that I begin with the premise that the current system has a significant flaw that we should try to fix.

Michalos, A.C.: 2005. Observations on the Proposed BC—STV Voting System.

A.C. Michalos (✉)
University of Northern British Columbia, Prince George, BC, Canada
e-mail: michalos@brandonu.ca

A.C. Michalos, *How Good Policies and Business Ethics Enhance Good Quality of Life*, DOI 10.1007/978-3-319-50724-8_18

Proportional representation (PR) voting systems of various kinds may be used to eliminate the flaw just described, and most democracies today do use such systems. In principle, we could obtain proportional representation using the single member constituencies we now have in BC plus some additional province-wide seats. In Germany, half their MPs are elected from single member constituencies and half from the country at large using party lists. We could and I think we should and one day will craft our own version of a so-called Mixed Member Proportional Representation (MMPR) voting system.

The BC Citizen's Assembly (CA) recommended a different system that would deliver something fairly close to proportional representation in our province, namely, the Single Transferable Vote (STV) system. The only choice BC voters will have in the referendum on electoral reform on May 17 is to accept the proposed BC STV system or the status quo. Although I believe the status quo is a flawed voting system in need of repair, I think it has fewer flaws than the BC STV system. Briefly, here are some of the flaws in the BC STV, drawn from several different sources. I regard each of these flaws as a reason to vote against the BC STV.

1. The BC STV system is not transparent and easy to understand.
2. Because most voters will not understand how votes are counted, we will be making elections less transparent at a time when people are generally demanding greater transparency from governments.
3. Because most voters will not understand how votes are counted, we will be encouraging voter suspicions, likely followed by anger and/or apathy.
4. The proportionality that the STV system delivers can be delivered with lower costs in an MMPR system.
5. Divisions of the distribution of people's ordinal rankings of preferences are not mathematically or substantively meaningful, e.g., giving 5 s choice candidates 19/45ths of Smith's "surplus" first choice is not meaningful. The preferential gaps between Smith's voters first two choices and Jones's may be very different, with the result that if we had real lumps of matter to distribute, 19/45ths of Smith's surplus might be more or less than 19/45ths of Jones's.
6. The increased geographical and population sizes of constituencies will make it more difficult for people to communicate with and know all candidates.
7. The increased geographical and population sizes of constituencies will make it more difficult for candidates to communicate with and know members of their constituencies.
8. The increased geographical and population sizes of constituencies will make it more likely that voters will focus on issues mainly of only local interest, with less attention to the general good or interest of BC residents.
9. If most voters focus only on local issues, one must assume or hope that the general or public interest will be served by some kind of 'invisible hand', but I think the best way to obtain the public good is for voters to aim for the greatest good for the greatest number.

10. The "quota" percentage of voters required for election to office varies with the numbers of representatives allowed from each constituency, e.g., each of 2 reps would need about 33% of voters, while each of 5 reps would need 17%.
11. Because each constituency will be represented by at least 2 people, each will have two voices which might be in conflict and effectively neutralize each other's strength.
12. The STV system is non-monotonic, meaning that it is possible to construct scenarios such that the more votes a candidate gets at different rounds of voting, the less likely that candidate is to win the election, i.e., voters might help their candidate most by not voting at all.
13. The STV system is not equitable because, depending on the rank ordering of candidates in different rounds, some voters' preferences will be counted several times while others will not be counted.
14. The system tends to reduce the strength of party discipline, including the ability of parties to deliver on their promises, at a time when all voters are sick to death of broken promises from politicians.
15. The system tends to reduce the strength of individual candidates to deliver on their promises, because they cannot count on party support.
16. The weakening of parties implies the weakening of broad-based, long-range, strategic planning based on a carefully thought through political philosophy.
17. The weakening of political parties implies the weakening of a political infrastructure that can be routinely mobilized for analysis, education and advocacy of programs and policies affecting the public good. (Among other things, the absence of such an infrastructure to mobilize support for the BC STV has practically doomed it to failure.)
18. It seems to be the case that where versions of STV are used (e.g., Ireland), it is more difficult for small parties to gain seats, but I think we should make it easier (as versions of MMPR would).

These reasons are not all or equally persuasive. The strength of some depends on diverse assumptions about representative government, good government, acceptable versions of democracy and people's levels of tolerance for uncertainty. For me, they are sufficient to vote against the BC STV proposal on May 17.

Addendum

I suspect that there is no ideal voting procedure that would satisfy everyone's conditions of adequacy for a perfect system. Indeed, it may be difficult to get agreement by everyone on exactly what conditions of adequacy ought to be adopted. The Voting Paradox reveals one reason for doubting that an ideal system is possible. It runs as follows.

Suppose we have:

1. At least three voters A, B and C.
2. At least three candidates, x, y and z.
3. For any two candidates, x is preferred to y if a majority of voters rank x above y.
4. Candidates are **weakly orderable** by voters' preferences. This means that all candidates are **comparable** in the sense that,

   a. For any pair, either x is preferred to y, or or y is preferred to x, or x and y are equally acceptable; and preferences for candidates is **transitive** in the sense that,
   b. For any three candidates, if x is preferred to y and y is preferred to z, then x is preferred to z.

Given these apparently plausible conditions, it is easy to show how we might find ourselves embroiled in self-contradiction.

For example, suppose we have 3 voters with preferences as follows.

A	B	C
x	y	z
y	z	x
z	x	y

So, according to condition 3, we know that x is preferred to y, and y is preferred to z.

So, according to condition 4b, it follows that x is preferred to z.

However, according to condition 3, we know that z is preferred to x.

Therefore, x is preferred to z and z is preferred to x, which is logically absurd.

The paradox apparently shows that there is no ideal system because such a system would have to include the weakly orderable conditions in order to guarantee a first choice election when a group actually has a first choice, but it would also have to admit the possibility of voter preferences of the sort just presented, which guarantees contradictory choices in some circumstances.

Chapter 19
Ancient Observations on Business Ethics: Middle East Meets West

Alex C. Michalos

Introduction

It is an interesting historical fact that the Age of Avarice, as I call the last quarter of the 20th century, simultaneously produced perhaps the most blatant self-consciously self-serving corporate behavior under the general rubric of globalization and the most prolific development of academic and non-academic literature on business ethics. To a large extent, the recent growth of the field of business ethics seems to have ridden on the tail of the growth of unbridled greed and notorious failures of moral leadership accompanied by widely publicized business failures. What is even more interesting to me is that when, roughly in the fifth and fourth century BCE, thoughtful people in the Middle East began to reflect on the nature of a good life and/or the life of a morally good person, unscrupulous and avaricious businesspeople provided a wide array of familiar examples of bad lives and bad people. It is fair to say that to some extent, 20–28 hundred years ago, the growth of the literature and field of ethics itself seems to have ridden on practically the very same tail. While it would be a gross exaggeration to suggest that without crooked businesspeople there would have been no need for the institution of morality or the study of ethics itself, it is not an exaggeration to say that such people were such familiar figures in the daily lives of the ancients that advocates for a good life (philosophers, poets, dramatists) could safely invoke the images of such people knowing that their listeners or readers would get the point.

Michalos, A.C.: 2008. Ancient observations on business ethics: Middle East meets West. Journal of Business Ethics, 79(1–2), pp. 9–19. © Springer 2007.

A.C. Michalos (✉)
University of Northern British Columbia, Prince George, BC, Canada
e-mail: michalos@brandonu.ca

A.C. Michalos, *How Good Policies and Business Ethics Enhance Good Quality of Life*, DOI 10.1007/978-3-319-50724-8_19

In this essay, I am going to provide a small sample of the kinds of images and examples of bad and good business behavior that were used by some relatively well-known and unknown ancient writers to help their contemporaries find a better life and become better people, morally speaking. The review is necessarily brief, but if it begins to reveal our common humanity with people across a vast amount of time (in human terms) it will have served its purpose. Regarding the theme of this conference, my story is rather more about the Middle East 20–28 hundred years ago meeting the West today than about the East today meeting West today, although, what is east or west, or even today for that matter, depends on one's perspective. From my home in British Columbia, Hong Kong is west and Paris is east.

Readers should be aware that for most of the ancient writers, especially the presocratics, we often have only bits and pieces of their thoughts, sayings and/or writings. There are fragments purported to be actual quotations, but often liable to be paraphrases or rough approximations of the philosophers' actual views. Often enough there is no way to confirm or disconfirm authenticity, and even when authenticity is relatively well established, there is often considerable controversy concerning the most appropriate interpretation of a fragment in its original language and the most appropriate translation of the original text. Add to these problems the number of centuries of reproductions, errors of omission and commission, and commentaries by more or less well-informed, well-intentioned (the main reports we have of the views of some philosophers come from hostile critics) and well-resourced researchers, and the difficulty of producing an accurate account of the work of our ancestors becomes clear. For reasons that will become clear as we proceed, I owe a particularly heavy debt to the translations and analyses of R.D. McKirahan.

Straight Dealing Leads to Observable Payoffs

The poems of Hesiod of Ascra (late eighth and early seventh century BCE) provide some insight into the lives of people of his generation and their assessments of what is good or bad. They lived in a world that was regarded as intelligibly ordered and fundamentally understandable, although filled with divine influences ranging from the purely mysterious to fairly anthropomorphic Olympian gods. The connotative range of the concept of divinity for ancient Greeks was significantly different from its range today. Anything imagined as immortal, ageless and capable of independent motion or power was regarded as divine. Hence, for example, when the sixth century BCE Milesian philosopher Thales posited water or Anaximander (sixth century BCE) posited some indefinite but spatially and temporally unlimited stuff as the ultimate building material of the world, that material would have been regarded as divine. Anaximenes (sixth century) is reported to have believed that the ultimate building material was air or "dark mist", and "gods and divine things" originated from that material (McKirahan 1994, pp. 31–48).

The following passages from Hesiod's *Works and Days* provide the earliest account that I have found indicating that straight dealing leads to prosperity and crooked dealing leads to disaster, i.e., in contemporary terms, there are greater profits to be made from morally good than from morally evil practices.

> Those who give straight judgments to foreigners and citizens and do not step at all aside from justice have a flourishing city and the people prosper in it. There is Peace, the nurse of children, throughout the land, and wide-seeing Zeus never ordains harsh war for them. Famine and Disaster never attend men of straight judgment, but with good cheer they feed on the fruits of their labors. For these the Earth bears the means of life in abundance… But for those who have thoughts of evil violence and cruel deeds, wide-seeing Zeus son of Kronos has ordained justice. Often indeed the entire city of an evil man suffers,… Famine and Disease together, and the people perish. Women do not give birth, but houses are diminished… (McKirahan 1994, p. 14)

According to Barney (2004, p. 2), this poem was "a very early and canonical text for traditional Greek moral thought". In Hesiod's view, as articulated in this poem, a "just man is above all a law-abiding one", and the driving motive of the unjust is greed. "The unjust man", Barney wrote, "is motivated by the desire to have more [pleon echein]: more than he has, more than his neighbor has, more than he is entitled to, and, ultimately, all there is to get". In a wonderfully succinct summary remark, Hesiod wrote, "…if one knows and is willing to proclaim what is just, Zeus far-sounding gives him wealth". Interestingly enough, in this remark the poet did not see a need to add any particular sort of action to knowledge and talk.

Unobservable Payoffs to Unobservable Souls

Pythagoras of Samos (c. 560–480 BCE) is one of history's most extra-ordinary people, brilliant, charismatic and enigmatic. He and his friends created associations that engaged in socio-economic, political, religious and academic activities. Although, he seems to have written nothing, so remarkable were his talents and character that incredible legends were attached to him, e.g., that he could walk on water and be in two different places at the same time. Economically and politically Pythagorean societies were relatively successful aristocracies, religiously they were relatively secretive and ascetic, and academically they nourished creative scientists and mathematicians. He is reported to have believed that the ultimate material of the universe was numerical in some sense, but the sense was quite unclear and Aristotle (384–322 BCE), among others, was quite critical of this feature of his metaphysics.

For present purposes, the details of the Pythagorean scheme are not as important as the general idea that the universe is not only intelligibly ordered but also constructed out of entities with geometrical shapes that, in principle perhaps, might be measurable. With the "mathematical solids" as basic building blocks, Pythagoras imagined that the universe, which he called the KOSMOS, was somehow held together or connected by HARMONIA, i.e., by some sort of principle of harmony.

He apparently believed that all living things (plants as well as animals) have immortal souls which at death transmigrate among diverse species, trading up or down as it were, depending partly on individuals' behavior and character. It is unclear if souls were supposed to be discrete, singular entities, aggregations of entities connected by the same principle of harmony holding the universe together, or merely that very same principle under a new name when it is applied to holding the parts of an individual's body together. The first of these alternatives would probably be the easiest to combine with a theory of transmigration. In any event, the aim of the relatively ascetic Pythagorean "way of life" was to bring increased harmony to an individual's soul, thereby improving that individual's chances for trading up rather than down and ultimately being released from the whole process. That "way of life" was pretty clearly divided into two main paths, the path of scholarship engaged in a variety of intellectual inquiries versus a path of religious asceticism engaged in following an array of more or less reasonable rules, e.g., eating in moderation and only vegetables, not eating beans, not keeping swallows in the house and not urinating facing the sun.

However one assesses the two distinct paths characterizing the Pythagorean "way of life", the philosopher's most important contribution to our subject lie elsewhere. This is his theory that the observable conditions of an individual's life and the individual's observable behavior have an impact on that individual's unobservable soul. Most importantly, by positing an unobservable immortal soul as the final recipient of any rewards or punishments justly visited upon an individual for his or her own behavior, Pythagoras directed our attention away from overt appearances to covert realities. After all is said and done, according to Pythagoras, the good life we seek is the unobservable harmony of that unobservable entity, the immortal soul. Thus, the contrast between these unobservable payoffs and the observable payoffs to individuals and communities resulting from straight dealing according to Hesiod writing roughly 300 years earlier could not be greater.

Trust, Social Cohesion and Social Capital

Michalos (1990) defended the theses that the world is to some extent constructed by each of us, that it can and ought to be constructed in a more benign way, that such construction will require more trust than most people are currently willing to grant, and that most of us will be better off if most of us can manage to be more trusting in spite of our doubts.

Trust was certainly one of the hottest topics in the field of good governance in the 1990s and it continues to attract researchers' attention in a number of areas. Putnam (1993, 1995, 1996) argued that social cohesion is the stuff of which social capital is made, and social cohesion is based on trust. In brief, to individuals' and communities' stocks of financial, physical and human capital, one may add social capital, and to some extent deficits of one sort may be compensated by surpluses of another sort. What's more, unlike physical capital stocks, for example, which tend to decrease with use, social capital stocks tend to increase with use. Exchange networks grow and communication becomes easier as trust builds with each successful exchange. In other words, social capital is a species of public good, like morality, love, knowledge, and art (Michalos 1995).

The general consensus seems to be that self-reported trust in institutions of various sorts as well as in one's neighbors is a good measure of social cohesion and capital. What is particularly interesting for present purposes regarding the significance of trust is that the Anonymous Iamblichus, writing around the late fifth and early fourth century BCE, had some brilliant observations. Iamblichus believed that the implications of living in communities that have good laws and law-abiding people (i.e., communities characterized by EUNOMIA) are quite different from those characterized by the opposite qualities (i.e., by ANOMIA). The following passages describe the sorts of social capital he envisioned.

> In the first place, trust arises from EUNOMIA, and this benefits all people greatly and is one of the great goods. For as a result of it, money becomes available and so, even if there is little it is sufficient since it is in circulation… Fortunes and misfortunes in money and life are managed most suitably for people as a result of EUNOMIA. For those enjoying good fortune can use it in safety and without danger of plots, while those suffering ill fortune are aided by the fortunate… Through EUNOMIA…the time people devote to PRAGMATA (a word which can mean 'government', 'public business', or 'troubles') is idle, but that devoted to the activities of life is productive. In EUNOMIA people are free from the most unpleasant concern and engage in the most pleasant, since concern about PRAGMATA is most unpleasant and concern about one's activities is most pleasant. Also, when they go to sleep, which is a rest from troubles for people, they go to it without fear and unworried about painful matters, and when they rise from it they have other similar experiences… Nor…do they expect the day to bring poverty, but they look forward to it without fear directing their concern, without grief towards the activities of life,… And war, which is the source of the greatest evils for people…comes more to those who practice ANOMIA, less to those practicing EUNO-MIA (McKirahan 1994, pp. 406–407).

In passages following the above quotation, Iamblichus described the implications of living in communities characterized by ANOMIA, which are essentially the opposites of those above. Besides being populated by people living with mistrust, fear and insecurity, such communities are the seedbeds for tyranny because those people have desperate needs for relief and turn to apparently strong but often unscrupulous leaders. In the end, as he remarked in the beginning, Iamblichus was sure that nobody would ever be strong enough to prevent the great masses of people from casting out tyrants and bringing justice for all.

Moral Relativity

Heraclitus of Ephesus (c. 540–480 BCE) was born to an aristocratic family and throughout his life maintained deep doubts about (if not disdain for) the capacities and character of those with less fortunate origins. Of the hundred or so remaining fragments of his works, those positing a world constantly undergoing changes while preserving identities are most frequently associated with his philosophy, e.g., "Upon those who step into the same rivers, different and again different waters flow" (McKirahan 1994, p. 122). He believed that the universe was not made but always existed, and formed a coherent unity displaying great diversity. The ultimate material building blocks were fire, water and earth, which were distinct but periodically transformed into one another. The fundamental principle of order was referred to as the LOGOS, which is a multi-purpose word connoting discourse, word, story, opinion, reason and cause, to mention a few.

Perhaps because he was so deeply impressed by the diversity of the world around him, he noticed that much of that diversity was constructed (to use a modern term) by observing the world from different perspectives or using different standards of comparison. For any of his contemporaries interested in defining "the" good life or "the" right way to live, the descriptive and evaluative relativism of some of his fragments would have been deeply disturbing. For example, consider the following.

> The sea is the purest and most polluted water: to fishes drinkable and bringing safety, to humans undrinkable and destructive.
>
> Pigs rejoice in mud more than pure water.
>
> We would call oxen happy when they find bitter vetch to eat.
>
> Physicians who cut and burn complain that they receive no worthy pay, although they do these things. The road up and the road down are one and the same.
>
> To God all things are beautiful and good and just, but humans have supposed some unjust and others just (McKirahan 1994, pp. 121–125).

Thus, safe drinking water is important to fishes and humans, but the same water is different for each species. It may be appropriate to think of rejoicing pigs and happy oxen, but different things produce these pleasant states in these different species. Pain and those who inflict it upon others are normally regarded as bad, but physicians inflict it upon their patients, believing it to be good and worthy of some valuable payment for services rendered. The gradient of a road may be advantageous or disadvantageous to a traveler depending on the direction of his or her travel, though the gradient is the same for all travelers. Most devastating of all, what appears just or unjust to humans is really uniformly just, beautiful and good to God. That is to say, everything in the world is really just, beautiful and good in some objective sense known only to God, although to humans (and presumably all other sentient species according to other fragments) some things appear to be unjust, ugly and bad.

In the presence of such complexity (or confusion), one might suppose that Heraclitus would have been unable and unwilling to provide any recommendations for living "the" good life. In fact, since vague and contradictory premises have unlimited implications, confused philosophical foundations provide fertile soil for practically any desired crop. Thus, besides valuing personal safety, justice, happiness and beauty as suggested above, according to Heraclitus, "Right thinking is the greatest excellence, and wisdom is to speak the truth and act in accordance with nature, while paying attention to it" (McKirahan 1994, p. 120). The "right thinking" or "wisdom" referred to is practical as well as theoretical. It is revealed in one's assertions and actions, which are guided by careful observation of the natural world followed by behaviour that is appropriate to the conditions of that world as well as to one's particular species. The good life is one lived in communities in which people willingly follow customs and obey conventional laws that are consistent with an ideal law sometimes referred to as "the divine law". It is a life relatively free of drunkenness, anger and violence. While there is a place for religion and religious rituals, there is no room for bathing oneself in blood or singing hymns "to the shameful parts [phalli]". Finally, Heraclitus believed that "It is not better for humans to get all that they want" (McKirahan 1994, p. 128). At a minimum, this last fragment implies that the mere maximization of desire satisfaction is neither necessary nor sufficient for the good life.

Granting the confusion and even logical incoherence of the total set of fragments remaining of Heraclitus's works, he is at least a candidate for the first philosopher to accept the relativity of moral views, i.e., of views about the good life and good people. The fragment about physicians being worthy of pay for burning and cutting people clearly implies that acceptable and even reward-warranting behaviour for some may be quite different for others. Unlike physicians, thugs are justly condemned and punished for engaging in acts of burning and cutting people. Presumably, because in the eyes of God the physicians' and thugs' behaviour are equally just and good, Heraclitus's acceptance of conventional ways of treating their behaviour must be regarded as his own way of accommodating differences in the world as it appears and as his metaphysics says it really is. If Heraclitus had been willing to treat the behaviour of physicians and thugs as equally just and acceptable as his metaphysics required, current advocates of special or particular moralities for diverse businesspeople and business practices might have regarded him as their earliest advocate.

The Relativity of All Assertions

Because of his prominence in Plato's (427–347 BCE) dialogue of the same name, Protagoras of Abdera (c. 490–420 BCE) is perhaps the best known of the so-called Older Sophists. Although, Protagoras had an aristocratic background, he made a living as an itinerant teacher of relatively advanced studies of rhetoric. Of the few fragments reliably attributed to him, the most famous is "A human being is the measure of all things—of things that are, that they are, and of things that are not, that they are not" (McKirahan 1994, p. 379). While we have just seen some elements of skeptical relativism in fragments attributed to Heraclitus, this fragment is a particularly bold statement of the relativity of all assertions, including those concerning what is just or unjust, beautiful or ugly, and even true or false. Diogenes Laertius added that "Protagoras was the first to declare that there are two mutually opposed arguments on any subject" (McKirahan 1994, p. 374). As if all this was not troublesome enough, in another bold fragment Protagoras professed a reasoned agnosticism.

> Concerning the gods I am unable to know either that they are or that they are not, or what their appearance is like. For many are the things that hinder knowledge: the obscurity of the matter and the shortness of human life (McKirahan 1994, p. 364).

The clear implications of such principles, then, are that the best life and the best sort of person to be are entirely dependent on individual preferences, and Protagoras certainly had his own preferences. According to Plato, Protagoras said that he could make people better in the sense of more excellent in managing their personal as well as public affairs. Perhaps more importantly for his commercial interests, Aristotle reported that Protagoras claimed the ability to make "the worse case the better" and to teach others how to accomplish the same feat. If he could deliver the product as advertised, his teaching would have been worth plenty to anyone with aspirations for a career in commerce, law or politics. Apparently enough people believed that he could deliver the product to make him famous, wealthy and politically influential.

Ethics Without Tears: Natural Pleasures Versus Conventional Pains

Although, there are several Antiphons cited by various authors in antiquity, Antiphon of Rhamnous (c. 480–411 BCE) seems to have been a relatively wealthy orator, statesman, philosopher, teacher of rhetoric and professional speech-writer. For present purposes, it is important to note that McKirahan (1994, p. 396) described him as "possibly the earliest advocate of hedonism in Greek philosophy". The remaining fragments of his work show that he carefully distinguished natural (PHYSIS) from conventional (NOMOS) phenomena, regarding the former as necessary and universal, and the latter as unnecessary and variable. Granting that it could be advantageous for people to live in accordance with conventional laws and customs, he argued that nature provided a more reliable guide to human well-being. The following passages capture the core of his position.

> Living and dying are matters of PHYSIS, and living results for them from what is advantageous, dying from what is not advantageous. But the advantages which are established by the NOMOI are bonds on PHYSIS, and those established by PHYSIS are free.
>
> And so, things that cause distress, at least when thought of correctly, do not help PHYSIS more than things that give joy. Therefore, it will not be painful things rather than pleasant things which are advantageous. For things that are truly advantageous must not cause harm but benefit. Now the things that are advantageous by PHYSIS are among these.
>
> <But according to NOMOS, those are correct> who defend themselves after suffering and are not first to do wrong, and those who do good to parents who are bad to them, and who permit others to accuse them on oath but do not themselves accuse on oath. You will find most of these cases hostile to PHYSIS. They permit people to suffer more pain when less is possible and to have less pleasure when more is possible, and to receive injury when it is not necessary (McKirahan 1994, p. 394).

A clearer foundation for attaining a good life without tears could not be constructed. Provided that things are "thought of correctly", what is pleasant is naturally, universally life-enhancing and what is painful is life-destroying. More precisely, provided that one thinks "correctly", one's experiences of pleasure and pain ought to be regarded as nature's reliable guides to appropriate human action. So, the best sort of person will make careful and accurate observations of nature, think "correctly" about what causes "distress" and "joy", successfully apprehend nature's guides to a long and pleasant life, and scrupulously follow those guides. Consequently, such a person will enjoy the best sort of life. In other words, the best sort of person will be able to distinguish a Fool's Paradise from Real Paradise, and live happily ever after in the latter.

Unfortunately, the good life achievable by Anti-phon's prescriptions is not necessarily morally good or just. Another part of the same fragment quoted above clarifies his view of justice and its relation to a good life.

> …Justice is a matter of not transgressing what the NOMOI prescribe in whatever city you are a citizen of. A person would make most advantage of justice for himself if he treated the NOMOI as important in the presence of witnesses, and treated the decrees of PHYSIS as important when alone and with no witnesses present. For the decrees of NOMOI are extra additions, those of the PHYSIS are necessary; those of the NOMOI are the products of agreement, not of natural growth, whereas those of PHYSIS are the products of natural growth, not of agreement (McKirahan 1994, pp. 393–394).

Since a transgressor of conventional laws may avoid "both disgrace and penalty" if there are no witnesses to the acts, while a transgressor of natural laws (so far as that might be possible) would suffer the consequences even if there are no witnesses, the former is a less serious matter than the latter. Therefore, in the pursuit of the good life, Antiphon advises each person to follow nature's directives favoring personal pleasure over pain.

Virtue Its Own Reward and the Principle of Transparency

Articulating the Stoic position through the voice of Marcus Cato, Marcus Tulius Cicero (106–43 BCE), writing roughly 400 years after Pythagoras, argued that morally right or good actions could only be properly performed for their own sake, not for any particular observable or unobservable payoff to anyone. The following passages provide a clear refutation of all our contemporary writers who try to defend business ethics on the grounds of its financial profitability. Cicero clearly saw that if morally right actions are finally only warranted by their financial profitability then they could be undermined and over-ridden by immoral actions whenever the latter promised greater profitability, a consequence that would effectively destroy the institution of morality.

> In friendship some profess that the Wise Man will hold his friends' interests as dear as his own, while others say that a man's own interests must necessarily be dearer to him; at the same time the latter admit that to enrich oneself by another's loss is an action repugnant to that justice towards which we seem to possess a natural propensity. But the school that I am discussing [i.e., Stoicism] emphatically rejects the view that we adopt or approve either justice or friendship for the sake of their utility. For if it were so, the same claims of utility would be able to undermine and overthrow them. In fact the very existence of both justice and friendship will be impossible if they are not desired for their own sake (Cicero 1931, p. 291).

In Book II of the same treatise, Cicero presents what we might now call a *Principle of Transparency* or *Publicity* as a fundamental guide or test of morally acceptable behaviour.

> Profess in any public assembly that the motive of all your actions is the desire to avoid pain. If you feel that this too does not sound sufficiently dignified and respectable, say that you intend both in your present office and all your life long to act soley for the sake of your own advantage, – to do nothing but what will pay, nothing in short that is not for your own interest; imagine the uproar among the audience! What would become of your chances of the consulship,… Will you then adopt a rule of life which you can appeal to in private and among friends but which you dare not openly profess or parade in public? Ah, but it is the vocabulary of the Peripatetics and the Stoics that is always on your lips, in the law-courts and the senate. Duty, Fair-Dealing, Moral Worth, Fidelity, Uprightnes, Honour…in that glorious array of high-sounding words, pleasure finds no place… In my view those opinions are true which are honorable, praiseworthy and noble – which can be openly avowed in the senate and the popular assembly, and in every company and gathering, so that one need not be ashamed to say what one is not ashamed to think (Cicero 1931, pp. 165–169).

Justice, Legal Compliance and Moral Rightness

Cicero's last treatise, *De Officiis (On Duties),* was written sometime in the 46–43 BCE period when he was fleeing for his life at the hands of followers of Julius Caesar and Mark Antony. He was not one of Caesar's assassins, but was a known sympathizer and was also known to have been sympathetic to the idea of eliminating Antony. So, in the year after Caesar's death in 44 BCE, Antony's people arranged Cicero's death. According to our translator, Miller, Cicero regarded this treatise as "his masterpiece", although "it was not written as a contribution to close scientific thinking…[but] as a means of occupation and diversion" (Cicero 1913, p. xiv).

Cicero shared many, if not most, of the views of his contemporary aristocrats. For examples, he believed that the chief purpose of government was to protect individual property rights, that it was acceptable to remove tyrants by assassination and that manual labor was unacceptable for a gentleman. He accepted the institution of slavery, but recommended that slaves should be treated as well as employees, though "they must be required to work". Of the four cardinal virtues, wisdom, justice, courage and temperance, he regarded justice as most important. In his view,

> …the duties prescribed by justice must be given precedence over the pursuit of knowledge and the duties imposed by it; for the former concern the welfare of our fellow-men; and nothing ought to be more sacred in men's eyes than that…every walk and vocation in life calls for human co-operation—first and above all, in order that one may have friends… So also to buyers and sellers, to employers and employed, and to those who are engaged in commercial dealings generally, justice is indispensable for the conduct of business. Its importance is so great, that not even those who live by wickedness and crime can get on without some small element of justice. For if a robber takes anything by force or by fraud from another member of the gang, he loses his standing even in a band of robbers… If, therefore, anyone wishes to win true glory, let him discharge the duties required by justice (Cicero 1913, pp. 159–213).

Many of Cicero's works contain excellent discussions of problems in business ethics. For example, in the third Book of his treatise *On Duties*, Cicero presents a case requiring a choice between what he calls "expediency" and "moral rectitude", which today we might say is a choice between legal compliance and moral rightness. It is a pedagogical gem, which I will quote in full.

> Suppose… a time of dearth and famine at Rhodes, with provisions at fabulous prices; and suppose that an honest man has imported a large cargo of grain from Alexandria and that to his certain knowledge also several other importers have set sail from Alexandria, and that on the voyage he has sighted their vessels laden with grain and bound for Rhodes; is he to report the fact to the Rhodians or is he to keep his own counsel and sell his own stock at the highest market price? I am assuming the case of a virtuous, upright man, and I am raising the question how a man would think and reason who would not conceal the facts from the Rhodians if he thought that it was immoral to do so, but who might be in doubt whether such silence would really be immoral.
>
> In deciding cases of this kind Diogenes of Babylonia [c. 240–152 BCE], a great and highly esteemed Stoic, consistently holds one view; his pupil Antipater [of Tarsus, second century BCE], a most profound scholar, holds another. According to Antipater all the facts should be disclosed, that the buyer may not be uninformed of any detail that the seller knows; according to Diogenes the seller should declare any defects in his wares, in so far as such a course is prescribed by the common law of the land; but for the rest, since he has goods to sell, he may try to sell them to the best possible advantage, provided he is guilty of no misrepresentation.
>
> 'I have imported my stock,' Diogenes's merchant will say; 'I have offered it for sale; I sell at a price no higher than my competitors—perhaps even lower, when the market is overstocked. Who is wronged?'
>
> 'What say you?' comes Antipater's argument on the other side; 'it is your duty to consider the interests of your fellow-men and to serve society; you were brought into the world under these conditions and have these inborn principles which you are in duty bound to obey and follow, that your interest shall be the interest of the community and conversely that the interest of the community shall be your interest as well; will you, in view of all these facts, conceal from your fellow-men what relief in plenteous supplies is close at hand for them?'
>
> 'It is one thing to conceal,' Diogenes will perhaps reply; 'not to reveal is quite a different thing. At this present moment I am not concealing from you, even if I am not revealing to you, the nature of the gods or the highest good; and to know these secrets would be of more advantage to you than to know that the price of wheat was down. But I am under no obligation to tell you everything that it may be to your interest to be told.'

> 'Yea,' Antipater will say, 'but you are, as you must admit, if you will only bethink you of the bonds of fellowship forged by Nature and existing between man and man'.
>
> 'I do not forget them,' the other will reply; 'but do you mean to say that those bonds of fellowship are such that there is no such thing as private property? If that is the case, we should not sell anything at all, but freely give everything away' (Cicero 1913, pp. 319–323).

Diogenes's last intervention was a huge and unwarranted leap. Antipater's demand that, from a moral point of view, one ought to be as concerned with the protection of other people's property as one's own certainly does not imply the destruction of the institution of private property. But there is no need to pursue this issue here. After describing this case, Cicero presents another case involving the sale of an "unsanitary" house, and then offers his assessment of what an honest seller would do.

> I must give my decision in these two cases; for I did not propound them merely to raise the questions, but to offer a solution. I think, then, that it was the duty of that grain-dealer not to keep back the facts from the Rhodians, and of this vendor of the house to deal in the same way with his purchaser. The fact is that merely holding one's peace about a thing does not constitute concealment, but concealment consists in trying for your own profit to keep others from finding out something that you know, when it is for their interest to know it. And who fails to discern what manner of concealment that is and what sort of person would be guilty of it? At all events he would be no candid or sincere or straightforward or upright or honest man, but rather one who is shifty, sly, artful, shrewd, underhand, cunning, one grown old in fraud and subtlety. Is it not inexpedient to subject oneself to all these terms of reproach and many more besides? (Cicero 1913, pp. 325–327).

A few pages later, after describing a third case, Cicero asserts that "a man deserves no great praise nor gratitude", morally speaking, if "he openly avows that he will abstain from doing for his own profit only what the law expressly forbids" (p. 333). He adds as well that

> In the laws pertaining to the sale of real property it is stipulated in our civil code that when a transfer of any real estate is made, all its defects shall be declared as far they are known to the vendor…any defect in a piece of real estate, if known to the vendor but not expressly stated, must be made good by him (Cicero 1913, p. 335).

These cases are followed by others involving the sale of spoiled wine, passing counterfeit money and selling slaves known to be "untruthful, or disposed to gamble, or steal, or get drunk" (p. 367). Quite generally, then, Cicero believed that such cases involved "criminal fraud" and that people "who do one thing while they pretend another are faithless, dishonest, and unprincipled scoundrels" (p. 329).

Summarizing his fundamental moral principle, Cicero wrote:

> This, then, ought to be the chief end of all men, to make the interest of each individual and of the whole body politic identical. For, if the individual appropriates to selfish ends what should be devoted to the common good, all human fellowship will be destroyed (Cicero 1913, p. 293).

More Ethics Without Tears: The Invisible Hand

If one begins with the fairly familiar, though not uncontroversial, idea that morally right actions are those that tend to produce the greatest good for the greatest number, then one might find another path to believing in ethics without tears. The most famous passages in Adam Smith's 1776 classic treatise on *The Wealth of Nations* involved the idea that purely selfinterested actions might, after all, be morally right or righteous if, as if guided by an invisible hand, general welfare was uniformly produced by such actions. In the presence of such an invisible hand, greed would indeed be good, not necessarily in its intention but in its consequences, which (unfortunately for pure consequentialist theorists) is all that matters, morally speaking. While Smith's invisible hand passages immediately became and have remained famous, the essence of the idea in those passages made its first appearance about seventeen hundred years earlier in Epictetus of Hierapolis's (c. 50–130 CE) *Discourses*. In the latter book we find the claim that Zeus "…has made the nature of the rational animal such that it cannot obtain any one of its own proper interests, if it does not contribute something to the common interest. In this manner and sense it is not unsociable for a man to do every thing for the sake of himself" (Long 1912, p. 61). Lest the point be missed by some inattentive reader, in a footnote to this passage, the translator (George Long) quotes an earlier commentator's (J. Schweighaeuser) remarks as follows.

> Epictetus means by 'our proper interests,' the interests proper to man, as a man, as a rational being; and this interest or good consists in the proper use of our powers, and so far from being repugnant to common interest or utility, it contains within itself the notion of general utility and cannot be separated from it.

Complementing this line of argumentation, Cicero recorded that Hecation of Rhodes (late second century BCE) might have claimed that "we do not aim to be rich for ourselves alone but for our children, relatives, friends, and, above all, for our country. For the private fortunes of individuals are the wealth of the state" (Cicero 1913, p. 333). That is, besides the fact that the wealth of individual citizens necessarily adds to the wealth of their states, individuals' motives for pursuing personal wealth may include genuine concern for their dependents, friends and so on. So, there is nothing inherently wrong about the pursuit of personal wealth and there may be something contingently if not inherently right about it.

Conclusion

What, after all, can we learn from this brief review of a tiny sample of ancient advocates of business ethics? Well, quite a bit, I think.

For 20–28 hundred years distinguished scholars have characterized the good life generally and a good person in particular using some common themes. Peace/security, prosperity/wealth, health, friendship/community, pleasure, happiness, wisdom, justice, courage and temperance are usually regarded as good. Their opposites, war/insecurity, poverty, illness, isolation, pain, unhappiness, ignorance, injustice, cowardice and intemperance are usually regarded as bad. In broad but very important strokes these common themes reveal our common humanity across hundreds of years and thousands of kilometers. We share a common heritage and a common future, requiring global collaboration in the identification of common problems and optimum solutions.

Across that same period of time there has been and remains some troubling diversity of opinion. The broad strokes of agreement cover up significant disagreements over details. In his great theoretical treatise, *Nicomachean Ethics*, Aristotle did not have much to say about business ethics in particular, but his opening remarks on happiness as "the highest good" apply to all of the common themes mentioned above.

> What is the highest of all the goods achievable in action? As far as the name goes, most people virtually agree; for both the many and the cultivated call it happiness, and they suppose that living well and doing well are the same as being happy. But they disagree about what happiness is, and the many do not give the same answer as the wise (Aristotle 1999, p. 3).

Clearly, the same might be said about justice, poverty, health and so on. What is even more disturbing is the fact that the disagreements are not merely between the "many" and the "wise", but among the presumed "wise" themselves. All of the writers in our small sample belong in the latter class if anyone does. And what did we find? Some thought that straight dealing does and should lead to observable prosperity and well-being, while others thought that it does and should lead only to unobservable well-being, and still others thought it should and does lead to both, or perhaps that it should whether or not it does. Others thought that straight dealing is warranted simply and only for its own sake, not for any subsequent observable or unobservable payoff.

The very nature of straight dealing or what is ethically required has been and remains contested, with some people believing that mere compliance with established laws being all that is ethically required and others believing that moral virtue extends beyond the law to some sort of mutual respect, concern and caring for all people.

In her excellent book comparing ancient and modern views on ethics, Annas (1993) remarked that modern moral theorists share many of the uncertainties about fundamentals that troubled men like Cicero. He struggled mainly with discrepancies among a variety of views of Stoics and Aristotelians, while we struggle with an even wider array of alternatives. Following Oakeshott (1989), she suggested that "moral self-consciousness itself' might be as high a moral ideal as one can hope for. That is, granting that our subject admits of no certainties, the commitment to reflection on the best sort of life to live and the best sort of person to be, morally speaking, might be all that is ethically required. Personally, I would follow Aristotle, supplemented by Mill (1863) more closely. More precisely, following Aristotle, I would say that such a commitment must be supplemented with action appropriate to the reflection, i.e., action following deliberation, proceeding from a disposition and an intention to do what is right because it is right in particular circumstances, reasonably anticipating certain consequences and experiencing personal satisfaction from living and acting that way. Following Mill, I would use some sort of consequentialist construction of the notion of good consequences to provide necessary but not sufficient criteria for identifying what is right.

Acknowledgements Paper written for Keynote Address at the World Business Ethics Forum: Does East meet West? held at Hong Kong Baptist University and University of Macau, 1–3 November 2006. I would like to thank Deborah Poff for helping me improve the discussion in several ways.

References

Annas, J. (1993). *The morality of happiness*. Oxford: Oxford University Press.
Aristotle. (1999). Nicomachean ethics. In T. Irwin (Ed.), trans. *Indianapolis* (2nd ed.). Hackett Publishing Co.
Barney, R. (2004). Callicles and thrasymachus. In E. N. Zalta (Ed.), *The stanford encyclopedia of philosophy (Fall 2004 Edition)*. http://plato.stanford.edu/achives/fall2004/entries/callicles-thrasymachus/.
Cicero, M. T. (1913). De Officiis ['On Duties']. In W. Miller (Ed.), trans. *Loeb classical library*. Cambridge: Harvard University Press.
Cicero, M. T. (1931). De Finibus Bonorum et Malorum ['On Ends']. In H. Rackham (Ed.), trans. *Loeb classical library* (2nd ed.). Cambridge: Harvard University Press.
Long, G. (1912). In G. Long (Ed.), *The discourses of epictetus with the encheiridion and fragments*, trans. London: Bell and Sons Ltd.
McKirahan, R. D. (1994). *Philosophy before socrates: An introduction with texts and commentary*. Indianapolis: Hackett Publishing Co.
Michalos, A. C. (1990). The impact of trust on business, international security and the quality of life. *Journal of Business Ethics, 9,* 619–638.
Michalos, A. C. (1995). *A pragmatic approach to business ethics*. Thousand Oaks: SAGE Publications.
Mill, J. S. (1863). *Utilitarianism*. Green, London: Longmans.
Oakeshott, M. (1989). The tower of babel. In S. G. Clarke & E. Simpson (Eds.), *Anti-theory in ethics and moral conservatism* (pp. 185–204). Albany: New York University Press.
Putnam, R. (1993). *Making democracy work: Civic traditions in modern Italy*. Princeton: Princeton University Press.
Putnam, R. (1995). Bowling alone: America's declining social capital. *Journal of Democracy, 6,* 65–78.
Putnam, R. (1996). The strange disappearance of civic America. *American Prospect, 24,* 34–48.

Chapter 20
The Monster of Supercapitalism

Alex C. Michalos

Introduction

When Robert Reich published his book on *Supercapitalism* in 2007, he would not have imagined that one of his central theses would be directly relevant to the theme of the Second World Business Ethics Forum in Hong Kong a year later. But it is. The theme of our conference is 'Rethinking the Value of Business Ethics'. Among other things, Reich argued that proponents of corporate social responsibility (CSR), or what some would call simply 'corporate responsibility' (CR) and we would call 'business ethics' are 'in earnest', 'sincere' and sometimes have a 'positive impact', but 'almost all' of what we have done 'has occurred outside of the democratic process. Almost none has changed the rules of the game' (Reich 2007, p. 168. Hereafter, when any page numbers appear without an author's name, they refer to Reich's book). Whether or not this view represents Reich's rethinking of the value of business ethics, he has managed to produce a treatise that may provoke some proponents to rethink its value. Although Reich is no Hume and I am very, very far from being Immanuel Kant, it is possible that like the latter, I have been enjoying a 'dogmatic slumber' to which I am not entitled. Therefore, it seemed to me that the founding and still Editor-in-Chief of the *Journal of Business Ethics* should 'hear this fellow out' as the British say and see if his thesis is well-warranted. Lest you die of suspense, I can tell you now that I intend to show that his thesis is not well warranted. I would also like to express my appreciation and thanks to Moses Pava

Michalos, A.C.: 2010. The monster of supercapitalism. Journal of Business Ethics, 91, pp. 37–48. © Springer 2010.

A.C. Michalos (✉)
University of Northern British Columbia, Prince George, BC, Canada
e-mail: michalos@brandonu.ca

A.C. Michalos, *How Good Policies and Business Ethics Enhance Good Quality of Life*, DOI 10.1007/978-3-319-50724-8_20

for calling my attention to Reich's book in a fine critique that will be published in the Journal in the near future (Pava 2008).

The structure of the essay is as follows. In the next section, I construct an argument that seems to provide the rationale for CSR proponents according to Reich. This is followed by a section introducing Reich's first and quite fundamental objection to the CSR proponents' basic argument. Two sections then follow that describe what I call *the Monster of Supercapitalism* and its alleged overpowering strength compared to democracy. After these sections, there is a section showing that if Reich's arguments for the strength of the Monster are sound, then they are also self-destructive, i.e. the baby goes down the drain with the bath water. In the final two sections before the conclusion, I show that Reich's understanding of democracy and democratic process are flawed, as is his understanding of CSR and its relation to the law.

The Efficiency Argument for CSR

Reich's case against CSR is largely oriented around, though not entirely limited to, a kind of efficiency argument that he supposes supporters of CSR would use to warrant their activities. In his words,

> These days, reformers often say they can find it easier to lobby corporate executives than to lobby politicians; they contend they can be more effective pushing certain large corporations to change their ways than trying to alter public policy. 'Government is failing to provide leadership on environmental concerns, and industry has grown more willing to address them,' says Jonathan Lash, president of the World Resources Institute... A major reason why government is failing to provide leadership is because, as we have seen, big corporations have become so effective in recent years at preventing government from doing much about the environment or any other issue that may require corporations to change in ways they'd prefer not to (Reich 2007, p. 169).

I would recast the *Efficiency Argument for CSR* as follows.

> *Premise 1*: In order to get socially appropriate behaviour out of big corporations concerning the environment or anything else, one must either directly motivate corporations to act or indirectly motivate governments to compel corporations to act appropriately.
>
> *Premise 2*: Since governments fail to compel big corporations to act because they are themselves manipulated by the corporations, the indirect route to changing the behaviour of the latter is effectively closed.
>
> *Conclusion*: Therefore, the only remaining course of action, dealing directly with corporations, must also be the most efficient.

Practically all of the 40 pages of the fifth chapter ('Politics Diverted') of Reich's book, are devoted to the presentation of about two dozen roughly distinct arguments designed to cast doubt upon the Efficiency Argument for CSR or some aspect of it. There are several versions of some arguments, some unclear cases of duplication, some arguments made famous by Friedman's 1970 classic article and at least one that is reminiscent of Adam Smith (1776) and Epictetus of Hierapolis (c. 50–130

CE; see Michalos 2008a, b). Add to all these the great number and variety of more or less familiar contemporary cases introduced to illustrate and/or support the arguments presented, and it is fair to say that the chapter is a veritable smorgas-borg of delicacies for business ethicists to chew on.

Objections to the Efficiency Argument for CSR

Reich's first objection to the Efficiency Argument for CSR would appear to be that it is a false dilemma because the direct route to changing the behaviour of big corporations is also effectively closed. 'In supercapitalism, the corporation as a whole must, for competitive reasons, resist doing anything that hurts—and will place a very low priority on anything that doesn't help—the bottom line' (Reich 2007, p. 169). Versions of this quoted sentence appear more often than any other sentence in Chap. 5, e.g. see pp. 170, 173, 177, 184, 189, 192, 195, 199, 203, 204, 207. An additional 14 versions appear outside of Chap. 5, giving us a reminder on about every eighth page of the text. The theme is clearly central to his critique of CSR and apparently, from his point of view, it cannot be repeated too often. While he believes that Friedman's view was that 'companies *should not* seek to accomplish social ends' (p. 173) and he also provides arguments for that view, his central theme is that companies *cannot* successfully seek to accomplish such ends. Why does he think that theme is true?

His detailed defense of the theme is contained in the second chapter of his book (pp. 50–87), and it is offered not as philosophical speculation but as a historically descriptively accurate account, i.e. he takes this important theme to be true as a matter of fact. The history is conveniently summarized as follows.

> The road to supercapitalism began [in the 1970s] with technologies that emerged from the Cold War – containers, cargo ships and planes, fiber-optic cables, and satellite communications systems. They allowed the creation of global supply chains. They also spurred the commercial development of computers and software that could produce items at low cost without large scale, and eventually distribute services over the Internet. All this shattered the old system of large-scale production and dramatically increased competition. It allowed big-box retailers to aggregate consumer buying power and push companies even harder for bargains. It also created profitable opportunities for entrepreneurs to knock down regulatory barriers in telecommunications, airlines, trucking, shipping, and financial services – which also increased competition. Together, emerging technologies and financial deregulation opened the way for investors to put their savings into giant mutual funds and pension funds that pressured companies for higher returns. CEOs who delivered were generously rewarded. Those who didn't were sacked. Finally, intensifying competition for consumers and investors put pressure on companies to cut payrolls, hitting unionized workers especially hard (Reich 2007, pp. 86–87).

In short, technological changes and deregulation created greater competition among producers and traders, and greater opportunities for consumers and investors to get better deals on consumer goods and higher profits. Supercapitalism is something like capitalism on steroids, finally delivering on the textbook promises of consumer and investor sovereignty.

Enter the Monster of Supercapitalism

Unfortunately, the consumer and investor sovereignty that has been delivered is not only limited, but not entirely benign. We find ourselves in a situation similar to that of Dr. Frankenstein, when he realized that limited human intelligence, scientific information and technological expertise, combined with relatively unlimited human appetites could produce a *practically* uncontrollable monster. I emphasized the word 'practically' because Reich clearly believes that the monster of supercapitalism is *theoretically* controllable (e.g. see his final chapter). The main burden of Chap. 5 is to convince us that the moral suasion coupled with voluntary action recommended by proponents of CSR is at worst a wasteful, worthless and dangerous diversion of resources and at best a poor substitute for the tedious and painstaking political work that is necessary to decisively and permanently tame the monster with legally binding laws and regulations. As we will see below, the exact nature of this political work is characterized in different ways in different parts of Reich's book, usually involving some sort of a healthy democratic process. Exactly why anyone would believe that the imperfect beings who produced the monster of supercapitalism would be any more successful than Dr. Frankenstein was at taming the monster is unclear. In fact, both the name, 'Of Two Minds', and the content of the third chapter of Reich's book suggest that he is not completely convinced that those imperfect beings, including himself, are up to the task. Nevertheless, so far as his first objection to the Efficiency Argument for CSR is concerned, since proponents of that argument are convinced that the indirect route to controlling corporate action through government action is closed, his first objection to that argument appears to be stronger or weaker depending on the strength of one's conviction that the monster of supercapitalism is directly practically uncontrollable. In Chap. 5, Reich seems to find this view compelling, i.e. the monster is directly practically uncontrollable.

Supercapitalism Versus Democracy

In Chap. 4, Reich suggests an *Efficiency Argument for Supercapitalism over Democracy* (Reich 2007, pp. 166–167), an argument which is offered as an 'explanation rather than justification or condemnation'. If this argument is sound, it would establish the truth of the antecedent of the second premise of the Efficiency Argument for CSR, i.e. 'governments fail to compel big corporations to act because they are themselves manipulated by the corporations'. Given the truth of that antecedent, its consequent would appear to follow fairly easily. The argument runs as follows.

> *Premise 1*: If all other things are equal and the monster of supercapitalism performs its tasks with lower direct costs to consumers and investors than a healthy democratic process

performs its tasks to citizens, then in conflict situations the monster may be expected to triumph over a healthy democratic process.

Premise 2: The monster thrives on millions of relatively small, low cost personal expenditures of a variety of resources that collectively move it in fairly predictable ways while a healthy democracy thrives on the work of relatively fewer people making relatively larger personal expenditures that collectively move it in relatively unpredictable ways. In other words, almost all adults engage in the market economy as shoppers and/or investors while relatively few engage in politics as political activists, and the few activists typically have relatively higher average personal costs per unit of engagement and more diverse goals that are achieved with more or less success than the many shoppers and investors. (A good example of the unpredictable nature of political engagement may be found on pp. 156–157 concerning phone and cable companies).

Conclusion: Therefore, in conflict situations in which the demands of the monster of supercapitalism can only be met by sacrificing the demands of a healthy democracy, the former may be expected to win.

Thus, even if one rejects Reich's historical analysis of the road to supercapitalism, one might be persuaded by this argument that in any contest between intentionally and directly moving the monster of supercapitalism by CSR in ways contrary to its nature versus intentionally moving governments by political action to move the monster in precisely those ways, the cards are stacked against moving governments. The relatively low-cost activities of individual consumers and investors, wittingly and unwittingly, strengthen the monster more than the relatively high-cost activities of individual political activists strengthen democracy. Therefore, over time one should expect the monster of supercapitalism to continue to flourish while democracy withers away.

In case anyone has doubts about the strength of the Efficiency Argument for Supercapitalism over Democracy, Reich has several real-life examples to illustrate the corporate control of big corporations over government operations. In his view,

> The fights that actually preoccupy Congress day by day… are typically contests between competing companies or sectors of an industry or, occasionally, competing industries. Companies have entered politics to gain or keep a competitive advantage over their business rivals. The result has been a clamor of competing business interests – a cacophony so loud as to almost drown out any serious deliberation over the public good (pp. 142–143).

Among other things, Reich notes that the U.S. President 'Bill Clinton's health care plan' failed because Clinton's own 'corporate sponsors were against it' and that Clinton strongly supported the North American Free Trade Agreement and the World Trade Organization because they were 'two items of central importance to big business' (p. 137). An apparent victory for environmentalists concerning a ban on oil drilling off the California coast was really a victory of 'major hotel and restaurant chains' over 'major oil companies, the American Gas Association, and manufacturing groups hard hit by rising fuel costs' (p. 149). 'Legislation barring credit card payments for Internet betting' was an apparent victory of anti-gambling lobbies, but a real victory for 'gambling casinos… which saw the huge growth in online gambling as a potential threat to their profits' (p. 149). Defeat of a bill allowing foreigners 'to gain control of American airline carriers' appeared to be a victory for those who wanted to protect American business interests, but was really a bill protecting the interest of cash-secure Continental Airlines over cash-short United Airlines (p. 151). Even knowledge is corrupted by the influence of corporate money. 'Time and again', Reich writes of his experiences in the U.S. Department of Labor in the 1990s, 'I saw well-respected professors and "senior fellows" at Washington think tanks make arguments in congressional hearings, regulatory proceedings, and even in the media that they must have known were specious. Scruples, like other marketable commodities, can be purchased if the price is right' (pp. 158–159). Summarizing his view of the U.S. Congressional activity, Reich claims that

> Legislation is enacted with public rationales that bear little or no relation to the real motives of the corporations and their lobbyists who pushed for them and legislators who voted for them. Regulations, subsidies, taxes, and tax breaks are justified as being in the 'public interest' but are most often the products of fierce lobbying by businesses or industries seeking competitive advantage over one another. The broader public is not involved. Citizen voices are drowned out. The public rationales mask what's really going on – which companies and industries gain and which lose (p. 297).

Baby and Bathwater Down the Drain

This is pretty heavy criticism. If Reich's observations are at all accurate, then the old joke that Americans have the best legislators that money can buy is no joke. What is worse, if one combines this view of the U.S. Congress with his view of the need to pass more laws to arrest the appetite of the monster of supercapitalism, then one must deal with the following very disturbing and, I think, fatal argument against Reich's critique. If corporations can only be legally right or wrong and held responsible for their actions according to the laws they must obey, and corporations ultimately control the legislative process, then corporations are ultimately only responsible to themselves. Like God Almighty, the monster of supercapitalism answers to no one but itself. If this is the world Americans live in today and the rest of us live in tomorrow, then it is indeed time to buy a fishing rod and just "fish until gunnin' season". In this mad world of the monster of supercapitalism, CSR is truly a diversion. But it is not a diversion from the serious work of law-making, which is controlled by the monster, but from all the leisure activities that promise nothing more than immediate pleasure.

Surely, one might think, I have misunderstood Reich. Before you judge, consider this advice from his final chapter, called 'A Citizen's Guide to Supercapitalism'.

> A citizen's guide to supercapitalism would begin by instructing the public to beware of any politician or advocate who blames corporations and corporate executives for the negative social consequences of supercapitalism, whether it be low or declining wages and benefits, job losses, widening inequality, loss of community, global warming, indecent products, or any other of the commonly voiced complaints. Corporate executives are responsible for

> obeying the law, and should be held accountable for any illegality. But they cannot and should not be expected to do anything more… As long as the deals [that corporations make] are legal, and as long as they satisfy consumers and investors, corporations and their executives will pursue them. This doesn't make them right, but the only way to make them *wrong* – the only way to stop companies from giving consumers and investors good deals that depend on such moves – is to make them illegal. It is illogical to criticize companies for playing by the current rules of the game; if we want them to play differently, we have to change the rules (pp. 213–214).

This from the man who gave us all kinds of reasons for believing that the monster of supercapitalism controlled government! Was he not reading his own material or was I reading too much into it? Did I correctly draw out the implications from his text or just smuggle them in when noone was looking. Was there a wink and a nod I failed to notice. If so, where?

That he remains ever hopeful is clear from the last two paragraphs of his book. That he understands the full implications of what he has written is less clear.

> The triumph of supercapitalism has led, indirectly and unwittingly, to the decline of democracy. But that is not inevitable. We can have a vibrant democracy as well as a vibrant capitalism. To accomplish this, the two spheres must be kept distinct… We are all consumers and most of us are investors, and in those roles we try to get the best deals we possibly can. That is how we participate in a market economy and enjoy the benefits of supercapitalism. But those private benefits often come with social costs. We are also citizens who have a right and a responsibility to participate in a democracy. We thus have it in our power to reduce those social costs, thereby making the true price of the goods and services we purchase as low as possible. Yet we can accomplish this larger feat only if we take our responsibilities as citizens seriously, and protect our democracy. The first step, which is often the hardest, is to get our thinking straight (pp. 224–225).

Quite so, and he should try to take that step as soon as possible.

At this point, what we have is an Efficiency Argument for CSR that might appear attractive to CSR proponents and a critique from Reich that suggests that the argument is a false dilemma because neither of the stipulated alternatives of the dilemma are live options. In Reich's view, it is a mistake to imagine that one must alter the behaviour of big corporations by direct or indirect means because under supercapitalism it is practically impossible to alter that behaviour at all. It is a mistake to imagine that any realistic course of action follows from the truism that action must be direct or indirect. If there were any realistic course of action to take, it would be direct or indirect, but in fact no such course of action exists. So, the Efficiency Argument for CSR is unsound and its proponents are mistaken. Score one point for Reich.

Then, we have my argument leading to the conclusion that Reich's critique of the Efficiency Argument for CSR is self-destructive because the arguments and examples used to support his critique equally undermine any hope of using any alternative to taming the monster of supercapitalism. In effect, his critique is such that the proverbial baby was tossed down the drain with its bath water. Score one point for the other side.

Democracy and Democratic Process

Having reached the fairly devastating conclusion that Reich's critique of CSR is fatally flawed, it seemed to me that I ought to look more closely at his understanding of politics, democratic process and CSR to see if a deeper examination of his views would reveal some misunderstanding on my part that would strengthen his critique or some other mistakes on his part that would strengthen my objections to it. (Figuratively, I want to either pull some nails out or drive more nails into his coffin).

Let us begin by asking, What exactly is Reich's understanding of politics in general and democratic process in particular? In Reich's treatise, politics in general, democracy and democratic process in particular are not clearly distinguished. Early on he says that,

> Democracy means more than a process of free and fair elections. Democracy, in my view, is a system for accomplishing what can only be achieved by citizens joining together with other citizens – to determine the rules of the game whose outcomes express the common good... Democracy is supposed to enable us to make... tradeoffs, or help us achieve both growth and equity or any other goals we share in common (p. 4).

Two ideas that he most frequently attaches to democracy and democratic process appear in this quotation, 'rules of the game' and making 'tradeoffs'. He regards the boycott campaigns against the government of South Africa and Shell Oil as having political goals insofar as the 'campaigns were designed to change the rules of the game'. As well, the goals were 'specific and political in the sense of altering the balance of power between owners and employees' (p. 181). One of his objections to CSR in general is that 'almost all (of it) has occurred outside the democratic process. Almost none has changed the rules of the game' (p. 168). He regarded 'moral' objections to American firms helping 'Chinese authorities suppress human rights in China' as a useless exercise because the firms 'All obeyed the prevailing rules of the game' and 'Framing the issue in moral terms... diverted attention from the harder but more important question of whether the rules of the game should be altered'. In his view, what is needed in such cases is 'specific legislation to change the rules' (p. 203).

Although the rhetoric of social responsibility may be employed by representatives of corporations and governments to alter the behaviour of the other side, 'in such contests real politics—the stuff of democratic conflict and deliberation—is nowhere to be seen... little legislation emerges to force the companies to behave any differently in the future' (pp. 190–195). 'Real politics' would create 'rules that balance the interests of consumers and investors with the broader interests of the public' (p. 196). What he calls 'faux democracy' involves misplaced moralizing about companies that is 'disconnected from any laws and rules defining responsible behavior' (p. 207).

Because Reich believes, as the immediately preceding quotation suggests, that 'responsible behavior' for companies (and presumably individuals, though he never says so) can only be assessed in the presence of generally accepted 'laws and rules', and he seems to find some sort of democratic process as the only legitimate source for such things, he objects to CSR enthusiasts insisting that big corporations or their CEOs should be engaging in such behaviour beyond that which is precisely required by law. That is, as Friedman claimed nearly 40 years ago at the dawn of the age of supercapitalism, Reich believes that 'companies exist only to serve consumers and thereby make money for investors. This is how they serve the public' (p. 207).

Reading these passages, I was reminded of some remarks by the Swedish sociologist, Gunnar Myrdal, concerning Americans' views about legislated laws. He said that Americans have

> ... a desire to regulate human behavior tyrannically by means of formal laws. This last tendency is a heritage from early American Puritanism which was sometimes fanatical and dogmatic and always had a strong inclination to mind other people's business. So we find that this American, who is so proud to announce that he will not obey laws other than those which are 'good' and 'just', as soon as the discussion turns to something which in his opinion is bad and unjust, will emphatically pronounce that 'there ought to be a law against...'. To demand and legislate all sorts of laws against this and that is just as much a part of American freedom as to disobey the laws when they are enacted. America has become a country where exceedingly much is forbidden in law... Actually today [1944] it is a necessity in everyday living for the common good American citizen to decide for himself which laws should be observed and which not (quoted in Michalos 1980, p. 4).

The American sociologist, Robert Park, confirmed Myrdal's impression when he remarked that 'We are always passing laws in America. We might as well get up and dance. The laws are largely to relieve emotion, and the legislatures are quite aware of that fact' (quoted in Michalos 1980, p. 4). Such remarks cannot be regarded as evidence refuting Reich's insistence on the necessity of laws, but they remind us that legislative remedies for human pathologies may be over-emphasized as well as over-rated.

More importantly, however, one should notice that Reich's tendency to think of democracy and democratic process as focused on formal rule- or law-making and conflict resolution is a very narrow view. Societies that have formal features of democracy and democratic processes have informal infrastructures or democratic cultures that are at least as important. The formal and informal aspects of democracy and democratic process are mutually supporting. In a background study prepared for the *Canadian Index of Wellbeing,* Moore et al. (2008, pp. 39–40) wrote,

> In contrast to political participation as a predictor of healthy democracy, civic engagement as the act of psychological and behavioural engagement has gained credence (Zukin et al. 2006). In the late 1960s, theorists began to explore the dimensions of democracy in greater detail... Political and sociological theorists began to expose a now commonly accepted notion that a participatory polity requires broader democratic participation than provided through the electoral process. Putnam, drawing on the observations of Alexis de Tocqueville's *On American Democracy* (1835), argues that American democracy is rooted in civil society; citizens' involvement in family, school, work, voluntary associations, and religion. Theorizing that 'civic virtue' is the basis of a healthy democracy, Putnam proposes that a civic community is made up of four elements: civic engagement; political equality; solidarity, trust and tolerance; and social structures of cooperation (Putnam 2000).

For present purposes, one should notice especially the moral implications arising in this quotation. 'The basis of a healthy democracy' is identified as citizen engagement in the institutions of 'family, school, work, voluntary associations, and religion' and such engagement is collectively labelled as 'civic virtue'. Such 'virtue' includes the assumptions that citizens have 'political equality', share some feelings of 'solidarity, trust and tolerance' and some 'social (i.e. not legal) structures of cooperation'. In short, the formal institutions of democracy are rooted in and depend upon the informal features of community. Add to this the fact that communities cannot exist without the institution of morality and one may immediately observe the error in Reich's efforts to show that the moralizing of CSR proponents is a misplaced diversion of resources. In the absence of a moral point of view adhered to by a community of individuals and articulated in the institution of morality, the democracy and democratic processes that Reich believes are essential to produce progressive and permanent change in the behaviour of the monster of supercapitalism are groundless.

In an essay called 'The Best and Worst Arguments for Business Ethics' that I wrote for Michalos (1995), I defended the claim that the institution of morality is necessary for community as follows.

> … what is being asserted is that communities or societies cannot exist without a minimum sort of morality based on at least two moral principles, one proscribing killing people at will and the other proscribing lying to people. In other words, in order for a community to exist, people must, at a minimum, adhere to the principles of not indiscriminately killing people and lying to them. To see that such a minimum morality is necessary for community, imagine the opposite. Imagine a community in which people are told that they ought to kill people at will and to lie to everyone and anyone. Such a community would be short-lived, if it could even get started. If members of the community did what they ought to do, they would literally destroy each other in the worst case and find it impossible to communicate with each other in the second worst case. If they literally destroy each other, there would obviously be no community. On the other hand, if they systematically lie to each other then there will be no useful communication and, what is worse, there may be danger in trying to communicate because everyone would be misleading everyone. So, in this case too there would be no community. Clearly, then, a minimum amount of morality is necessary for community (Michalos 1995, p. 55).

It is counter-productive for Reich or anyone else to abandon demands for CR because the latter is necessary for human communities to exist and when the latter disappear, the monster of supercapitalism will have nothing left to feed on and not only the monster, but its more benign brother, capitalism itself will also disappear. In brief, this is the argument developed in Michalos (1995, pp. 54–57). It is less complicated (sophisticated) than the argument found in Marx and Engels (1849) about the bourgeoisie producing 'it own grave-diggers', but it shares some natural affinities.

If my understanding of the relationship between the institution of morality on the one hand and democracy and democratic process on the other is accurate, then Reich's belief that proponents of CSR should commit more resources to the latter and less to the former is false. Since the institution of morality is a necessary foundation for democracy and democratic process, any investments made in the former are bound to strengthen the latter, just as any investments withheld from the former are bound to weaken the latter. Precisely because investments in CSR are investments in the institution of morality, they cannot be diversions from the important work of taming the monster of supercapitalism by strengthening democracy and democratic process. Score one more point for my side, add one more nail to Reich's coffin.

The Nature of CSR and Its Relation to the Law

What exactly is Reich's understanding of CSR? Since the main burden of Chap. 5 is to convince readers that CSR is a diversion from the more important, productive and permanent work of making rules and laws through democratic processes, one would expect a clear articulation of the concept of CSR. Unfortunately, it never quite appears. Generally speaking, he seems to regard CSR as a direct descendent of some ideas of what he calls 'democratic capitalism' that flourished in the early years of the twentieth century in America.

> While Europeans set up cartels and fussed with democratic socialism, Americans went right to the heart of the matter – creating democratic capitalism as a planned economy, run by business... As early as 1914, the popular columnist and public philosopher Walter Lippmann called on America's corporate executives to be stewards of the entire nation. "The men connected with [the large corporation] cannot escape the fact that they are expected to act increasingly like public officials... Big businessmen who are at all intelligent recognize this. They are talking more and more about their 'responsibilities,' and their 'stewardship'." (p. 26).

Although 'a planned economy, run by business' sounds more like an oligarchy than a democracy, in time it was transformed along the lines of stakeholder theory.

> 'The job of management,' proclaimed Frank Abrams, chairman of Standard Oil of New Jersey, in a 1951 address that typified what other chief executives were saying, 'is to maintain an equitable and working balance among the claims of the various directly affected interest groups... stockholders, employees, customers, and the public at large. Business managers are gaining professional status partly because they see in their work the basic responsibilities [to the public] that other professional men have long recognized in theirs' (p. 45).

For Reich, democratic capitalism, regarded as a kind of 'equitable and working balance' of diverse interests arrived at voluntarily through negotiations among rational stakeholders as sketched by Abrams seems to be close to what he supposes CSR proponents would like to see. While this is probably an accurate assessment of what many if not most CSR proponents would like to see, it would appear to characterize democratic socialists as well as democratic capitalists. As the former United Auto Workers president said, 'If fighting for equal and equitable distribution of the wealth of this country is socialistic, I stand guilty of being a Socialist' (p. 33). Without trying to split hairs between the capitalists and socialists who all regard themselves as good democrats, as a CSR proponent, I do believe that the law is a very blunt instrument for crafting social change and that it should be our last resort, while reasoned debate coupled with moral suasion should be our first resort. Unfortunately, in Reich's view the creation of the monster of supercapitalism led to the destruction of our first resort. In his view, the very possibility of that sort of democratic capitalism or socialism is gone and those who can see the world as it really is must recognize that our last resort, the law, is all that is left. As just shown, this is a mistake. Since there can be no law produced from a healthy democratic process without a minimum institution of morality, if there is law, it cannot be all that is left.

Granting that Reich is right in supposing that the *aim* of CSR proponents is some sort of democratic capitalism or socialism, we still do not have a clear view of his understanding of the *nature* or *practice* of CSR. We are heading downtown, but in what sort of vehicle? Interestingly enough, for me anyhow, the main clues to his view of the nature or practice of CSR are revealed in his critique of what I called in Michalos (1995, p. 57) the worst argument for business ethics, i.e. 'In brief, a businessperson ought to be morally good because there is money in it or, at least, there is more money in moral goodness than in moral evil'. A critique of this argument may be found in an essay by Cicero written in the first century BCE (Michalos 2008a). Here is Reich.

> One popular argument is that 'socially responsible' companies are more profitable. Dow Chemical reduces its carbon emissions so it can lower its energy costs. McDonald's employs more humane slaughtering techniques, which prevent costly worker injuries and yield more meat… All these steps may be worthwhile but they are not undertaken because they are socially responsible. They're done to reduce costs. To credit these corporations with being 'socially responsible' is to stretch the term to mean anything a company might do to increase profits if, in doing so, it also happens to have some beneficent impact on the rest of society. Taken to the logical extreme is the textbook economics argument that whenever a company increases its profits it has a positive effect on society because it thereby utilizes assets more efficiently, releasing those that are no longer needed to be used more efficiently elsewhere. In this sense, all profitable companies are socially responsible… For many years I have preached that social responsibility and profitability converge over the long term… But I've never been able to prove this proposition nor find a study that confirms it. More important from the standpoint of the modern firm, the long term may be irrelevant. Under supercapitalism, the 'long term' is the present value of future earnings (p. 171).

Reflecting on these passages, it seems to me that he is clearly asserting that if a company engages in some behaviour *because* it produces profits then it cannot be regarded as and praised for engaging in that behaviour *because* it is socially responsible. This seems uncontroversial. The action is not motivated by a desire to do the morally right thing because it is morally right (however that is specified), but to do the most profitable thing because it is the most profitable thing to do. However, consider the following.

> In general, corporate initiatives that… generate higher profits and higher returns for investors, are not socially virtuous. They're just good management practices that should – and, given the competitive pressures of supercapitalism, will – be undertaken regardless of how much or how little they benefit society (p. 173).

In these passages, not only motives but human agency itself has practically disappeared, replaced by the hidden hand of the monster of supercapitalism, delivering the goods as theoretically promised. However, supposing that motives are essential components of any plausible analysis of human action, one must ask, Why can't the agent for a company be motivated by profits and moral virtue at the same time? Is the world so perversely structured that one can never 'do well and do good at the same time' (p. 171)? Of all the diverse mixed motives out of which people can act, are the motives of corporate profits (or even personal gain) and moral goodness necessarily mutually exclusive? Presumably, that is Reich's position. Should it be ours?

At a minimum, from the point of view of motives alone, we seem to have four options to consider. One might be:

1. Motivated to do the right thing (morally speaking) and motivated to make a profit, e.g. craftspeople like William Morris and CSR proponents.
2. Motivated to do the right thing and not motivated to make a profit, e.g. at least some not-for-profit organizations like Oxfam.
3. Not motivated to do the right thing but motivated to make a profit, e.g. agents for big corporations under supercapitalism.
4. Not motivated to do the right thing and not motivated to make a profit, e.g. possibly some artists and scholars who pursue beauty or truth for their own sakes.

This is not an argument, but it seems to me that all four options are logically possible and that there are real-life examples of all four as suggested above. I can't think of any arguments that would be more persuasive than those examples. However, I suspect that the logical possibility of *mixed motives* was not high on Reich's agenda. Regarding the latter, his primary concern would be about *motives and payoffs* in the real world. From the point of view of motives and payoffs, the four options of primary concern to Reich would be as follows. Agents for a company might be:

1. Motivated to do the right thing (morally speaking) and actually make a profit, e.g. 'Great Britain's economy is not markedly less successful than America's, although its citizens tend to live in smaller houses and drive less. But people there still remain in their jobs longer, and if they lose them they have more generous unemployment insurance than in the United States' (p. 105).
2. Motivated to do the right thing and actually not make a profit, e.g. Cummins Engine, Dayton Hudson, Levi Strauss, Polaroid, Marks and Spencer, Body Shop, Ben and Jerry's and Merck (pp. 173–174).
3. Not motivated to do the right thing and actually make a profit, e.g. ExxonMobil, tobacco companies, 'Firms producing alcohol and firearms, companies relying on revenues from gambling, and firms producing lurid magazines and videos have all done reasonably well on Wall Street—most even outperforming the S and P 500 Index' (p. 175).

4. Not motivated to do the right thing and actually not make a profit, e.g. Enron; '... it seems doubtful Enron's commitment to social responsibility was any more sincere than its dedication to its investors' (p. 174).

In Michalos (1992), I explained some complications of following an Aristotelian analysis of human actions into intent (motives), content and consequences (payoffs). Because the three components are essential, the discussion here is oversimplified. Hopefully, further reflection and discussion will help clarify the role of a reasonable consequentialism in the kinds of issues that we are considering.

The point that Reich makes concerning all of the companies that were motivated to do the right thing and actually did not make a profit (Case 2) is that 'Under supercapitalism, a commitment to social virtue is no substitute for obsessive dedication to shareholder value' (p. 174). Regarding those that were not motivated to do the right thing but actually made a profit (Case 3), he observed, 'investors don't punish profitable companies or industries notably lacking in social virtue' (p. 174). As well, I suppose Enron is a paradigm case of a firm not motivated to do the right thing and failing to make a profit (Case 4).

I could not find any examples in Reich's book of companies that were motivated to do the right thing and actually made a profit (Case 1). However, there certainly are countries in which the wealth is shared more equally among workers, consumers and investors than in the USA, e.g. Great Britain, as Reich suggested. Presumably, in our globalized market, there would be no wealth to share in such countries unless they had some internationally competitive companies. According to Jackson (2008, p. 9),

> Economic studies have shown again and again that countries with high rates of unionization have much more equal wages and thus more equal societies, with no negative impacts on economic performance. Some of the most successful economies in today's world, notably the Scandinavian countries, have unionization rates of 80% and more. They do well because workers are well trained and highly productive, and, as importantly, the gains from a strong economy are fairly shared.

According to Pava (2008, p. 808).

> The best run businesses search actively and imaginatively to find and invent solutions that produce more profits *and* better social outcomes simultaneously (see Savitz and Weber 2006, and Porter and Kramer 2006, for especially good, contemporary descriptions of the link between competitive advantage and corporate social responsibilities).

Pava (2008, p. 807) also lists several examples from Vogel (2006) of '*positive* and quite *significant* changes in corporate behavior' that at least he and Vogel believe were 'produced' by proponents of CSR. A good meta-analysis of 52 studies on the association between 'corporate social/environmental performance (CSP) and corporate financial performance (CFP)' may be found in Orlitzky et al. (2003). These authors concluded that

> Theoretically, portraying managers' choices with respect to CSP and CFP as an either/or trade-off is not justified in light of 30 years of empirical data. This meta-analysis has shown that (1) across studies, CSP is positively correlated with CFP, (2) the relationship tends to

> be bidirectional and simultaneous, (3) reputation appears to be an important mediator of the relationship, and (4) stakeholder mismatching, sampling error, and measurement error can explain between 15 percent and 100 percent of the cross-study variation in various subsets of CSP-CFP correlations. Corporate virtue in the form of social and, to a lesser extent, environmental responsibility is rewarding in more ways than one (p. 427).

My guess, and it is only a guess, is that in Reich's view the nature or practice of CSR would be specified by the first and/or second cases in the two sets of four options. I am confident about the first conjunct of these four options, i.e. the nature or practice of CSR requires at a minimum that agents are motivated to do the right thing, morally speaking. I suspect that Reich accepts the fact that agents can have mixed motives because that is often what being 'of two minds' is about. Since he is not interested in not-for-profit organizations, I suppose we can ignore the second case involving agents who are motivated to do the right thing and not motivated to make a profit. So, what we are left with to characterize the nature or practice of CSR is Case 1 considering motives alone, and Cases 1 and 2 considering motives and payoffs.

Notwithstanding all his examples and arguments in support of the view that under supercapitalism companies motivated to do the right thing morally speaking cannot make a sustainable profit (i.e. Case 2 involving motives and payoffs), it appears that some companies can, i.e. it appears that Case 1 is possible. Sometimes Reich seems to want to dispose of such possibilities by definition as, for example, when he says that in spite of Wal-Mart's apparent generosity following Hurricane Katrina, 'You don't have to be a cynic to suppose Wal-Mart is doing the least it must do… to counter the anti-Wal-Mart camp's negative effects' (p. 189). That is, he immediately transforms an apparent Case 1 into a real Case 3. Presumably, Reich would insist that companies that actually share the wealth more equally sacrifice efficiencies, perhaps lose some of 'the potent incentive of great wealth' as well as some innovation, just as the companies did in the 'not quite golden age' covering a period from 1945 to 1975 (p. 48), but they survive. (On the slippery and much abused notion of 'efficiency', see Michalos 2008b). Even under supercapitalism, they satisfy enough consumers and investors to make sustainable profits. After all, then, the monster of supercapitalism is not invincible, contrary to all the evidence Reich assembled to convince us otherwise. Therefore, the first premise of the Efficiency Argument for CSR does contain at least one live option, namely, direct dealing with corporations. Therefore, that argument cannot be rejected on the grounds that it offers no live option. Accordingly, it may well be a sound argument. Score another and final point for my side.

Conclusion

The analyses contained in this article certainly do not exhaust the great variety of interesting arguments and examples presented in Reich's book. There are several more for others to consider. Reich is clearly a man of the world, an insider who has seen the unseemly side of politics and big business, and has taken the time to give us the benefit of his observations, conclusions and recommendations. We have to take such things seriously and after proper reflection, act according to our convictions. Like Reich, I am ever hopeful that the monster of supercapitalism can be tamed. Unlike Reich, I believe that CSR is at least as necessary and useful for that task as anything else. I also believe that Zukin et al. (2006, pp. 206–208) should have the last word.

> Because government matters, participation in civil society – through contributing to charitable causes, volunteering in one's local community, joining civic organizations, and the like – cannot substitute for voting, working for a party or candidate, or contacting one's elected official about a policy concern. At the same time, because civil institutions matter, participation in the electoral and policy process can not substitute for engaging in this aspect of our society. There may be times and circumstances in which one type of engagement is preferable to another, but over time and across groups, both are crucial. In short, each is a necessary but not a sufficient requisite if citizens are to have an authoritative and equal voice in the democratic process.

References

Jackson, A. (2008). Canada needs stronger unions to close the growing gap. *The CCPA Monitor 15*(2), 9. Marx, K., & Engels, F. (1849). *The Communist Manifesto* (London).

Michalos, A. C. (1980). Crime, justice and politics. In *North american social report*, Vol. 2. Dordrecht: D. Reidel Publishing Co.

Michalos, A. C. (1992). Ethical considerations in evaluation. *Canadian Journal of Program Evaluation, 7*, 61–75.

Michalos, A. C. (1995). *A pragmatic approach to business ethics*. Thousand Oaks: SAGE Publications.

Michalos, A. C. (2008a). Ancient observations on business ethics: Middle east meets west. *Journal of Business Ethics, 79*(1–2), 9–19.

Michalos, A. C. (2008b). *Trade barriers to the public good: Free trade and environmental protection*. Montreal: McGill-Queen's University Press.

Moore, K., Swystun, L., Holden, B., & Bernardin, H. (2008). *Final report for the democratic engagement domain*. Saskatoon: Prairie Wild Consulting and Holden and Associates.

Orlitzky, M., Schmidt, F. L., & Rynes, S. L. (2003). Corporate social and financial performance: A metaanalysis. *Organization Studies, 24*(3), 403–441.

Pava, M. (2008). Why corporations should not abandon social responsibility. *Journal of Business Ethics, 83*(4), 805–812.

Porter, M. E., & Kramer, M. R. (2006). Strategy and society. *Harvard Business Review* 78–92.

Putnam, R. D. (2000). *Bowling alone: The collapse and revival of american community*. New York: Simon and Schuster.

Reich, R. B. (2007). *Supercapitalism: The transformation of business, democracy, and everyday life*. New York: Alfred A Knopf.

Savitz, A. W., & Weber, K. (2006). *The triple bottom line*. San Francisco: Jossey-Bass.

Smith, A. (1776). An Inquiry into the Nature and Causes of the Wealth of Nations. Chicago: University of Chicago Press.

Vogel, D. (2006). *The market for virtue: The potential and limits of corporate social responsibility*. Washington: Brookings Institution Press.

Zukin, C., Keeter, S., Andolina, M., Jenkins, K., & Carpini, M. (2006). *A new engagement? Political participation, civic life, and the changing American citizen*. New York: Oxford University Press.

Chapter 21
The Business Case for Asserting the Business Case for Business Ethics

Alex C. Michalos

Introduction

The BC and ABC Theses

The business case for business ethics is the thesis that being morally good is materially good for business. I will call this the BC thesis. The thesis of my essay is that *asserting* the business case for business ethics is materially good for business. I will call this the ABC thesis.

Some people may recall that in Michalos (1995, p. 57), I argued that the worst argument for business ethics was the argument that "a businessperson ought to be morally good because there is money in it or, at least, there is more money in moral goodness than in moral evil." As articulated in that article, the worst argument was just another formulation of the business case for business ethics, i.e., for the BC thesis.

Some people might also recall that in Michalos (2008a) I showed that this bad argument was first identified and demolished by the philosopher-statesman Marcus Tullio Cicero in the first century BCE. In case your reading list has not included either the particular piece by Cicero or me, his demolition of the BC thesis took the form of pointing out that if your primary reason or motive for action is self-interest or profits, then, when there is more to be gained by morally evil than morally good action, you will prefer the former, which would be morally wrong in itself and undermine the institution of morality. In short, the BC thesis is plainly a morally deficient argument for business ethics. Incidentally, it is probably worthwhile to emphasize that given the unsoundness of what I call the Loyal Agent's Argument (Michalos 1999; Poff 1999), whether the bottom line is one's own or a corporation's profits, the BC thesis is morally deficient.

A.C. Michalos (✉)
University of Northern British Columbia, Prince George, BC, Canada
e-mail: michalos@brandonu.ca

A.C. Michalos, *How Good Policies and Business Ethics Enhance Good Quality of Life*, DOI 10.1007/978-3-319-50724-8_21

The ABC thesis that I want to defend in this essay, namely that *asserting* the business case for business ethics is materially good for business is a variant of a thesis that will be familiar to anyone who has read Niccolo Machiavelli's *The Prince* (1980). Here are the crucial passages.

> A prince… ought to take great care that nothing goes out of his mouth which is not full of the five qualities… all pity, all faith, all integrity, all humanity, and all religion. Nothing is more necessary than to have this last quality. For men, universally, judge more by the eyes than by the hands… Everyone sees what you seem to be, but few touch what you are… And with respect to human actions, and especially those of princes where there is no judge to whom to appeal, one looks to the end. Let a prince then win and maintain the state—the means will always be judged honorable and will be praised by everyone; for the vulgar are always taken in by the appearance and the outcome of a thing, and in this world there is no one but the vulgar" (Machiavelli 1980, p. 109).

Recasting Machiavelli's target-student from an aspiring prince in the early sixteenth century to an aspiring corporate leader in the early twenty-first century, one might say that in his view there were two necessary conditions for success. First, it is necessary to appear morally virtuous and second, to make a sustainable profit. For Machiavelli, the way to appear to be morally virtuous was to talk a good game, i.e., to preach pity, integrity and so on, whatever one practiced. As someone once said, "Sincerity is everything. If you can fake that, everything else is easy." If you can also make a profit over some reasonable length of time while talking a good game then no one would ever question the reality of your virtue. "Where there is no judge to whom to appeal, one looks to the end." For a prince, the end was "to maintain the state." For our contemporary corporate leader, the end is to maintain a sustainable profit.

Machiavelli assumed that his two necessary conditions were matters of fact, based on historical evidence. In *The Prince* and his longer *The Discourses on the First Ten Books of Titus Livius* (Machiavelli 1970), this was his primary mode of defending claims. He would state his thesis and then present one or more historical examples that were consistent with it. I don't know if anyone has ever done any rigorous empirical testing of his thesis concerning two necessary conditions for success. It is, of course, easy to think of additional examples that are consistent and others that are inconsistent with the thesis. It would be difficult to find persuasive real-life cases of leaders who are uniformly "making it by faking it," i.e., cases of leaders who always or usually deliberately merely pretend to be morally good agents and who always or usually generate a sustainable profit however that is defined. People like Bernie Madoff often end as he did. Since we cannot open up people's heads or hearts to observe their deepest intentions, we can only judge their intentions by their behavior (verbal and otherwise) and its consequences, which is unfortunate to say the least.

Validation and Vindication

In the middle of the twentieth century, the positivist philosopher of science, Herbert Feigl, expanded Machiavelli's observation that in the absence of a judge, "one looks to the end" in a somewhat famous article (Feigl 1950). In that article, among other things, Feigl was grappling with the so-called problem of induction. Briefly stated, the problem was how to justify inductive inferences, i.e., inferences from the observed to the unobserved. The justification for accepting the conclusions of deductively valid arguments on the basis of their premises was plain for all to see. If the premises of such arguments are all true and there are no methodological flaws, then anyone accepting the premises and rejecting the conclusion would be guilty of self-contradiction. In such cases, the conjunction of the premises and denial of the argument's conclusion would be a self-contradictory or logically false proposition. For inductively valid arguments no such transparently acceptable justification was or is available because by definition (as suggested above) the conclusions of inductive arguments always go beyond the information contained in their premises. For example, even if every observed duck has died sooner or later, the generalization that *all ducks die* is not logically guaranteed by the premise because that generalization applies to all observed and unobserved ducks and nobody knows or can know how or even if the all unobserved ducks end their lives. In short, the conjunction of the premise that all observed ducks have died and the denial of the generalization that all ducks die (i.e., there is some duck that does not die) is not self-contradictory.

Feigl argued that in the absence of a rule (i.e., a criterion by which to judge one's inferences as well as one's rules for warranting inferences), one ought to proceed pragmatically and justify one's inferences and rules on the basis of their consequences. He called our standard rule-following procedure for justifying inferences by showing that they were patterned after deductively valid argument forms with all true premises and no methodological flaws *validation*. Justifying the rules themselves by the pragmatic procedure of showing that, in my terms, their acceptance produces at least as many benefits as costs, all things considered, he called *vindication*.

I think that Machiavelli's observation was accurate and that Feigl's distinction between validation and vindication is a useful elaboration of it which has direct application to ethics in general (a point emphasized by Feigl) and to the ABC thesis in particular. As you might have expected, there is a bright and a dark side to the story. The good news is that very often the justification for moral decisions or judgments proceeds by validation. For example, there is wide-spread, general acceptance of the moral maxims condemning harm to innocent people by things like murder, assault, theft or blatant lies. As well, there are often fairly clear cases in which such moral rules are deliberately violated or not, and there are generally accepted procedures to follow to make appropriately justified decisions regarding guilt or innocence leading to moral blame or praise.

The bad news is that often enough particular cases are not easily subsumed under generally accepted rules or different rules might be applied and/or applied in different ways leading to different decisions. As Aristotle famously observed over 2,300 years ago, different subject matters, and he referred to political science generally or what we would call ethics in particular, do not lend themselves to the same sort of rigor as other matters. Hence, the "educated person," he wrote, "seeks exactness in each area to the extent that the nature of the subject allows" (Aristotle 1999, p. 2). If he had read Feigl, then he might have said that, where ethical issues are concerned, one should often expect justification to take the form of vindication.

Well, you might ask, what's so bad about that? In a word, plenty. I am, as many people know, a pragmatist. I confess I was a teenage logical positivist and I suppose some of the boy remains in the man. In fact, many positivists were and probably still are pragmatists. Pragmatists by definition believe in judging propositions, human actions, events, theories and institutions by their consequences. The one great problem that pragmatists have is that there is no generally accepted rule book that tells us which consequences to count and how to count them. That is why you can find thoughtful, apparently well-intentioned pragmatists in bed with practically anyone from Adolf Hitler to Jesus Christ. You can also find ill-intentioned pragmatists committing the Fallacy of Special Pleading (Michalos 1970), making their consequentialist cases by advertising and counting only features favorable to their cases and neglecting features that are unfavorable. Over many years I have spent a lot of time and energy thinking and writing about this great problem, e.g., Michalos (1978, 1985, 1997, 2003). All of my work on measuring the quality of life has been and is motivated by my desire to find a generally acceptable, rigorous, quantitative solution of the pragmatists' problem of precisely specifying a good way, if not the very best way, of counting consequences to press into the service of pragmatic justifications or, in Feigl's terms, vindications. I suppose that like Moses, I will not see the promised land, but I hope others will.

Motives and Profits

In my presentation (Michalos 2010) at the Second World Business Ethics Forum at Hong Kong Baptist University in 2008, I spent some time examining Reich's (2007) book and how he seemed to address first, the four logical possibilities involving the *mixed motives* of doing something because it is morally right versus doing something because it will make a profit, and second, the following four possibilities involving *motives and actual payoffs*.

1. Motivated to do the right thing (morally speaking) and actually make a profit.
2. Motivated to do the right thing and actually not make a profit.
3. Not motivated to do the right thing and actually make a profit.
4. Not motivated to do the right thing and actually not make a profit.

I did not consider the more complicated cases involving *both* mixed motives and actual payoffs, i.e., an agent (person or company) might be

1. Motivated to do the right thing (morally speaking) and motivated to make a profit and actually make a profit (Successful CSR agent).
2. Motivated to do the right thing and motivated to make a profit and actually not make a profit (Unsuccessful CSR agent).
3. Motivated to do the right thing and not motivated to make a profit and actually make a profit (Reich's supposed unlikely or non-existent CSR agent).
4. Motivated to do the right thing and not motivated to make a profit and actually not make a profit (Reich's real CSR agent).
5. Not motivated to do the right thing and motivated to make a profit and actually make a profit (Successful pure capitalist agent).
6. Not motivated to do the right thing and motivated to make a profit and actually not make a profit (Unsuccessful pure capitalist agent).
7. Not motivated to do the right thing and not motivated to make a profit and actually make a profit [An agent (e.g., artist, scholar, athlete) pursuing beauty, truth or excellent performance for its own sake and receiving excellent material rewards].
8. Not motivated to do the right thing and not motivated to make a profit and actually not make a profit (A pure hedonist agent?).

It may be noticed that the above eight alternatives just sketched do not include Machiavelli's insistence on appearance versus reality. If you recall your truth-table exercises from elementary logic, then introducing the motive of *appearing to be motivated* in one way or another to our matrix would increase its length from 8 to 32 options (2^5). To keep matters as simple as possible, I am not introducing this motive here.

Faced with the set of eight possibilities, it seems to me that Reich would insist that a corporate agent is only doing the right thing morally speaking if he or she is motivated to do the right thing and not motivated to make a profit and actually does not make a profit, i.e., Case 4. For Reich, virtue must be its own *and only* reward. If a virtuous agent actually profits materially from his or her morally good acts, he would not regard the agent as morally praiseworthy. Whenever such an agent actually makes a profit, as in Case 1 or Case 3, Reich would assume that he or she is only doing what a good capitalist ought to do (i.e., make a profit regardless of other considerations), is *not* motivated by a desire to do the right thing morally speaking and therefore is not entitled to moral praise. That is, by definition, Reich rules out the kinds of mixed motives (Cases 1 and 3) that might make sense of the very idea of being ethical in business or operating a business in a socially responsible way. In place of Cases 1 and 3 Reich insists on Case 5. Such a priori destruction of the very possibility of business ethics or CSR seems to me unwarranted and inconsistent with the widely held view that people routinely have mixed motives.

I cannot pursue all the interesting historical antecedents of the view that virtue must be its own and only reward.

I suspect the view would have been attractive to some of the ancient Stoics (Annas 1993) and probably to Immanuel Kant (Michalos 2001). In *The Prince,* Machiavelli argued that given the choice between the virtue of being generous and the vice of being miserly, a prince ought to prefer the latter because the former would be unsustainable without excessive taxation which would finally lead to his being hated and overthrown. On the other hand, one might argue for anonymous generosity on the grounds that it removes the possibility of the actor being intentionally rewarded for his or her acts of generosity. Psychological hedonists claim that people naturally pursue pleasure and ethical hedonists claim that people, morally speaking, ought to pursue pleasure (Brandt 1967). In both cases, the ultimate payoff of human action, including virtuous action, is pleasure. While pleasure is not a material reward, it is a reward beyond the act of doing the right thing because it is the right thing to do. Plato and Aristotle both took pleasure very seriously as an important by-product of virtuous action. Summarizing their views, I wrote,

> Although Plato clearly rejected the idea that the good life was identical to a life of pleasure, he believed that pleasure had a useful role to play in a good life, and he recognized at least five theories of pleasure's origin,… a desire satisfaction theory, a needs satisfaction theory, a harmony theory, a true pleasures theory, and a class theory of pleasure… Plato's greatest student, Aristotle, believed that EUDAI-MONIA, happiness, "living well and doing well" is achieved insofar as one deliberately engages in the unimpeded excellent exercise of one's capacities for the sake of doing what is fine, excellent, or noble, provided that the deliberation and activities are undertaken from a virtuous character and accompanied by an appropriate amount of external goods and pleasure (Michalos 2012).

In the *Republic* and other treatises, Plato referred to goods like "good reputation" and pleasure as "handmaids to [moral] virtue," never as proper and sufficient reasons for virtuous action (Michalos 2012). In any event, as this cursory review suggests, the idea that virtue must be its own and only reward is questionable and has been rejected outright by some excellent philosophers.

Corporate Social Responsibility Report 2010

I have taken a lot of time to warn you that in my defense of the ABC thesis, you should not expect more and you will not get more than a rough vindication. I stumbled over the ABC thesis while reading some articles in Canada's most widely circulated, popular, weekly magazine called *Maclean's Magazine.* There were four articles in the June 21, 2010 issue with provocative titles, "Corporate Social Responsibility Report 2010: Good For Business" (*Maclean's* 2010), "Ethics: A Conscience Choice" (Gohier 2010), "Crisis Management: When Things Get Messy" (Kirby 2010), and "The Top 50: Raising The Bar" (Jantzi-Sustainalytic analysts 2010).

The short lead article introduced the whole set of articles with the assertion that "for the second year in a row, *Maclean's* has partnered with Jantzi-Sustainalytics, a global leader in sustainability analysis, to present the country's Top 50 Socially Responsible Corporations" (*Maclean's* 2010, p. 37). The fact that two *for-profit* organizations had "partnered" in producing and marketing a report on the "Top 50 Socially Responsible Corporations" *for profit* struck me immediately as clear supporting evidence for the ABC thesis. Of course, I do not know if the report actually made a positive contribution to *Maclean's* and Jantzi-Sustainalytics's financial bottom line, but since it is the second report, it seems likely that it did. If so, that report would satisfy one of Machiavelli's necessary conditions for success. I also have no way of knowing if those responsible for the whole project (assessments and publication) were motivated by a desire *to appear* to be motivated by a desire to do the right thing (i.e. reward moral virtue) or if they were genuinely motivated by a desire to do the right thing or both. The titles and the content of the articles certainly give the appearance of coming from a motivation to do the right thing. Hence, Machiavelli's other necessary condition for success was also satisfied. Thus, the "Corporate Social Responsibility Report 2010" seems to provide a clear win–win–win scenario for *Maclean's,* Jantzi-Sustainalytics, and Machiavelli, not to mention the 50 award winners themselves.

Maclean's and Jantzi-Sustainalytics' understanding of CSR is not very clear. It seems to be essentially connected to their idea of sustainability, which is also never spelled out, but seems to be very close to what most people would regard as efficiency. Sustainable practices or policies are often practices or policies that do or probably will produce greater benefits with the same or fewer costs, e.g. the Bank of Montreal's plan "to be carbon neutral by the end of 2010" should produce an increased environmental benefit that "dovetailed nicely with cost-cutting" in dollars (Gohier 2010, p. 38). The idea of efficiency is very attractive to pragmatists and moral consequentialists, but its strengths and weaknesses are practically the same as those concerning the counting of consequences. Efficiency measures are fundamentally ratios of benefits to costs, or outputs to inputs, and what they tell us depends, among other things, on what one counts as benefits or costs, outputs or inputs (Michalos 2008b). In Michalos (1978), I explained how workable accounts of rationality and morality could be provided in terms of a robust account of efficiency, but few if anyone found my explanations compelling. Nevertheless, my main point here is that in principle there is nothing wrong with thinking about sustainability as efficiency. It all depends on what one loads into one's notion of efficiency, and it is worth noting that so far as many business people are concerned, such relatively non-material things as "reputational benefits" are acceptable candidates for inclusion in efficiency calculations (Gohier 2010, pp. 38 and 40).

Jantzi-Sustainalytics' methodology for evaluating corporations for their CSR performance is no clearer than their account of sustainability. The long quotation below provides the essentials as reported in *Maclean's.*

> The Top 50 Socially Responsible Corporations in Canada were selected on the basis of their performance across a broad range of environmental, social, and governance (ESG) indicators... The selected companies rank at the top of their respective peer groups in Jantzi-Sustainalytics Global Platform. These companies have demonstrated strong performance in areas such as environmental initiatives, impact on local communities, treatment of employees and supply-chain management. Some are notable for their development of products or services that contribute directly to sustainability.

> Each of the companies featured is either Canadian-listed or a wholly owned subsidiary of a foreign-listed company with significant operations or brand presence in Canada…
>
> Given that Canadian subsidiaries of foreign companies are inextricably linked to their parent companies, the evaluation is based on the performance of the foreign corporate entities. Jantzi-Sustainalytics' research process includes a thorough examination of company documents, media sources, online databases, government sources and NGO research, as well as direct communication with key stakeholders. Analysts use a Best-of-Sector™ methodology to compare companies within a given peer group to industry best practices… (Jantzi-Sustainalytic analysts 2010, p. 54).

It is worth noting that if Canadian subsidiaries can be evaluated on the basis of "the performance of the foreign corporate entities," then the evaluation game has some attractive fixed costs as one takes the game from Canada to the USA, to Europe, and anywhere else where transnational corporations operate in a network of commercial and/or political jurisdictions. Analyses done for transnationals like Adidas Group, Honda, L'Oreal, and Sony Corp., for example, can be used in many different contexts, attracting benefits over and over from a single investment.

Following the suggestion at the bottom of the text just quoted, I visited http://www.sustainalytics.com for "more information on the rating criteria," and on June 20, 2010, I sent the following message to the company.

> Can you send me a copy of the procedures and criteria used to get the Corporate Social Responsibility Report 2010 that was featured in June 21 articles, or the report itself if possible?
>
> On June 22, I received the following reply.
>
> Jantzi-Sustainalytics provided the research for the *Maclean's* list, which you can view on their website. There is also a section on the site which outlines the research methodology which you can view by clicking the link below.
>
> http://www2.macleans.ca/2010/06/14/jantzi-macleans-csr-report-2010/
>
> If you have any further questions, please feel free to contact me.

I went to the *Maclean's* website, did not find what I needed, but did find these interesting comments.

> Our second annual survey of companies in Canada that prove it pays to have a conscience… The underlying goal is the same: make the world a better place. As well as the Top 50 list… we look into how CSR might help with major PR problems, like BP's oil spill, and whether the recession made the business world any less socially responsible.

A few minutes later I wrote back to Jantzi-Sustainalytics.

> Hi… Thanks very much for the additional information. When I went to the website to find the methodology and criteria, all I got was the entry to all Jantzi products. I could not find a button to press that would give me the methodology and criteria. Can you please direct me right to that spot. The company website is huge.

Having had no response, the next day (June 23) I wrote again.

> Hi again… Were you able to find directions to the methodology and criteria for me?

A few minutes later the following reply came.

> Unfortunately, the link at the bottom of the Maclean's page was misleading. There is no additional information on the Sustainalytics website pertaining to the criteria and rating for the 50 Most Socially Responsible Corporations list. The methodology used for the Maclean's list is based off of Sustainalytics' regular research methodology and was modified for this project. The link below provides some information about our regular research process. http://www.sustainalytics.com/sustainalytics-global-platform.
>
> I'm sorry I couldn't be of more help. Please feel free to contact me if you have any further questions.

At http://www.sustainalytics.com/indexes, among other things, I found this.

> In January 2000, Jantzi Research launched the Jantzi Social Index^{R}, partnered with Dow Jones Indexes. The JSI, a socially screened, market capitalization-weighted common stock index modeled on the S&P/TSX 60 consists of 60 Canadian companies that pass a set of broadly based environmental, social, and governance rating criteria. The JSI has begun to generate the first definitive data on the effects of social screening on financial performance in Canada.

From the second sentence in the preceding paragraph, it appears as if there are 60 companies in the dataset from which 50 made their way to the Top CSR performers. If that is indeed the case, then 50/60 = 83% of the CSR competitors rose to the top of their "peer group." That would suggest that the bar for achieving distinction as a top CSR performer was very low, too low in fact to warrant any sort of praise, moral or otherwise, for those companies. Hopefully, someone at *Maclean's* or Jantzi-Sustainalytics will be able to tell us exactly how many CSR competitors were in the dataset from which the top 50 were chosen.

At the same website, we are given some questions used by the analysts in their selection of "rating criteria" for the JSI. They included such things as "Is each rating criterion researchable?... measurable?... Is there a business, corporate social responsibility, and/or scientific foundation for each rating criterion?" No specific indicators are given, although we are told that there are some "exclusionary indicators" such as "the production of nuclear power, the manufacture of tobacco products, weapons-related contracting."

At http://www.sustainalytics.com/sustainalytics-global-platform, among other things, I found this.

> The Jantzi-Sustainalytics Global Platform is the foundation of the research we offer to asset owners, plan sponsors, investment managers and other stakeholders... Jantzi-Sustainalytics provides clients with comprehensive analysis on corporate ESG performance... The Jantzi-Sustainalytics model incorporates between 60 and 100 indicators, weighted according to the industry in which they are operating. These include a broad range of core and industry-specific indicators that address sustainability policies, management systems and performance outcomes.

In sum, this is all the information I could find about the procedures and criteria used to get the Corporate Social Responsibility Report 2010, according to *Maclean's* and Jantzi-Sustainalytics websites.

Auditing the CSR Report

At http://www2.macleans.ca/2010/06/14/social-responsible-corp-2010/, there are a number of comments posted on the web concerning the *Maclean's* articles. Here is a sample.

> Jana de Lottinville: "… For corporations, social responsibility is no longer an ancillary activity but an integral part of their business models. It's 'doing well by doing good" and more companies are committed to this both because it's the right thing to do and because it's good for business.

> Hosertohoosier: "Corporations do good by making profits, paying taxes, obeying the law, creating jobs, and conducting research. The impact of a few do-gooder deeds pales in comparison to the social benefits of things like the invention of the PC, television or the automobile." Pdpd: "… we can recycle good-old 'yay-CSR/boo-profit" or Friedmanite 'boo-CSR; it's bad for the economy' arguments, but at the end of the day whether CSR is good or bad for a given situation (or company) is probably entirely contextual… there is no solid data on profitability. Companies that invest heavily in CSR tend to perform similarly to peers in that respect… Firms 'doing' CSR is almost always a clear 'net social benefit' at the local level, and should be applauded as such. But it is entirely possible that CSR can act as a cynical PR campaign tool to frustrate more formal regulation. So that's what I meant by the importance of context."

> Duff Conacher: "The title of the report is misleading because the information and factors used to rank some of the companies is dangerously incomplete (especially for 10 or so financial services companies listed)… Anyone who digs into the details will soon realize that the information and factors used to measure the companies does not, in many cases, measure the impact of the companies' fundamental activities. For example, no one knows the details of the more than $1 trillion in outstanding loans and investments and insurance policies held by the 5 big Canadian banks, 3 other banks and 2 insurance companies that are included in the top 50 list, nor any details about their customer service record, because these financial institutions are not required by law to disclose any details (as the federal government continues to protect them from actual accountability by refusing to pass a law requiring disclosure.) A law requiring at least some disclosure of this information has existed in the U.S. for more than 20 years… As long as the people and organizations who produce these so-called corporate responsibility reports without having the key information they need to actually measure the level of responsibility of the companies, the reports will continue to provide cover for irresponsible activities by corporations."

These comments suggest that different people have different ideas about exactly what should be counted as CSR activities and the value of praising or blaming companies for their performance of such activities. There is not a great deal of agreement on the meaning of basic concepts connected to CSR, on appropriate assessment criteria, data availability, measurement, aggregation, and auditing procedures. In short, the field is ripe for exploitation, and no one should be surprised if companies like *Maclean's* and Jantzi-Sustainalytics find a profitable niche in the field.

Having explored and explained some of the philosophical foundations of the ABC thesis and some of the practical problems I and others encountered in trying to assess the methodological foundations of the Maclean's/Jantzi-Sustainalytics Corporate Social Responsibility Report 2010, I set out to provide a kind of auditing overview of the top 50 CSR performers based on a subset of the eight alternative kinds of agent motives and payoffs sketched earlier, and the information provided by the *Maclean's* articles on the top 50 performers. Since I did not have access to any of the "60–100 indicators," their "weights" or the aggregation procedures used to distinguish the top 50 companies from some others, I knew that I could not produce any sort of detailed audit of the adjudication process leading to the Report. All I could do was work with the *Maclean's* articles and the extra material found on the websites to try to get some sense of how the various companies performed according to our eight alternatives. This proved to be an unproductive exploration for several reasons.

First, since I did not have access to the inner workings of the minds of those who produced and/or implemented the policies and programs leading to their companies' inclusion in the top 50 CSR performers, I was left with appearances as my working data for the first two conjuncts of each of the eight alternatives, i.e., I was left guessing real motives on the basis of activities that appeared as if they were motivated by the aims of doing the right thing and making a profit. Second, while in principle one might know exactly the financial payoffs connected to the various policies, activities and/or products described in the articles, in fact I did not have access to those payoffs. Hence, again, I was engaged in guess work for the third conjunct as well. Third, because each of the 50 companies listed in the *Maclean's* article (Jantzi-Sustainalytic analysts 2010) has 2 or 3 bullets highlighting some activity, policy, or program that is supposed to indicate some kind of good CSR performance, I thought I might be able to sort the total 139 bullets into some useful categories. We are not told how these activities, policies, or programs are connected to any of the "60–100" particular indicators or even if these activities, policies, or programs are counted as indicators in themselves. But they are apparently supposed to illustrate good CSR performance, e.g., General Mills Inc. "Stimulates sustainable agriculture by developing best-in-class agricultural practices, using conventional hybrid crop varieties to gain greater yields, and improving the environmental performance of production scale farming practices" and Xerox Corp. "Engaged in a 3-year partnership with the Nature Conservancy, focused on sustainable forest management in Brazil, Canada, Indonesia, and the U.S." After several hours over several days, it became clear to me that, from one sitting to another, I was replacing bullets from one category to others inconsistently. What looked like a good guess at one time as an item for one category, at another time looked like a good guess as an item for some other category. Fourth, many of the bullets simply described the particular products produced by the various companies. For example, BMW "introduced the ActiveHybrid X6 and the ActiveHybrid 7, which consume 20% less fuel than conventionally powered models" and Stantec Inc. "Develops building designs with energy and resource efficiencies that exceed the standards of those outlined in the Model National Energy Code of Canada…" If BMW and Stantec were only interested in making material profits, they might very well produce and sell such products and make such profits, i.e., these companies would be good examples of successful pure capitalist agents (Case 5). They might as well be good examples of successful CSR agents (Case 1). Fifth, and finally, it occurred to me that practically any company might be operating as a Case 1 or Case 5 agent, and there would be no way of knowing which, with a reasonable amount of confidence. Quite apart from the companies in the Report considered here, this comment applies to every company, anywhere, at any time, including the several companies that have published the *Journal of Business Ethics* for nearly 28 years. The vast majority of successful companies apparently do produce goods and services that people need and/or want, everything from automobiles to zippers. Granting that companies also spend a lot of money crafting advertising campaigns to artificially create needs and/or wants where none naturally existed (Michalos 1980), it would be silly to imagine that all the goods and services sustaining more or less successful capitalist economies are useless devices designed by single minded (motivated) pure capitalists. People like HosertoHoosier have a limited but not nonsensical view of good business.

Reflecting on the combination of all these issues, I reached the conclusion that I could not produce the detailed sort of audit that I thought would be possible after the first couple of readings of the *Maclean's* articles. I was prepared to produce an audit that could only be regarded as "vulgar" in Machiavelli's terms (i.e., dealing only with appearances), and I thought that such an audit might be better or worse than nothing. It would have been better if the vulgarity of my efforts provoked others to do better by creating better measures of CSR performance and using them in more transparent ways than *Maclean's* and Jantzi-Sustainalytics. It would have been worse if the vulgarity of my efforts provoked others to seek their own profitable niches in the field of CSR assessment with no better results than *Maclean's* and Jantzi-Sustainalytics or, worse still, if my efforts merely helped others "provide cover for irresponsible activities by corporations" as Conacher suggested or simple special pleading in the interests of increasing profits. In the end, I thought and still think my first impression was mistaken. Even a vulgar audit could not be produced given the information at my disposal. The most I could hope for would be a kind of rough vindication of my assessment of the value of the Maclean's/Jantzi-Sustainalytics Report and through it, a vindication of the ABC thesis. As vulgar as the report is, I think its success supports my claim that the ABC thesis is true.

Conclusion

The upshot of this article of mine is that while there are almost certainly personal and corporate material payoffs to be made from asserting the business case for business ethics, such payoffs can at best be only "handmaids of [moral] virtue" in business and at worst, serious threats to individuals' understanding of and action consistent with moral virtue, as well as threats to the very institution of morality. Whatever business case there is for business ethics itself or for the assertion of the business case for business ethics, such business cases are not moral arguments and are no more morally praiseworthy than the business cases for selling any other product from automobiles to zippers.

On September 3, 2010, I sent the following message to *Maclean's* and Jantzi-Sustainalytics; so far no reply has been received.

> I much appreciated the pieces of the June 21 on the top 50 CSR performers. I will be presenting the enclosed article in Macau in a couple of months and would appreciate knowing if I have correctly presented Maclean's and Jantz-Sustainalytics material.

References

Annas, J. (1993). *The morality of happiness*. Oxford: Oxford University Press.

Aristotle (1999). *Nicomachean ethics* (Irwin, T., 2nd ed. Trans.). Indianapolis: Hackett Pub. Co.

Brandt, R. B. (1967). Hedonism. In P. Edwards (Ed.), *The encyclopedia of philosophy* (pp. 432–435). New York: Macmillan Publishing Co.

Feigl, H. (1950). De Principiis non disputandum.? On the meaning and the limits of justification. In M. Black (Ed.), *Philosophical analysis: A collection of essays* (pp. 113–147). Englewood Cliffs: Prentice-Hall.

Gohier, P. (2010, June 21). Ethics: A conscience choice, *Maclean's Magazine*, pp. 38 and 40.

Jantzi-Sustainalytic analysts. (2010, June 21). The top 50: Raising the bar. *Maclean's Magazine*, pp. 42, 44, 46, 48, 50, 52–54.

Kirby, J. (2010, June 21). Crisis management: When things get messy. *Maclean's Magazine*, pp. 40 and 42.

Machiavelli, N. (1970). *The Discourses* (B. Richardson, Trans.). London: Penguin Books.

Machiavelli, N. (1980). *The Prince* (L. P. S. de Alvarez, Prospect Heights, Trans.). Illinois: Waveland Press.

Maclean's (2010, June 21). Corporate social responsibility report 2010: Good for business. *Maclean's Magazine*, p. 37.

Michalos, A. C. (1970). *Improving your reasoning*. Englewood Cliffs: Prentice-Hall.

Michalos, A. C. (1978). *Foundations of decision making*. Ottawa: Canadian Library of Philosophy.

Michalos, A. C. (1980). Advertising: Its logic, ethics and economics. In J. A. Blair & R. H. Johnson (Eds.), *Informal logic* (pp. 93–111). Inverness: Edgepress.

Michalos, A. C. (1985). Multiple discrepancies theory (MDT). *Social Indicators Research, 16*, 347–413.

Michalos, A. C. (1995). *A pragmatic approach to business ethics*. Thousand Oaks: Sage Publication.

Michalos, A. C. (1997). Combining social, economic and environmental indicators to measure sustainable human well-being. *Social Indicators Research, 40*, 221–258.

Michalos, A. C. (1999). The loyal agent's argument. In D. C. Poff & W. J. Waluchow (Eds.), *Business ethics in Canada* (3rd ed., pp. 196–202). Scarborough: Prentice-Hall Allyn and Bacon Canada.

Michalos, A. C. (2001). Ethics counselors as a new priesthood. *Journal of Business Ethics, 29*, 3–17.

Michalos, A. C. (2003). *Essays on the quality of life*. Dordrecht: Kluwer Academic Publishers.

Michalos, A. C. (2008a). Ancient observations on business ethics: Middle East meets West. *Journal of Business Ethics*, *79*(1–2), 9–19.

Michalos, A. C. (2008b). *Trade barriers to the public good*. Montreal: McGill-Queen's University Press.

Michalos, A. C. (2010). The monster of supercapitalism. *Journal of Business Ethics, 91*(1 Supplement), 37–48.

Michalos, A. C. (2012). The good life: Eighth century to third century BCE. In K. C. Land, A. C. Michalos, & M. J. Sirgy (Eds.), *Handbook of social indicators and quality of life research*. Dordrecht: Springer.

Poff, D. C. (1999). The loyal agent's argument revisited. In D. C. Poff & W. J. Waluchow (Eds.), *Business ethics in Canada* (3rd ed., pp. 203–204). Scarborough: Prentice-Hall Allyn and Bacon Canada.

Reich, R. B. (2007). *Supercapitalism: The transformation of business, democracy, and everyday-life*. New York: Alfred A Knopf.

Chapter 22
Public Policy Letters to Editors 1989–2001

Alex C. Michalos

Citizens Forum: Stop Cruise Missiles Over Canada

Guelph Daily Mercury, January 26, 1989, p. 4

It is time to stop flying cruise missiles over Canadian skies.

When the Liberal government agreed to allow these weapons to be test flown in 1983, we were told that the flights would be stopped when "concrete results were achieved in INF negotiations: namely, results that would decrease the level of missile deployment in Europe".

Precisely such results were achieved in the INF treaty last year. More recently, the Soviet Union announced that it would make troop and tank withdrawals from Europe. And troops have been withdrawn from Afghanistan.

When the Defence Department's White Paper came out in 1987, every peace group in the country was appalled by its cold war tone and doctrine designed for the 1950s. Still, some people said let's wait and see what actually happens in Afghanistan and at the INF table.

We did wait and all indications have been favorable. There is a fresh wind of peace blowing across the world. But not across Canada.

In 1985 the United Nations report on Unilateral Nuclear Disarmament Measures argued that the arms race might be reversed by "gradually creating an atmosphere of mutual trust and confidence … through unilateral initiatives … such as reductions in military expenditures, reductions in the number of troops, cuts in the number of certain types of weapons, establishment of nuclear-weapon-free zones (NWDZs) and a wide variety of restrains in military programs."

By-August 1987 there were 166 NWFZs in Canada, including Toronto, Vancouver and Hamilton. An active group in Guelph hopes to have our city included in the near future.

A.C. Michalos (✉)
University of Northern British Columbia, Prince George, BC, Canada
e-mail: michalos@brandonu.ca

A.C. Michalos, *How Good Policies and Business Ethics Enhance Good Quality of Life*, DOI 10.1007/978-3-319-50724-8_22

Ending cruise missile flights in Canada would certainly be a modest unilateral initiative. But international confidence-building "measures" are supposed to be modest. They are not supposed to threaten anyone's security.

Halting the flights in the presence of the current international climate would be an excellent signal of Canada's willingness to keep up the momentum and it would not threaten anyone's security.

When the UN asked us to send peace-keepers in the middle east, our response was swift, affirmative and consistent with our prior commitment to stop the missile flights. "A promise made is a debt unpaid".

Citizens Forum: Marching Against Ontario Poverty

Guelph Daily Mercury, March 17, 1989, p .4

On April 4, around 5:00 p.m., Guelph will be visited by a group of people marching from Windsor to Queen's Park to demonstrate their concern for poor Ontarions.

By Statistics Canada's definition, people are poor when more than 58.5% of their gross income is spent on food, clothing and shelter. Using this definition, then, the poor need not always be with us. Poverty can be eliminated when everyone's income is high enough to allow them to spend less that 58.5% of it on necessities.

In 1986, the last year for which we have statistics, there were 216,200 poor families and 292,600 poor unattached individuals in Ontario. That was about 8.7% of all families and 28.3% of all unattached individuals.

In the same year, the Ontario government established the Social Assistance Review Committee, chaired by George Thomson. The mandate of the Committee was to examine the objectives of our social assistance system, to measure its effectiveness and efficiency at meeting those objectives, and to recommend strategies to improve it.

According to the Committee's report, "The objective for social assistance...must be to ensure that individuals are able to make the transition from dependence to autonomy, and from exclusion on the margins of society to integration within the mainstream of community life."

Among the 274 formal recommendations of the Committee, there is this one: "Within six months of the release of this report, the government should issue a statement indicating what action it intends to take in response to our recommendations."

The six month period ends on Good Friday, this month. The march against poverty begins the same day. It is important that the government is reminded of its commitment to the poor. In particular, it is important for the government to announce its strategies of action on such crucial innovations as opportunity planning and perverse tax-back policies.

The current tax-back rates for the working poor are such that in many cases "for every dollar earned from income, the welfare recipient loses more than a dollar in benefits."

With the recommended opportunity planning system, "a skilled staff person and the welfare recipient will develop a plan that identifies strategies to enable the recipient to leave social assistance or to live more independently in the community. It will require assessing the individual's skill's aptitude, and aspirations and linking the recipient to appropriate services, programs, and supports".

Most poor people do not receive any social assistance, and "for the majority of recipients, social assistance meets a temporary need often created by a life crisis". On average, employable recipients leave the system after seven months, single parents (85% of whom are women) leave after three or four years and those with disabilities after five years.

Thirty-seven per cent of all beneficiaries of social assistance are children under 18, 32% are disabled, and another 30% are single parents. Thus, the myth of the undeserving poor living off the sweat of other people's brows is clearly just a myth.

The Thomson Committee carried out its mandate in splendid fashion. The demonstrations at the end of this month are not intended as criticisms, but as visible reminders of the vital task that lies before the government.

We hope many Guelphites will join the marchers, the rally, the music, and the supper in the square on April 4. Anyone interested in getting more information about the non-partisan Campaign Against Poverty in Ontario should call 822–5504.

Citizens Forum: Overwhelming Case Against Buying Submarines

Guelph Daily Mercury, March 1, 1989, p. 4

The government is still thinking about buying nuclear submarines. But I still think the case against buying them is overwhelming.

The Department of Defence's (DND) original estimates were $8 billion over-25 years for 10–12 subs, in 1986–87 dollars. With no cost overruns and a 4% inflation rate, that $8 billion becomes more than $21 billion. But weapons systems are notorious for cost overruns of 200 to 300%. So, virtually all experts outside DND guesstimate costs of at least $20 billion.

DND's White Paper talked about the efficient patrol of three oceans, sometimes about defending Canada's sovereignty in three oceans. NATO and the Warsaw Treaty countries each have almost 200 active subs. At any given time neither side knows where half of the other side's subs are. So, even if we could keep three subs sailing all the time in the three oceans', what difference would it make to either our sovereignty or our security?

DND says that with the new subs we could detect and even destroy intruders, especially in the Arctic. Again, the numbers are such that for every one we could delect, there would be dozens undetected. But apart from that, what sense does it make to say we could just destroy intruders?

DND claims our armed forces should have state-of-the-art equipment. But the British and French subs they are thinking about buying are at best yesterday's state-of-the-art. They have been described as "obsolete death traps" and "noise-makers" that will be as dated as our current, Oberon-class subs are by the time the first one is delivered. By the time the last one is delivered a quarter of a century from now; it will be as useful as the Maginot Line. DND claims there were no nuclear accidents in 34 years of submarine service. But the U.S. Center for Investigative Reporting found 29 accidents, including the 1963 sinking of the USS Thresher with 129 seamen and the 1968 USS Scorpion with 99 seamen. The Royal Navy reported 712 "minor" accidents between 1962 and 1979.

DND tells us that we are not violating any nuclear non-proliferation treaty by having nuclear-powered subs, because they are not carrying nuclear weapons. But we criticized Argentina and India for wanting nuclear-powered warships without nuclear weapons.

DND has also claimed that we need nuclear subs to protect "sea lines of communication". In the Second World War we had convoys and needed protection against submarines. But there are not going to be any convoys in a nuclear war. The US, for example, has no plans for convoys resupplying forces in Europe. They are not figuring on a WW II type of war.

Considering all these issues, the obvious thaw in the international Cold War, and all the real threats to our security from scarcities of raw materials, environmental degradation and the severely unequal distribution of the world's wealth, the purchase of nuclear subs would be a colossal mistake. Last December a national poll found that 69% of Canadians came to precisely this conclusion. Let's hope the new government represents that majority.

Nuclear Energy Should not Be a Priority

Guelph Daily Mercury, March 30, 1989, p. 4

Bruce Laplaunte's articles on nuclear energy (March 18) gave a good account of the issues from the producing industry's point of view, but there is a lot to be said against the building of new nuclear reactors. Among other things, it should be remembered what increasing the number of reactors implies.

1. Increasing the risks of life and health from accidental high-level and routine low-level exposure to radiation;
2. Decreasing opportunities to develop alternative forms of energy production because of the high capital demands of nuclear energy;
3. Increasing opportunities for the development and deployment of nuclear weapons (e.g., by selling Americans tritium from Darlington);
4. Increasing opportunities for sabotage, terrorism and theft at reactor and waste disposal sites;
5. Increasing need for paramilitary personnel to secure reactor and waste sites;
6. Increasing the training and sustaining to technical elites to run reactor systems;
7. Increasing the sales and integrational availability of uranium for weapons;
8. Increasing social and psychological stress accompanying the introduction of nuclear facilities into communities;

9. Feeding the illusion of limitless energy and shifting the focus away from conservation;
10. Leaving future generations the problems of genetically-induced disabilities, technological systems and social structures that they may find highly debilitating;
11. Creating unfair distributions of risk for people living near and working around reactors;
12. Destroying aquatic life and its dependents in the water bodies adjacent to reactors;
13. Increasing the tendency toward dense urbanization as a result of the centralization of power centres;
14. Increasing the magnitude of the still unsolved nuclear waste management problem.

Some of these difficulties are more serious than others. Personally, I find the ominous signs coming from from Queen's Park regarding the sale of tritium to the United States most disturbing. The more tritium we put in the hands of the Americans, the more bombs they will make and the more insecure the world will become. Even if our tritium is only used for peaceful purposes, whatever we sell them frees U.S. producers to supply greater quantities to their military, dragging us deeper into their bloated military industrial complex.

Until the tritium business appeared on the scene, my main concern was nuclear waste management. For 50 years the nuclear industry has claimed this is a technical problem to be solved sometime in the future. In fact, their proposed solution of burying the waste is practically identical to their ostrich-like approach to the whole problem.

According to an article in the Toronto Star last June, most Canadian radioactive waste is stored at Chalk River in "concrete silos about 10 metres across and 10 metres deep … laid out in nine rows of 11; when they are full they are capped with 20 tonne concrete blocks".

When it comes to the steel reactors themselves, as opposed to spent fuel, pipes and other parts, if we follow the American practice, we will simply encase the huge reactors in concrete and walk away. After their 50 years or so of active life, the reactors at Pickering, Bruce and so on will stand for the foreseeable future like giant tombstones along our lakes.

Of course we can't keep damming rivers and burning fossil fuels, and turning the globe into a hothouse. But it is not helpful for energy producers to give us moderate reminders to conserve energy while they are threatening us with blackouts and shortages if we don't build more reactors. Ontario Hydro has a long history of threats of shortages followed by increased development followed by increased sales of power to the United States followed by still more threats.

Virtually all authorities agree that it costs 10 times as much to build new generating power for a watt of electricity as it does to get that watt through conservation. So, when we talk about energy development, our first consideration should be development through conservation. Ontario Hydro's slogan is Conservation First, but that doesn't seem to be their first priority.

Citizens Forum: Abortions Are not 'on Demand' Basis

Guelph Daily Mercury, April 5, 1989, p. 4

Contrary to the March 10 Mercury editorial, the Law Reform Commission's incubator view of pregnant women is not an acceptable compromise. It implies that pregnant women have the full protection of their Charter "right to life, liberty and security of the person" until their 20th week of pregnancy, and then the women become human incubators and their rights are negotiable. The very point of having Charter rights is to prevent them from being negotiated away.

For 20 years, since the 1969 Criminal Code Amendment Act, therapeutic abortions have been legal in Canada provided that they are performed by a licensed medical practitioner, in an accredited hospital, with a committee of at least three physicians certifying that the continuation of the pregnancy would be likely to endanger the life or health of the pregnant women.

On Jan. 23, 1988 the Supreme Court struck down section 251 of the old Act. That removed the requirement to have committee certification and to have abortions performed in hospitals. Section 252 remains intact. It is still illegal for unlicensed hacks to "supply a drug, instrument or other noxious thing to procure an abortion". Besides S. 252, there are provincial laws prohibiting unlicensed practitioners and requiring accepted medical standards by licensed practitioners. So, it is quite misleading to suggest that there are no laws regulating abortions or that there is some urgency to create new legislation.

The 1969 law allows that a pregnant women's circumstances might be such that in order to protect her life or health, a pregnancy can be legally terminated at any time throughout the nine month gestation period. In fact, our statistical records show that about 99.5% of therapeutic abortions are performed within 20 weeks of conception. That is because such abortions are surgical procedures made by licensed medical practitioners regulated by sound medical criteria in consultation with their patients.

In the fourteen months since the court's decision and since 1976 in Quebec, there as been no change in standard medical practice and no change in the relative frequency of abortions performed after 20 weeks.

Considering the approximately half of one percent of therapeutic abortions that are obtained after the 20th week of gestation, they are mainly allowed because of serious fetal deformities, danger of the pregnant woman's life or health, or the unavailability of an earlier abortion. I can find no justification to risk the health or life of a woman for a fetus or to maintain seriously deformed fetuses. And the appropriate response to the problem of insufficient access to early abortions is to provide sufficient access.

In September 1983, a gallup poll found that 89% of Canadians favoured allowing abortions "if the woman's health is endangered by the pregnancy". That is precisely what the current laws allow.

There is no responsible group in Canada asking for "abortion on demand". The federal and all provincial advisory councils on the status of women, the National

Action Committee on the Status of Women, Canadian Abortion Rights Action League, Canadian Medical Association, Society of Obstetricians and Gynaecologists and The Canadian Psychiatric Association all endorse the current laws. They all have spoken out against the introduction of new legislation.

The majority of therapeutic abortions are given to women who were practicing some form of birth control that failed, and most of the others were given to women or girls who were the victims of incest, rape or ignorance. There is no evidence of the widespread use of therapeutic abortion as a method of birth control and no evidence that Canadian women decide to have abortions in a mindless, heartless, or generally frivolous way. It is preposterous to imagine that a woman would routinely subject her body to surgery to terminate unwanted pregnancies rather than use the variety of relatively harmless preventive measures in the form of pills, jellies, condoms and so on.

Because it is preferable to prevent anomalies rather than to take remedial action after they occur, it would be preferable to have no pregnancies resulting from failed contraception, incest, rape or ignorance. So, those who support the current legislation also strongly favor increased funding for research on accessibility to reliable contraception, family planning, sex education, birth control information and counseling, and for the reduction of incest and rape.

Obviously we must have more public debate about therapeutic abortion and much of it will probably have to go on in the press. For now I only want to emphasize again that current laws do not allow "abortion on demand", women are not asking for it and medical practitioners are not offering it.

Citizens Forum: Settle All Native Land Claims First

Guelph Daily Mercury, April 28, 1989, p. 4

There is something bizarre about giving people a licence to do things without knowing how the things will be done. Imagine giving someone a driver's licence without knowing how well the person can drive.

Strange as it sounds, that is the sort of task before the National Energy Board right now.

Three Calgary-based firms, Esso Resources Ltd., Shell Canada Ltd. and Gulf Canada Resources Ltd., have asked the Board for a licence that would allow them to export up to 9.2 trillion cubic feet of natural gas from their reserves in the Mackenzie delta over 20 years starting in 1996. That is about 90% of the proven reserves in the area, and as near as I can determine, about nine per cent of all Canada's estimated gas reserves.

The Board is operating on a two- step procedure. First, it is supposed to review the costs and benefits of granting a licence to export the gas, and then it is supposed to review the costs and benefits of building a pipeline through which the gas is to be exported. Presumably, the idea is that if we are opposed in principle to exporting the gas, then it would be pointless to talk about building an acceptable pipeline.

Fair enough. But on the other hand, if there is no acceptable plan for a pipeline, then it is pointless to talk about how we feel in principle about exporting the gas. The gas in question is not going anywhere without a pipeline.

The companies say that they will not invest the funds required to prepare an acceptable pipeline plan unless they have an export licence. The trouble is, what is acceptable to the companies may not be acceptable to Canadians, including the Native Metis, Dene and Inuit, and the environment, including the porcupine, caribou and the beluga whales.

Most of the local stakeholders favor development provided that the government of the Northwest Territories is given "full control and management" of the resources, there are guarantees of employment and other long term economic benefits to the local people and guarantees of protection for the environment. But the companies have not offered such guarantees and the federal government has not agreed to abandon it's share of the action.

For those of us far from the scene, the crucial issues involve the security of supply of gas in the future and the wisdom of allowing the oil companies to determine the shape and pace of the development of our resources.

Considering the supply, because of last year, the Mulroney government eliminated the so-called "surplus test" that required a producer to have a 25-year supply of gas available for sale in Canada before exports would be approved, the Board is left pretty much on its own to determine a new policy regarding acceptable risks of total depletion. Exactly how a three-member unelected Board is supposed to make such a politically charged policy decision is at best unclear.

Considering the wisdom of allowing the oil companies to determine the shape and pace of the development of our resources and the Arctic region surrounding it, one must support Bill Erasmus, the president of the 15,000 member Dene nation. Last week, he reminded the Board that the companies had promised major benefits to the Native people from the Norman Wells, N.W.T. pipeline, and precious little came of the promises. In the light of our history of government and industry's dealings with Native people, wisdom is certainly on the side of delaying any licence approvals until the Native claims are settled not merely in principle but in fact.

Citizens Forum: Readers Oppose Low-Level Flights

Guelph Daily Mercury, October 19, 1989, p. 4

If the current federal government has its ways, Goose Bay, Labrador, will have a new NATO base and there will be 40,000 low-level bomber flights over Labrador and Quebec every year. At the very time when the governments of West Germany and the Netherlands have announced significant cuts in such flights over those countries, the Mulroney government continues to barter for a new base, increased flights and a continuance of the cold war.

The proposed new war zone is the homeland of 10,000 Innu people of Labrador, who for thousands of years have shared the land with caribou, beaver, marten, mink, migratory waterfowl and a rich variety of other wildlife.

With a full NATO base, 27,500 flights a year would be at altitudes less than 500 feet, and about 1,000 flights would be at night. No one could have a permanent home on the land beneath these flights because neither animals nor humans can tolerate the intense sonic booms generated by military jets at such levels.

But sonic booms are not the worst of it. Once the base is installed, frequent combat exercises will be held using the complete range of conventional weapons. Live bombs, missiles, machine guns and cannons will be used. Enormous craters will be blasted in the ground and the earth will be turned into an immense metal-strewn junkyard. This is not prophecy! It is an accurate report of the nature of tactical training areas around the world.

Besides destroying the habitat and the way of life of the Innu, a new military base built to accommodate visiting servicemen will certainly bring physical, sexual and economic exploitation of women. That too is historical fact. The sexual abuse of women by military men for their "rest and recreation" occurs worldwide. The women usually come from poor families, using prostitution to escape poverty. Servicemen often leave single women to raise "souvenir babies" in third world countries, and it will happen here.

A few Innu people are currently going across Canada to try to get support for their efforts to save their land and their way of life. Clearly, all Canadians have a stake in their struggle. We cannot hope to have international peace and security, and sustainable development in a livable environment if we allow our eastern coast to be turned into a war zone. We cannot go peacefully forward into the 21st century carrying the military hardware and mental set of mid-20th century cold warriors.

On Nov. 3 Guelph will be visted by some of the Innu. They need our financial and moral support. Their lives and livelihoods are on the line. They will return to a battleground, while we will be lucky enough to return to our daily routines in relative safety.

Please help our local committee of the Canadian Alliance in Solidarity with Native Peoples by calling Sharon O'Sullivan, 824-5179. And by all means join us on Nov. 3 in welcoming the visiting Innu.

Letters: Recession to Deepen with New Tory Budget

Guelph Daily Mercury, March 2, 1990, p. 4

When Michael Wilson's budget came out in April last year, I predicted that if he could stick to his game-plan, we would be in a recession within a year. Two weeks ago the Royal Bank and Wood Gundy announced that we are in a recession. The budget tabled last Tuesday is bound to drive us into an even deeper recession, in the coming year.

He knows and has told us that his policies will increase unemployment. So, the numbers of needy people will increase. Still, government assistance to the needy will be cut. Cut from previous decisions regarding unemployment insurance, child care, family allowances and old age security, and from new cuts in transfer payments to the provinces for health care and post-secondary education.

He continues to claim that high inflation rates are driving high interest rates at the Bank of Canada, although Statistics Canada's most recent report on this issue claims that he has it roughly backwards. High interest rates are producing much of the inflation, along with some increased food costs resulting from a relatively bad year in agriculture.

Lest anyone suppose that high interest rates are punishing everyone, it should be noted that the assets of our chartered banks have increased over 2000% since 1965. No Liberal or Tory prime minister since John Diefenbaker has tried to prevent the banks, through the bank, from ripping us off.

While the government is withdrawing its helping hand, its other hand is going to be picking our pockets with the new goods and services tax. Virtually everyone except members of the Tory government admits that the GST's relative tax bites on the wealthy will be smaller than the bites on low and modern-income earners. What's worse, this has been typical of most Tory tax reform since they came into office in 1984.

The sale of Petro-Canada, like the sale of Air Canada, will be another giant step toward increasing the wealth of Canada's privileged few. Only about 10% of Canadians have any substantial investment money. So, when a crown corporation is put on the block, it just provides a new opportunity for those with investment funds to take control of new chunks of our economy.

Reductions in transfer payments to provinces for health and post-secondary education will either be made up by provinces with new taxes, by purchasers of particular services or the services will be allowed to continue deteriorating. If there are increased user fees for health and education, these also tend to increase the gap between rich and poor Canadians. Those who cannot pay the extra price will fall behind in getting more education or better health care.

The clear result of taking more from and giving less to those with the relatively greatest need will be substantial increase in the concentration of wealth in Canada. In brief, the 10% of Canadians who now own 51% of this country, will certainly own more four years from now if Wilson's plan works.

Wilson and his corporate friends continue to talk about the necessity of trimming annual deficits and the national debt, and that is certainly a laudable exercise. But many of us think there are better ways. Consider some options that Wilson neglected. He might have:

(1) lowered the bank rate or at least arrested it, which is the main reason for the uncontrollable annual deficits and the national debt;

(2) called in some of the $30 billion in outstanding deferred corporate taxes;
(3) taxed all capital gains, dividend and interest income at the same rate as labor income;.
(4) returned to the 10 income tax brackets of some years ago and increased the spread so that middle income earners are not hit harder than everyone else;
(5) put a 20% minimum income tax on all corporations instead of the modest capital-base tax that was introduced last year;
(6) introduced a one per cent net wealth tax on the wealthiest 10% of Canadians;
(7) re-introduced inheritance and gift taxes;
(8) introduced a net wealth tax on the chartered banks or at least taxed some part of the spread in the interest between loans and deposits;
(9) introduced differential interest rates in different regions of the country or for special purposes such as industrial innovation and export industries (which are very successful in Japan);
(10) brought back the troops from Europe;
(11) reduced RRSPs that benefit primarily the wealthy.

The plain fact is that Michael Wilson and the Mulroney government are serving relatively privileged Canadians much better than the rest of the population. In spite of their rhetoric, that is the clear implication of their preferred policies. When Statistics Canada takes its next wealth survey in 1991, this fact will be abundantly clear. Unfortunately, by then a lot of people will have been irreparably harmed.

Health Care Still a Political Football

Guelph Daily Mercury, August 22, 1990, p. 7

Dear Editor

One might think that comprehensive health care should not be a partisan political issue. After all, everyone should want the best care available and affordable.

Unfortunately, such care has been a political football at least since the '40s in Saskatchewan when Tommy Douglas and the CCF tried to make it available for all Canadians. It took them about 20 years to introduce public medical insurance in that have-not province, and some extra years to get the federal government to come around.

Much as we cherish it today, the plan was resisted by the Liberals and Progressive Conservatives, and bitterly fought by the Canadian and American Medical Associations. In the end, Douglas won the battle and was subsequently turfed out of office.

I mention this brief history to inform readers that the current battle for a comprehensive health care facility in Guelph is only our most recent battle in a war that is not over. It should not be a partisan battle, but Rick Ferraro has defined it as such in his summer report to his constituents. The first three pages of his report are devoted to hospital redevelopment, and he is clearly proud of his contribution to solving this difficult problem.

Speaking as one member of Guelph's non-partisan Coalition for Comprehensive Health Care, I want to say that his proposed solution is totally unacceptable for several reasons.

The most objectionable aspect of the solution was emphasized in Virginia Wilson's article in the Mercury of August 3, 1990, pg. 3A. Wilson reported that the Sisters of St. Joseph were going to meet with the bishop of Hamilton diocese in order to find out exactly what sort of health care could be delivered in their hospital.

That is, of course, proper procedure for the Sisters, but it is highly offensive and undemocratic for those of us who do not share the Sisters' faith. The bishop is not an elected representative of his community and has no mandate to make policy for us.

The Roman Catholic Church is one of the world's greatest opponents of full reproductive rights for women. The Sisters and the official hierarchy have made it perfectly clear that they intend to continue their opposition in any new hospital that they manage in Guelph.

This opposition is contrary to the expressed wishes of the vast majority of Canadians, to the Canada Health Act recognizing therapeutic abortion, and to recent judgements of the Supreme Court recognizing women's rights to equal access to all kinds of health care and to the security of their persons.

It makes as little sense to have our hospital run according to the demands of a minority religious faith as it would to have our schools run that way. Indeed, you can substitute practically any words for "religious faith" and the problem remains. In a democratic country no unelected minority should be able to dictate policy for the majority.

It is precisely this principle that underlies the non-partisan nature of our coalition. The group includes Catholics and non-Catholics, Liberals and non-Liberals. The main issue is not religion or political stripe, unless a commitment to democratic rule through majorities is regarded as a brand new political doctrine.

Ferraro has written that if his constituents don't like his way of handling this issue, they should throw him out. Personally, I would have given him his walking papers for many things besides the hospital issue. But some members of the coalition don't feel that way. They just want him to take democracy and his obligation to all members of this community seriously.

Whatever the bishop decides this time, those who do not share his faith are disenfranchised. We have no voice and no vote in his community.

In the Roman Catholic Church, women are second class citizens. In the Canadian Charter of Rights and Freedoms, there are no second class citizens.

The freedom of religion enshrined in the Canadian Charter must allow all citizens freedom from the demands of other people's religion, and such freedom must be granted in the fundamental areas of health care and education.

If the final word on the development of Guelph's future health care facility is going to come from the Roman Catholic hierarchy, then males as well as females outside the faith are going to be turned into second class citizens. And that is as morally wrong as anything can possible be.

In brief, Rick Ferraro is kidding himself if he thinks most of us just want to end the controversy and get on with building some kind of new hospital. No one can just dismantle the democratic process and the charter of Rights and Freedoms, and expect the rest of us to roll over and play dead. Mulroney and Winegard couldn't do it with Meech Lake, and Ferraro and Peterson can't do it with a new hospital.

I urge anyone who agrees with the views expressed here to phone the coalition at 843-5006. Don't wait until it's too late.

Towards the Renunciation of War

Guelph Daily Mercury, January 19, 1991, p. 6A

"The Commons was less than half full," Carol Goar wrote in the Jan. 16 edition of The Toronto Star, and most of those present seemed little interested in serious debate on a war in the Gulf.

Now we are at war. As I write these sentences, the radio is reporting a third wave of air strikes against Iraq.

Thurday, Goar says that Brian Mulroney "has some of the attributes of a good wartime leader". Maybe so. Unfortunately, his most salient attributes are those of an ingratiating charlatan.

The man who spent his life courting the rich and powerful to become a branch plant manager is on his way to becoming a branch plant prime minister. With the help of sympathetic Tory colleagues, American trains now run where VIA once ran, American airlines fly where Air Canada flew, American postal service is used where Canada Post became too unreliable and expensive, and thanks to the trade deal, the Canadian work force is being restructured to accommodate the American corporate agenda.

As bad and unforgiveable as all these assaults on our country are, they cannot compare to dragging us into an undeclared, unnecessary and unjustified war.

The United Nations was functioning as the thoughtful voice of the world community and the economic sanctious of that community were working. Saddam Hussein's aggression was contained.

Virtually all of his armaments were imported. So, his capacity to make war had to decrease over time, and reasonable people might have hoped to see results in 12–18 months.

U.N. Resolution 678 did not commit any nation to war, but it did allow such action. For the self-proclaimed world's most violent society, the United States, a licence to kill is an irresistible opportunity. Having granted the licence, members of the U.N. cannot escape responsibility for what has happened. It was predictable.

I think it was also predictable that Brian Mulroney would adopt the American point of view. Since his first election, almost his entire foreign policy and much of his domestic policy has been a reflection of that of the U.S.A. In a word, the overall agenda of the Mulroney government has been the Americanization of Canada.

No one should have been surprised to discover that somewhere along the way, Canadians would be told that it is morally right to engage in some war, some place, for some obscure reason. That is the American way, and now is has become our way.

Goar remarked that Arabs must perceive a double standard at work when now there is a rush to war when no one went to war to enforce the 1967 U.N. Resolution 242 calling for withdrawal of Israeli troops from the West Bank and Gaza Strip.

Had she stepped back in history another 20 years, she would have found that no one went to war to enforce the U.N. Resolution 181(2)A of 1917 either. At that meeting, the General Assembly endorsed the so-called Plan of Partition with Economic Union according to which Palestine was to be divided into "Independent Arab and Jewish States and the Special International Regime for the City of Jerusalem."

The history of the United Nations is a record of endless negotiations followed by resolutions followed by more or less successful attempts at implementation. At no time in that history was there ever such widespread international agreement about the need for an implementation mechanism, and at no time was there ever such widespread action by members of the world community. There was an excellent chance that sanctions would have worked, and the world would have been a better place for it.

Whether this war is long or short, it is important for all of us to keep the vision of peace alive by continuing to nourish it. Obviously, we have again failed to prevent war. So now we must press for the earliest possible suspension of hostilities.

If you believe that the world must renounce war as a method implementing public policy, then let your voice be heard. Today such voices are being raised all around the world, and one day they will drown out the barking dogs of war.

Opinion: Canada Helps Outfit World's Warriors

Guelph Daily Mercury, February 5, 1991, p. 7A

The hypocrisy of members of the Mulroney government is almost beyond belief.

According to a report in The Toronto Star (Jan: 25) External Affairs Minister Joe Clark told a meeting of the Conference of Defence Associations that while Canada's arms exports to Persian Gulf countries was closely controlled, other countries had been "less scrupulous".

In his important book, Arms Canada (1987) Canada's premier peace researcher, Ernie Regehr, said that "What is clear is that Canada makes no effort to control the sale of weapons with Canadian components".

In the December 1990 issue of the Ploughshares Monitor Regehr explained government's most recent policy of disclosing arms sales to foreign countries. Because the new policy does not reveal the specific kinds of equipments or the quantities sold, it is useless to anyone interested in determining exactly what was used for what tasks, including tasks involving the repression of civilian population.

The government's main arguments against full disclosure are that sales would be decreased and that commercial confidentiality would be violated. Both arguments assume that it is acceptable for Canadians to be in the business of selling arms abroad and that the manufacture and sale of arms is simply like any other commercial product.

In my little book on Militarism and the Quality of Life (1989), I showed that these arguments and many others used to defend arms manufacturing are seriously defective, and I documented the fact that since 1984 the government has relentlessly pursued increased production and export of military armaments.

Two years ago some residents of Guelph were among those arrested for peaceful demonstrations against the government funded ARMX 89 display in Ottawa. ARMX 89 was the fourth biennial Canadian exhibition sponsored by our Department of National Defence.

According to the pre-registration brochure, "Manufacturers' and suppliers of Defence Equipment, Systems and Subsystems for Air, Land and sea Forces" should attend in order to take advantage of "A great opportunity for foreign corporations to sell to Canada and a great opportunity for Canadian companies to promote export capabilities and offer their products to the Canadian government".

At this very moment plans are under way for ARMX.91, to be held in May at Carp Ontario.

Since the ARMX series began in 1983, it cannot be blamed on the Canada/US trade deal. However, the trade deal makes the future expansion of ARMX more likely because apart from subsidies to oil and gas companies (Article 906), subsidies "relating to the traffic in arms, ammunition and implements of war" are allowed to both countries (Article 2003). All others subsidies are negotiable. In Maude Barlow's recent book on the trade deal she has some horrifying speculations regarding multinational companies that pressed for the deal in the interest of increasing arms sales.

In 1987 Defence Minister Perrin Beatty boasted that "The Department of National Defence has seen steadily increasing funds for research and development-directed contracts in Canadian industry. In the last 10 years the expansion has been almost sevenfold".

Because Canada and the United States agreed to have a rough balance of arms trade through the 1963 Defence Production Sharing Arrangements (DPSA) Canada must sell roughly as much as its buys from the States. So no long term economic gains may be expected from selling arms to our main purchasers. Hence, continued increases in the production and export of arms must rely on overseas markets.

Because Europeans tend to insist on exchanges similar to those of the DPSA the most promising markets are those of the Third World. This is why virtually all arms manufactures actively pursue the Third World market and that is one reason why there have been more than 100 wars since 1945 fought in developing countries, producing more than 20 million combat deaths.

People who argue for increases in the Canadian production and export of arms almost always retreat to the point of claiming that our contribution to the world's supply is and will be relatively insignificant. In my little book, I calculated that in 1986 about $2.5 billion of our GNP was involved in arms production. Then I wrote "Two and a half billion dollars that you would have matched the Federal government's expenditures for Family Allowances and for Research and Development (R&D in the natural sciences): it would have been six-times the Federal governments expenditure on the environment, 13 times the expenditure for R&D in the social sciences and three times the expenditure on recreation and leisure. It would have just about matched the country's expenses on community colleges and it would have added another 22,676 new or renovated housing units to the 56,659 units funded by the Federal government in 1986."

Clearly Canada's involvement in the production and export of armaments is not insignificant, and no one in the Mulroney government should be crowing about the blood on others' hands.

Pay Equity—the Other Side

Guelph Daily Mercury, March 12, 1991, p. 7A

Dear Editor

Derek Nelson's article against pay equity (March 6, The Daily Mercury) was reminiscent of his articles on the same subject on March 6, 1990 and Feb. 7, 1989.

It looks as if he is engaged in an annual ritual of pay equity bashing. Ritual or not, I must say I have found his articles useful for my course in business ethics. As you can imagine, in my course he represents the other side.

Until the University of Toronto Press published Carl Cuneo's excellent book, Pay Equity, last year, one really had to scramble to construct a comprehensive account of the subject. Cuneo carefully documents all the arguments and evidence for and against pay equity, and is generally supportive of the idea. Unfortunately, virtually every concrete realization of the idea has been seriously defective.

Besides recommending that Nelson and others interested in the subject should read Cuneo's book, I want to respond briefly to three points he has made at one time or another.

First, he (Nelson) cited a study by Walter Block in 1982 for the Fraser Institute that concluded that "marriage and children are what bring down total female income". Block's evidence was a 1979 study by Peter Koch and Walter Haessel of 1971 Census data.

However, Margaret Denton and Alfred Hunter analyzed the 1973 Canada Mobility Study and published a study in 1984 claiming that "marital status is an inconsequential determinant of earnings for both men and women… As a result, the major argument in Block… is turned on its head" (according to Cuneo).

Second, Nelson again follows Block in claiming that pay equity will merely eliminate jobs that needy women or men might have found useful. According to Cuneo, there are studies by economists on both sides of this issue. In some places, at some times pay equity legislation seems to have increased employment, while in another places and times it has had the opposite effect.

Third, Nelson seems to think that wage scales are either the result of relatively objective market forces or of relatively subjective decisions by bureaucrats. I say "seems" because he apparently thinks that market forces are reducible to relatively subjective consumer choices.

This is just a false dichotomy because, among other things, in fact everything under and including the sun can be a market forces; Academics are notorious for trying to carve out chunks of the complex, interdependent and interactive real world and to claim them for their very own. In the case of economists, one of these chunks is called market forces.

Market forces are supposed to be separable from other forces, to operate according to their own laws and to be only really understood by economists. Governments, civil servants, and other do-gooders can intervene in such forces, but they can't be such forces. More importantly, whenever outside forces intervene, the result is bound to be disasterous.

The trouble is, when the question is raised, what is market force?, the most plausible answer is that it is any force that has an impact on markets. So, for example, if the sun shines or fails to shine enough, that effects agricultural productivity and that is therefore a market force. If employers can get their employees to produce more per hour by giving the latter pep talks or pop machines, then talks and pop machines are market forces. If people work harder to the glory of God, General Motors or, Oh Canada, then all of the latter become effective operators in the market place.

Clearly, then, Nelson and others are fooling themselves if they imagine that any kind of government legislation, whether it is in the interests of improving the lot of disadvantaged workers or of our physical environment, is somehow outside of and foreign to market forces.

The question is not what is inside and good, or outside and bad. Rather it is how much are Canadians prepared to pay for social justice, a clean environment, good education, and so on. The costs of such things must be finally be rolled into some prices somewhere. Instead of knee jerk resistance or support, we have to take one case at a time and weigh its likely overall net benefits and costs.

NAFTA Hearing Exposes Costly Flaws

Guelph Daily Mercury, December 14, 1991, p. 4A

Dear Editor:

With about a dozen other people of various political persuasions, I presented a brief on the North American Free Trade Agreement to the Parliamentary Sub-Committee on International Trade of the Standing Committee on External Affairs and International Trade meeting in Halifax.

The whole affair created a feeling of deja vu for me. I vividly recalled our MP Bill Winegard chairing the 1988 Committee Hearings on the Canada-U.S. trade deal. I remember complaining to him about the haste with which the hearings were conducted and I remember his replying that it was all part of a longer process.

1 began my current brief by complaining again about the secrecy and dispatch with which this neo-conservative constitution for North America is being rammed through Parliament.

Following that, I repeated some objections to the deal regarding its subversion of sovereignty and its anti-conservation/anti-environmentalism.

As I hoped I would, I learned more than I taught. One of the most interesting things I discovered was that no-one seemed to have read the deal itself. Even the MPs seemed to be working from summary sheets or even less, more trust that others in their party had studied the deal.

People on both sides of the issue for and against NAFTA did not feel obliged to cite relevant passages or to focus in any particular way on the deal.

The most useful brief (for me at least) was offered by a local economist who gave a detailed analysis of NAFTA's Chap. 19 dispute settlement mechanisms. The provisions of this Chapter are the same as those in Chap. 29 of the first deal with one important difference.

In the first deal, both countries agreed to take up to seven years to work out a precise definition of unacceptable subsidies to business. In NAFTA the pursuit of a precise definition is abandoned.

By abandoning the pursuit of a precise definition of unacceptable subsidies, NAFTA permanently enshrines the Canada-U.S. subsidies code until GATT (the General Agreement on Tariffs and Trade) or some other agreement is made.

One of my biggest complaints about the first deal and now of NAFTA is that the only acceptable subsidies recognized in both deals are for the manufacture and export of armaments and for fossil fuel exploration.

Thus, the primitive subsidies codes in these two deals effectively guarantee two things.

First, Canadian industrial and regional development subsidies will be increasingly directed to military hardware (e.g., jam-free radios, antisubmarine helicopters). In other words, Canadian development will become more militarized like American development.

Second, Canadian taxpayers' will continue to be required to pay more than Americans for any fuel discovered here with the help of government subsidies to multinational oil and gas companies. Because the two deals prohibit export taxes on energy resources, investment losses of our tax dollars for exploration for such resources simply have to be absorbed by Canadians.

A Regressive Trade Deal

Guelph Daily Mercury, March 8, 1993, p. 4A

Dear Editor

The North American Free Trade Agreement (NAFTA) is a dangerous piece of anti-labor legislation because:

1. It has no minimum labor standards, nothing like a minimum wage requirement, occupational health and safety regulations.
2. It recognizes no labor rights: no rights regarding organizing, collective bargaining, child labor, forced labor, racial or sexual harassment prohibitions.
3. Neither labor unions nor individual workers have any standing in NAFTA's dispute settlement procedures.
4. There are no mechanisms for labor complaints, no rules of procedure or regulatory codes to be enforced.
5. Because the prescribed risk assessment procedure includes balancing economic benefits and costs against those of health and safety, worker safety may be traded off against high profits.
6. Because greater freedom is given to corporations in the investment chapter to move jobs at will, there is less job security for workers, more pressure to depress

wages, more pressure to reduce benefits and taxes, and therefore less social security available for workers.

7. The only recognized unfair trade practices in NAFTA are those that destroy expected or real corporate profits, not those that destroy people's lives, the quality of people's lives or even whole communities.
8. Governments must compensate corporations for trade profits lost if Crown corporations are established, but there is no required compensation to workers or communities for runaway corporations.

A progressive trade deal would protect worker rights and prevent job losses resulting from the exploitation of the most vulnerable people.

Instead of forcing working people into a self-destructive race to the bottom, it would encourage the upward harmonizing of labor standards and a higher quality of life.

No Guarantees

Globe and Mail, March 10, 1993, p. A16

Re NAFTA In Principle (editorial—March 1):

Increases in productivity do not guarantee increases in standard of living. Louisiana has higher levels of productivity than Michigan, but Michigan workers have a higher standard of living. Workers at the Ford plant at Hermosillo, Mexico, are at least as productive as Ford workers in Ontario, but the Mexicans still make one-seventh of what the Ontarians make.

Increases in trade do not guarantee increases in standard of living. Mexican trade with the rest of the world has increased in the past decade, but the real wages of Mexicans have decreased. Cheaper prices for consumers do not guarantee increases in consumer spending. When Canadian producers moved their operations south to enjoy the benefits of the free-trade agreement, they left many Canadians behind without jobs and with a decreased capacity to consume anything.

Increasing patent protection for transnational corporations does not open trade. On the contrary, such protection guarantees the continued underdevelopment of Third World countries by preventing more rapid dissemination of new discoveries at modest cost.

Increasing protection for investors does not guarantee increased protection for workers. Both the FTA and North American Free Trade Agreement increase investors' security by decreasing workers' job security and, by further decreasing government tax revenues, social security as well.

Finally, calling international treaties "free trade agreements" does not guarantee that they are not highly protectionist deals and that they do not subvert democratic freedoms.

Massed Ottawa Rally Left a Great Feeling

Guelph Daily Mercury, May 21, 1993, p. 4A

Dear Editor

It was both exhilarating and disturbing to be in the very front line of 100.000 people marching up Parliament Hill.

Many of us from the Guelph area arose at 4 a.m. to make the Ottawa rally against NAFTA and the FTA.

Travelling up the 401, there were a dozen buses in our group, a dozen of 600 coming from all directions.

All the buses and people convened in the Ottawa flats. Bus after bus squeezed into its allotted space, and people scurried away in all directions to avoid being crushed.

I walked up Wellington St. and spotted a small group at a traffic light waiting for the parade. To my delight, the corner gang turned out to include Audrey McLaughlin, Nancy Rich, Bob White and Michael Cassidy.

We exchanged greetings and I walked up a few more blocks. When I returned a while later, there were thousands of people in the street leading up to the comer gang.

Some people were standing on one of the 20 foot-long banners that were to lead the parade. So I picked up one end and the next thing I knew Audrey picked up the other and we were on our way.

Immediately after thinking how lucky I was to have such a privileged place in the line, I started to worry about the batteries failing one of the people in the three wheelchairs in front of us.

I wondered if 100.000 people would come to a sudden halt or make a speedy detour. Would the group notice if anyone collapsed?

On the hill, the speeches and music were suitably inspired and inspiring. It was a great feeling being with so many people who so obviously gave a damn about our country's future.

One of the most impressive things about the whole meeting was the fact that it was taking place on the front lawn of the Parliament Buildings.

A speakers' tent and platform were erected. Elaborate sound systems were in place and virtually every speaker at the microphone criticized government incompetence, especially the Mulroney government.

Moral philosophers have often written about the so-called Paradox of the Good Samaritan, which is simply that in order for some people to do some kinds of good deeds, some other people have to be bad off in some way.

Regarding the case in point, it took a lousy government to provoke so many people to exercise their democratic right to peacefully assemble and protest.

I hope their spirit and energy can be pressed into service in the next election, and of course I really hope it will be in the service of my own campaign.

Business Ethics: Not Giving up on the Pony

Globe and Mail, March 2, 1994, p. A19

Re Business Ethics An Awfully Hard Sell (letter—Feb. 19):

J. Richard Finlay says that after 20 years of working in the area of business ethics, he concluded that "the only way it can be sold to business decision- makers is on the basis of bottom-line results, i.e., bad ethics equals lost dollars".

I hope he is wrong, because this is probably the worst possible argument anyone could use in support of business ethics.

The argument runs: Rational business people ought (prudentially, in their own self-interest) to do whatever is profitable for business. It is profitable to conduct business in accordance with principles of morality. So, rational business people ought to conduct business in accordance with principles of morality. In brief, a business person ought to be morally good because there is money in it, or at least there is more money in moral goodness than in moral evil.

The danger in this argument comes from the fact that it clearly makes profits or increased money-making capacity the reason or motive for doing what is morally required and being morally good. This raises two problems.

Insofar as one is acting primarily in the interest of increasing profits, is trivially true that one's primary interest is not in doing what is morally right. So, there would be nothing morally praiseworthy about one's motive for action. Consequently, one of the most important features of virtuous action, namely a morally virtuous or good intention, would be absent.

Second, since profits are accepted as legitimate motives even for moral action, in all those cases where estimated greater profits were connected with morally evil deeds, it would be acceptable for business people to engage in the latter. In other words, the trouble with making the bottom line in a business sense (increasing profits) the bottom line for moral purposes is that the two lines are not the same. So, in conflict situations when both cannot be realized, morality would be abandoned in favour of profits, which is precisely the opposite conclusion that a defender of business ethics would want to see.

Without getting into what I think are the best arguments for business ethics, let me mention two reasons for being optimistic about business ethics. I introduced our introductory business ethics course at Guelph about 15 years ago to a class of three students, one with no visible signs of a mind. For the past three, or four years I have taught this course twice a year averaging about 250 students per year.

Deborah Poff and I founded the Journal of Business Ethics a dozen years ago as a quarterly, and after a few years it grew to a monthly publication.

I have followed the output of the World Economic Forum since the beginning, including its dangerously silly annual Competitiveness Reports. A cynic might say that it finally allowed some discussion of business ethics because it is now completely confident that some open discussion of such issues cannot possibly arrest the powerful right-wing forces unleashed in the Reagan-Thatcher-Mulroney era.

Maybe so, I offer my optimistic tidbits for those who, like me, continue to believe in the pony beneath the manure pile.

Another Perspective Alex Michalos: No Place for Scrooge

Globe and Mail, December 18, 1995, p. B7

"MARLEY was dead, to begin with … Old Marley was as dead as a door nail".

With these words, Charles Dickens began the most beloved Christmas story in English literature.

From its publication in 1843 to today, generations of people laugh and cry with the transformations of Ebenezer Scrooge on Christmas morning from "the squeezing, grasping, scraping, clutching, covetous old sinner" to the warm-hearted and generous old man, "as good a man as the good old City knew".

Among other things, *A Christmas Coral* is a brilliant endorsement of philanthropy.

Marley's ghost said it all "Mankind was my business. The common welfare was my business; charity, mercy, forbearance, and benevolence were all my business".

Since Scrooge was the sole owner of the warehouse bearing the name "Scrooge and Marley," he was giving away his own money. If he had stockholders and had been living in the United State, he would have been doing something illegal.

Six years before the publication of Dickens's masterpiece, a U.S. court had laid down the law making corporate philanthropy illegal.

According to Mark Sharfman, in *Business and Society*, in the 1837 Charles River Bridge case, the courts found that corporate acts were contractual, limited and specific and that any act beyond chartered powers was prohibited.

Remarkably, 70 years later, in 1963, the U.S. Supreme Court refused to hear the case of A.P. Smith Manufacturing Co. v. Barlow, effectively making corporate philanthropy legal.

Today, of course, such philanthropy is not only legal, but it is often assumed that measures of corporate philanthropy may be used as measures of good corporate citizenship.

I believe this assumption is wrong and that the 1837 decision was right.

When businesses lobby governments for favourable tax treatment, their expenses are tax-deductible, which means they are tax expenditures in government accounts. Such expenditures must then be paid by other taxpayers.

When businesses lobbying efforts are successful, then other taxpayers are beaten a second time because they must cover any shortfalls resulting from the new tax regime.

Since favourable tax treatment effectively subsidizes the total cost of bringing a product to market, the market price gives a misleading signal to potential purchasers and consumer sovereignty is undermined.

Insofar as a community funds important public services through corporate philanthropy instead of through fair taxation, it is allowing its services to be designed by an unelected group of relatively privileged people, with no mandate or promise to serve the public interest.

Besides buying public services, corporate philanthropists are buying private acquiescence to corporate mischief in the form of trade in cigarettes, war machines and usurious interest rates.

The purpose of public services in education, health care, family assistance and housing is to empower relatively underprivileged people, to strengthen their voices, and to help them become full participants in civil society.

To make such services depend on the whims of corporate philanthropists, as we are increasingly doing in Canada, is a moral outrage.

When businesses make tax-deductible contributions to their favourite charities (creating more government tax expenditures), they usually ask for and get special recognition as generous benefactors, even though the sums involved are typically lower than sums they would have had to pay in a system of taxation that was not biased in their favour as a result of their lobbying.

In the light of these considerations, it is ironic that corporate philanthropists get special recognition as benefactors. It would be more accurate to recognize such businesses as successful self serving subverters of our mixed market economy and egalitarian democracy.

All things considered, from the point of view of strengthening democracy and our economy, it would be preferable to prohibit all forms of corporate philanthropy and make corporations pay a fair share of taxes.

To those who find this suggestion laughable, I would remind them of Dickens's concluding remark that Scrooge "was wise enough to know that nothing ever happened on this globe, for good, at which some people did not have their fill of laughter in the outset."

And, of course, "God Bless Us, Every One!".

Building a Healthier Community

Prince George Citizen, March 3, 1997, p. 13

Practically all research from around the world shows that the most miserable people on earth are those who think of themselves as in the labor force but are unemployed.

These people sincerely want to work for a living but, for one reason or another cannot find work.

Since the turn of this century when research in social sciences began in earnest, a major compliant from outsiders has been that such research tells us little that we do not already know. The trouble is, it is unclear which "we" really knows what and, as someone once said, it's the things we know that aren't true that give us the most grief.

Well, there is no mystery in the misery of unemployment for anyone who has been there or known someone who has been there, The first thing that happens to working people when they lose their jobs is that their self-esteem is shattered. After all, in our society, one of the first things we use to identify ourselves is what we do for a living.

Especially in a mixed market economy like ours, what one does to earn one's keep to some extent justifies one's existence. Even those who are young enough or old enough to be outside the active earning stage of their lives are not entirely freed from the requirement of doing something useful with their lives. If they are not employed earning money then they are still expected to be employed at something preparing for an active/productive career at one end and dispensing wise counsel and stability at the other.

As one's own self-esteem unravels, one's close relationships follow. Whether or not those who love the displaced worker are financially dependent upon him or her, they share the loss. Their loved one is not the person he or she used to be and the social network or family that they once formed is no longer what it was.

No wonder that families with an involuntarily unemployed person suffer extraordinary stress. Increased tension, arguments, physical violence, drug and alcohol abuse, depression, despair and even attempted suicides are all disproportionately represented in such families.

There have been times in which virtually anyone who wanted paid employment could find it, but we are not living in such times.

There were not 30,000 alternative jobs waiting for Maritimers when the fishery collapsed and there are not thousands of new jobs waiting for displaced forestry workers. When a new hotel opened in Niagara Falls with a call for 200 employees, 4,000 people lined up for work.

In fact, in the first week of February 1997, Canada's national newspaper reported that our country has not had such a long period of high unemployment since the depression of the 1930s.

The great difference between then and now is that our country has never had as high a national income level as it currently has, has never has as many people with such great wealth and such a big gap between the rich and the poor.

However, just as it was predictable and predicted that Canada's unfair tax regime of the past 20 years would produce great inequalities in income and wealth, which would decrease mass consumer spending and total tax revenues, which would then increase the national debt and create a weaker social safety net at the very time more Canadians needed a stronger one, it is today quite certain that a fairer tax regime could reduce the inequalities and alleviate much unnecessary suffering.

It would be unwise and unfair to blame any government for all our ills or even for all our unemployment, but I do believe successive federal governments have made bad situations worse.

We live in a country in which the richest 10% of the population owns over half the wealth, and the richest 20% owns over 70%.

And we live in a world in which for every dollar invested in the production of real goods and services (real wealth), over $100 dollars is spent on redistributing that wealth through trading in international currency markets.

It is not unreasonable or unfair to ask the government of Canada to introduce an annual net wealth tax on those whose net holdings are over $1 million to provide more help to less fortunate Canadians. It is equally fair and reasonable to ask the international community, through the United Nations, to introduce a financial transactions tax on foreign currency exchanges to provide more funds for helping the less fortunate across the whole globe.

Tax Freedom Day a Clever Strategy of Corporate Spin

Victoria Times-Colonist, July 9, 1997, p.10

AS OUR NATION'S premier advocate for free market capitalism, the Fraser Institute has been spectacularly successful at undermining the notion of a public good and the belief that there are goods and services that people ought to provide for each other collectively.

Perhaps the Institute's greatest triumph has been its invention of the idea of Tax Freedom Days.

In the spring of every year for many years, the Institute makes a solemn pronouncement of the precise day on which Canadians become tax free.

After this day, we are "working for ourselves" and before this day we are working for federal, provincial and municipal governments.

(This year, the Fraser Institute calculated it was June 30.)

It is ironic that taxpayer support for governments and public institutions that guarantee our civil society is routinely described as working for someone else.

Under the same political rug, the Fraser Institute's concept of Tax Freedom Days sweeps the fact that government revenues are used to build hospitals, schools, universities, court houses, roads, bridges and airports, and to pay the salaries of doctors, nurses, teachers, professors, engineers, judges, legislators, administrators, crown attorneys, police officers and fire fighters, to mention only a few.

And under this rug lies the fact that the jobs just listed are created by governments making good use of tax revenue, jobs that in most cases involve long term commitments.

Working for someone else indeed!

Granting all these objections to the idea of Tax Freedom Days, there remains one shred of truth in it that will not go away.

That truth is that the Fraser Institute has managed to make Canadian taxpayers pay for its own self-serving activities, since corporate contributions to the Institute are tax expenditures in our government's accounts.

Since the Institute lives off tax expenditures, it is fair to say that Tax Freedom Day is really the day the Institute and its corporate sponsors stop freeloading on the rest of us.

The Institute's corporate sponsors are even bigger freeloaders than the Institute because besides making the rest of us pay for their propaganda machine, they beat us a second time since any shortfalls resulting from beating us the first time must be covered by revenue drawn from other taxpayers.

All things considered, the day should be renamed the Freedom from Corporate Freeloading Day.

What is worse, from the point of view of free marketers, is that because the Institute's corporate sponsors are allowed to advertise and sell their free market philosophy at the expense of Canadian taxpayers, the real price of their products is effectively subsidized.

In other words, besides undermining public services, the Fraser Institute has been successful at undermining capitalism too, since the greatest virtue of free market capitalism is a price system determined by sovereign consumers.

Week in and week out, year in and year out, the Institute sends out its taxpayer subsidized, free market message to millions of Canadians who unwittingly pay for it and who therefore cannot fairly judge whether it is worth the price.

Would Canadians be willing to pay for the message if they knew its full price? I doubt it.

Will the Fraser Institute ever abandon tradition and announce the Freedom from Corporate Freeloading Day? I doubt that too.

Since it is impossible to seriously question whether the Institute has made accurate calculations to identify a Tax Freedom Day without making the wrong-headed assumptions indicated above, the most reasonable response to the annual pronouncements is to remember the assumptions, condemn them and move on to more important things.

Alex Michalos is a professor and chairman of the political science program at the University of Northern British Columbia, and a research associate with the B.C. office of the Canadian Centre for Policy Alternatives.

NDP Convention: A Delegate's View

Prince George Citizen, September 4, 1999, p.4

Dear sir:

Some of your readers may be interested in hearing a local delegate's view of what happened at the federal NDP convention in Ottawa last weekend. I was one of two delegates sent from Prince George Peace River.

All the news reports I saw told the story of a traditionally moderately leftist party moving to the political right, led by its elected leader, Alexa McDonough, and resisted by trade union leaders like Buzz Hargrove and relatively loose cannons like Svend Robinson.

It never happened. Buzz and Svend never had to prevent Alexa and the party from moving to the right because neither of the latter were ever inclined to make such a move. The most accurate assessment of the party's current tendencies may be found in the Federal Council's discussion papers and recommendations dealing with health care, job creation, fiscal policies and a vision of Canada's future.

Careful reading of these documents reveals a fairly traditional agenda. New Democrats believe that taxes should be levied according to people's ability to pay. Following this principle, they want tax decreases for relatively low and middle-income earners and tax increases for relatively high-income earners.

When the Liberals reduced the number and spread among income tax brackets in the 1970s, they shifted the burden of taxes from the relatively wealthy to everyone else. When the Progressive Conservatives brought in the GST, they shifted the burden still further. The NDP resisted those changes at the time and last weekend the NDP re-affirmed its commitment to make the federal tax system more progressive, in particular by such tactics as gradually winding down the GST and adding a couple of tax brackets for high-income earners.

When the Tories and Liberals reduced transfer payments for health and education, the NDP resisted again. When the country was persuaded to adopt something like the NDP'S medicare program from Saskatchewan, the federal government was committed to paying half the cost. Today, the federal share is down to 15%, which means people in relatively poorer provinces cannot get the same kind of health insurance coverage that those in richer provinces get. Last weekend, the NDP re-affirmed its commitment to 50/50 cost sharing for health care and called for the federal government to immediately increase its share to 25%.

The main change I saw in our policies concerns electoral reform. A number of New Democrats have recommended some system of proportionate representation for many years. In my case, about 25 years. At long last the party now has a Committee on PR which will consider alternative systems and make recommendations to the party. The BC party also has such a committee and in due course it too will have recommendations.

In 1922, Robert G. Good, an Ontario farmer, was elected to Parliament in the Progressive Party. Thirty years later he wrote a book called 'Citizen Farmer' in which he showed that almost every election held in Canada since Confederation was undemocratic in the sense that a majority of seats went to parties that did not get a majority of votes.

It was, and remains, a national scandal, duplicated in provincial elections. I am glad to report that my party finally seems to be headed in the right direction on this issue. Unfortunately, none of the other parties have seen the light yet.

Democratic decision-making is damn slow.

The Ugly World of the WTO (A UNBC Professor Tells of his Visit to the Seattle Convention)

(EDITOR'S NOTE: The following is a bit of a departure from the usual for Mailbag —especially its length—but we thought Prince George residents would like to read a protester's account of the WTO, through the eyes and pen of UNBC professor Alex Michalos).

Prince George Citizen, December 3, 1999, p. 4

Dear sir:

I went to Seattle to support the trade unionists, environmentalists and others protesting against the World Trade Organization (WTO).

In the five years of its existence, the WTO has undermined many more years of work and legislation designed to create livable working conditions and healthy environments and governments accountable to the electorate.

Foolish elected officials and faceless bureaucrats serving the interests of greedy corporations have crafted rules and used them in such a way that Canadians and Americans have to breathe toxic fuel additives, Americans have to roll back laws protecting endangered species (sea turtles) from extinction, native South Africans are prevented from using indigenous plants for medicine and Mexican farmers face a reduction in biodiversity as their seed corn is overrun by genetically modified corn, followed by increased dependence on transnational seed producers.

At one of the workshops I was appalled to hear that Canada is using WTO rules to force France to abandon its law against the use of asbestos products. The speaker wryly remarked that the difference between the Canadian government's view of land mines and asbestos mines is determined by the fact that we have corporations in the latter business but not in the former.

As I walked from my hotel to the site of the workshop, I was struck by the number of private and public security people along the way. Every intersection had police officers and every major hotel had its own security forces hanging around its entrances.

When I tried to enter the Westin Hotel to have lunch, I was told no one could enter without a WTO identification card. In fact more than a dozen buses had literally been used to form an impregnable wall around the Westin.

More than anything else, including the violence that erupted on Tuesday, being prevented from entering a restaurant because I lacked WTO credentials symbolized the world order constructed in that deal.

There are many more people in Seattle and around the world who lack WTO credentials. But in Seattle and the rest of the world, the full force of the law is used to exclude them from its proceedings while binding them to its decisions.

One speaker at the labour rally said that anyone who produces a good product in good working conditions and sells it at a fair price doesn't need a WTO with secret tribunals cutting secret deals that threaten people's livelihoods and their very lives. Another speaker said there must be something wrong with an agreement that makes the rich richer and the poor poorer.

Of all the lies U.S. President Bill Clinton has told, there is no bigger lie than that the WTO makes everyone a winner.

Last month I was at a conference in Ottawa and happened to share a luncheon table with a man who claimed to have been 'at the table' writing the WTO rules. I told him three rules had implications for workers' rights, the environment and democracy that made the deal unacceptable to everyone who worked for and believed in such things.

He said the people who wrote the deal, including himself, intended to prevent such things from being used as barriers to trade. In his view, commercial profits were more important than workers' rights, a livable environment and democracy itself. In his view, systems of public education and public health care are barriers to trade, and ought to be dismantled.

This is the incredibly narrow mind-set that produced and continues to support the WTO. Confronted by such destructive narrow-mindedness, those who marched and spoke out against the WTO were right. The world of the WTO is an ugly world, and those who challenge it are right to challenge it.

It was a privilege to march again with the usual suspects, Bill Blakie (federal NDP Trade Critic), Ken Georgetti (President, Canadian Labour Congress), Maude Barlow (Director, Council of Canadians), the B.C. Nurses Union, the B.C. Teachers Association, the steelworkers, etc. in a cause worth fighting for.

It was a pity to have our peaceful protests marred by masked thugs who, among other things, tried to intimidate me into joining them instead of going on to the labour rally, and then proceeded to smash windows, loot stores, get themselves gassed and finally arrested.

Still, all things considered, it was a worthwhile trip to Seattle. Meeting old friends and idealistic young people full of hope and energy made it easy to believe a new day is dawning for the human race, and for government by and for people rather than by and for insatiable corporate monsters.

A nice Christmas present, eh?

Vote New Democrat for a Change

Prince George Citizen, October 24, 2000, p. 4

Dear sir:

I met the Most Reverend Njongonkulu Ndungane, the man who replaced South Africa's apartheid-fighting Archbishop Desmond Tutu at his retirement.

We were in Montreal to participate in a conference on international finance. Walking back to our hotel after dinner, I said to Ndungane in my best Canadianese (after asking one more time how to pronounce his name). So you had some big shoes to fill, eh?'

'Yes', he said, very big shoes'. Asked what his strategy was for fighting organized evil, he said, Tutu had three principles. 'Mobilize. Mobilize. Mobilize.'

The conference was devoted to assessing the impact of the International Monetary Fund (IMF), World Bank and World Trade Organization (WTO). Speaker after speaker listed the colossal failures of these institutions. Promising financial stability, security and prosperity, their neo-liberal policies of privatization, deregulation, globalization and structural adjustment brought the world increased instability, insecurity and poverty. Promising increased trade and technological transfers, they brought third world countries increased restrictions to trade and new technologies, and still more poverty.

Ultimately the conference became a forum for crafting strategies for reforming the institutions.

Oscar Olivera, a man who could not have measured five feet tall standing on his toes, described his struggle against the IMF/World Bank's plan to privatize the water of his city, Cochabamba, Bolivia.

After three years, the Bolivian government had to tell the IMF/Bank that they were sorry, the poor and politically unsophisticated Bolivians back home simply would not tolerate it. It is inspiring and empowering to meet modem Davids who triumphed over apparently invincible Goliaths.

One speaker remarked on how ironic it was that following the collapse of the various ideologically driven left-wing regimes of Eastern Europe, the world now has to suffer the ideologically driven right-wing proponents of the IMF, World Bank and WTO.

It also struck me as ironic that as we sat around trying to find some reasonable ways to save the world from the excesses of the ideological right-wingers, a few miles away the prime minister was calling an election in which our relatively right-wing Liberals were mainly contesting the relatively farther right wing Canadian Alliance. It is difficult to see what good can come of such a fight, unless of course, Canadians see its futility and vote New Democrat for a change.

Recruit and Retain a Simple Equation

Prince George Citizen, August 15, 2001, p. 5

Dear sir:

I was invited to give a lecture at the Pentagon, well, in Pentagon City across the highway from the Pentagon.

About 100 U.S. military personnel came to hear six academics and a Canadian colonel talk about the nuts and bolts of measuring the quality of life of America's armed forces. As you can imagine, it was easier for the brass to come out to us than it would have been for us to go into them.

Because quality of life is one of those catchy phrases that means different things to different people, I am never quite sure what people expect me to talk about when they send me an invitation. Fortunately, I have so few colours in my paintbox that it is not much of a trick to pick one or two to paint a picture worth seeing, even if not worth remembering.

When I told my host I guessed there was no point in talking about poverty in the U.S. military, she said "Not necessarily." She had read some reports of service personnel qualifying for food stamps. As it turned out, there was quite a bit of discussion about why we were all there. Some thought the issue was a simple moral one. We have a moral obligation to be good to "people who put themselves in harm's way for our benefit". These were clearly the doves.

Others thought it was a matter of combat readiness. American forces had to be "ready to defend American values and the American way of life at all times" and the quality of life of the military was nothing more or less than the quality of its readiness to perform that task. Obviously the hawks.

A majority seemed to think the issues were recruitment and retention. After all, the last thing anyone wants to see in an army is a bunch of bitter bozos with lethal weapons who can't get jobs anywhere else.

Aha, I thought. Recruitment and retention. That's something we understand in Prince George. Maybe I should tell them to hold a rally at their Civic Centre, form a Task Force and raise hell in Washington.

At one of the breaks an air force officer told me his son sat down with a pile of brochures from the various services, weighed the perks in each one and then joined the army.

"You are not joining the air force?" his dad asked. "No." he said, "Here, add 'em up yourself and you'll see you wouldn't either".

"I see." I said to the officer. "Maybe this recruitment and retention stuff is a lot simpler than it appears."

Appendix

History in Photographs

See Figs. A.1, A.2, A.3, A.4, A.5, A.6, A.7, A.8, A.9 and A.10.

Fig. A.1 Wolfgang Zapf and Wolfgang Glatzer in Frankfurt 1980

A.C. Michalos, *How Good Policies and Business Ethics Enhance Good Quality of Life*, DOI 10.1007/978-3-319-50724-8

Fig. A.2 Meeting of Working Group 06: Social Indicators of the International Sociological Association in New Delhi, India 1986. Front row: Alex, Wolfgang Glatzer, Rudolf Andorka; Standing from right side: Ruut Veenhoven, Arne Mastekaasa, unknown, Bruce Headey, Torbjorn Moum, Hanneke de Haes, unknown, Denis F. Johnston

Fig. A.3 Alex campaign ad 1988 Federal Election

Fig. A.4 Alex displaying 4 volumes of the *Global Report on Student Well-Being* in 1993

Fig. A.5 Alex receiving Distinguished Quality of Life Researcher Award from Ed Diener, President of the International Society for Quality of Life Studies (ISQOLS) at annual general meeting in Prince George, British Columbia 1996

Fig. A.6 Members of ISQOLS celebrating at home of Deborah and Alex in Prince George 1996. *From left* Joachim Vogel, Torbjorn Moum, Ferran Casas, Alex, Wolfgang Glatzer and Valerie Moller

Fig. A.7 Ed Diener, Robert A. Cummins and Richard J. Estes at ISQOLS meeting in Williamsburg, Virginia 1998

Fig. A.8 Alex and Bruno Zumbo at the University of Northern British Columbia in 1999

Fig. A.9 Alex representing Canada at the Round Table on the Basic Sciences of the 33rd Session of the UNESCO General Conference, Paris, France October 2005

Fig. A.10 Simon Ho, Alex, Gabriel Donleavy and Joanna Kit-Chun Lam at the World Business Ethics Forum in Hong Kong and Macau, China 2006

MIX
Papier aus verantwortungsvollen Quellen
Paper from responsible sources
FSC® C105338
FSC
www.fsc.org

If you have any concerns about our products,
you can contact us on
ProductSafety@springernature.com

In case Publisher is established outside the EU,
the EU authorized representative is:
Springer Nature Customer Service Center GmbH
Europaplatz 3, 69115 Heidelberg, Germany

Printed by Libri Plureos GmbH
in Hamburg, Germany